Studies in Islamic Economics

A Selection of Papers,
presented to
The First International
Conference on Islamic
Economics
held at Makka under the
auspices of King Abdul
Aziz University, Jeddah

February 21–26, 1976
(Ṣafar 21–26, 1396 H.)

Edited by
KHURSHID AHMAD

**International Centre
for Research in Islamic Economics
King Abdul Aziz University, Jeddah
and
The Islamic Foundation, United Kingdom**

Reprinted 1981

ISBN (Hardcase) 0 86037 066 6
ISBN (Paperback) 0 86037 067 4

Views expressed by different writers represent their personal views and do not necessarily represent the views of the International Centre for Research in Islamic Economics, King Abdul Aziz University, Jeddah.

Produced by
The Islamic Foundation
Leicester, U.K.

For
The International Centre for Research in
Islamic Economics,
King Abdul Aziz University,
Jeddah

Printed and bound in Great Britain by
Robert MacLehose & Co., Ltd.
Printers to the University of Glasgow.

بسم الله الرحمن الرحيم

Contents

Part II

SURVEYS ON ISLAMIC ECONOMICS

APPENDICES

Foreword

Islamic Economics represents one of the emerging social disciplines and the publication of *Studies in Islamic Economics* is destined to strengthen and advance this process. King Abdul Aziz University had the unique honour and privilege of organising the first International Conference on Islamic Economics in February 1976 at Makka. This conference provided Muslim economists and *Sharī'ah* experts (*'Ulamā'*) with the opportunity jointly to participate in discussions on major issues and themes in economics. It was the first time in contemporary history that these two streams of expertise, represented by professional economists and traditional Islamic scholars, had a chance jointly to reflect on problems of common interest. The Conference constitutes a watershed in the history of Islamic Economics which began in the twentieth century as a branch of *Fiqh* and *Kalām*, and emerged from this conference as a category of economics. A child with the prospect of a great future.

Selected papers from the Conference are being published in two volumes, one in English and the other in Arabic. *Studies in Islamic Economics*, which contains some of the English papers, has been edited by Professor Khurshid Ahmad, who was also Vice-President of the Conference. The companion Arabic volume contains selected Arabic papers and has been edited by Dr. Muhammad Saqr, who also acted as Secretary of the Steering Committee of the Conference. King Abdul Aziz University, its International Centre for Research in Islamic Economics, and I personally take great pride in the publication of these two volumes and pray that Allah may accept these efforts of our colleagues and enable us to continue to serve the cause of Islamic *Da'wah*. I also take this opportunity to express our gratitude to H. E. Shaikh Hasan Al-Shaikh, Minister for Higher Education, for his guidance, support and encouragement and to Dr. Muhammad Omar Zubair, President of the Conference and Former President of King Abdul Aziz University, for the dynamic leadership he provided in organising the Conference and promoting research in Islamic Economics.

(Dr) Abdullah Omar Nasif

President,
King Abdul Aziz University,
Jeddah

28th February, 1980
11th Rabī' al-Thānī, 1400

Preface

The publication of *Studies in Islamic Economics* and its companion volume in Arabic are to me, as was the organisation of the First International Conference on Islamic Economics in February 1976, parts of a dream translated into reality. It has been one of my ambitions in life to help and participate, in however humble a way, in the promotion and development of Islamic Economics as a rigorous academic discipline. I know we have a long way to go; yet I am happy we have at least made a small beginning. It has been one of the chief pleasures of my life to have been associated with these efforts. I hope and pray that our steps will forge ahead and that all of us who are engaged in this creative effort will realise that we have done no more than started to collect pebbles on the shores of Islamic economics. The discipline is in the early phases of its infancy. We must not relax our standards and should be even more critical, albeit constructively, than our critics and adversaries. It is only through sustained research, innovative reflection, meaningful criticism, and careful experimentation that the little 'chick' of Islamic economics, which is just emerging from the egg-shell, will be able to grow to maturity.

I take this opportunity warmly to thank H. E. Hasan Al-Shaikh, Minister for Higher Education for his personal interest in promoting study and research in Islamic economics and to all my colleagues in King Abdul Aziz University, the Steering Committee of the Conference, and the participants to the Conference for their support and co-operation. I hope the publication of these selected conference papers will help in illuminating some of the grey areas and will provide scholars and researchers with fresh incentives to step up their efforts.

The credit for these publications goes to our colleagues in the International Centre for Research in Islamic Economics and I wish them every success. I also thank the Islamic Foundation for help in editing the manuscript and particularly for undertaking the painstaking task of the publication of this book.

(Dr) Muhammad Omar Zubair

Introduction

Contemporary Islamic resurgence, although still in the initial phases of articulation, has begun to influence the theme and language of the ideological dialogue of our times. An old and neglected issue has moved to the centre of the debate: the relevance of God and His guidance to the politico-economic life of mankind.

Western Civilisation is based on the principle of separation of Religion and State. Man is assumed to be self-sufficient. As such, the social, economic, political and technological questions of human civilisation are grappled with without any reference to God and His guidance. God may be worshipped in one's personal life. Nonetheless the affairs of society and the economy are to be conducted according to Man's own discretion and sovereign 'wisdom'. The conquest of nature has become the main target of human effort. The stream of civilisation, however, seems to run its course without reference to the values and principles communicated to mankind by God through His prophets.

The Muslim world is no exception to this state of affairs. The models of economy and society developed during the last two hundred years or so, are steeped in the traditions of western secularism. The last three decades have witnessed the emergence of over forty independent Muslim states yet the politico-economic systems obtaining in these countries continue to be based on western models. This is the contradiction which resurgent Islam has tried to challenge.

Contemporary Islamic resurgence is neither a transient political articulation of militant Islam nor simply an angry outburst against western nations. On the contrary, it heralds the Muslims' positive and creative response to the ideological challenge of western civilisation. For the Muslim world it is an attempt to try to reconstruct society and the economy by drawing primarily upon its own rich but neglected religio-cultural sources.

The ultimate objective of this exercise is to establish a just social order in which the material and the spiritual aspects are welded together, with the result that "progress" and "prayer" do not represent two watertight compartments but two sides of the same coin, with prayer acting as a stepping stone to human progress and progress leading to the glorification of the Creator.

Islam is a complete way of life and the divergence between the values and principles of Islam and the secularism-ridden social reality lie at the root of the tension that permeates the Muslim world today. Resurgent Islam represents a new approach – that is, to strive to reconstruct the economy and society in accordance with Islamic ideals and values and the needs of contemporary life.

There is a new quest to discover the true meaning and message of Islam by drawing upon the original sources of Islam – the Qur'ān and the *Sunnah* of the Prophet (peace be upon him) – and upon the historical experience of the Muslim people. Efforts are being made in almost every area of individual and social life – literary, educational, political, socio-cultural, economic and technological – to assess the relevance of Islam and to find out ways and means of transforming this consciousness into socio-economic reality. The nascent social discipline of Islamic Economics represents one such creative response from the Muslim economists and '*Ulamā*'.

I

FROM ECONOMICS TO ISLAMIC ECONOMICS

If crisis in a science is symbolised by its continued inability to meet the challenges that confront it, then few would disagree that economics is in the throes of a deep crisis. The phoenix-like rise of macro-economics from the charred debris of the crash of the 1930's had generated a new confidence and a new valour among the economists. The solution of almost every problem seemed within sight. All looked green in the valley of economics.

This confidence was proved false and short-lived. Not only did the old problems remain unsolved, new ones emerged with threatening overtones. Mass poverty; frustrated take-offs in development; increasing disparities at regional, national, and international levels; co-existence of hunger and affluence; irrational use of non-renewable resources; incongruity between technology and developmental needs; unsuitability of production and consumption processes to environmental needs; exploitation of the poor and the afflicted by the rich and powerful; inflation and stagflation; structural deformities in relations between developed and developing countries; all of these and many more problems fail to be tackled within the framework developed by post-Keynsian economics. This is being realised even by those economists who had earlier thought that their sophisticated economic models could provide answers to all the perplexing questions.

Noble Laureate Paul Samuelson of MIT laments the disarray into which economic theory has fallen. He warns "there are no signs that we are converging towards a philosopher's stone that will cause all the pieces to fall neatly into place". Professor Otto Eckstein of Harvard says "we are always one inflation too late in specifying the exact form of the price-forecasting equation". Robert Heilbroner goes a step further when he says "Economists are beginning to realise that they have built a rather elaborate edifice on rather insubstantial narrow foundations.[1]

The predicament of economics has been searchingly examined in a recent study, *Economics in the Future: Towards a New Paradigm.*[2] The near consensus that emerges in this book is that what is needed to salvage economics from the throes of crisis in which it is caught is not just some new interpretation of this or that economic theory or some changes within the current paradigm of economics, but that the *need is to change the paradigm itself* and move towards a new paradigm under which economic problems are not studied in isolation but in the context of an entire social system.

This background constitutes a point of departure for the Muslim economist. Islam is not a religion in the limited sense of the word, interested only in man's salvation in the life to come. Islam is a complete way of life and aims at constructing the entire fabric of human life and culture in the light of values and principles revealed by God for man's guidance. Human life is looked upon as an organic whole and its problems are approached, not in a purely mechanistic way, but in the light of the moral values and social ideals that Islam expounds. The purely positivistic vision of social sciences developed in the West becomes obsolete in this new context.

Man is treated as a human being, possessing a moral personality, and not just a complex of molecules. The world has suffered from the folly of the social sciences following almost unreservedly the model of the natural sciences, with the result that technocratic solutions are being imposed in the name of science, often legitimising the status quo to the neglect of all moral, ideological and political options available for social policy. Muslim economists believe that re-orientation of approach and a reconstruction of the entire framework of economic analysis and policy are needed to harness economics once again to the service of humanity. During the last fifty years over eight hundred books and journal articles have been written by Muslim economists articulating different aspects of the new paradigm they want to develop.[3]

The Muslim economist starts from the assumption that economics neither is, nor can be, totally value-free. Economic literature, produced in the last two centuries, is rife with vigorous protestations of 'objectivity' and 'scientific positivism', but in the last analysis, there is very little of economics that can really be described as totally value-neutral.[4] And what is more important, this is hardly desirable.

The social sciences have to have their own stance *viz-à-viz* human objectives and values. To pretend to follow exactly the methodology of the physical sciences in the field of social sciences, without regard to the latter's unique subject matter and the dynamics of the human situation is unrealistic.[5]

Socialist economics does not claim to be ideologically neutral. It is committed to a certain ideology and set of values. It stands or falls with them. Although there is a lot of prattle about positivism and objectivity, there are no pretensions of ideological neutrality, but this assertion is no more than a myth.

Classical economics was based on a hierarchy of values derived from the 18th century philosophies of individualism, naturalism and utilitarianism. Its alleged 'universal principles' of 'utility maximisation' and 'profit maximisation' are assumptions rooted in philosophic and ideological beliefs and not in objective reality.[6] Its concepts of 'competition', 'price-mechanism' and of the 'invisible hand' are related to the specific purposes it was made to serve in the rise and growth of capitalism.[7] The entire corpus of classical and neo-classical economics is derived from a set of assumptions and postulates, albeit through meticulous application of rigorous deductive logic supplemented by results of empirical investigations. The myth of objectivity and value-neutrality deserves to be exposed and the philosophic assumptions of modern economics laid bare.

In contradistinction to this, the assumptions and values of Islamic economics are clearly stated from the very beginning and the function of the Muslim economist is to explore and elucidate their relationship to economic life, theoretically as well as empirically. The Muslim economists do not wish to conceal these assumptions and values under the facade of false objectivity. To them, objectivity consists in honest expression of their values and consistent pursuit of these social ideals through logical analysis as well as empirical investigation.

It can hardly be over-emphasised that such an effort must be made with academic rigour and scholarly detachment. Nonetheless, it would be idle to assume that this theorising can take place in a climate of positivistic objectivity and value-neutrality. Most of the economic thinking that masquerades as value-neutral turns out, on closer scrutiny, to be otherwise. The result of this approach, however, is that its value-assumptions remain apparently hidden. They remain implicit and as such, are not susceptible to evaluation in an ordinary way.[8]

This is unfair and improper. We agree with Myrdal that "efforts to run away from valuations are misdirected and foredoomed to be fruitless and damaging" and that "the only way in which we can strive for objectivity in theoretical analysis is to lift up the valuations into the full light, make them conscious and explicit, and permit them to determine the viewpoints, the approaches and the concepts used. In the practical phases of a study the stated value premises should then, together with the data established by theoretical analysis with the utilisation of those same value premises – form the premises for all policy conclusions".[9] This is what Muslim economists are trying to do.

One of the major contributions of Islam lies in making human life and effort purposive and value-oriented. The transformation it seeks to bring about in human attitudes and *pari passu* in that of the social sciences is to move them from a stance of pseudo-value-neutrality towards open and manifest value-commitment and value-fulfilment. The first premise which we want to establish is that economics in an Islamic framework operates with its feet firmly rooted in the value-pattern embodied in the Qur'ān and the *Sunnah*. We study human behaviour as it articulates itself in different value-backgrounds and also how to influence it to fulfil the norms to which the society is committed. All the technological relationships between inputs and outputs are to be analysed and investigated in this framework. The attitude, tastes, motives, social customs, etc., which are ordinarily treated and given as 'constant' become 'variables', subject to policy manipulations. The scope of Islamic economics is wider than that of economics. Its approach has to be more global and holistic. The widening of the scope takes place at both levels, horizontal as well as vertical or inter-temporal. This represents a new approach to the study of the economic problems of man.

II

THE 1976 CONFERENCE AND ITS IMPACT

The First International Conference on Islamic Economics was held at Makka from Ṣafar 21–26, 1396 (February 21–26, 1976) under the auspices of the King Abdul Aziz University, Jeddah. It was attended by two hundred economists and '*Ulamā*' from all parts of the world. The Conference discussed over thirty papers presented in English or Arabic. The Conference elected the following as its officers:

President:	Dr. Muhammad Omar Zubair
Vice-Presidents:	Dr. Hasan Abu Rukba
	Professor Khurshid Ahmad
	Professor Sabahuddin Zaim
Rapporteur:	Dr. Monzer Kahf

Papers were presented at sectional meetings each dealing with a specific theme. Major areas covered were as follows:

1. Concept and Methodology of Islamic Economics.
2. Production and Consumption in an Islamic Economy.
3. The Role of the State in an Islamic Economy.
4. Insurance within the Framework of the *Sharī'ah*.
5. Interest-free Banking.
6. *Zakāt* and fiscal policy.

7. Economic Development in an Islamic framework.
8. Economic co-operation among Muslim countries.

A general session was held in which two survey articles on Islamic Economics were presented. A symposium was organised on the Teaching of Islamic Economics. Each section held organisational meetings to deliberate upon problems of future study and research in Islamic Economics as well as about possibilities of extending facilities for its teaching at College and University levels.

The Conference provided the Muslim economists with a rare opportunity, the first in recent history, to address themselves to the problems of Islamising economics including an effort to elucidate the basic concepts of Islamic economics and deliberating upon ways and means of implementing them in the contemporary world. It was highly rewarding for the Muslim economists to meet each other and develop personal and professional contacts directed towards promoting research in the nascent social discipline of Islamic economics. It was also a unique experience for the professional economists to co-operate at such close quarters with the '*Ulamā*' and mutually avail themselves of each others' expertise in the promotion of a common cause.

One of the major contributions of the Conference was the proposal to establish an International Centre for Research in Islamic Economics at the King Abdul Aziz University, Jeddah. The Centre has, by the grace of Allah, come into operation. The Centre is responsible for the production of many publications including the present work: *Studies in Islamic Economics*, containing selected papers from the 1976 Conference.

It is also encouraging to note that Islamic economics is now being taught at a number of universities in the Muslim world.[10] The Association of Muslim Social Scientists, U.S.A. has organised a number of conferences in which papers have been presented on different aspects of Islamic economics. The Council of Islamic Ideology, Islamabad, The Islamic Foundation, Leicester, The Pakistan Institute of Development Economics, Islamabad and the Institute of Policy Studies, Islamabad, among others are promoting research on many themes related to Islamic economics. Islamic economics is heading towards a real breakthrough.

III

INTERNATIONAL CENTRE FOR RESEARCH IN ISLAMIC ECONOMICS

As we have noted, the First International Conference on Islamic Economics recommended that the King Abdul Aziz University should consider the establishment of an International Centre for Research in Islamic Economics. Consequently, in Jumāda Al-Thānī 1397 H. (1977) the Centre was established to co-ordinate and to support research at the highest level of scholarship.

The Centre is expected to direct its efforts to achieve the following objectives as recommended by the Conference:[11]

(a) The establishment of a specialised library that would collect scholarly works in the field of Islamic economics in various languages and issue catalogues to research scholars everywhere.
(b) Conduct and support theoretical and applied research in various fields of Islamic economics, publish text-books in this field for the use of Muslim Universities and organise training courses needed by Muslim economic establishments.
(c) Provide research facilities and scholarships for visiting Muslim scholars to undertake research in their fields of interest.
(d) Promote co-operation in the field of Islamic economic research among various universities and institutions.
(e) Publish research papers and periodicals in Islamic economics.
(f) Help establish chairs for the teaching of Islamic economics, provide scholarships for research in this field and promote lectures, conferences and regional symposia in this field.

Since its establishment it has been possible to initiate a number of activities to achieve its objectives. An International Seminar on "Monetary and Fiscal Economics of Islam" was held in October 1978 under the auspices of this Centre. The Centre has already published a booklet entitled *Monetary and Fiscal Economics – An outline of some major subjects for research* as well as a bibliography, namely *Contemporary Literature on Islamic Economics*. Another booklet on *Suggested Research Topics on Development and Distribution in an Islamic Framework* will soon be published. A number of other research works are also in course of preparation.

The Centre intends to engage in the following activities:—

(a) Conducting pure and applied research in various areas of specialisation in Islamic economics.
(b) The production, distribution and translation of teaching materials in Islamic economics;
(c) Organising guest lectures and workshop activities;
(d) The publication of professional journals and bulletins;
(e) The publication of occasional papers and monograph series;
(f) Organising and conducting seminars and conferences here and abroad;
(g) The exchange of scholars;

(h) The offering of in-service training facilities;
(i) Awarding fellowships for doctoral and post-doctoral studies to young Muslim economists.

In line with its overall objectives, the Centre has invited research proposals from scholars of the Muslim World interested in conducting research in various areas of Islamic economics. Under this programme, grants are to be awarded to individuals, research agencies and universities to carry out scientific research for eventual publication in the form of monographs, occasional papers and text-books from the Centre. About three dozen research projects approved under this scheme till the writing of these lines are in progress. The Centre has a programme of translation of standard works on Islamic economics involving several languages. As a first step a number of important papers originally written in English have been translated into Arabic. The Centre wishes to establish professional links with other institutions and agencies engaged in theoretical or applied research in Islamic economics and related areas.

The Supreme Advisory Council of the Centre, composed of eminent Muslim scholars in Economics and *Sharī'ah* drawn from the Kingdom of Saudi Arabia and other Muslim countries, has already been set up. The Centre has a Director, a number of Research Professors and a small Administrative Staff.

IV

ABOUT THE BOOK

Now a word about the present volume. *Studies in Islamic Economics* contains some of the papers presented at the first International Conference on Islamic Economics. All papers have been revised in the light of discussions that took place at the Conference. In view of the space constraint only half of the papers presented in English are included in this volume but care has been taken to include at least one paper from each section of the Conference. A Companion Volume is being produced in Arabic containing papers presented in the Arabic language. This Arabic volume has been edited by Professor Muhammad Sakr, University of Jordan. It contains the following papers.

METHODOLOGY OF ISLAMIC ECONOMICS

Dr. Mohammad Sakr	Islamic Economics – Basic concepts
Dr. Mohammad Shawqi al-Fanjari	Islamic Economic Doctrines
Sheikh Manna' Qattan	Meaning of Islamic Economics

PUBLIC INTEREST AND THE JUST PRICE	
Dr. Hasan O. Balkhi	The Just Price in Islam
Dr. Mohammad Anas al-Zarqa	Social Function and Consumer Behaviour: An Islamic Formulation of Selected Issues.
ROLE OF STATE IN THE ECONOMY	
Sheikh Muhammad al-Mubarak	Economic Role of the State in Islam
ZAKĀT AND TAXES	
Dr. Yousuf al-Qardawi	Role of *Zakāt* in the Solution of Economic Problems
Dr. Atif al-Sayyed	The Concept of Justice in Taxation and *Zakāt* during the Early Islamic Period
Dr. Muhammed Saied Abdus Salam	Role of Financial and Accounting Theory in the Implementation of *Zakāt*
BANKS WITHOUT INTEREST	
Dr. Ahmad al-Najjar	Our Approach to a Distinct Theory of Islamic Economics
INSURANCE	
Sheikh Mustafa al-Zarqa	Insurance and its Place in Economic Life
Dr. Husain Hamid Hassan	The Position of *Shari'ah* on Insurance Contracts
Dr. Jalal al-Sayyad	Insurance and Some Doubts Relating to it
ECONOMIC CO-OPERATION	
Mr. Hasan Abbas Zaki	Economic Co-operation Between Muslim Countries

These two volumes taken together contain the essence of contemporary Muslim thinking on major economic issues. The discipline of Islamic economics is still in its larval stage and as such a number of ideas and formulations are tentative. More research and greater sophistication in formulating and presenting one's ideas are needed. The Muslim economists do not suffer from any complacency; they offer their submissions in great humility and with the realisation that they have a vast area to cover. The real contribution of the Conference, and of the present volume, lies in identifying issues and themes for further study and research so as to enable the little sapling of Islamic Economics to grow into a mature tree. Much will depend on the way the Muslim economists accept the challenge that confronts them and produce creative thought and rigorous reformulation of economics to serve the social objectives of Islam.

I am grateful to brother Azmatullah Khan of the Islamic Foundation, Leicester for assisting me in editing the manuscript, and to Mr. E. Fox for improving the language and proof-reading. My sincere thanks are due to Dr. Muhammad Omar Zubair and Dr. Abdullah Omar Nasif for all the encouragement they have given in producing this volume and for contributing Preface and Foreword to the book and to my brothers and colleagues Professor Dr. Muhammad Sakr, Dr. Anas Zarqa and Dr. Nejatullah Siddiqi for many valuable suggestions. I would also like to thank Dr. Ghazi Madani, Director, International Centre for Research in Islamic Economics for his generous support and co-operation. I would also like to place on record my sincere gratitude to Brothers Khurram Murad and Dr. Manazir Ahsan of the Islamic Foundation for supervising the publication of this volume. I hope and pray that this book may be helpful in elucidating some areas of Islamic Economics and more important in provoking newer thinking and research in areas not properly covered so far.

KHURSHID AHMAD

Institute of Policy Studies,
Islamabad

20 Rabī‘ al-Thānī, 1400
8th March, 1980.

Notes

1 See: Wilfred Beckerman, "Crisis in Economy or Economics?" *New Statesman*, London, Jan 23, 1976
2 *Economics in the Future: Towards a New Paradigm*, edited by Kurt Dopfer; Contributors: Jan Tinbengen, Harvey Leibenstein, Sir Roy Harrod, Gunnar Myrdal, William Kapp and Shigeto Tsuru, London: Macmillan, 1976.
3 See: Muhammad Nejatullah Siddiqi, *Contemporary Literature on Islamic Economics*, Research Report No. 1, International Centre for Research in Islamic Economics and the Islamic Foundation, Leicester, 1978.
4 See: Walter A. Weisskopf, *Alienation and Economics*, New York: E. P. Dutton & Co., 1971, Gunnar Myrdal, *The Political Element in the Development of Economic Theory*, London: Routledge & Kegan Paul, 1953: idem, *Value in Social Theory*, Routledge & Kegan Paul, 1958; and *Asian Drama*, Pantheon, New York, 1968, Vol. 1, Prologue pp. 5–35.
5 The Cambridge economist, Professor Joan Robinson, writes: "Every human being has ideological, moral and political views. To pretend to have none and to be *purely objective* must necessarily be either self deception or a device to deceive others . . . to eliminate value judgements from the subject matter of social sciences is to eliminate the subject itself, for since it concerns human behaviour, it must be conceived with the value judgements that people matter". Joan Robinson, *Freedom and Necessity*, London: George Allen & Unwin, 1970, p. 122.
6 Modern investigations into the real behaviour of the 'economic man', and of utility

and profit functions confirm this point. See: Von Newman and O. Morgenstein, *Theory of Games and Economic Behaviour*, Princeton, 1947: Simon, H. A. "Theories of Decision-Making in Economics and Behavioural Science", *Surveys in Economic Theory*, Vol. III, London, 1967: Ch. IX: Papandreau, G. A.: "Some Basic Problems in the Theory of the Firm", *A Survey of Contemporary Economics*, Vol. II, Homewood II, 1952. H. A. Simon, *Models of Man*, New York, 1957: See also Katona, G.: "Rational Behaviour and Economic Behaviour", *Psychological Review*, New York, July, 1953, pp. 307–318.

7 Economists of the German historical school and some institutionalist economists have dwelt upon this relationship. See: Schumpeter, *A History of Economic Analysis*, New York, Macmillan, 1948. See also Myrdal, G., *The Political Element in the Development of Economic Theory*, op. cit.

8 Gunnar Myrdal writes in *Asian Drama* (op. cit. vol. I, p. 32), "The problem of objectivity in research cannot be solved simply by attempting to eradicate valuations . . . every study of a social problem, however limited in scope, is and must be determined by valuations. A 'disinterested' social science has never existed and never will exist. Research like every other rationally pursued activity, must have a direction. The viewpoint and the direction are determined by one's interest in a matter. Valuations enter into the choice of approach, the selection of problems, the definition of concepts, and the gathering of data, and are by no means confined to the practical or political inferences drawn from theoretical findings. The value premises that actually and of necessity determine approaches in the social sciences can be hidden. In fact, most writings, particularly in economics, remain in large part simply ideological . . . Throughout the history of social studies hiding of valuations has served to conceal the inquirer's wish to avoid facing real issues."

9 Myrdal, G., *Asian Drama*, op. cit., p. 33.

10 These include: Al-Azhar, King Abdul Aziz University, Jeddah and Makka; University of Jordan, Amman; Umm Durman University, Khartoum; University of Karachi, Karachi; University of Punjab, Lahore; Islamic University, Bandung, etc.

11 Taken from the Brochure of the Centre.

PART I

Contributions to Islamic Economics

CHAPTER ONE

Islamic Economics: An Approach to Human Welfare

*Dr. Anas Zarqa**

"Al-Hadi! Lord! The way is hard, and we, Thy creatures, have none other 'Guide' than Thee."

—Sir Edwin Arnold
—*Pearls of Faith*

THERE has been a considerable amount of writing in the last twenty-five years on the broad economic aspects of the Islamic system. The main thrust of that writing has been in three directions:

(a) Comparisons giving broad outlines of the Islamic economic system *vis-à-vis* capitalism and socialism;
(b) Critiques of non-Islamic economic systems and philosophies; or
(c) Substantive expositions on a certain economic issue, *ribā* (usury and interest), and related questions.

A noted thinker and acute observer of the Islamic intellectual arena, Professor Muḥammad Al-Mubarak, recently expressed the view, justified in my opinion, that a sufficient amount has been written on (a) and (b), and that the time has come for going deeply into the Islamic economic system itself, understanding thoroughly its characteristics and giving it a modern formulation.[1] An effort is being made in the present paper to shed some light on certain methodological and philosophic aspects of Islamic Economics and to illustrate its unique approach by reflecting upon an Islamic social welfare function.

Can there be an Islamic Economics?

Economics, it is often emphasized, is a positive science, while Islam, being a religion, is normative *par excellence*. One may conclude that we

---

* Dr. Anas Zarqa, educated at the Universities of Damascus and Pennsylvania, is presently Associate Professor of Economics, King Abdul Aziz University, Jeddah. The author acknowledges his debt to Professor Mustafa A. Zarqa for extensive and helpful discussion and comments and to Mrs. S. Tayara for stylistic improvements in the paper.

cannot have meaningful *Islamic* economics any more than we can have Islamic mathematics or Islamic atomic physics.

I shall argue in this part and elsewhere in this paper that distinct and meaningful Islamic economics is possible, nay, necessary. Briefly, my argument is that economics is not as innocent of value judgments as we are often led to believe, nor can it ever be. Neither is Islam devoid of positive assertions about economic reality. We can then replace non-Islamic value judgments by Islamic ones, and add to the economists' stock of positive assertions Islamic assertions, then work out the consequences.

This, to be sure, is a task easier said than done. It is no less than building an almost new theory. But this, as Muslims, we must do if we are to contribute genuine Islamic solutions to human problems and if we are to stop acting as "free-loaders" in the social sciences of today.

I shall also argue that what is classified as a "value judgment" rather than a "positive statement" is occasionally a function of our limited knowledge and even of our religious beliefs.

Value Judgements in Economic Theory

Economics, it is said, is a positive science, and has become so by exorcising itself of any ghosts of value judgments that were occasionally reported on its premises. But it is now increasingly believed that the economics mansion is haunted by several unexorcisable "resident ghosts". Thus values are involved in:

(*a*) *Choice of topic to be pursued.* Thus when more resources are devoted to one theory fewer are left for another. "This applies in training new scientists, time in class, space in books and periodicals. Even devoting equal time is not value-free."[2]

(*b*) *Choice of variables and assumptions.* Economic reality varies greatly in time and space, or equivalently, is influenced by many variables. Without theory, purely empirical analysis of data using multiple regression and related techniques proves association but cannot separate cause from effect. Hence, no universal conclusions about the causes, effects and paths of economic phenomena can be reached by empirical methods without "strong theoretical guidance".[3]

This theoretical guidance entails surveying the variables that are conceivably relevant to the phenomena under study. They are usually large in number and often non-economic in nature. By a mysterious process of reasoning and guesswork we classify the variables into three pigeon holes:

(a) irrelevant to the phenomena,
(b) exogenous to the phenomena, i.e. affecting it without being affected by it, and

(c) endogenous variables that interact with one another and are also affected by the exogenous variables. These are the variable that are deemed important to explain and predict.

Thus the choice of variables and their classification, and the subsequent puzzles that are posed and solved theoretically or empirically cannot but be affected by the investigator's culture and beliefs, as well as his worries about man and society.

(*c*) *Choice of method.* Any method of investigation in theoretical or empirical areas reveals a certain conception of the world, and encourages certain modes of emphasis.

Quantitative methods, for instance, give prominence to the well-defined, and the easily or inexpensively measurable. Such techniques in the social sciences will work better "if the participants will only be willing to make rational, deliberate choices with criteria whose arguments are limited in number and easily quantifiable".[4] Problems and concepts that can be fitted into this framework receive the most serious professional attention, at the expense of other problems and concepts. Alternative methods of investigation are possible, and may be desirable in certain fields.[5]

(*d*) *Choice of ends and means.* Some important concepts in economics become meaningful only after an end or goal is specified. Benjamin Ward, for instance, noted that value judgments are crucial to the notion of *efficiency* where we must classify variables as either inputs or outputs. "If some kinds of labour are indeed satisfying one would want to classify them as outputs" along with more conventional outputs. "The classification is based on a . . . judgment as to what is valued and what is disvalued in a society."[6]

The concept of gross national product is similarly based on certain value judgments as a measure of output and *a fortiori* as a measure of performance and welfare.

Conclusion. There are thus several areas in economic theory where value judgments have a crucial role to play, and in these areas we can make a distinct contribution as Muslims.

Needless to say, several areas of economics are truly positive and cannot be different in an Islamic or in any other framework (such as first and second order conditions for achieving a given amount of production with minimum costs, given factor prices and a production function).

Positive Economic Statements in the Qur'ān and the *Sunnah*

Islam, though primarily normative, is not devoid of positive economic statements or hypotheses. The quotations that follow illustrate this idea from the Qur'ān and the authentic sayings of the Prophet, upon whom be blessings and peace.

(a) "Beautified to mankind is the love of lusts – woman, off-spring, heaped-up heaps of gold and silver, horses of mark, cattle and tillage, that is the enjoyment of the present life; but God-with Him is the fairest abode." (3: 14)

"Surely man is passionate in his love for wealth." (100: 8)

Man is depicted in these verses as having a strong and insatiable love of wealth. This hypothesis is in agreement with what economists usually assume in this regard.

(b) "Had I knowledge of the unseen, I should have abundance of wealth, and adversity would not touch me." (7: 188)

"No soul knoweth what it will earn tomorrow . . ." (31: 34)

These two Qur'ānic verses, among several others, emphasize the assumption of uncertainty about the future consequences of present actions. Few would doubt the realism of this assumption. Nevertheless, significant parts of economics, especially in the theories of capital, interest and the firm, are still based on the opposite assumption of perfect foresight.

(c) "If God were to enlarge the provision for His servants, they would indeed transgress beyond all bounds through the earth; but He sends (it) down in due measure as He pleases. For He is with His servants well-acquainted, watchful." (42: 27)

"Nay, verily man is overbearing, because he sees himself possessed of riches." (96: 6–7)

These two verses indicate one effect of a substantial increase in wealth and income on human behaviour. Economists do not seem to have taken note of this relationship.

(d) "And in no wise covet those things in which God hath bestowed His gifts more freely on some of you than on others: to men is allotted what they earn, and to women what they earn: but ask God of His bounty. For God hath full knowledge of all things." (4: 32)

"Nor strain thine eyes in longing for the things We have given for enjoyment to parties of them . . ."

It is related in authentic *ḥadīth* that the Prophet, upon whom be blessings and peace, said:

> "Observe those less fortunate than you are and do not observe those more fortunate than you are – by doing so you will be less likely to feel ungrateful for Allah's bounty."

The two Qur'ānic verses above imply among other things, that an individual's demand for goods is affected by the consumption of others (even though he is encouraged to overcome this tendency). The quoted *ḥadīth* implies that the utility a consumer derives from a good is affected by his relative position as compared to others (income wise and otherwise). The individual is encouraged, however, to overcome this tendency.

Many more quotations can be given to illustrate the fundamental Islamic assumption that individual utilities are highly interdependent and endogenous. This contradicts the assumption of autonomy and independence of utilities which is basic to much of the theory of consumer behaviour and welfare economics.

We have thus seen that Islam has something to contribute to the positive side of economic analysis (not only to the normative side) – a fact not yet generally appreciated even by Muslim economists. The positive hypotheses that are derivable from the Qur'ān and the *Sunnah* may either confirm (as in (a) above) or contradict (as in (b) and (d)) what is assumed in traditional economic analysis. Such hypotheses may, alternatively, call attention to relationships not yet recognized in economics (as in (c) above).

Normative Statements that are Nearly Positive and Vice-Versa

There is a difference between positive and normative statements. In view of the widely held pre-conception that religious injunctions are usually normative, I find it important for a Muslim economist to recognise that on occasion this distinction is dangerously misleading. An example will be necessary.

Statements in this example are preceded by N if normative, and by P if positive. Only the latter may be true or false.

Some years ago, a North African politician is reported to have said roughly that:

P1. "Fasting in Ramaḍān reduces effort and hence production."
N1. "More production is a vital national goal."
N2. "Therefore, in such a poor country fasting is against the national interest."

Let us complete the picture with other statements:

N3. "O Believers, prescribed for you is the Fast,
P2. . . . haply you will be godfearing . . ." (2: 179)
(Note that this Qur'ānic verse is partly N and partly P.)

In view of the general feeling that P1 is very probably true, those who accept N1 (perhaps also N2) and still decide to fast (N3) are clearly expressing a value judgment that obeying God is more worthy of consideration than some loss of production. But they are put on the defensive and probably would feel uneasy or unhappy.

P3. The Secretary-General of the United Nations stated in a Note on *Crime Prevention and Control* (19 September 1973) that "Many countries face the problem of bribery and corruption, which represents economic and social costs of serious proportions". (par. 68.) It is generally believed that this (North African) country is no exception.

P4. Starting from N3 and P2 one may reason that fasting promotes godfearing, which in turn improves moral standards, reduces corruption and negligence, and thus increases production later on.

Assume now that a research organisation checked P1 and P4 and found them both true – P1 in Ramaḍān, and P4 in other months. Their separate quantitative effects on national income were estimated. Assume further that everyone accepts N1.

If fasting turned out on balance to have a negative effect on production, then none of the above statements would change its character from N to P, or vice-versa.

But if the positive effect of fasting on production turned out to be greater, then several fundamental changes would take place:

P1 would be strongly qualified by P4, and
N2 would become positive and false.
N3 would become what I would call a "mixed" statement, N with strong P element in it, or vice-versa.

Let us read the whole Qur'ānic verse:

"O Believers, prescribed for you is the Fast, even as it were prescribed for those that were before you – haply that you will be Godfearing . . . and that you should fast is *better for you if you but know;* . . . God desired ease for you, and desires not hardship for you. . . ."
(Emphasis added.) (2: 183–84)

Conclusions on Methodology

What is often classified as a normative statement – implying sometimes that the opposite statement should be given equal weight – is a function of our knowledge or lack of it. This is particularly true of all "Do's" and "Don't's" that we meet in Islam. They are "mixed statements" that are apparently normative but imbued with positive consequences. Acts of devotion – often thought of as normative – are also prime examples of mixed statements.

Man's behaviour, economic and otherwise, is affected, among other things, by his outlook, beliefs and moral standards, so anything affecting those variables must inevitably have far-reaching economic consequences.

Some economists, most notably P. A. Samuelson, over-emphasise the positivist outlook which attaches great significance to distinguishing normative from positive statements.[8] Fretting over this distinction is justifiable only in the rare cases where we intend to spend the time and money to test a statement *before* we accept it.

Real life is, however, very different. It is often the case in practice that we *accept* a positive statement and invite others to do so without having the slightest intention or the time and money to test it. That North African politician enunciated his statement with full knowledge that even though it is positive and refutable, no one will try to refute it. I ask: What is the practical difference between such a statement and a normative one which no one can refute?[9]

It is suitable here to recall how Islam teaches us to view its injunctions.

Firstly, there is no claim that what is prohibited is all bad and what is enjoined is all good. Rather, as stated by Al-Shāṭibī, every Islamic injunction may have both desirable and undesirable effects, and Islam bases its rules on the predominant effects.[10]

Secondly, if man had adequate knowledge of the direct and indirect consequences in both the short and long run of his actions and attitudes, and if these consequences had the same dimension, there would have been no point in religion's concerning itself with social matters. But man's knowledge, alone, is inadequate.[11] The Omniscient and Merciful God, out of His concern for man's welfare, provided him with landmarks and guideposts to save him the tragic costs of falling a victim to his limited knowledge and occasionally to his conceit and passions. The Divine Guidance is meant to enable man to start out in the right direction on his social and intellectual endeavours. It is not meant to stultify nor displace such endeavours which constitute an important part of man's mission on earth. God has provided a type of small scale map on the basis of which man must fill in the detail. Had man perfect knowledge and no biases, he would come to conclusions identical to God's injunctions and guidance.

This line of thought is supported by verses in the Qur'ān too numerous to present here.[12]

Philosophical Underpinnings of Neoclassical Economics

The title of this section would be meaningless if one subscribed without reservations to the "widespread view . . . among economists that basic economic theory is value-neutral, that it can be applied in any society, and that in principle it can be made to serve almost any political ends".[13] I do not believe that such a view is entirely correct, as the arguments of this paper would hopefully demonstrate.

The secular world-views within which economists have developed their ideas may be summarised as follows:

> Man is a being (not a creature), a product of nature. His existence need not have any ultimate meaning – he is simply, here, and that is that.
> Humanity is the ultimate reality, and the significance and ultimate aims of this life, if any, ought to be sought *within* life itself and not beyond it.
> The perfectibility of the human race is attainable without superhuman aid.

The traditional liberal conception of man may perhaps be summarised in four principles: hedonism, rationalism, individualism and freedom.[14]

Hedonism is the pleasure–pain principle of Jeremy Bentham: man is under the governance of two sovereign masters, pain and pleasure, and pleasure is the supreme end of life. Man is naturally indolent, i.e. averse to exertion and that which he considers painful.

"*Rationalism* is means–ends orientation, the use of deliberate choice among alternatives in seeking the satisfaction of man's wants."

"*Atomism* is the assertion of the essential separateness and autonomy of each man from every other, with the consequent stabilisation of values by means of processes internal to the individual human organism."[15]

I prefer to call it *individualism* rather than atomism.

Freedom is the assertion that man is initially, totally free. The basic limitation on his freedom stems from his socialisation with others, who are equally free. "Thus each person is the negation of the freedom of others."[16]

These concepts are very much alive today. What they practically mean for the consumer is illustrated in the two quotations that follow.

E. Shils wrote that the hedonistic attitude came to mean, among other things, that it is:

> "An obligation of government to try to support progressive, populistic hedonism: . . . all or most members of a given national society should be gratified in their material wants and this gratification should be continuously extended. The goal is a continuous increase in the supply of products available for the gratification of needs."[17]

Given such a framework, the definition of what makes a "good life" is not difficult to anticipate. S. F. Singer, an eminent professional, writing in 1971, tried to define the quality of life:

> "In our society (U.S.A.) where material comforts are important and contribute to what people perceive as happiness, a loose definition (of the quality of life) might be 'having as much money as possible left over after taking care of the basic necessities; and having the necessary time and opportunities for spending it in a pleasant way'."[18]

Neoclassical Assumptions about Consumer Behaviour

Economists assume that an individual consumer is strongly and primarily motivated by the desire for personal consumption and leisure. It is also assumed that this desire is insatiable and that the consumer goes about satisfying it in a rational way to the maximum possible extent.

It is also not difficult to see the affinity between the economists' assumptions about the consumer's utility function and the principles of individualism and freedom (the utility function summarises the ways in which an individual's satisfaction is affected by his consumption of different goods).

Thus all non-economic factors which affect consumer behaviour are lumped together and given a clever none-of-your-business name: tastes. They enter the utility function as exogenous variables, and thus can affect the consumer's behaviour but are neither affected by it nor by that of other consumers.[19] Tastes include not only demographic and other personal characteristics of the consumer, but also and most importantly for us, his beliefs and moral values. These values can presumably be anything, but they should not be so bizarre as to contradict the aforementioned assumptions nor that final assumption, the hallmark of selfish egoism: an individual's utility is independent of that of others.[20]

One shouldn't fail here to note that economists too numerous to mention have scored their objection to the assumption of independence of utilities – only to continue using it in their analyses. A few did work out the implications of relaxing it but then only in a particular case.[21]

Dropping this assumption has implications that are both far-reaching and complicated to handle, the latter being the usual excuse for neglecting an honest analysis of the matter – not a convincing excuse, one must add, in view of the fact that economists find it occasionally worth their while to pursue complicated but trivial questions.

Islamic Tenets and Economic Behaviour

Islamic tenets that are relevant to economic behaviour are too numerous to cover here. I shall demonstrate the relevance of two such tenets: God is the owner; and life is a test.

God is the Owner

An understanding of the concept of property in Islam is one of the foundations of behaviour for both the consumer and the firm.

When man is born, he is, figuratively speaking, ushered into the cosmic banquet that is prepared for men by God. The banquet includes not only the material things of the earth and the universe, but also natural laws (God's law), man's own body, senses and mental abilities, etc. All these are the creation and the property of God alone.

The only thing that man can truly claim to be "his" is his will, which, by the leave of God, is free.[22]

What man, individually or collectively, achieves or acquires in the present life is the result of using his will to press the right buttons and let the laws of God act upon the property of God. Even when man obtains something by "the sweat of his brow" he is in fact directing his will to use his body and senses, which are God's creation and property, and in that process man is using up God's food and breathing God's air. Whatever man owns, in the conventional legal sense, is something he is allowed to "have", even though it is God's rightful property.

> ". . . to Him belongs all that is in the heavens and the earth, and all that is between them, and all that is underneath the soil." (20: 6)

> "Praise belongs to God, the Nurturer of all Being, the All-Merciful, the All-Compassionate, the Master of the Day of Doom." (1: 1–4)

When the concept that "God is the Owner" settles in a man's heart, be he a producer or a consumer, he feels honoured and grateful that some of God's wealth has been put in his trust. A man is then inclined to acknowledge God's right to define for him the proper limits for the enjoyment and use of that wealth, and also to acknowledge God's right to designate other individuals or the community as the *rightful* claimants to a share of that wealth.

> "Believe in God and His Messenger, and expend of that unto which He has made you trustees. And those of you who believe and expend shall have a mighty wage." (57: 6)

> ". . . and give them of the wealth of God that He has given you." (24: 33)

One Aim of Life: To Test Man

> "Blessed be He . . . who created death and life, that He might try you which of you is fairest in work. . . ." (67:2)

Life is a test through which we do not go equally prepared, and justly enough, we are not questioned equally on the Day of Judgement. God has endowed people differently and in many ways: in mental or physical ability, in material and social environment, in power, knowledge, wealth, etc. Some of these ways an individual is born with; some are acquired by effort, and still others come by circumstances, but each individual is accountable to God for all the ways in which he has been preferred over others. Everyone, on the Day of Judgement, shall be questioned concerning:

> . . . his life, how he expended it, and his youth, how he used it up, and his wealth, from whence he did earn it and whereto he did spend it, and what use he did make of his knowledge. (Authentic saying of the Prophet.)

"It is He who has appointed you viceroys in the earth, and has raised some of you in rank above others, that He may try you in what He has given you. Surely thy Lord is swift in retribution; and surely He is All-Forgiving, All-Compassionate." (6: 165)

We conclude, then, in agreement with Dr. Ahmad Al-Naggar, that nothing that a man uses (as a consumer or as a producer) is morally free, even if it is economically free.[23] It must be paid for by being thankful to its Creator and Owner, i.e. we must be mindful of Him in its use, and share some of its fruits with other rightful claimants.

An Islamic Social Welfare Function

That hard-to-pin-down concept of a social welfare function that modern economists long for, received more than 800 years ago original formulation from two Muslim thinkers and jurists: Al-Ghazālī (died 505 H.)[24] and Al-Shāṭibī (died 790 H.)[25]. The first gave the original formulation and the second greatly developed and refined the concept. Excellent surveys of their ideas are provided by several prominent modern jurists: M. Abu Zuhra, M. A. Al-Zarqa (on whose work I shall draw), A. W. Khallāf and M. M. Dawālib'ī.[26] The starting point is that Islam sets goals for human life.[27] All matters (be they activities or things) that help in achieving these goals increase social welfare, and are called *maṣāliḥ*, or utilities; the opposite are *mafāsid* or disutilities.

Al-Ghazālī, and later Al-Shāṭibī, by surveying Islamic teachings and injunctions in the Qur'ān and *Ḥadīth*, came to the conclusion that social utilities in Islam may be divided into a three-level hierarchy: Necessities, Conveniences and Refinements.

Necessities. Necessities comprise all activities and things that are essential to the *preservation* of the five foundations of good individual and social life according to Islam: Religion, Life, Mind, Offspring and Wealth. To preserve these foundations is one of the first goals of the religion of Islam.

Examples in this category include actions, in amount sufficient to preserve the five foundations, and injunctions related to such actions, such as: (1) establishment of the five pillars of Islam (Belief, Prayer, Fasting, *Zakāt* and Pilgrimage) and calling to the way of God; (2) Inviolability of human life and related sanctions, the permission, or rather, injunction to earn a living, to eat and drink, to have clothes and a home, and related matters such as buying and selling; (3) prohibition of wine and other mind-attacking matter; (4) the institution of marriage and the prohibition of fornication; (5) protection of wealth, in its wide sense, and prohibition of the destruction of wealth (even one's own), prohibition of transgression against the property of others; and (6) fighting to defend those goals; the acquisition of basic knowledge and education, and establishing sufficient economic activities (e.g. food production) to preserve the five foundations.

Conveniences. Conveniences comprise all activities and things that are not vital to the preservation of the *five foundations*, but rather, are needed to relieve or remove impediments and difficulties in life.

Examples include the use and enjoyment of things that man can do without, but with difficulty, such as entering into contracts of various kinds.

Many crafts, industries and economic activities are included here, to the extent that their products or services are considered conveniences, i.e. to the extent sufficient to relieve or remove difficulty. For instance, some type or other of floor covering is difficult to do without when it is cold; hence, the production of a simple covering such as straw mats is a Convenience. When such mats are available, carpets and the carpet-making industry become Refinements.

Change in the mode of life may move certain activities or things from one category into another. Thus when population was dispersed in rural communities, sewerage was a Refinement. But in densely populated urban centres that are now common, sewerage becomes a Convenience, for without it significant difficulties including health hazards are faced. Similarly, public transportation in small communities is *not* a Convenience but a Refinement, even when it is considered a Convenience for the purpose of travel among such communities. However, in urban centres extending over a relatively large area, public transportation is a Convenience. If it is available, private means of transportation become Refinements.

Conveniences also include activities and things that help to *promote* and develop rather than *preserve* the "five foundations". Instances of this include:

—printing books that promote some Necessities, e.g. calling to the Way of God, or imparting any kind of Necessary knowledge. It is implied here that such Necessities can be preserved by other means that are simpler than printing, such as by word of mouth;

—protection of health and promotion of physical education to strengthen the body. Notice that protection of *life* is a Necessity.

Finally, Conveniences include, among other things, acquiring knowledge, promoting education, and developing wealth (both public and private) to the extent required for the achievement of Conveniences. This is one application of the well-known Islamic juristic principle: whatever is indispensable for the performance of a duty is also a duty.

Refinements. This category includes activities and things that go beyond the limits of Conveniences. More specifically, it includes matters that do not remove or relieve difficulties but rather those that complement, brighten or adorn life.

Injunctions characteristic of this category are those related to politeness in behaviour and speech, observance of Islamic etiquette in eating, drinking, clothing, salutation, cleanliness, etc.; moderation in general, a particular instance of which is moderation in expenditure (" . . . neither prodigal nor parsimonious but moderate, in between") (25: 67). Improving the quality of one's work and production belongs to this category (according to the saying of the Prophet, peace be on him, "God loves for one of you, if you do a job, to do it perfectly".[28]

Other actions in this category are rest, innocent hobbies, recreation and kindred activities in amounts adequate to provide rest for body and mind, and to restore one's energies.

Refinements also include those innocent things taken in moderation that provide comfort, such as carpets, good quality furniture, painting one's home, i.e. things that one can forego without difficulties. Included also in Refinements are moderate amounts of objects of enjoyment and ornamentation such as flowers and jewellery.

Going beyond Refinements into prodigality and self-indulgence is considered by Islam a disutility for individuals and society alike, and is strongly disapproved.

Rules of precedence. We have given above a brief description (based on the works of Al-Ghazālī and Al-Shāṭibī) of a set of objectives that Islam defines for man and society. The attainment of these objectives increases social welfare.

Valuable as it is, the definition of these objectives comprises only the first component of social welfare function as conceived by modern economists. For this function to exist the second component should be provided: a set of *rules of precedence* which help to resolve conflicts among different social objectives. The two components together make up the social welfare function. An explanation of this idea is perhaps in order.

The social welfare function should help us choose from among well-defined social (or economic) situations that alternative which enhances welfare most, or that which is least harmful. It is often the case in such choices that the attainment of one objective takes us away from some other worthy objective. Thus choice often involves the resolution of conflicts among social goals. For a social welfare function to be worthy of the name, it must provide rules of precedence that help resolve a conflict of goals.

Do Al-Ghazālī and Al-Shāṭibī furnish rules of precedence, i.e., do they complete the specification of a welfare function? Yes, indeed.

To start with, one should recognise that these two jurists provide not only a mere set (collection) of Islamic goals, but rather they provide what in mathematics is called *an ordered set*, i.e. one whose elements have a hierarchy. Thus at the highest level are Necessities, followed by Conveniences, then Refinements. Al-Shāṭibī provides many insights and details about ordering the elements within each category. (He does not and no one can provide a complete ordering.)

The simple and fundamental rule of precedence according to these two scholars is not difficult to anticipate:

> Actions or things related to a lower-level category (e.g. Refinements) are disregarded if they conflict with the objectives of a higher-level category. To the extent that ordering is provided within a category, this rule is also useful there.

A classic example in Islamic jurisprudence about this ordering is the permission to uncover any part of the body for medical examination or treatment. For even though covering certain parts of the body is emphatically required, it is nevertheless a Refinement, whereas medical attention is a Necessity (if needed to save life, or a Convenience otherwise) and must have precedence.

This rule, even though very powerful and simple, is far from sufficient given the complexity of real life and the multiple effects that any action has. So where do we go from here?

We go to Islamic jurisprudence (*fiqh*) which at first sight might seem an unlikely source of help for a social welfare function. Both Al-Ghazālī and Al-Shāṭibī are renowned jurists, and both clearly refer to the numerous precedence rules contained in the whole tradition of *fiqh*.

Thus we have at our disposal that magnificent and rich source for defining priorities and resolving conflicts among social aims or individual interests. It is not only an intellectual heritage but, more importantly, it is a detailed value system solidly based on Divine Guidance. To a Muslim this is the only valid source of value judgments and interpersonal comparisons.

It is interesting to note that Benjamin Ward proposed that economists base social welfare judgments on the Anglo-American legal heritage and legal process. Professor Ward points out some difficulties that such an attempt must overcome, but concludes that it is ". . . a worthy goal, both morally and in terms of its prospective feasibility".[29] It may be noted in passing that the difficulties Ward foresees are largely absent from Islamic jurisprudence because Muslims believe in its Divine origin.

Relationship between Islamic Jurisprudence and Economics

The possibility of specifying a reasonably well defined social welfare function in Islam is a matter of momentous significance to society, policy-makers, and especially to Muslim economists and jurists. For a hint of this significance, let me quote from a well-known Muslim scholar, Professor Muhammad Al-Mubarak, who recently wrote, in a different context: "Production and profit are (in an Islamic system) not ends but means. The moving force of current systems is profit, but in an Islamic system it is human welfare".[30] So to define this welfare from an Islamic viewpoint must be the *sine qua non* for making practical Islamic recommendations on any social or economic issue.

Turning now to the subject of the present subsection, we should note that the idea of an Islamic welfare function throws considerable light on the proper relationship between Islamic economics and jurisprudence.

Muslim jurists have a central role to play in defining in collaboration with other social scientists, including economists – details of a social welfare function relevant to present-day society. Once such a social welfare system is so defined, Muslim economists need no longer wander about aimlessly. They could begin from this function and choose for positive economic studies those problems, variable and inter-relationships most relevant to that welfare.

> "There has come to you from God a light, and a Book Manifest whereby God guides whosoever follows His good pleasure in the ways of peace, and brings them forth from the shadows into the light by His leave; and He guides them to a straight path." (5: 15-16)

Economists could then present to Muslim jurists alternative economic policies, clearly stating the effects of each policy on variables relevant to Islamic welfare. Then and only then can jurists and economists use the welfare function and its supporting heritage of *fiqh* to provide society with Islamic solutions to current problems.

Al-Ghazālī and Al-Shāṭibī made a sterling contribution by deriving a social welfare function which is implied by the Qur'ān and the Tradition of the Prophet (peace be on him). Though still relevant and having considerable insight, their contribution would not directly answer all the questions we want to pose in this last quarter of the twentieth century.

Al-Ghazālī and Al-Shāṭibī have done their share. Have we?

Notes

1. Al-Mubārak, Muhammad, *Niẓām al-Islāmī al-Iqtiṣād Mabādī wa Qawā'id 'Āmmah*, Beirut: Darul Fikr, 1974, pp. 9–10.
2 Roberts, J. Marc, "On the Nature and Condition of Social Science", *Daedalus*, Summer, 1974, p. 54. This point is also emphasised by Ward, Benjamin: *What is Wrong with Economics?*, London: Macmillan, 1972, p. 193 and by Lindbeck, A.: *The Political Economy of the New Left*, Harper, 1971, pp. 9–21. The latter considers the choice of topic to be the only subjective element in positive economics.
3 Adelman, Irma: *Theories of Economic Growth and Development*, Stanford, Stanford University Press, 1961, p. 6, in reference to the phenomena of economic developments. For further relevant discussion, see Samuelson, P. A., *Foundations of Economic Analysis*, New York, Athenum, 1965, pp. 319–320. Schumpeter, J. A., *The Theory of Economic Development*, Cambridge, Mass.: Harvard University Press, 1949, Ch. i, and Henderson and Quandt, *Micro-Economic Theory: A Mathematical Approach*, New York: McGraw-Hill, 1958, pp. 1–2.
4 Ward, op. cit., p. 158.
5 A good case for "storytelling" as an alternative is made by Ward, op, cit., pp. 179–190, which also calls attention to the roughly equivalent position of S. Shaeffler,

The Failures of Economics: A Diagnostic Study (Cambridge: Harvard University Press, 1955).

6 Ward, op. cit., p. 211.

7 Throughout this paper, quotations that are followed by numbers in this form: 42: 27 are from the Qur'ān – e.g. *Surah* 42, verse 27.

8 Notably, Samuelson in *Foundations of Economic Analysis: passim.*

9 Ward holds that many of the economists' positive beliefs were not established by empirical tests before being accepted, and that empirical testing, when carried out, is seldom decisive (see Ward, pp. 98 and 173–177).

10 See for example The Qur'ān 2: 219 and 5: 90 concerning drinking and gambling. Al-Shāṭibī, Vol. 2, pp. 26–27; well summarised in Mustafa Al-Zarqā (in Arabic), Vol. I, pp. 104–105.

11 For a brilliant discussion of the limits to man's knowledge in social matters, see Muhammad Baqir Al-Sadr, *Man and the Social Problem* (in Arabic).

12 See, for example, verses 2: 184 on fasting; 2: 219–22 and 4: 25–28 on marriage; 2: 219 on drinking wine and gambling; 2: 102 on sorcery; 2: 10–13; 4: 83; 22:47; 23: 1; 28: 43–47; 28: 50–51, 30: 41 on various general ideas.

13 Ward, op. cit., 27.

14 Ward, op cit., pp. 24–25, includes only the first three principles, and I shall roughly follow his explanations of them. But I find it necessary to add freedom as a fourth and fundamental principal. I use the word 'individualism' where he uses 'atomism'.

15 Ward, op. cit., pp. 24–25.

16 Al-Sadr, op. cit., p. xii.

17 Shils, E., "Faith, Utility and Legitimacy of Science", *Daedalus*, Summer, 1974, pp.2 ff.

18 Singer, S. F., "Governmental Policies and Optimum Population" in *Is There an Optimum*, ed. by S. F. Singer, p. 400.

19 See, for instance, Henderson and Quandt, op. cit., Ch. 2, and Singh, H. K. M., *Demand Theory and Economic Calculation*, London: Allen and Unwin, pp. 120 ff.

20 See Graaff, J. de V., *Theoretical Welfare Economics*, London: Cambridge University Press, 1967, pp. 43–45, 160–170; cf. Samuelson, p. 224; Henderson and Quandt, pp. 212–214, work out the implications only for the static Pareto optimality.

21 For example Duesenberry, J. S., *Income, Saving and Theory of Consumer Behaviour*, 1949.

22 Mahmud, Mustafa, *Hadīth 'alā al-Talfizurin al-Urdunī fī Tafsīr badh Sūrah al-Fātihah*, Amman, 24-12-1974.

23 Al-Najjār, Ahmad, *Al-Madkhal Ilā al-Nazariyah al-Iqtisādiyah fī al-Manhaj*, Beirut: Darul Fikr, 1973, pp. 32 ff.

24 Al-Ghazālī, Abū Hāmid, *Al-Mustarfa' fī 'ilm al-Usūl*, Cairo: Maktabah al-Tijāriah al-Kubrā, 1937, Vol. I, pp. 139–144.

25 Al-Shāṭibī, Abū Ishāq Ibrāhīm, *Al-Muwafiqāt fī usūl al-Sharī'ah*, Cairo: Maktabah al-Tijāriah al-Kubrā, Vol. II, pp. 8–25 and 176–186.

26 Abu Zuhra, Muḥammad, *Mālik*, Cairo: Matba' al-I'timād, 1365 H.; Al-Zarqā, Mustafā Ahmad, *Al-Madkhal al-Fiqh al-'Am*. Damascus. Matba' al-Hayat, 1964, (Vol. I, pp. 100–103, Vol. II, pp. 604–605); Khallāf, Abdul Wahhāb, *Usūl al-Fiqh*, Cairo: Matba' al-Nasr, 1361, pp. 163 ff.; al-Dawālibī, Muhammad M'arūf, *Al-Madkhal ilā 'ilm usūl al-Fiqh*, Damascus, 1955, pp. 412–418.

27 I am deeply indebted to Professor Al-Zarqā, my father, for extensive discussions on this part of the paper. He was also kind enough to check the examples and to provide several valuable ones. Building on his help I did not hesitate to give, where necessary, modern examples to clarify the ideas of Al-Ghazālī and Al-Shāṭībī.

28 An authentic tradition of the Prophet (peace be upon him). See: Ibn Taymīyyāh, *al-Kalām al-Taiyyab*, Beirut: al-Maktab al-Islami, 1385, p. 11.

29 Ward, op. cit., p. 235.

30 Al-Mubārak, op. cit., p. 29.

CHAPTER TWO

A Contribution to the Theory of Consumer Behaviour in an Islamic Society

*Dr. Monzer Kahf**

THE "utility" analysis developed by the Austrian marginalist school and by Alfred Marshall has its roots both in "economic rationalism" and in "utilitarianism". These two sources had great influence in the formation and emergence of the "new capitalism" in the Europe of 17th, 18th and 19th centuries. During the 19th century Marxism too grew up in the same atmosphere, one may indeed say in the very lap of the new capitalism. Because of this, it could never shake off the philosophical basis of that brand of capitalism. That does not mean there are no dissenting voices. Max Weber, a leading sociologist, has very rightly maintained in his well known book *The Protestant Ethic and the Spirit of Capitalism* that "economic rationalism" is not the only form of rationalism that can explain the economic phenomena. Thus, for instance, it may be pointed out that Islamic rationalism is another form of rationalisation.

Islamic rationalism is founded on the ideological belief in the Oneness of God and in the oneness of religion and the Book. In accordance with this belief, human life is conceived as one whole, oriented towards *one* ultimate goal. This goal has many expressions in the Islamic faith and literature, such as, serving Allah, "entering the Paradise", "worshipping Allah", "seeking salvation in order to escape Hell", "passing the trial on the Day

---

*Dr. Monzer Kahf, Chairman, Economist Group of the Association of Muslim Social Scientists, U.S.A. Dr. Kahf was educated in Syria and the United States and holds a Ph.D. in Economics with specialisation in International Economics. Amongst his recent publications is *The Islamic Economy*, North American Trust, Indianapolis, 1978.

The author would like to acknowledge that in this paper, he has utilised material from two of his earlier unpublished papers entitled "The Islamic Economics" and "The Economic View of Ibn Taimiyyah". Section IV in this study has drawn upon another paper of the author, namely, "A Model of the Household Decision in an Islamic Economy", which was presented at the annual convention of the Association of Muslim Social Scientists, held in May, 1974, in Gary, Indiana, U.S.A. The English translation of the Qur'ān by Yusuf Ali has been the main source for citations of the meaning of the Qur'ānic verses.

of Judgement", etc. In fact all these expressions may be said to be that of "obtaining the consent of Allah".

The affirmation of one goal for human life has the effect of unifying human behaviour (not to mean standardisation) and denying the artificial dichotomy so distinctive of the philosophy and thinking of the "new capitalism". Islamic rationalism succeeded in handling many problems of human behaviour that the western economic rationalism failed to explain, and because of its historical background the capitalist rationalism is alien to the Islamic economic scheme and behavioural attitudes under Islamic influence. Despite this, Islamic rationalism has not ignored the importance of man's material wants, needs and satisfactions. In this matter, both the economic rationalism of capitalism and the superstitious philosophy of the European Middle Ages could not explain the assorted behaviour of man. This was largely due to the fact that the two systems took diametrically opposite positions in viewing the workings of human behaviour.

Additionally, Islam is never satisfied by only awakening human consciousness and putting it on the right track; but rather, it always creates the environmental conditions that are necessary for the proper functioning of this consciousness. Therefore, a study of Islamic rationalism must be supplemented by an analysis of the socio-economic framework and atmosphere provided by Islamic teachings.

Throughout history, societies imposed, and are imposing, certain limitations and constraints on their members in respect of the set of goods and services made accessible to the consumer. The use of certain commodities is sometimes forbidden by legislation, prohibited by religion, or simply unavailable because of the level of the development of current technology. A comparative study of the sets of attainable goods and services in different societies and under different cultural systems has its own merits and benefits, but, this paper will not enumerate the lawful and prohibited kinds of beverages and food from an Islamic point of view. The principal focus of this paper will be on the *impulses that motivate, and the goals that are pursued by the consumer in his choice among the goods and services contained in the attainable set, and on the macroeconomics of this behaviour, given the axiomatic system of Islam.*

Section I will briefly highlight the ideas on consumer behaviour developed under the capitalist and the Marxist systems. Section II will analyse consumer rationality under the Islamic axioms. Section III will be devoted to the consumer's decision to allocate his income between saving and final spending. Section IV will derive the macromodel of income allocation in an Islamic society. The fifth and last section will summarise the findings and the conclusions. This paper will show, for example, that *Zakāt* and the prohibition of *Ribā* have a central role in the macroeconomic theory of Islamic economics, especially in the analysis of investment-saving relationship, economic policy and economic growth. It is the opinion of this writer that such a study ought to be based on some observations and empirical evidence concerning the consumer behaviour in an Islamic society, but the practical impossibility of observing and collecting data, at this time, forced him to deal with the topic on a purely theoretical basis.

I

THE THEORY OF CONSUMER BEHAVIOUR IN CONVENTIONAL ECONOMICS

The theory of consumer behaviour developed in the West after the rise of capitalism is an offspring of a duality, namely, "economic rationalism" and "utilitarianism". Economic rationalism interprets human behaviour as being founded on a "rigorous calculation, directed with foresight and caution toward economic success".[1] Economic success is strictly defined as the "making of money out of man". The acquisition of wealth, whether in terms of money or in terms of commodities is the ultimate goal of life and at the same time the yardstick of economic success.

The ethics of this philosophy is related to and derived from "economic success". Success in making money is the result and the expression of virtue and proficiency. Utilitarianism is the source of moral values and attitudes. "Honesty is useful because it assures credit; so are punctuality, industry, and frugality."[2]

From this dual origin emerged the theory of consumer behaviour. This theory considers the maximisation of utility as a postulated objective of the consumer. The utility to be maximised is that of a "homo-economicus" whose sole goal is to achieve the highest level of economic acquisition, and whose only stimulus is the "sense of money". The theory of consumer behaviour under the capitalist system has passed through two stages. The first stage is associated with the marginalist theory, according to which the utility of consumer is rigorously measurable in cardinal units. The consumer reaches his equilibrium when he maximises his utility subject to an income constraint; that is, when the ratios of marginal utilities of the different commodities equal the ratios of their money prices. The second and more modern stage rules out the measurability and the cardinality of utility. However the conditions become now the equality between the marginal rates of substitution, i.e., the slope of the indifference curve, and the ratios of money prices, i.e., the slope of the income constraint.[3]

The Marxist economics never deviated from the doctrine of "homo-economicus". In fact, one aspect of the dialectical materialism of Marx is that it is a mere "restatement" of this doctrine in a historical perspective; therefore, some of the latest trends in Marxist economics betray increasing influence of early marginalist formulations of the utility theory as an explanation of consumer preferences;[4] while the contributions of John R. Hicks in the field of techniques of consumer utility maximisation are reflected in the writings of some other socialist economists.[5] Marxist economics continues to move in the same grooves.

Section II will show that this concept of rationalism, which may be termed as "communo-capitalist" does not coincide with the Islamic doctrines, nor do the alternative behavioural patterns which dominated the economic relationships in Europe before the rise of the economic rationalism, such as the "hand-to-mouth of peasant" or the traditionalism of the guild craftsman.[6]

II

MOTIVES AND GOALS OF CONSUMER BEHAVIOUR UNDER THE ISLAMIC CULTURE

The economic behaviour of human beings in the Islamic culture is dominated by three general principles: The belief in the Last Day, the Islamic concept of success, and the Islamic concept of riches.

1. Islam associates the belief in the Day of Judgement and the life in the hereafter with the belief in Allah. This extends the time horizon of Muslims beyond death. Life before death and life after death are closely interrelated in a sequential manner. This has two effects as far as consumer behaviour is concerned: first, the outcome of a choice of action is composed of two parts, its immediate effect in this life; and its later effect, in the life to come.[7] Therefore, the utility derived from such a choice is the total of the present value of these *two* effects. Second, the number of alternative uses of one's income is increased by the inclusion of all the benefits that would be gained only in the hereafter. Examples of such alternative uses are free of charge lending (القرض الحسن), giving to the poor and needy, care of animals, spending for the welfare of future generations, improvement of communal life even when this has no immediate benefit for the individual,[8] promotion and perpetuation of goodness, etc. These uses of income are excluded from the Max Weber rationality unless they have some immediate utility. Thus, many alternative uses of one's income may have positive utility in the Islamic culture; whereas their utility benefits in the communo-capitalist rationalisation may be zero or negative.

2. Success is defined in Islam in terms of the "consent of Allah" and not in those of the "accumulation of wealth".[9] Virtue, righteousness, and the fulfilment of the servanthood to Allah are the key to His consent. Virtue and righteousness can be achieved through good actions and purification of human behaviour from evil and vice.

Service and obedience to Allah may be rendered by the positive use of

human capabilities and resources, given by Allah. This inclu
and exploitation of everything given to mankind by Allah. Ac..
Islamic teachings, if a man really wants to serve Allah, the utilization oi the natural and human resources made available to him is not only a privilege but also a duty and obligation prescribed by Allah[10]. Therefore, material progress and perfection are in themselves moral values in Islam.[11] Abstention and withdrawal from enjoyment and satisfaction from material life is in direct opposition to Islamic doctrines.[12] Efficiency and the value of time are concepts made alive in the human consciousness by the religion of Islam.[13] After all, Islam urges and requires people to spend part of their time and energy for the remembrance of Allah, the improvement of spiritual and moral surroundings, the propagation of virtue and goodness, etc.; all this can only be done if part of human resources can be spared and liberated from the pursuit of consumption.[14]

3. The concept of wealth and income (*Māl* المال) is unique in Islam. *Māl*, whether looked at as wealth or income, is a bounty from Allah; it is not an evil. Heaven is not only open to the poor, but it is also and equally open to the rich. *Māl* is a tool that may be used for good or for evil.[15] Poverty is, in some instances, associated with disbelief and riches are considered a gift from Allah.[16] Since riches are a bounty from Him, they must be used for the benefit and satisfaction of human wants. This is an implication of humble service to Allah (*Subhānahū Wa Ta'ālā*). The Prophet is reported to have said: "Verily, Allah likes to see the trace of His bounty on His servant". The relationship between income or *Māl*, and consumption is defined by the Prophet in the following saying: "The Prophet (peace be upon him) asked once: Who among you, the *Māl* of his heir is dearer to him than his own *Māl*? They answered: every one sees his *Māl* dearer than his heir's. Then, the Prophet said: your *Māl* is what you use up and your heir's *Māl* is what you leave".[17]

That is, since *Māl* is a tool to buy goods and services which bring about satisfaction, it should be spent for that purpose and not hoarded. The concept of real income appears in another saying where real income is defined as the total of what is used for the purchase of goods and services that produce immediate satisfaction in this life plus that which is given away for causes that enrich one's lifeafter.[18]

In the light of these three principles, consumer behaviour in an Islamic society can be described as a maximisation of success, *Falāḥ*.[19] Success may be defined, in the narrow sense, corresponding with consumer choice, as the level of obedience to Allah derived from the satisfaction of one's material wants and the exhibition of the effect of Allah's bounty by extracting enjoyment of the *Māl* given by Allah, and the enrichment of one's lifeafter. The maximisation of success of the consumer is subject to an income constraint determined by the level of "spendable income". The latter is defined as total income minus planned change in wealth.

The exhibition of the trace of Allah's bounty affects the consumer's behaviour by raising the proportion of final spending to income;[20] because it implies an increase in spending on material wants and/or enrichment of one's life in the hereafter at each level of income. Consequently, at each level of income, final spending in the Islamic household is expected to be higher than that in the non-Islamic family.[21] Therefore the maximisation problem may be reduced to a problem of two objective functions: one for the satisfaction derived from the consumption of goods and services, and the other for the enrichment of the life in the hereafter by spending for the sake of Allah. These are maximised subject to the spendable income given the set of accessible goods and services and the relative prices.[22] The solution of the maximisation problem, i.e., consumer equilibrium, can be found by making use of the well-known mathematical techniques.

This section studied the rationality of consumer behaviour as derived from the Islamic ideology. It concluded that the goals of the consumer include the enrichment of one's life in the hereafter as well as the enjoyment obtained from material consumption. Very little was said about the decision of allocating income between saving (change in wealth) and final spending. Section III will address itself to this aspect of choice.

III

INCOME-ALLOCATION DECISION

Before proceeding to examine the consumer's decision of income allocation between saving and final spending, we must define the terms used in this discussion. Consumption function is usually defined in the communo-capitalist literature as the relationship between income and consumption of goods and services. These goods and services constitute only one part of our term "final spending", namely, spending on goods and services that bring about immediate satisfaction in this life. The second component of final spending, i.e., the spending for the sake of Allah is not accounted for in the consumption function mentioned above. That is why I avoided the use of the term consumption in the previous section. The term final spending refers to these two components together. Final spending is distinguished from investment in that the latter affects the level of wealth, whereas the former does not.

Saving is conceived in this study as a positive act that has its own purposes rather than a mere residual, after consumption has taken place. People save for a variety of reasons such as precaution for the ambiguity and uncertainty of the future; to provide for future consumption; to accumulate wealth for their heirs;[23] to increase their future income; etc.

These motives compete with the impulses of final spending discussed in the previous section for the given income. The stronger the drive or tendency for final spending, the larger is the part of income allocated for final spending. This drive may be so strong that final spending may exceed income; in that case, saving becomes negative. This may happen at a very low level of income where the needs for consumption exceed current income, or at a very high level of religious consciousness about the afterlife where one may give away even all one's wealth for the sake of Allah; this is exemplified by the choice of Abū Bakr when he brought all his accumulated wealth to the Prophet to finance one of his battles. On the other hand, the greater the desire to save, the higher the proportion of saving to income. Therefore, on the saving-final-spending scale of Figure 1, one can locate all the points of combination of saving and final spending that produce the same level of satisfaction to the consumer. The locus of these points will be called the income-allocation indifference curve I. It has a negative slope for the reasons mentioned above. We will assume that it is also convex to the origin, i.e., the marginal rate of substitution of saving for final spending (the slope of I) is decreasing as final spending increases. This means that the higher the final spending, the greater becomes the desire to save; and the higher the rate of wealth accumulation, the stronger becomes the desire for final spending. One more assumption is still to be made; that is, the higher

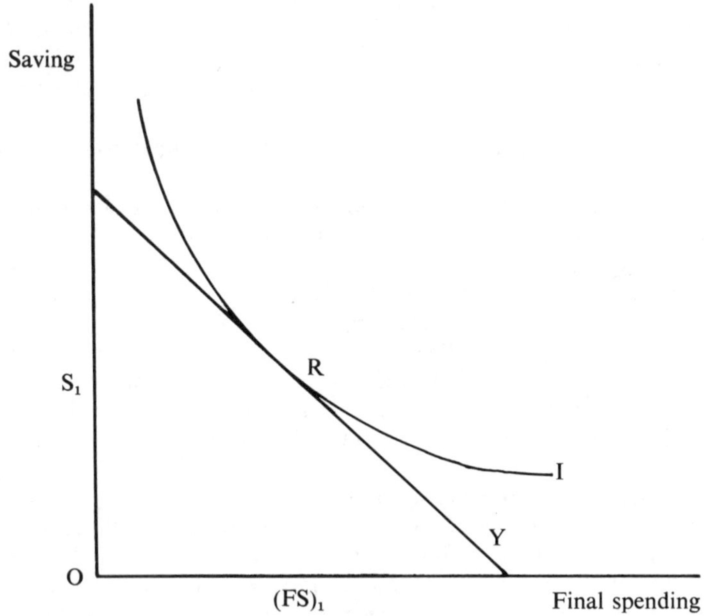

Figure 1

the income-allocation indifference curve, the better off is the consumer with no saturation point.[24]

The income constraint can be shown in Figure 1 as a straight line, Y, whose intercept equals total income. The slope of the income constraint depends on the trade off between the current purchasing power and the future purchasing power of the unit of income. For operational simplicity, let income be measured in money terms and let money prices remain constant. The equilibrium of the consumer is at the point *R* in Figure 1 where the marginal rate of substitution equals the slope of the income constraint.

Section IV will discuss the determinants of the slope of the budget line and investigate the macroeconomics of the behaviour of the consumer in an Islamic economy; it will also compare it with a non-Islamic economy.

IV

THE MACROECONOMICS OF CONSUMER BEHAVIOUR IN AN ISLAMIC SOCIETY

In order to derive the macro function of final spending in an Islamic economy, certain assumptions must be made.

1. An Islamic economy is defined as an economy where the Islamic laws and institutions prevail; and where the majority of its individuals believe in the Islamic ideology and practise its way of life. This makes such a society quite different from the contemporary "Muslim" societies.

2. More specifically, the institution of *Zakāt* is assumed to be a part of the socio-economic structure and that it is collected and distributed in accordance to the Islamic injunctions; that there exists a *Zakāt* Fund as a department of the executive branch of the government; that *Zakāt* is considered as a constant ratio of net worth; and that there are no restrictions on the collection and distribution of *Zakāt* as to whether it is done in real terms or in money terms, or concerning the percentage given to each of the eight worthy destinations. The ownership of *Zakāt* must be transferred to one or more of these eight categories mentioned under this footnote;[25] it should not remain in the hands of the authorities. However, *Zakāt* can be collected or dispensed with in the form of consumer's goods or producer's goods.

3. The third assumption is that in the given Islamic economy *Ribā* is prohibited by law. Every interest on credit is considered *Ribā*. This means that the rate of interest on loans should always be zero. There is no discrimination, as far as the prohibition of interest is concerned, between producer's credit and consumer's credit. However, this study is more concerned with the loans for investment rather than with consumption loans.

4. The fourth assumption being that *Qirāḍ* does exist as a legal economic institution. *Qirāḍ* is defined as the act of injecting money assets in the production process through the co-operation of the entrepreneur who provides his entrepreneurial skill and *Muqāriḍ* who furnishes his funds.[26] The net income of the project is divided between them. The reward of *Muqāriḍ* will be called *profishare*, and the reward of the entrepreneur will be called profit.[27] The crucial difference between profishare and interest on capital is that the former is a percentage of net income of the firm; whereas the latter is a fixed cost of production.

5. Fifthly, developed monetary markets for producer's goods, consumer's goods, and especially financial instruments are assumed.

6. And sixthly the consumer is assumed to maximise the satisfaction of his income as described in the previous section. Additionally, and in accordance with the implications of the saying of the Prophet (peace be upon him) which reads: "Invest the *Māl* of the orphans so that it does not vanish because of the deductions of *Zakāt*," it is assumed that consumers are interested in preventing the level of their wealth from declining after the payment of *Zakāt*.

The Final Spending Decision

Now that the assumptions of the Macro model are made clear, we can investigate the effects of the *Zakāt* institution and the prohibition of *Ribā* on the decision of income allocation between saving and final spending. *Zakāt* influences both its payer and its recipient. The effects of *Zakāt* on the *Zakāt* payer are as follows:

(a) The payment of *Zakāt* entices the payer to raise saving ratio at each level of income. Since *Zakāt* is imposed on accumulated net worth and not only on income, the wealth-owner-consumer must increase his saving ratio in order to prevent the level of his wealth from decreasing. For example, if the rate of return on capital is 10% the wealth owner needs to save more than 25% of his income in order to keep his wealth constant. On the aggregate, almost all wealth owners are taxed by *Zakāt* since the minimum exempted level, *Niṣāb*, is very low. This effect of *Zakāt* on saving is positive: the introduction of *Zakāt* raises the saving-income ratio. This effect is called "the saving effect". It must be observed that this is a once and for all rise in the saving function since the *Zakāt* rate is not variable. This means that as a result of the saving effect, the saving-income ratio must be higher in an Islamic society than in a non-Islamic society.

(b) *Zakāt* penalises idle wealth, whether this is held in terms of "Argent sterile" or in terms of "waiting" means of production. This effect tightens the relationship between saving decision and investment and brings these two decisions closer to each other as far as the time span between them is concerned.

On the other hand, the effect of *Zakāt* on the income-allocation decision of *Zakāt* recipients is to increase their disposable income, hence, increasing both saving and final spending together. It must be noted, however, that not all the recipients of *Zakāt* are in the classes characterised by low saving ratio, since only three kinds of *Zakāt* recipients have immediate consumption necessities; these are: the poor, the needy and the wayfarer. In addition, the economic policy, concerning the collection and the distribution of *Zakāt* in terms of producer's goods, money, or consumer's goods, affects the income-allocation decision of the recipients and limits their degree of choice.

Consequently, the aggregate effect of *Zakāt* must be a higher saving-income ratio since it represents an upward shift of the saving function (on the part of *Zakāt* payers) and a rightward movement along the curve (on the part of *Zakāt* recipients).

Moreover, the prohibition of interest raises current final spending in relation to saving. In the construction of Figure 3, we assume that neither saving nor final spending is inferior.

If the rate of interest is more than zero, the slope of the income constraint must be more than one (absolute value). In Figure 3, the budget line YY has a slope of -1, it represents the zero interest rate. YY′ has a slope of $-\left(\frac{1+i}{1}\right)$, where $i > 0$ is the rate of interest. The point *C* measures the level of final spending when current money income is equal to the distance

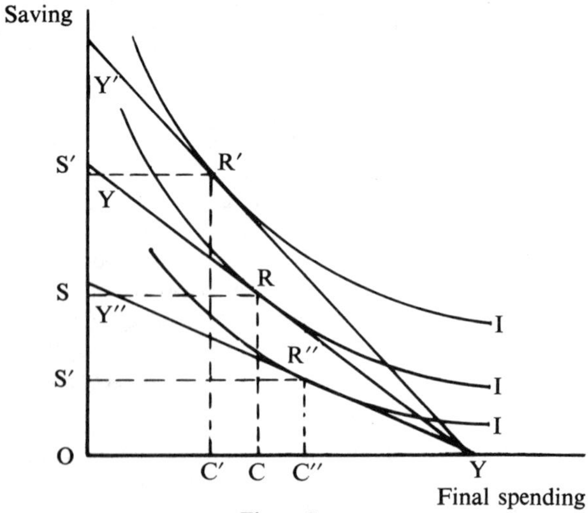

Figure 3a

OY and the rate of interest is zero; whereas, point C' measures final spending for the same level of current income but for a positive rate of interest. In Figure 3b, the final spending function (FS) is derived from the points which are similar to point R in panel 3a for different level of current income. By the same token the final spending function (FS)′ is derived from points similar to R'.

Assume that savings are not invested. The part of money income that is not used for current final spending in period t must decrease in period $t + 1$ by the amount of *Zakāt*. Consequently, the Islamic institutions do not only reduce the absolute value of the slope of the income constraint to unity by having prohibited interest, but they reduce it further to less than one by taxing savings at the rate of 2.5% annually. The combined effect of the prohibition of *Ribā* and the imposition of *Zakāt* is to shift the final spending function to (FS)″ in panel *b* of Figure 3. This positive effect on final spending will be called "the final spending effect".

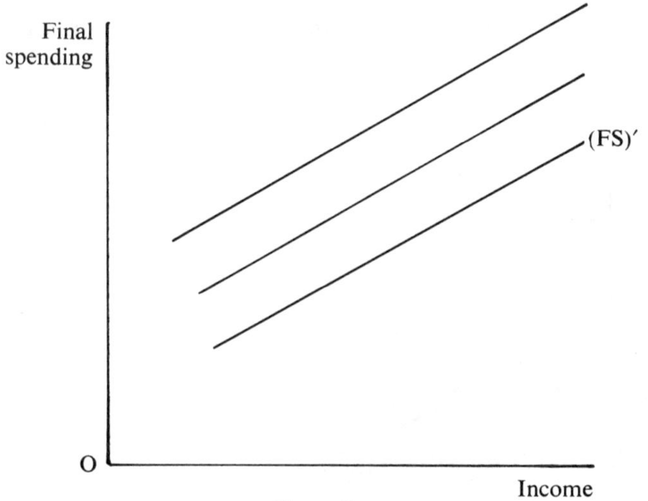

Figure 3b

The Investment Decision

The foregoing analysis has two apparently contradictory effects: the saving effect and the final spending effect. This section attempts to resolve this apparent contradiction and to explain how these two effects can be consistent with each other and with the dynamics of the system. The household, as an income earner is interested in increasing the ratio of current final spending to income, because the higher the saving ratio, the lower the income-allocation indifference curve. This may seem as negating the conventional wisdom, but the subsequent analysis will show its rationalisation.

Assume that one's income is *Y*, it is received at the beginning of the period, say a year; assume also that *s* is the percentage of Y that is saved for the whole period; savings will be used at the end of the period for final spending; and the next-period current income is zero. Total final spending of this individual in the two periods is:

$$FS = (Y - S) + (S - Sz),$$

where *FS* is total final spending, *S* is total savings, and *z* is the rate of *Zakāt*. Then:

$$FS = (Y - sY) = (sY - zsY), \text{ or:}$$
$$FS = Y(1 - zs).$$

Thus, the relationship between total final spending and the saving ratio is negative. There exists an inverse relationship between FS and *s*. This is shown in Figure 4 where $s_1 > s_2 > s_3$, and the slope of the Y's is $-\left(\frac{1-z}{1}\right)$. The higher the saving ratio, the lower is the attainable basket of total final spending.

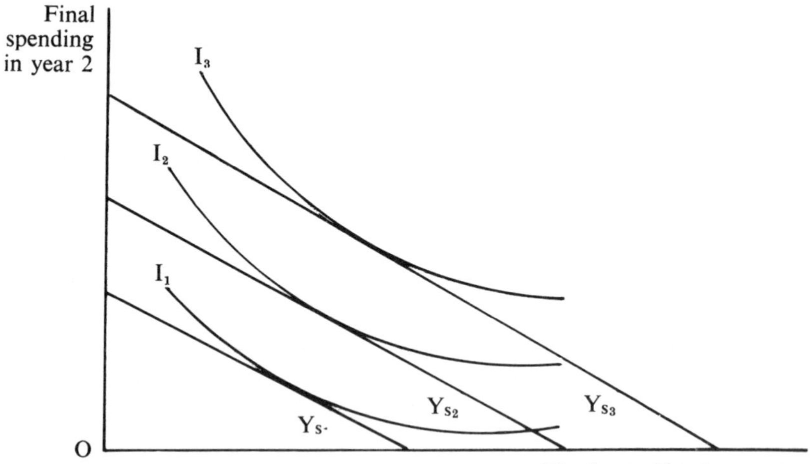

Figure 4

The household, as a wealth holder, is concerned about at least maintaining its wealth intact. This is done by raising the saving ratio in order to compensate for the *Zakāt* payment.

Consequently, the behaviour of the household can be described as a maximisation of consumer's satisfaction subject to two constraints: the amount of income, and the maintenance of wealth, that is:

$$\text{Max } U = U(FS,S).$$

$$\text{Subject to: } FS + S = Y, \text{ and}$$

$$DW = S \geqslant z(W + S),$$

where U is consumer satisfaction, W is the consumer's wealth, and D is the time derivative. For simplicity, let income be generated from only one source, profishare; that is: $Y = (QR)vW$; where Q is the rate of profishare, R is a rate of return on projects, and v is the rate of wealth utilisation. The income received at the beginning of each period is the result of the economic activity during the previous period: hence, it is a historical datum for the period of the study. This implies, in Figure 5, and is given from the time period $t - 1$. It was shown, in Figure 4, that at higher saving ratios, the *Zakāt* payment will be higher; consequently, the part of income left at the disposal of the household is smaller. This means, in terms of Figure 5, that the higher the ratio of saving to income, the flatter the income constraint. In fact, the slope of the income constraint is bounded from below; that is:

$$-1 \frac{dS}{d\,(FS)} = \frac{-(1 - z)}{1}.$$

Figure 5 shows the relationship between the saving decision and the investment decision. If the decision to save is not accompanied by a decision to invest, i.e., if $v < 1$, the consumer will be on a lower indifference curve such as 1″.

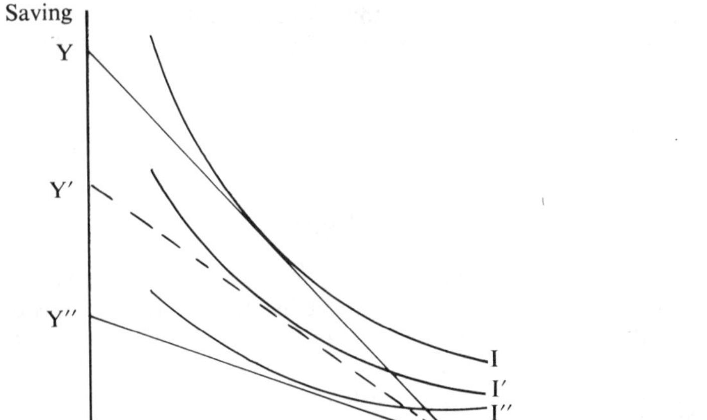

Figure 5

The slope of the Y's is determined by the rate of utilisation of savings, v, the rate of profishare on investment, Q, the rate of return on projects, R, and *Zakat* rate, *z*, which is institutionally constant. For a given income and s = 0, current final spending will be at the point *Y*. For s = 1 and v = 0, the slope of the budget line becomes $-\left(\frac{1 - z}{1}\right)$, the applicable budget line is YY″ and the equilibrium of the consumer is at the lowest indifference curve. At higher rate of utilisation of savings, the slope of the income constraint increases (in absolute value). The slope of the income constraint is calculated by the following equation:

$$\frac{dS}{d\,(FS)} = -\frac{(+\,QR)\,(1 - z)}{1}\,v.$$

When v = 1, i.e., when savings are utilised immediately in the productive process, the level of the consumer's satisfaction depends entirely on the rate of profishare on investment and the rate of return on projects, since *z* is constant. It must be noted that the absolute value of the slope of the income constraint is positively related to the rate of savings' utilisation, the rate of profishare, and the rate of return on projects.

Two conclusions follow from the discussion of this section: first, the Islamic system is characterised by the phenomenon that unless investment considerations are integrated in the decision to save, consumer's welfare is negatively influenced by saving. And second, the consumer-saver's welfare is directly influenced by the state of affairs in the society. A decline in the economic activity reduces the rate of return on projects, *R*, the thing which reduces the profitability of investment and lowers the absolute value of the slope of the income constraint, this in turn, reduces the saving ratio through the consumer's endeavour to reach a higher level of indifference; consequently, saving is positively related to the rate of return on projects.

V

CONCLUSIONS

In view of the preceding facts and arguments, it may be concluded that:

1. In contrast to the communo-capitalist theory, the Islamic theory considers the consumer as a maximiser of *Falāḥ*. *Falāḥ* is the success in this life and in the afterlife. Muslims say in their daily prayers: "Our Lord, grant us good in the life on this earth and good in the lifeafter".

2. The Islamic economic system, by virtue of the very nature of its institutions, maintains a high rate of saving. It must be noted that the maintenance of wealth is not a cost of production like the maintenance of capital (allowance for depreciation). The reduction of the individual wealth by *Zakāt* does not necessitate an increase in the rate of depreciation for the economy as a whole. In fact, the deduction of *Zakāt* from the

individual wealth leaves intact the volume of capital in the economy, no matter whether *Zakāt* is paid in terms of consumer's goods such as food and shelter, or whether it is paid in durable or perishable commodities.

3. The inherent forces of the Islamic system make the perspectives of investment an integral part of the saving decision. This has some significant effects on the comparative statics of the system. Saving is positively related to the investment opportunities and expectations. This sort of relationship implies that, at times of declining investment expectations, saving will decline and consumption will rise. This in turn increases aggregate demand and improves expectations.

In the interest system, the decision to invest is completely separated from the decision to save. Such a dichotomy provides a major cause for fluctuations in the economic activity.

This conclusion, gives an economic interpretation of verse 275 in *Sūrah* 2 which reads: "And Allah hath permitted trade and forbidden *Ribā*".

4. At the same time that the consumer-wealth owner is encouraged to (at least) maintain the level of his wealth by increasing his saving (investment), the distribution of *Zakāt* increases the disposable income of the recipients, thus raising their consumption, i.e., the system provides for an increase in output (resulting from the attachment of the decision of saving to the decision of investment) and an increase in aggregate demand at the same time.

5. The Islamic system secures larger resources for growth and development than can otherwise be done. This is achieved by the automatic forces of the system even without any deliberate economic policy.

6. The system mobilises non-active wealth by dissolving and reintroducing it into the economic circuit.

7. The system puts the hand of the economic policy on a big portion of the society's output. *Zakāt* has to be collected and distributed every year, giving the economic authority, through the *Zakāt* Fund a hand in influencing the trends of economic activity as well as its level through proper administration of the *Zakāt* Fund.

8. This study has also shown the significance of *Zakāt* as a tax on the accumulated net worth rather than a tax on income alone. Although it did not discuss the distributive effects of *Zakāt* or its role with regard to social welfare, the study has proved that this kind of tax plays an important role in the functioning of the Islamic system, even as an incentive for investment.

At the end, I must admit that this paper does not tackle the issue of a fiscal and financial system in Islam. That is to say that this paper does not attempt to claim that there must be no other taxes but *Zakāt*.

Notes

1 Weber, Max, *The Protestant Ethic and the Spirit of Capitalism* (New York: Charles Scribner's Sons, 1958), first published in German 1904–5, p. 76.

2 *Ibid.*, p. 52.
3 Shows, E. Warren and Burton, Robert H., *Macroeconomics* (Massachusetts: D. C. Heath and Company, 1972), pp. 49–88.
4. Sremuilin, S., "Fifty years of Social Progress in the USSR", Voprosy Ekonomiki, 1969 No. 11 translated in "Problems of Economics", 8 (June 1970): 3–34; and "Natural Resource Evaluation", "Problems of Economics" 10 (April 1968): 19–30.
5 Andorka, R., *Mikromodellek* (Micromodels). (Budapest: Kozgazdasaries Jogi Konyykiado, 1970), Reviewed in Acta Economica 7 No. 2, 1971, pp. 239–241.
6 Weber, Max, *ibid.*, p. 76.
7 In this regard, the Qur'ān talks about the enjoyment in the lifeafter in so many verses that any specific quotation is useless. However, there are several verses in Al-Qur'ān that refer to the measurability and the comparability of the postponed and immediate effects. For example, verse 261 of *Sūrah* 2 says: "The parable of those who spend their *Māl* in the way of Allah is that of a grain, it groweth seven ears, and each ear hath a hundred grains. Allah giveth manifold increase to whom He pleaseth, and Allah careth of all and He knoweth all things".
8 Among a good number of Sayings of the Prophet and verses of the Qur'ān, one is impressingly amazing as an extreme example of communal improvement. The Prophet (peace be upon him) is reported as saying: "If the Day of Judgement has come to one of you while he has a small plant in his hand, he should plant it".
9 The Qur'ān gives a detailed example of the Islamic view on the relation between success and riches in the story of "the owner of the two gardens" in *Sūrah* 19, verses 32–44.
10 Verse 15 in *Sūrah* 67 reads: "It is He who has made the earth manageable for you, so traverse ye through its tracts and enjoy of the sustenance which He furnishes you, but unto Him is the resurrection".
11 The Prophet is reported as saying: "Verily, Allah likes you, when you make something, to make it with perfection". Narrated by Al-Baihaqī.
12 The Prophet is reported as objecting to the act of abstention from the lawful enjoyment of material living.
13 The Qur'ān emphasised efficiency in several verses, such as "And those foremost will be foremost." Thus giving efficiency a religious content that touches the heart of the believer. Additionally, the Prophet is reported asking Allah: ". . ., and protect me from deficiency (or inaptitude) and laziness, . . ." Narrated by Al-Ḥākim and Al-Baihaqī. Additionally, Islam prescribes five prayers in a day, as if it is telling that a day is a very long period that must be calculated by hours and minutes.
14 Muhammad Nejatullah Siddiqui; *Some Aspects of the Islamic Economy* (Delhi: Markazī Maktaba Islāmī, 1972), p. 19.
15 The Qur'ān classifies spending (and not *Māl* itself) as an act of goodness or an act of evil in *Sūrah* 2 verse 265 and *Sūrah* 3 verse 117.
16 The Prophet (peace be upon him) is reported as saying: "Poverty is almost disbelief". Also with respect to showing His bounty upon the Prophet Muḥammad Allah asked: "Did He not find thee an orphan and give thee shelter, and He found thee wandering and gave thee guidance, and He found thee in need and made thee rich". *Sūrah* 93, verses 6–8.
17 Narrated by Al-Bukhārī in *Al-Adab Al-Mufrad.*
18 The Prophet (peace be upon him) is reported as saying: "You don't really possess of your *Māl* but that you eat and use up, that you dress and wear up, and that you spend on charity and preserve (for the lifeafter)". Narrated by Muslim and Ahmad.
19 Maximisation or making the best out of limited resources is an Islamic concept emphasised in many sayings of the Prophet. Generally, the idea of maximisation is related to the belief in the upcoming Judgement and the consideration of this current life as a "life of testing". The concept of maximisation is plainly mentioned

in the following saying of the Prophet: "A believer does never reach saturation of good till he reaches his end, Heaven".

20 Final spending is defined later.

21 The Islamic injunction in this regard is that one should not be avaricious. If one is rich, one should enjoy a higher level of spending on one's material wants and on the prosperity of one's lifeafter. Looking through the social history of Islam, you may find many applications of this injunction. For example, Abū Hanīfa used to enjoy good clothing; and 'Abdullāh Ibn Al-Mubārak used to pray to Allah asking Him to give him richness, and he was a big spender on charity.

22 This is a problem in i to n commodities and j to m ways of spending for the sake of Allah. Money prices of the n commodities are assumed known. The subjective prices of the m ways are determined by three factors: First, the objective weights given to the j way in the Islamic teaching, and their weight in relation to the i commodity; second, the capitalisation period of the lifeafter's enjoyment; and third, the degree of religious consciousness of the individual consumer. For example, while Muslims were preparing for the battle of Tabūk, 'Uthmān preferred to give away for *Jihād* all his newly imported business; at the same time he was offered double or triple of his cost as profit. He did that on the ground that he had a better offer, ten times. He was referring to verse 161 in *Sūrah* 6 of Al-Qur'ān. In this example, the capitalisation period was zero for 'Uthmān and the level of religious consciousness was very high; consequently, the subjective price of spending for *Jihād* was equal to its objective relative weight given in Al-Qur'ān.

23 The Prophet is reported advising his companion Sa'd "you better leave your heirs rich than leaving them poor and dependent on asking other people". Narrated by Al-Bukhārī and Muslim.

24 See the saying of the Prophet mentioned in footnote 19.

25 These are mentioned in *Sūrah* 9 verse 61 in the Qur'ān, as follows:

"Poor, needy, employees of the Fund of *Zakāt*, those whose hearts have been recently reconciled, those in bondage and in debt, in the Cause of Allah, and wayfarer."

26 The terms used here do not bear the same contents as in jurists' literature. The definitions given above suit better the analysis in this paper.

27 The distribution of the net income of the firm (project) between *Muqāriḍ* and the entrepreneur is outside the scope of this paper. However, something must be mentioned about it in order to remove the confusion which may arise about the working of the system. In the capitalist theory of income distribution, input markets determine the share of inputs, capital and labour. These are considered as costs of production. Similarly, the commodity market determines the prices of output. The share of the entrepreneur, profit, is simply the residual; i.e., the difference between total revenue and total cost.

In the Islamic theory, this is not exactly so. The cost of labour is determined in the factor market; but since interest is prohibited the cost of labour equals total cost of production in a simplified two-factor model. The difference between total cost and total revenue is distributed between the entrepreneur and *Muqāriḍ*. This is achieved in *Qirāḍ* market, where the entrepreneur and *Muqāriḍ* meet. Figure 2 describes this market; the vertical axis measures the percentage of the net income of the firm (TR-TC) which is given to *Muqāriḍ*. This percentage is the rate of profishare. The horizontal axis measures the flow of *Qirāḍ* funds, i.e., net investment. The supply of *Qirāḍ* funds is a function of consumer preferences as well as the profishare rate and the expected rate of return on projects. At a higher rate of profishare, the supply of investment rises, indicating that the supply curve is upward sloping to the right. A change in consumer preferences toward more saving implies an upward shift in the supply of investment and a rise in the expected rate of return on projects shift the supply curve downward.

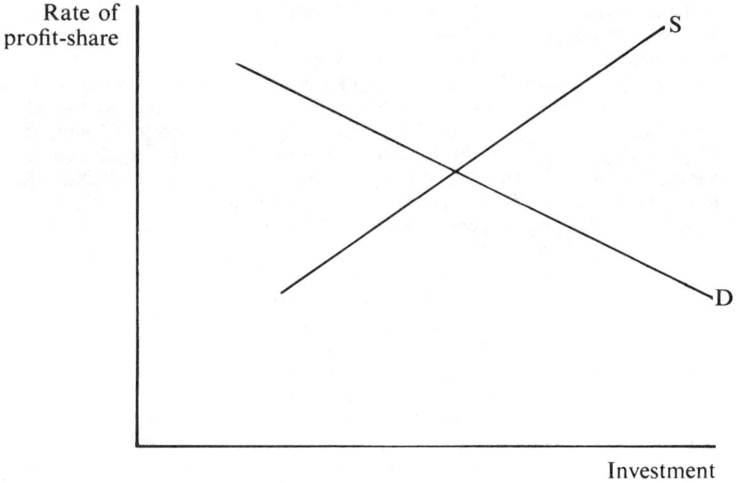

Figure 2

The demand for investment is a function of the rate of profishare, the expected rate of return of the project (i.e., the rate of net income to total investment), and the entrepreneurial skills. At a higher rate of return on the project, the demand curve shifts upward whereas an increase in the entreprenurial skills, say by an exogenous increase in inventions shifts the demand curve upward because it increases the rate of profishare offered for each level of investment. The slope of the demand curve is negative because at higher rate of profishare the desire of the entrepreneur to make new ventures declines. The entrepreneurial skills affect the demand for investment through the capital-entrepreneurship ratio.

It must be noted that this market only determines the shares of *Muqāriḍ* and the entrepreneur in the net income of the firm; but it does not determine the rates on return or investment or on entrepreneurial skills. To determine these rates of return, we need to know the rate of return on the project. One result of the presence of *Qirāḍ* market in the Islamic theory is that it makes the share of the entrepreneur, profit (as well as the share of *Muqāriḍ*) deterministic through the functioning of the supply and demand rather than being left as a residual. However, the full implications of changing the share of capital, from being considered a fixed cost of production to becoming a percentage of net income, still have to be investigated.

CHAPTER THREE

Some Conceptual and Practical Aspects of Interest-Free Banking

*Dr. Muhammad Uzair**

BANKING is an important financial intermediary and vital institution in the economic structure of any country. It mobilises savings and idle funds in an economy and makes them available to those who can make better and fuller use of them. In this way, banking effects a re-allocation of the capital funds. Besides this main function, the banking system makes possible a most convenient method of making payments through chequing facilities, and renders many other subsidiary services. An important question that agitates the minds of those who think on Islamic economics, whether proponents or critics, is the feasibility of interest-free banking. It is proposed to discuss here, briefly, certain conceptual and practical aspects of the issue.

At the very outset it is desirable to lay down the axioms or assumptions for the following discussion. The first axiom is that interest in all its forms is prohibited by the Holy Qur'ān. This also implies that there is no room or justification to introduce various interpretations on the term *Ribā* as has been attempted by some scholars. The second axiom is that the Muslim society in an Islamic State is genuinely interested in eliminating *Ribā* and sincerely desires to introduce a system of interest-free banking, not as a supplement to, but as a substitute for the prevalent system of banking. This means that the members of the society and the State are not only interested in making the change, but are prepared to bear the inconvenience and the difficulties that would be unavoidable in the transitional phase of the changeover. These two axioms have been mentioned in the beginning because it is not only a scientific system of analysis and writing according to research techniques, but is also the approach of the Holy Qur'ān itself.

*Dr. Muhammad Uzair, Consultant, Investment Corporation of Pakistan, is amongst the pioneers of *Ribā*-free banking. He has also served as Professor of Economics, University of Karachi; Director, Institute of Business Administration, Karachi; and Member, Monopoly Commission, Govt. of Pakistan.

In the very beginning of the Holy Book, preconditions have been laid down regarding the people who are likely to benefit from the guidance, from the code of life, given in the Qur'ān.

I. Redefining the Factors of Production

In the light of the above-mentioned axioms, let us now look at the need to modify the conceptual framework of economics to suit the requirements of Islamic economics. The beginning will have to be made by redefining the factors of production.

A postulate which is essential for the analytical framework of Islamic economics is that capital as a separate factor of production does not exist, but is a part of another factor of production, namely enterprise. This means in essence redefining the term "enterprise" in a broader way so as to include "capital" as a part thereof. This, it may be mentioned, is not difficult to reconcile. With the passage of time and technological changes in methods of production, the definitions of other factors of production have also gone through changes. Land, for example, does not mean land in the limited sense any more, but for all practical purposes land today is synonymous with the term "natural resources". Similarly, the term "labour" has become wider, to include not only the industrial worker in the limited sense, but white-collared personnel, as well as the managerial personnel in any productive unit. Thus, for all practical purposes the term "labour" now denotes all "human resources". Moreover, considering the modern methods of production, along with an assessment of the qualitative process of production, suggests the need for considering technology as an important factor of production. Technology plays its role whenever there is a relationship between natural resources and human resources. The production resulting from a combination of natural and human resources is also determined by technology. It needs no proof or effort to establish that, given the same inputs of natural and human resources the quality of the "enterprise" factor and the quality of the "technology" factor will lead to different outputs in two productivity units, or indeed in two different countries. In the text books of economics one finds that whenever there is a discussion of economic laws, such as the law of diminishing marginal utility or the law of diminishing marginal returns, a qualification is mentioned that the quality of the commodities and the inputs respectively remain the same or unchanged. However, in practical life we find that except in a very primitive society things do not remain the same and the qualities of commodities or inputs invariably change over a reasonable span of time. This in other words means that in the present day, technology has become such an important factor that the quality of products and the quality of the natural resources, as well as the quality of the human resources applied, always change with the passage of time, except perhaps in a very short run or at one point of time in a limited sense. The importance of technology thus has to be recognised as a factor of production and assuming that this factor remains constant means laying down an assumption which is not relevant to the facts of practical life.

The postulate of combining capital with enterprise is conceptually not too difficult to reconcile. The definition of the term "interest" in the economic literature has already been broken down into two parts on a conceptual level. A distinction has been made between the return on the capital, and the "risk premium" to take care of the risk or uncertainties in recovery and other things. This distinction implies that conceptually speaking interest and profit have some resemblance, in that interest includes reward for risk while profit constitutes a reward for uncertainty. This, in other words, means some resemblance between capital and enterprise. Moreover, the formation of large corporations and companies with a large number of shareholders – sometimes more than a million – and the institution of raising share capital of joint stock companies from the general public have tended to combine the functions of enterprise and capital in the same persons. Entrepreneurs, therefore, are not only the small number of promoters who conceive and initiate a particular project but also the large number of shareholders who join the sponsors or promoters and also become entrepreneurs. All that these large number of entrepreneurs are doing is to provide capital, or more precisely "risk capital" and agreeing to accept the return or profit on their investment which is not predetermined but has some uncertainty regarding the rate of dividend likely to be declared, and be mentally prepared for the extreme possibility of not receiving any dividends if the performance of the company or the project is not nearly as satisfactory and fruitful as was anticipated by the people who subscribed to the share capital.

With the passage of time the concept or definition of a bank has also undergone many changes. The modern-day banks are no longer operating on the classical lines of commercial banking, namely short term loans of 90 days in the nature of "self-liquidating" loans or bills. The classical concept of a commercial bank as providing only short term capital for three months has undergone changes. The modern banks, not only in developed countries but also in developing countries, are engaging themselves in a big way in financing industries and agriculture. This financing, moreover, is not confined to short term capital but includes credit facilities to help in acquisition of fixed assets for intermediate terms as well as long terms of maturity. Thus, the distinction between commercial banks and development banks is fast disappearing because of the structural changes in the economic activities of most of the countries. Commerce is no longer the most important sector for the banks. The relative importance of this sector has declined in all countries, including the developing countries. Similarly, the investment operations regarding the earning assets of the banks have increased. Investments by banks are not confined to short term treasury bills or even long term government bonds bearing interest. Commercial banks have started making investments in the equity shares of enterprises, so enabling the banks to collect dividends on those shares. Thus, it will be noticed that the water-tight compartmentalisation of commercial banks and investment banks is also disappearing gradually. In brief the commercial banks are moving from purely commercial banking to development and investment banking, thus getting used to examining carefully the profitability of the projects or the scripts in which they use their funds. Scientific financial and credit analysis are in practice in all the good banks. Thus, the banks should not find it difficult from a practical point of view to shift from interest-earning bodies to profit-sharing or dividend-receiving bodies.

II. Flaws in the Theory of Interest

The theory of interest has always been a very difficult area in economic literature. The application of a marginal productivity approach has not been found to be very helpful in the case of interest. Complex explanations have been attempted to explain the rationale of charging interest, the rate of interest and the supply of capital funds. Some of the explanations which have been given are: (a) Time Preference Theory, (b) Abstinence Theory, and (c) Liquidity Preference Theory.

The most formidable treatment of the theory of interest has been given by Austrian economist Bohm-Bawerk. He tried to explain the rationale of interest and the rate of interest in terms of time preference, namely the concept of technical superiority of present over future. This implies that an average person prefers present over future and if he is required to forego the present comfort or use of his funds, he is entitled to some remuneration known as interest. However, the explanation of capital formation is rooted in the "roundaboutness" of the method of production.

This complex concept takes us to a primitive society, and an explanation of capital is given in terms of "physical capital" formation, or to be more exact, accumulation of "capital goods". Naturally, an explanation of the origin of accumulation of capital goods cannot be used to explain capital formation and allied rationale for charging interest in a period when cash capital or "capital funds" are used. Moreover, Bohm-Bawerk – who tried to offer a counter-thesis to the concept of Karl Marx – by emphasising the roundaboutness of production ends up with an explanation of capital formation in terms of primitive capital which in turn brings his thesis very near to the labour theory of value expounded by Marx.

Similarly, the concept of abstinence given by some other thinkers is untenable in the present society. In the practical life of today, we do not see any abstinence on the part of those who provide the bulk of the savings or the capital funds. This can perhaps be possible in a very primitive society where the government may force the people to save, thus causing an abstinence or sacrifice on the part of those who save, providing capital funds, thus entitling them to a reward for the abstinence or the sacrifice in the form of an interest payment. The concept of "forced saving" of the modern variation is even less applicable in the case of a saving process making available the capital funds and justifying the payment of interest thereon.

The Keynesian concept of "liquidity preference" as a justification or rationale of interest on the supply side is accompanied by a concept of marginal efficiency of capital on the demand side. In the Keynesian framework these two concepts determine the rate of interest. The determination of interest by liquidity preference is not exactly the same thing as determination of interest by supply of savings or investible funds. However, doubt has been expressed about the validity of this explanation. It has not been established whether the supply of liquid funds or savings in general are determined by the rate of interest, though they may be partially affected by that phenomenon.[1] Thus we find that economists have been hard put to explain the rationale of interest and the rate of interest.

Perhaps the theory of interest is the least clear part of the entire economic theory. This is so because an effort has been made to explain something which is difficult to justify. Those who have tried to give some rationale, taking into account and criticising other theories and explanations had ultimately to use the concept of opportunity cost. The rate of interest according to them consists of three parts: (a) the basic interest rate, (b) a risk premium, and (c) administrative costs involved in the lending process. The combination of the first two components, namely the basic rate and the risk premium constitute the opportunity cost.[2] However, no valid and sound explanation has been given regarding the basic rate itself. The basic or the minimum rate has been taken as the rate of interest charged by the government on their securities which have practically no risk of non-recovery.

The basic rate of interest or the opportunity cost has been identified as the government rate of interest on its securities wherein no risk is involved. This is hardly a satisfactory conceptual explanation. This rate paid by the government is an arbitrary decision, and a constant rather than a variable explained in the normal economic powers.

Another practical difficulty in explaining the rationale of interest and its rate is the fact that capital funds actually used for investment purposes come from different sources. On an *ex post facto* basis the total investment and the total saving are supposed to be equal not only in the Keynesian framework but also in the analysis of those who partially differ with Keynes. However, on *ex ante* basis the investment and savings may not be equal according to the economists. The difference is because of the fact that investment is supposed to be the function of the entrepreneur, while saving the supply of capital is the function of the capitalist or the saver.

For the economy as a whole, though, what really matters is investment or the saving actually used. Thus the real thing of significance is the capital funds. The courses of supply of capital funds in the present-day economy are various:

(a) The most important source for the supply of capital in modern industrialised society is the "retained earnings" or the reserves built by various productive units. In many advanced countries, the retained earnings constitute more than half of the additional funds required. This portion of available capital funds naturally is not determined by the rate of interest but is a function of other variables such as possible uses and expected rate of return on the investible funds accumulated in the form of retained earnings by the corporations and companies.
(b) Capital funds made available and used in the form of equity investment, namely new investment in shares issued by various productive units or companies. At present, with joint stock companies as the typical form of business ownership and organisation, an important and significant part of total capital funds, and utilisation of savings of the people, takes this shape.
(c) Capital funds available in the form of lending on the basis of interest. This shape or form of savings may be used in government securities, debentures or bonds of the private sector, and deposits in the banks.

Looking at these three alternative sources of supply of capital funds one is bound to realise that at present, two out of these three alternative sources of capital funds originate without any consideration of interest. One finds that the bulk of the total capital funds take the shape of equity investment in one form or the other. This development, therefore, leads us to justify the merging of the two factors of production, namely enterprise and capital into one single factor. Thus consequent elimination of interest as a form of reward for capital is justified for two reasons: Firstly, that conceptually a sound and correct explanation of interest as a remuneration has not been possible by the economists who have thought little on the subject. Secondly, looking at the practical operation of the present-day economy we know that the sharp line of distinction between capital as a factor of production, and enterprise as a factor of production, is not tenable, as it would be in a primitive society where everything can be explained in terms of labour theory, as done by Karl Marx.

Under the present analytical framework of modern economic theory capital is a factor of production entirely different from all other factors of production. The differences between the characteristics of capital and other factors are:

(a) Unlike other factors of production, capital is itself the result of production, or a produced means of production. This does not apply to other factors like land, labour and enterprise.
(b) The origin of capital, and the accompanying justification for its remuneration, are derived from the accumulation of physical capital or capital goods in a primitive society. However, the same justification for reward or remuneration is applied to cash capital or capital funds. This is a unique treatment and creates confusion.
(c) Factors of production other than capital lose some degree of productivity and utility with the passage of time. While other factors of production wear out or depreciate with usage, capital in the sense of "cash capital" as different from "physical capital" does not wear out or lose its value over time.
(d) While in the case of other factors of production, there is always some unavoidable difference in quality between one unit and the other units, capital in the sense of "cash capital" is of uniform quality as far as various units are concerned.

These differences between capital and other factors of production naturally raise a question as to whether the capital is a factor of production at all, or is it only a tool or means for another factor of production, namely enterprise. It is known that pre-enterprise in the sense of enterprise without having some capital along with it, does not exist in practical life. This means that there are capital funds available in two forms and in two manners, namely capital which goes automatically with enterprise, usually known as the "risk capital", and the pure capital or credit which is available at a certain rate of interest. Logically, therefore, capital should be merged with the other factor of production known as enterprise.

The separation of enterprise and capital has created not only conceptual problems but has caused practical problems in the operation of the economy. According to monetary theories of trade cycles, most of the cyclical fluctuations have resulted from an over-investment or under-investment of "cash capital" in the economy. The lack of synchronisation between saving and investment on *ex ante* basis has created the problems. Through the borrowed capital, which has no relationship with the voluntary saving, there is always the possibility of over-expansion resulting in lack of synchronisation between saving and investment. Hayek, a leading proponent of the monetary theory of trade cycles, points out:[3]

> "Nobody has ever asked them to pursue a policy other than that which, as we have seen, gives rise to cyclical fluctuations; and it is not within their power to do away with some fluctuations, seeing that the latter originate not from the policy but from the very nature of the modern organisation of credit. So long as we make use of bank credit as a means of furthering economic development, we shall have to put

> up with the resulting trade cycles. They are in a sense the price we pay for a speed of development exceeding that which people voluntarily make possible through their savings and which, therefore has to be extorted from them."

Thus, if capital is merged with the factor of enterprise, over-expectations and, therefore, over-expansion of credit can be eliminated. The defects of the banking system on a credit basis, pointed out by Hayek, can be overcome if the banking business is reorganised in such a manner that capital and enterprise move together. If there is this merger of capital with enterprise, the possibilities of over-expansion of credit will also be eliminated. This means that all capital becomes "risk capital", or a part of enterprise. The decisions of the members of entrepreneural groups will then not be in a vacuum and on a presumption that bank credit will be available on a contractual basis and at a rate of interest which is substantially lower than the rate of profit. If banking business is reorganised in such a manner that the depositors interested in earning some income on their deposits are required to share the profit and loss with the users of the capital funds or the entrepreneurs, a better equilibrium will emerge and a more harmonious relationship between *ex ante* savings and investment will be possible.

III. Basis of Interest-Free Banking in an Islamic Framework

We have seen earlier that capital is an instrument of enterprise both from a conceptual point of view and from a practical point of view. We will now have a look at the conceptual basis of interest-free banking in the framework of Islamic tenets. As mentioned in the beginning, we start from an axiom or assumption that "interest" as a form of payment for use of capital funds is prohibited. The Holy Qur'ān ordains the prohibition of "interest" (*Ribā*) at least five times in the second *Sūrah*. This prohibition of interest has been put as (i) Madness (*Takhabbuṭ*), (ii) a thing God wants to "destroy" (*Maḥq*), (iii) a thing which if not abandoned deserves a "war" (*Ḥarb*) from God, (iv) a thing which is anti-thesis of faith (*Īmān*) or in other words infidelity (*Kufr*), and (v) a thing if persisted in which calls for permanent abode in hell (*Khulūd fin-Nār*). These aspects of *Ribā*, as it is looked upon in the Qur'ān,[4] have been mentioned only as examples.

As interest is prohibited for all purposes and in all its forms as far as the Islamic framework of thought is concerned, we have to look for guidance for a system of banking which is in consonance with Islam. The conceptual basis for a better banking system even according to general economic theory would be the one wherein capital is a part or partner or instrument of the factor of production known as enterprise. Thus, we have to look in Islamic literature for a permissible form of business relationship between those who provide capital funds and those who use the same, on the basis of sharing profit or loss as the case may be. In this connection we find a mention of the institution of *Muḍārabah* or *Qirāḍ* or *Muqāraḍah*. According to a great Muslim jurist, Imām Sarakhsī, the definition of the institution of *Muḍārabah* based on the Qur'ān and the *Sunnah* is as follows.[5]

" املاء المضاربة مشتقة من الضّرب فى الأرض وانما سمى به الآن المضارب يستحق الربح
بسعيه وعمله نحو شريكه فى الربح ورأس المال الضرب فى الأرض والتصرف وأهل
المدينة يسمون هذا العقد مقارضة ذلك مروى عن عثمان بن عفان رضى الله عنه
فانه دفع الى رجل مالا مقارضة وهو مشتق من القرض وهو القطع فصاحب المال قطع
هذا القدر من المال عن تصرفه وجعل التصريف فيه الى العامل بهذا العقد فسمى به
ويضربون فى الأرض يبتغون من فضل الله " .

Translation: "The word *Muḍārabah* is derived from "*Ḍarb* on Earth". It has been so named because the *Muḍārib* (user of others' capital) qualifies to get a share of the profit on account of his endeavours and work. He thus participates in the profit as well as having the right to use capital, and strive according to his discretion. People of Madinah call this contract *Muqāraḍah* which is derived from the word *Qarḍ*, meaning "surrendering". The owner of capital, thus, surrenders his own rights over that portion of capital, to the *Āmil* (user of capital). This is how it has been so named. We have, however, chosen the former name as it conforms to what occurs in the Book of Allah saying 'and others strive on earth seeking the gift of God' . . . "

The legality of this kind of partnership between the supplier of capital and user of capital is also recognised by other jurists of Islam such as Burhānud-Dīn 'Alī b. Abū Bakr al-Marghīnānī (in his work *Hidāyah*) and 'Alā'ud-Dīn Abū Bakr b. Mas'ūd al-Kāsānī (in his work *Al-Badā'i' was-Sanā'i' fī Tartīb ash-Sharā'i'*). Actually the institution is one of those that prevailed in Arabia before Islam, but was found to conform with the Islamic principles and was thus retained in the Islamic framework. Ibn Rushd says about *Muḍārabah:*[6]

" ولا خلاف بين المسلمين فى جوانى القراض وانه مما كان فى الجاهلية فأقره الاسلام
وأجمعوا على أن صفته أن يعطى الرجل المال على أن يجريه على جزء معلوم
يأخذه العامل من ربح المال أى جزء كان مما يتفقان عليه ثلثا أو ربعا أو نصفا . "

Translation: "And there is no difference of opinion among the Muslims about the legality of *Qirāḍ*. It was an institution in the pre-Islamic period and Islam confirmed it. They all agree that its form is that a person gives to another person some capital that he uses in

> business. The user gets, according to conditions, some specified proportion of the profit, i.e. any proportion they agree, one third, one fourth or even one half."

The two above-mentioned extracts from leading jurists of Islam indicate the legality of a partnership between the saver, or the supplier of the savings, and the user of the savings or the investors. Before we proceed further it may be mentioned that the term "user of capital" as used in the above quotations does not mean only physical worker or labourer in the limited sense but would include entrepreneur or the person who uses the investable fund according to his abilities, experience, and expertise. This difference between society of that particular type and the present-day business framework explains the reason why the user of capital would now include the entrepreneur rather than workers or labourers alone. Moreover, even in those days some of the users of capital were not workers or labourers in the limited sense but were businessmen who used the capital for actual investment purposes. Thus the contract or the arrangement of *Muḍārabah* or *Muqāraḍah* is actually an arrangement of partnership or profit sharing between the supplier of capital and the user of capital who work together as partners and share the profit or loss as the case may be. This is in brief the foundation of partnership between capital and enterprise in the Islamic framework.

We have now to apply the above-mentioned principles of partnership between capital and enterprise in the field of banking. It may be mentioned that in the case of interest-free banking in an Islamic Society there will be three parties: (1) The actual user of capital or entrepreneur; (2) The bank which serves as a partial user of the capital funds and as an intermediary link; and (3) The supplier of savings or capital funds, i.e. depositors in the bank. Thus, there is a triangular relationship between the actual entrepreneurs, the banks, and the depositors. One tier of *Muḍārabah* partnership will be between the depositors and the bank; and the other tier will be between the bank and the ultimate or actual user of the fund or the entrepreneur. There may be for example an arrangement that the entrepreneur (or the borrower in the present-day banking system) and the bank would share the profit in a ratio of 50 per cent each, or 60 per cent for the entrepreneur and 40 per cent for the bank, or any such ratio which may be agreed upon between themselves may be regulated by the government or the central bank. Similarly, there will be an arrangement between the bank and the supplier of capital (depositors in the present banking system) for sharing the profit in the ratio of 50 per cent each or 60 per cent for the bank and 40 per cent for the supplier of capital funds or the depositors. This may seem at first sight to be a complex arrangement, but once the system is introduced and begins to operate in practical life, it will become as mechanical and routine as the present-day system wherein banks charge a higher rate of interest on certain categories of deposit while paying nothing to some types of depositors, e.g. the Current Account depositors. The source of profit for the bank is the difference between the interest it receives and the interest it has to pay to the depositors. Similarly, in the changed framework required for interest-free banking, the entrepreneurs and the bank would share the profit on an agreed percentage or ratio, a higher proportion going to the entrepreneur *vis-à-vis* the banks; and the depositors would share a smaller proportion of what comes to the bank. Variation in ratios may reflect different tiers of the system.

Whether percentage or the ratio for sharing the profit between the entrepreneurs (borrowers) and the banks on the one hand, and that between the banks and the depositors on the other, should be determined in the normal course of business activities and bargaining or should be regulated by the government or central bank as a policy variable or a political decision by the government either arrangement would serve the purpose as far as the conceptual framework is concerned. The decision will have to be taken in the light of the actual circumstances prevailing and the inclination of the people who make the decision. On the face of it, it may seem that a ratio of two thirds for the users (65 per cent) and one third for the suppliers (35 per cent) would seem to be a reasonable arrangement because this would be a good via media. In the extract given, one extreme being the 50 per cent for each party, and the other extreme being one quarter for the supplier and threequarters for the user of capital. However, the central bank of the country can be empowered to introduce slight modifications in the details of the terms and conditions from time to time, depending upon the overall economic situation and the expansionary or contractionary policy pursued by the central bank in the interest of the overall national economic well-being of the country. This power would be analogous to the power to change the "bank rate" in the present system.

The above arrangement would take care of the main profit-earning activity of the banks in an interest-free banking system. To be more precise, the arrangement pertains to what could be described as the "investment account" deposits in the banks. As far as the demand deposits or the demand liabilities are concerned, the matter is simpler as will be discussed a little later. Similarly, subsidiary services or the activities of the banks will remain unaffected. These subsidiary services which are not the main profit-earning activities from the point of view of the banks themselves, constitute an important service for the clients of the banks. The subsidiary services are: remittance facilities, safe vault arrangements and many other relatively smaller services. The real question regarding the feasibility of the interest-free banking system relates to the main profit-earning activities of the bank, namely the loans made available to the industrial and business sectors for whom the bank finance constitutes an important activity. This main business of banking we have already analysed above.

We will now turn to discuss the operational aspects of interest-free banking.

IV. Structure of Banking Business

Having discussed the basis and character of long-term loans in Islamic banking we have to analyse the practical structure of banking operations in interest-free banking. In this connection let us first discuss briefly the deposits of various categories in a commercial bank under any system, and then see how things would stand in an interest-free banking system. The analysis will be based on an approach of sources and uses of funds, namely inflow of deposits and the generation of earning assets therefrom. In the analysis of deposit types, we can also use the Keynesian approach of "motives" of "liquidity preference" and savings. The deposits in commercial banks are of three broad categories, namely: (a) Fixed Deposits or Time Deposits, (b) Savings Bank Account Deposits, and (c) Current Account Deposits. The motives of the deposits and depositors in the three categories are different.

The motives of the depositors in the first category, namely fixed deposits, is "investment motive" or "finance motive", that is to earn on the idle funds some income during the period that they themselves do not utilise those funds in their normal business operations. In the changed framework of banking the deposits in the Fixed Deposits or Time Deposits category will become "Investment Deposits". These deposits will be invested by the banks by making these funds available to the parties who need these investment funds to generate and earn income thereon. These investment funds or loans would constitute the main earning activity of banks in interest-free banking. In case of excess demand for loans, part of the funds can be obtained from the next category of deposits, as we will discuss in the next paragraph. However, in case of even more demand, the bank can resort to borrowing from the central banks as is done at present. Needless to say the availability of the funds from this source will depend on the monetary policy of the central bank, which is quite understandable. The profit or dividend earned on these funds can be utilised by the banks for distribution among the "investment depositors". The income or dividend earned from these funds can be credited on a pro-rata basis to the depositors in this category.

The second category of deposits, namely the Savings Bank Account category is also motivated by the desire to save some funds and to earn some income. The main difference between Fixed Deposits and Savings Bank Deposits is the nature and kind of depositions. The Fixed Deposits are the deposits by the business community and other sections of the population which are well off and have idle funds for which they themselves cannot think of a direct investment, either because of lack of information about opportunities or because of lack of initiative and a desire to avoid taking any risks. The primary motive is "investment motive" or "finance motive" while the secondary motive may be "precautionary motive". The depositors in the Savings Bank category on the other hand are people in the middle class and the motive of these depositors is saving for a primarily "precautionary motive" while the secondary motive may be "investment motive" or "finance motive". The people in this category prefer to deposit in a Savings Bank Account instead of a Current Account because their motive may be to earn a little income on it during the period that these funds are deposited with the banks. The banks invest these funds by giving loans to other parties or by buying some securities of either the public or private sector. In the changed framework the banks can invest these funds as they do now and credit the income thus earned to the accounts of depositors on a pro-rata basis.

The third category of deposits, namely the Current Account Deposits are owned by different sections of the population with primarily the "transaction motive" of keeping the excess liquidity readily available so that the depositors can write cheques on these accounts, thus finding a convenient method of spending and making payments. Since the motive of the depositors in this category is not to earn any profit or income, the banks generally do not and need not pay any return on this category of deposits. In the changed framework the funds available with the banks in this category will not be invested for making loans or investment and other securities. However, the banks can use this short term excess liquidity of the depositors to make very short-term loans to the parties which run out of liquidity because of unavoidable problems in cash management and lack of synchronisation between inflow and outflow of cash resources. Thus, the funds in this category do not require the banks to make any payment of profit or dividends to the depositors. In fact the modern banks in many countries realise moderate "service charges" besides the cost of the cheque books, from the depositors in this Current Account or Chequing Account. The rationale for this charge, besides recovery of unavoidable costs, is that the banks make available the convenient service of making payments, enjoyed by the depositors in this category. Logically, therefore, the very short-term loans made out of the funds in this category do not entitle the banks to charge anything from the parties which borrow for very short term purposes to balance the liquidity position rather than to make investment in profitable ventures.

This treatment of the Current Account Deposits solves the fundamental problem which arises in the minds of people with regard to interest-free banking. The banks will not charge anything on the loans made out of the funds in this category of deposit. However, the banks can recover from the clients a moderate amount as service charges to take care of the cost which is incurred in making book-keeping entries and such other activities which are unavoidable in the process of making short-term loans.

If, however, the banks still have some excess liquidity – after taking into consideration the cash resources and compulsory liquidity required by the central bank – they can make use of the funds in this category for holding near cash items like government treasury bills, of course without interest. Even in the present situation the interest on treasury bills is very nominal, and a changeover from the present system to the interest-free banking system will not involve any serious problem. Inter-bank lending on a short term can also be made out of the excess liquidity in this category of deposits.

In the light of the above picture of the structure of banking without interest, the financial viability and operational feasibility can be seen clearly. With the help of this outline a Balance Sheet (or position statement) and a Profit and Loss Account (or Income Statement) can be easily drawn up to show that the banking operations can be as smooth and profitable in an interest-free system as in the present one. The discussion, it is hoped, would be convincing not only for economists but also for the practical bankers.

V. Some unresolved Practical Problems

After discussing the overall structure of banking, let us look, in greater detail, at some practical problems which agitate the minds of students and critics of interest-free banking.

(a) Short-Term Credit

An important unresolved question in the literature on interest-free banking is that of very short-term loans. We know for a fact that in spite of the structural changes that have taken place in the banking business, an important segment of its activities is the provision of short-term loans or overdrafts. Sometimes these short-term loans may be for a period of much less than three months or the classical 90 days transactions.

A genuine question arises as to how can the banks be rewarded or remunerated for these short-term loans for which the determination of profits is impracticable and even irrelevant. It has been argued by some writers that this should be a free service which the banks provide to their clients. This, however, does not seem to be a very realistic approach to the problem. We have to prove the feasibility and viability of the interest-free banking system as a business institution rather than a relief organisation. Any assistance by a bank to any party involves incurring certain costs for which a bank, being a business institution, has to be compensated. The solution for this problem has to be found on business lines rather than as a goodwill gesture from a partner. Moreover, there is no denying the fact that the party which borrows for a short-term period is going to put the borrowed funds to some use from which certain earnings can be, and usually are, derived. The bank has a right to share in the same with the borrowing parties or the clients. Perhaps a realistic approach would be that the bank classifies these short-term loans into various categories. Let us have a look at the various categories of short-term loans and their respective treatment in interest-free banking.

(1) *Short-term loans for one year or a quarter thereof.* This category would include loans for a period of three months, or a quarter of a year, up to one year. This period is adequate for determining the actual profitability of the funds used by the borrowing unit. Many firms draw up quarterly accounts for internal purposes of budget control and managerial efficiency. If this is done, or can be done by the borrowing firms the problem can be solved for the banks. Alternatively, the average annual rate of profitability for the borrowing firm can be used as a criterion for a quarterly period and can be applied for two to three quarters as the case may be. The annual rate of profitability of a particular borrowing party is known to a bank and can be determined very easily and, therefore, can be used in case it is not possible to determine specifically the actual return earned on the borrowed funds in as much as they become a part of total funds used by the borrowing party.

(2) *Short-term loans for one month to three months.* For this period there are again two possibilities:

(a) Either we can apply the annual rate of return criterion to the small fraction of a one year period, i.e. one month to three months; or
(b) We can try to determine the specific rate of return on the borrowed funds. In case these short-term loans for one to six months maturity are obtained for the classical type of "self-liquidating" bills, namely financing the import or purchase of any particular goods such as spare parts, industrial raw material, and such other purposes, the specific profitability resulting from the additional funds can be determined without any difficulty.

(3) *Short-term loans for less than one month.* Loans for a period of less than one month are usually meant for improving the liquidity position of the borrowing firm. In the cash management of the borrowing firm or persons, there may be some unavoidable difficulties of synchronisation of inflow and outflow of the cash resources, thus necessitating additional liquidity. With the passage of time the cash management of the borrowing parties or funds can be improved so as to minimise the need for borrowing funds for this purpose. To the extent, however, that this becomes unavoidable for the borrowing firm, it can make use of the credit facilities from its bank. Since the nature of the problem is to supplement or improve the liquidity position rather than investment in the real sense, the criterion of

rate of return is neither relevant nor feasible. The bank can guard as well as remunerate itself by doing two things:

(a) There will have to be a "limit" on the amount or the standing "line of credit" or overdraft for the short-term liquidity requirements, based on the average deposit balance or credit of the borrowing party for the entire year.
(b) The bank can compensate itself for the cost incurred on the transaction, that is first debiting the account of the borrowing party and later crediting the account. For this purpose the bank can recover a "service charge" based on scientific lines. This service charge, on a per transaction basis, will be different from interest because it will not be tied down to the length of time within one month or to the amount borrowed. Moreover, realising service charges is not new for the banking business.

(b) Consumer Credit

Another unresolved issue in the context of interest-free banking is that of consumer credit or non-productive credit, which has always been an unavoidable phenomenon in any kind of society. Mostly this phenomenon has been pertinent to the poor and the needy in the low income brackets. The purpose has been mostly to meet certain unanticipated exigencies for personal or family purposes. Today, however, the phenomenon of consumer credit has gained a new dimension. Present-day consumer credit is characterised by two phenomena. First, it is not confined to the poor and the needy in the lower income groups but has become a practice or phenomenon for the middle class. Secondly, the purpose of consumer credit in the new context is not meant only to meet certain exigencies, but is a conscious and deliberate attempt to raise the standard of living, wherein consumer credit is required to finance the purchase of durable consumer goods, house building, etc. Higher demand for consumer credit today is the result of a conscious and planned effort on the part of the producers and sellers of durable consumer goods. In other words the created demand for the newly developed durable consumer items has tempted the people of the middle class to raise their standard of living in advance of higher income expected in the future, or sometimes even without this expectation. In the latter cases the repayment is made out of the salaries of the people over a period of time. A question, therefore, arises as to what will be the solution of the problem of consumer credit in an interest-free banking system.

The question of consumer credit can be examined on the basis of the different segments of population from which the demand for such credit emanates. Let us first take the case of consumer credit for the low income groups. The segment of population in this category might consist of two sub-sections, one consisting of the people employed in government agencies or in the private sector, and the second consisting of the self-employed people and farmers in the agricultural or rural sectors. As for the employed people they can meet their requirements of consumer credit from their respective employers. In cases where schemes of a contributory provident fund or pension fund exists, this can be done even more conveniently. As far as the self-employed people and the rural people in the agriculture sector are concerned this may be done through co-operative banks or such other specialised agencies created by the government.

Coming to the consumer credit of today used by people in the middle class, a fundamental question arises at the outset. The question is whether it is desirable to encourage people to live beyond their means in a race for raising their standard of living. From the socio-economic point of view, perhaps this may seem quite undesirable in any society including the high consumption societies of the West. Many sociologists and economists in those countries are worried about this phenomenon in the rich countries. While the sociologists are concerned about the desirability of "living within one's means", the economists are concerned about the excessive credit expansion and susceptibility of the economy to the cyclical fluctuations. The case in developing countries or relatively poorer countries is slightly different and may seem desirable and unavoidable from a socio-economic point of view. Here again the people concerned may be either employed or self-employed. The employed people can again use the facility of borrowing from their employers to finance the purchase of durable consumer goods. As for the credit meant for house building purposes, this can also be partly met from the employers as is the practice in government agencies and the private sector in most of the countries. However, there can be also a specialised institution sponsored by the government to provide housing facilities on a hire purchase basis. Alternatively there can be private agencies which make available houses on a hire purchase basis. The self-employed people can use the facilities of the specialised housing agencies in the government or in the private sector.

In spite of alternative available sources there may be a residual demand for consumer credit which has to be met by the commercial banking system. This residual demand can be met by the commercial banks partly by financing the commercial houses or agencies which supply the goods on hire purchase or on an instalment basis. In other words, instead of meeting the demand side, the commercial banks would mostly finance the supply side and share the profit with the agencies selling the durable consumer goods on hire purchase or on an instalment basis. Thus, by a process of elimination there will be a very small section of the population which may approach the commercial banks for consumer credit because no other alternative sources are available. A commercial bank in an interest-free banking system will meet this residual demand on the merit of the cases, out of the residual fund available to them. The residual funds with the banks may be in the Current Account deposits or Savings Bank deposits. The banks can charge a small amount as service charges from the borrowers in order to cover the administrative expenses involved in the activity.

VI. Summary and Conclusions

The theory of interest is the weakest and the haziest part in the economic theory. No proper explanation and no satisfactory interpretation is available to explain the rationale of the present-day interest on capital funds. The justification of payment for capital is usually based on accumulation of physical "capital goods" in a primitive society, which cannot be justifiably applied to the present day "capital funds" or "cash capital". Moreover, the existence of interest in its present form as a reward for capital has created problems in the economic operations in the industrialised societies of today. According to many theorists, the recurrence of trade cycles and fluctuations in economic activities is explained by the phenomenon of interest and the operation of banking in its present form.

From a conceptual point of view it is difficult to establish a justification for separate existence of capital as a factor of production. It seems desirable and pertinent that capital should be treated as a tool or instrument of enterprise, the dichotomy between enterprise and capital is resolved, and they jointly become one factor of production. This will mean that profit will be a reward for enterprise including capital. This will be a neat and harmonious arrangement because the bulk of the capital in the present-day economies of the world is made available in the form of risk capital or equity capital from the entrepreneur in one form or the other.

After merging capital as a part of enterprise and establishing profit as the only form of reward for the joint factors of production, the basis of banking has also to be revised. Banks being the mobilisers of the savings or capital funds can serve as an intermediary link between the savers or the suppliers of the capital and the actual users of the funds or the entrepreneurs. In the framework of interest-free banking, there will be a triangular relationship of the three.

In the Islamic framework, interest-free banking can be run on the basis of *Muḍārabah* or profit-sharing arrangement, between the suppliers of the capital and the users of the capital. There will be a two-tier arrangement of profit sharing between the entrepreneurs or the ultimate users of the investible fund and the banks and at the same time there will be a profit-sharing arrangement between the banks and the depositors who are the savers or suppliers of the funds. The percentage or ratio of the profit sharing can be two-thirds for the users and one-third for the suppliers of the funds. The banks will thus get a share of one-third from the profit earned by the actual investors. Similarly, the depositors will get one-third from the share received by the banks. This will apply to the main profit-earning activities of the bank. The arrangement may seem to be complex at first sight, but will become mechanical and routine after a while.

As for the very short-term loans required by the clients of the banks, they can be made available out of the idle funds available in the Current Account category of the commercial bank in an interest-free banking system. No interest will be charged on very short-term loans for periods not exceeding one month. However, the banks can recover a service charge from the borrowers to cover the cost of operations and the appropriate portion of overhead expenses. For the periods between one month and one year, there are two possibilities. Either the actual profitability of the funds used by the actual investors can be worked out to serve as the basis of profit sharing; or alternatively an average annual rate applicable to the overall business of the entrepreneur can be applied. This will resolve a very pertinent question which is asked about the feasibility of the interest-free banking system.

As for the question of consumer credit, already there are doubts expressed by sociologists and economists in the developed countries as to whether it should be encouraged or should the people be asked to live within their means. To a large extent, the genuine demand for consumer credit can be met by other sources of borrowing such as specialised agencies sponsored by the government or by borrowing from their employers, in the case of employed people. There will be thus, by a process of elimination, only a residual demand for the consumer credit which may have to be met by the commercial banks. Interest-free loans can be made available by the commercial banks for this purpose out of the Savings Bank Account deposits, wherein the motive of the saver or depositor is not to earn profit. However, banks operating an interest-free banking system will be entitled to recover from their clients a service charge to cover the operational expenses involved in making the loans and recover the relevant portion of general overheads allocated to that department of the banks.

In this way, a conceptual and workable framework can be developed for interest-free banking, which will not only be according to Islamic tenets, but will also eliminate a conceptual defect in the present-day economic theory.

Postscript

In response to discussion that followed the presentation of this paper at the Conference, the author adds the following notes:

(1) Only the principles and guidelines of an operation framework of interest-free banking have been discussed in the paper. The basis of allocation and distribution which seems different or difficult in discussion will become a simple matter of routine operation when

implementation is started. After all, insurance companies deal in large numbers too. They determine and distribute their "bonus" or share of profits to a very large number of policy-holders who opt for "policies with profit". With the facilities of computerisation, now available to practically all the banks, there is hardly any problem in distribution of profits in place of interest. Moreover, commercial banks in the present-day system of supposedly simple operations, on the basis of interest, have also to go into complex computations. This is especially involved in calculation of interest for exact amount of balance and "number of days" on saving bank deposits, as well as "overdraft" or "running credit".

(2) The outline of banking operations in a system free of interest has been presented naturally in a skeleton form rather than in the form of a detailed scheme in view of the scope and limitation of the paper. Some readers may possibly point out that the operational framework of banking operations in the above discussion has a greater orientation towards "investment banking" rather than "commercial banking". This, however, would not be very correct. Investment in shares or securities has been suggested only as one of the uses of funds or only a partial operation of banking in an interest-free system. Even in the present day system of banking, "investments" constitute usually 25 to 30 per cent of the total "earning assets" of a typical "commercial bank". Moreover, the elimination of interest from banking – in an Islamic framework – inevitably involves the principle of "profit-sharing" or "equity-participation". There may be some apparent resemblance with "investment banking". This is not by accident but by design in view of the conceptual framework of banking in an interest-free system. Every society and economic system is bound to have its own model and guidelines for detailed operations. To an outsider the form and operations of an institution in a new system may seem different from its counterpart in the present system; but this is the way it has to be. By the way of analogy it may be mentioned that combination of "economic motives" or the so-called "rational economic behaviour" with Islamic injunctions and value system is unavoidable in an Islamic system distinguished from the present day pattern in other systems. So is the case with other institutions such as system of government, philosophy of criminal laws, orientation of punishment, etc. Thus, any resemblance between "commercial banking" in an Islamic system with "investment banking" in the present-day Western system is understandable. In fact, it is because of the institution of "interest" that a dichotomy between commercial banks and investment banks has developed in the modern capitalistic societies, exactly as "capital" has developed as a factor of

production, independent of and distinct from the factor "enterprise". Since the institution of interest is to be eliminated in an Islamic society, the detailed shape of "commercial banks" will be naturally different from that of the existing commercial banks.

(3) In the 1970s, the problem of inflation has assumed a significant magnitude and constitutes an important economic problem. It is, therefore, quite natural that people may wonder about the position of interest-free banking in the context of inflation. Substitution of the principle of "profit-sharing" for a fixed and predetermined "interest" eliminates the problem of a very limited return to depositors in the existing banking system. The rate of interest is predetermined and is not revised quite as frequently as the general price level keeps rising in inflationary situations. Thus, the savers face a little problem in spite of upward revision in the rate of interest from time to time. In a system of interest-free banking this disadvantage to the depositors will be easily eliminated, and there should be no problem in mobilisation of savings. The share of the deposits will rise in the same proportion as the profits to the users of the funds or investors. In fact in the present day situation of rapid inflation, commercial banks are making unjustified "inflation profits" because the rate of interest they charge from the parties are revised and varied not only from case to case but from time to time, whereas the rate of interest paid to the depositors remains relatively stable, the bank thus enjoying the profit between these two rates. Moreover, in an inflationary situation businessmen generally gain from inflation to the extent that prices of their products or commodities rise very rapidly, thus widening the "margin of profit" in spite of higher rates of interest charged by the commercial banks. In an interest-free economy there is a permanent tie-up among the three parties, namely the depositors, the bankers and the clients obtaining funds from the banks, thus eliminating the possibility of undue advantage or disadvantage to anyone among these.

Notes

1 Keirstead, B. S., *Capital, Investment and Profits* (New York: Wiley, 1959), p. 50.
2 Keirstead, *loc. cit.* p. 52.
3 Hayek, F. A. von, *Monetary Theory and Trade Cycle*, pp. 189–190.
4 See Holy Qur'ān, *Sūrah al-Baqarāh*.
5 Imam Raḍī-al-Dīn Muhammad Muhammad al Sarakhsī *Al-Mabsūt* (Cairo: Matba' Sa'adah) Vol. XII, p. 17.
6 Abū al-Walīd Muḥammad Ahmad b. Rushd Al-Qurtubī, *Bidayātu'l Mujtahid wa Nihāyatu' l-Muqtasid* (Cairo: 1329), p. 205.

CHAPTER FOUR

Money, Interest and *Qirāḍ*

*Professor Dr. Mahmud Abu Saud**

ECONOMICS is a social science that constitutes an integral part of the ideology which prevails in a certain society. It is dangerous to adopt an economic system that does not emanate from and correspond with the ideology, in fact such a trial is doomed to be a failure. Thus, there is no "Islamic Economics" *per se* unless there is an Islamic ideology prevailing and applied in a Muslim community.

Islam is based upon the principles of Oneness of God, the liberty and dignity of men, their equality as creatures and servants of God and justice among them and in their reward. These elements, *inter alia*, are reflected in the economic concept of Islam, money included.

I

MONEY

In the so-called free-economy or capitalist economy, money has acquired a privileged status over all other commodities. By the definition arbitrarily given to it, it has become superior to man himself, it implies some qualifications that are not supposed to be within its jurisdiction and which have evolved and become as if they were really genuine, despite the fact that they have no physical existence.

Most of the economists define money by its four classical functions: (a) means of exchange, (b) measure of value, (c) medium of deferred value, and (d) store of value.[1] Day and Peza explain the nature of money as follows: "The real significance of money is that it is a claim which can be used by its owner to buy things".[2]

A. Means of Exchange

Accepting such definitions as correct, the fact remains that such functions are not intrinsic or inherent in money. Practically speaking, exchange, which is the main function, can be undertaken and is taking

* Professor Mahmud Abu Saud is a director of the North American Trust and a Senior Egyptian Economist. He has served as Professor of Economics at the Universities of Cairo and Kabul and as Economic Adviser to the State Bank of Pakistan.

place in many a case without the mediation of money. Samuelson, stressing this fact, adds that money "*is an artificial social convention*".[3] Originally, people intend to exchange goods against goods, and utilise money as a medium to facilitate this exchange. Yet, in barter, or direct exchange, nobody concedes his goods to another person without getting some goods in return. When money intervenes, the operation is split into two parts: selling goods against money and buying goods against the withheld money. This split enables the money-holder to sit on the withheld money for any period he opts for without risk or cost – other things being equal. The implication here is that by sitting on the proceeds of sales, the exchange operation is interrupted and the function of exchange is suspended incomplete. To keep such proceeds is actually to bar somebody in the society from selling his products, which is a violation of Samuelson's "social contract".

If this function of money is fully operative, i.e. whosoever exchanges his products against other products through the mediation of money without an unnecessary time gap between selling and buying, most of the economic discrepancies experienced in liberal economies could be eliminated. Hicks hinted at this, stating that:

> "One of the advantages that is gotten from the use of money is that people do not have to pass it on immediately; they can choose the time of their purchases to suit their convenience. If they use this facility moderately, it is useful to them; and it does not harm other people."[4]

Hicks does not mention those who withhold money indefinitely and live on it. Nor does he tell us what "moderately" means, and who is the judge of moderation. What Hicks did not say was expressed by Prudhon when he was asked:

> "Why are we short of houses, machinery and ships? He answered: Because money is a sentinel posted at the entrance to the markets with orders to let no one pass. Money you imagine, is the key that opens the gates of the market (by which term is meant the exchange of products); that is not true – money is the bolt that bars them."[5]

And in fact one would ask: Why is it that money supply is on the increase while recession is besetting the markets? The answer is that a great part of that supply is not used to meet the "transactional demand" in the Keynesian sense. By holding the greater part of money supply for precautionary and speculative purposes, people are checking the main function of exchange and are rather incapacitating the role of money.

We should like to emphasise from the very beginning that money *per se* cannot be considered equivalent to fully-fledged goods, mainly because all goods embody a utility which satisfies some human economic demand.

This innate natural property is artificial in money, as demand for it – as a means of exchange – is a derived one imputed to the original need for the exchange of products. If money ceases to function as such means, i.e. if no exchange of real products takes place through the mediation of money, its *raison d'etre* disappears. Without real exchange through money – if it exists – money would be an illusion causing harm and a lie distorting facts.

B. Measure of Value

This qualification is derived from the previous one, because the means of exchange must determine the value of the exchanged goods as related to itself. Thus, money acts as a common denominator to all economic goods, and the value relationship of their exchange is expressed in terms of money units. This implies that money is the standard measure for all values.

However, this function is a feigned qualification, all known standards of measurement are fixed in themselves except money. The metre, the ton, the volt, etc., do not change in relation to what is measured by them. Yet money does change. "From its use as a measure of value flows the practical maxim that money ought to have a constant value, however constancy may be defined. It is a strange fact that after so many centuries of experience in so many countries man has not yet succeeded in providing for himself a money with stable value."[6]

In my opinion, the failure is due to the malfunctioning of money as a means of exchange, and to the artificial attributes bestowed on money, allowing people to withhold it without charging them any cost for such a violation of the "social contract". Creating money out of thin air by means of creating credit has created what Irving Fisher called "money illusion".[7]

C. Store of Value

"When money is held, it is a store of value whose ultimate worth depends on the trend of prices."[8] This is a disputable statement, because holding money is only holding a title or a claim to some goods which we may opt to procure in the future. It is not storing any real goods or real values. On the contrary, holding money is keeping half the exchange transaction in abeyance. Thence, to qualify money as a "store of value" is to vitiate the main cardinal function of money as a means of exchange. If it is claimed that money gives its holder the choice of exchanging goods at present or storing the value to be acquired in future, our answer is that that exactly is the fallacy. One acquires money by liquidating (selling) an asset or selling one's goods – which means ridding one's self of the real value which would have incurred some cost if one had wanted to store it. Having exchanged his asset against money, such a person has procured a claim on goods which can arbitrarily be stored without charge or cost – an advantage bestowed on the person who has done harm to his society by abstaining from buying from others.

D. Standard of Deferred Payment

Consequent upon the three previous functions, future transactions are expressed in terms of money. Having explained to what extent money is not a standard of value in practical life, we need not go into any detail pointing out the risks and difficulties in deferred payments. This function is necessarily tied up with the passage of time during which the ratios among the relative values of goods change, and the ratio among these and money changes, not only on account of the change of the relative value of goods, but also because the "standard of value" in itself is not stable. Such instability of the measurement complicates all future economic transactions and gives vent to illegitimate claims, the worst of which is the payment of interest.

Is Money a Commodity?

There is a difference of opinion among economists about the nature of money as we know it at present, i.e. fiat money and bank credits. The argument is about whether such money is a part of a nation's wealth or is it a debt incurred by its issuer and which is offset by the credit counterpart of the holder.

Patinkin, Tobin, Gurley and Shaw, Pigou, Metzler and Haberler are amongst the economists who do not include the whole of fiat money and its attributes in wealth. Friedman, Martin Baily, Pesek and Thomas Saving ignore the "money as debt" argument and flatly state that money is a part of what we economically call relevant wealth and of net worth.

The issue has been blurred by the unnecessary argument about whether fiat money is a debt or not. It is common knowledge that no issuing bank in our present time would pay any tangible countervalue to any paper currency it issues when presented with it. Thus, indebtedness is fictitious and illusory. Professor James Tobin objects to considering fiat money a part of wealth in the following terms:

> "The community's wealth now has two components: the real goods accumulated through past real investment and judiciary or paper 'goods' manufactured by the government from thin air. Of course, the non-human wealth of such a nation really consists only of its tangible capital. But as viewed by the inhabitants of the nation individually, wealth exceeds the tangible capital stock by the size of which we might term judiciary issue. The illusion can be maintained unimpaired as long as the society does not actually try to convert all of its paper wealth into goods."[9]

Pesek and Saving categorically admit that money – any money – is not totally identical with other goods:

> ". . . money is in one respect identical with and in another respect completely different from all other commodities. It is different . . . in

that it has a technical property of yielding its owner real income that depends on the price ratio between other goods and money. It is identical with all other commodities in that it is a claim of the owner on the resources of others, but it is not a debt of others to the owner."[10]

Don Patinkin took up the Pesek-Saving theory and tried to prove its fallacy. He corroborated with M. Kalecki in the latter's view that money is a component of wealth. "The stock of money relevant for the real-balance effect was not the usually defined hand-to-hand currency plus demand deposits, but the monetary base alone."[11] He went on to confirm that the view became accepted without question in the literature, and received its highest degree of formalisation in the Gurley-Shaw distinction between outside money – money that is backed by foreign governments (which is part of the net wealth of the community), and inside money based on private domestic securities (the inside money includes created money and all other institutional credits – all of which are not a part of net wealth).

To sum up, money can be a quasi-commodity at best, and even if one considers it a commodity having a demand and a limited supply, there will be some undeniable differences between the usual commodities and money:

(i) Money has a technical (or artificial) property of yielding its owner real income simply by holding it, i.e. without exchanging it against other goods.
(ii) It has no carrying cost, no production cost (almost so) and no substitute having complete liquidity.
(iii) Demand on money is not genuine as it is derived from demand for goods that money can buy.
(iv) Money is exempt from the law of depreciation to which all goods are subjected.
(v) Money is the product of social convention having a purchasing power derived mainly from the sovereignty as against the intrinsic value of other goods.

Once the meaning and nature of money has been clarified, the study of interest will be easier to follow.

II

INTEREST

What is Interest?

Economists have given different definitions of interest, each trying to fit his definition to his theory justifying the payment of interest. To me, interest is the excess of money paid by the borrower to the lender over and above the principal for the use of the lender's liquid money over a certain period of time. In their effort to define interest, many economists treated "money capital" as equivalent to capital goods, a subtle mistake which helps them find a warrant for charging interest on borrowed money. Let us have some examples.

Samuelson states that "Interest is the *price* or *rental* of the use of money".[12] Thus he equates the price with the rental use of money considering its service exactly as the service of a medical doctor or of a tractor. His concept of money as a means of "transforming one good to another by exchange rather than by production" forces him to treat money like any other commodity that has a price or a rental. If we recall Samuelson's concept of money, immediately we recognise why he subtly tried to treat money as a fully-fledged commodity. However, we would find some difficulty in reconciling his description of money as a means of "transforming one good to another by exchange rather than by production" with his view about interest. When money is sold, one should pay a "price" according to Samuelson, and if borrowed, one should pay a rent. To *sell* money, there *must* always be some exchange of one *good* against another good – according to Samuelson. But here, you sell your money for exactly the same money. Why then the price at all if it is a "selling" transaction?

As for considering interest as rent for money, the first objection is that every rent comprises an element of depreciation (even in static conditions, i.e. everything being equal). First, money as a means of exchange is not supposed to depreciate. Second, when one uses the doctor's or the tractor's service, both of them remain almost intact. You don't rent something that perishes or disappears once you use it. But when you use money once you lose it forever. How can it then be rented? Finally, if we apply Samuelson's previous maxim of "exchanging one good for another" how can we accept the idea of rent?

Don Patinkin gives the following more confused definition: "Interest is one of the forms of *income from property*, the other forms being dividends, rent and profits. The term 'interest' sometimes has the broader connotation of *all income* from property. This is the case when we speak of the 'interest charge on capital' which denotes the alternative income that can be earned on a given quantity of money-capital."[13]

Here, Patinkin considers interest as a part of the functional share earned by capital goods as well as money-capital. It is strange that Patinkin did not give labour any share of the resulting income, while he allotted interest a share of the yield. It is clear that this is not true, because interest is paid to the lender irrespective of the yield and perhaps even before the income is realised. Here, again, Patinkin treats capital goods as synonymous to money-capital.

Y. S. Bain states that "Interest paid for invested money is thus a third distributive share, in addition to wages and rents. It is paid for the services of invested money and it is earned by capital goods in which the funds are invested."

Professor Bain does not mention "profits" here and equates "the loanable funds" with capital goods. If interest was a functional share of the investment process as he alleges, it would be negative if the process yields a loss – which is not the case. Besides, as long as the lender is not the investor, we cannot by any means tie up interest with the investment process.

J. M. Keynes did not define interest, but mentioned the rate of interest as "Money rate of interest is the percentage of excess of a sum of units of money contracted for forward units of time over spot or cash price of the sum thus contracted for forward delivery".[14] In the course of analysing the reasons that make money rates of interest more acceptable than commodity rates, Keynes mentioned that "... the power of disposal over an asset over a period may offer a potential convenience or security, which is not equal for assets of different kinds, though the assets themselves are of equal value. There is, so to speak, *nothing to show for this at the end of the period in the shape of output*, yet, it is something for *which people are ready to pay something*".[15] The words I have put in italics refute Patinkin's and Bain's idea of interest as a residue or function of income or investment. However, Keynes tried to find a justification relevant to his liquidity preference theory and came up with nothing in the output which is something for which people are ready to pay something. This part was critically criticised by some leading economists; Harrod wrote:

> "We are told that the reason why people require interest on bonds is to compensate them for the sacrifice of liquidity, which sacrifice consists essentially in the risk that, when they want to realise their assets, the bonds may have fallen in capital value, i.e. that the rate of interest may have risen.
>
> "Keynes thus exposed himself to the criticism of Professor J. R. Hicks that he has 'left the rate of interest hanging by its own boot straps'. And D. H. Robertson has the following amusing passage: 'While there are hints here and there of a broader treatment, in the main his (Keynes) plan is to set the rate of interest in the direct functional relation only with that part of the money stock which is held for what he calls "speculative reasons", i.e. because it is expected to become other than it is; if it is not expected to become other than it is, there is nothing left to tell us why it is what it is. The organ which secretes it has been amputated, and yet it somehow still exists – a grin without a cat'. Mr. Plumptre of Toronto, in an unpublished paper, has aptly compared the position of the lenders of money under this theory with that of premium, the only risk against which it ensures

them being the risk that its premium will be raised. If we ask what ultimately governs the judgements of wealth owners as to why the rate of interest should be different in the future from what it is today, we are surely led straight back to the fundamental phenomena of productivity and thrift."

I believe Sir Roy Harrod was unique in describing interest as something untrue. He wrote: "And so why is there interest? . . . Surely there are some phenomena of the minds, the resultants of thoughts and opinions, hopes and fears, itself only a promise, finally indeed an act, but one solely originating in the will of the two parties, not a physical phenomenon at all. Surely there are mental phenomena to which the dictum may correctly be applied *that there is nothing true but thinking makes it so*".[16]

In short: Interest is only a fiction.

III

MUḌĀRABAH OR *QIRĀḌ*

What is *Qirāḍ*?

Linguistically, both words, *Muḍārabah* and *Qirāḍ* are used to signify the same idea: "To give somebody out of your capital a part to trade in, provided that the profit is shared between both of you, or that an apportioned share of profit is allocated to him . . . accordingly, the active partner is called *Ḍārib*, because he is the one who travels and trades. It is also possible that both capitalist and active partner are called *Muḍārib* or *Muqāriḍ* as both share the profits with each other".[17]

Historically, *Qirāḍ* was widely practised in the pre-Islamic era as a form of partnership. The Makkans were depending on commerce for their livelihood; and those who could not exercise commerce by themselves, travelling long distances and leaving their homes for long periods, used to give capital to those able and willing to trade against a certain percentage of net profit. The consequence of jurists' opinion is that such a practice was approved by the Prophet. There is almost a unanimity on the legitimacy of *Qirāḍ*.[18]

Qirāḍ in Islamic Jurisprudence

It is related that many companions of the Prophet practised *Qirāḍ*. Even the Prophet acted as *Muqāriḍ* before Revelation.

Despite the unanimity on the legitimacy of *Qirāḍ*, there is nothing ascribed directly (*Marfū'*) to the Prophet himself except what Ibn Mājah related on the authority of Suhaib who said that the Prophet (peace be upon him) said, "Three are blessed: deferred sales, *Muqāraḍah* and mixing wheat with barley for home use and not for sale". In its lineage there are Nasr Ibn al-Qāsim on the authority of 'Abdal-Rahim Ibn Dāwūd, both of them are unknown. Ibn Hazm stated in his book *Marātib al-Ijmā'* that all chapters of *fiqh* have basis from the Holy Book and *Sunnah*, except *Qirāḍ*, for which we have found no similar basis whatsoever. Nevertheless, there is genuine solid unanimity on it, and one can categorically say that it was practised during the days of the Prophet, who was aware of it and who approved it, otherwise it would not have been legitimate.[19]

As there are no fast rules set by the *Sunnah* defining the terms of *Qirāḍ* other than the Prophet's approval to what was being exercised in his time, jurists have differed widely on such terms. Some of them were more inclined to restrict its meaning while others were more lenient and tolerant. Both parties supplemented their views by established Islamic rules, if not directly pertaining to *Qirāḍ*, they related to material transactions, especially those which refer to the terms of association and partnership and the laws for usurous dealings. Jurists who adopted analogy considered *Qirāḍ* as a special "Contractual Act" having its own special terms and conditions, though they have naturally differed among themselves as to the nature and terms of this contract. Those who dismissed analogy in jurisprudence were constrained to figure *Qirāḍ* in its narrowest limits. Having no texts to rely on, they resorted to some general Islamic rules to determine the act of *Qirāḍ*, some of them in our view were appropriate while others were not.

Thus, we have to treat all the forthcoming divergent views of Muslim jurists in this respect as personal opinions which do not and cannot commit Muslims in any way. If a jurist is carried by his own analogy to the conclusion that such and such a type of *Qirāḍ* is prohibited (*Ḥarām*) or even undesirable, all that we should do is to consider his logic, analogy and juristic proof to the plea, but we are not bound by his verdict.

Subject of *Qirāḍ*

According to "Zāhirīyah", *Qirāḍ* must comprise a contribution of cash money, which is the capital. If the capitalist wants to give the active partner (*Al-Muqāriḍ*) goods instead of cash money, he must specifically ask him to first sell these goods, and utilise the proceeds of sale in his *Qirāḍ*. Ibn-Ḥazm claims that there is unanimity on this view.[20]

As a matter of fact all Ḥanafīs do agree that the participation of the capitalist must be in coins, while they disagree about the validity of the contract if this participation is in non-minted silver and gold.[21] As for giving goods as participation, they claim that this vitiates the *Qirāḍ* and makes it void.

Ḥanbalites and Shāfi'ītes are of the opinion that participation must be by means of a definite amount of minted coins, while the contract is vitiated if participation takes the shape of either non-minted gold and silver or any other goods. Mālikites are divided among themselves about the validity of goods as capital for *Qirāḍ*, some agree and some object. Ibn Qudāmah, an eminent exponent, states that "*Muḍārabah* is valid if the subscribed capital is determined, whether it is in coined or precious metals or goods". He supports his view by the views of Abū-Bakr, Abū al-Khaṭṭāb, Mālik, Ibn Abī Layla, Tāwūs, Al-Awzā'ī and Ibn Abī Sulaimān. Those justify their opinion on the plea that "the main objective of *Muḍārabah* which is a sort of association, is that both parties dispose of both capital and labour and participate in the profit earned by the partnership. Such profit-sharing takes place whether the capital is in money or in goods".

The idea behind forbidding *Qirāḍ* unless the participated capital is in coined gold or silver is that the trading capital must be unequivocally determined so that every partner can assess his share in profits in accordance with his participation in the partnership. This is quite an acceptable logic, it was adopted by those who allowed goods as capital, provided that the capitalist asks his partner to sell the goods, determines their price and uses the same as capital. Al-Shawkānī is of the opinion that *Qirāḍ* is one form of association where all sorts of participations are allowed. Consequently, if anyone claims that the prescribed capital in *Qirāḍ* can only be in cash money he must produce evidence to support his claim.

Al-Shawkānī[22] came to the same conclusion, i.e. any goods of determined value can be subscribed as capital in *Muḍārabah*. He, however, based his judgment mainly on the "*Sāhil Ḥadīth*" quoted in Al-Bukhārī on the authority of Jābir Ibn 'Abdullāh where "the Prophet (peace be upon him) sent an expedition of 300 soldiers under the command of Abū 'Ubaidah Ibn al-Jarrāḥ in the direction of the sea-shore. I was one among them. On our way, the expedition's supplies were exhausted. Abū 'Ubaidah gave an order to collect all supplies with the soldiers which supplies totalled two '*Mizwad's*' of dates. He started rationing them among us till they came almost to an end and he began distributing them one by one. I asked him what one date could help, and he answered that it was something instead of nothing".[23]

Al-Shawkānī also referred implicitly to "*Ash'ariyyin Ḥadīth*" where the Prophet (peace be upon him) said "If the *Ash'ariyyin* went far for conquest or if their fortunes in Madinah dwindled, they amassed whatever they had in one bag and divided it equally among them; so they belong to me and I belong to them".[24] Personally, I don't think that the analogy is relevant because *Qirāḍ* is different than such benevolent voluntary co-operation. Here there is no *act* of agreement between capital and labour to enter into partnership for gain, and the objective is quite different. In both *Ḥadīths* indeed, the whole idea of any gain or trading association is completely absent.

There is also a difference of opinion about whether the acts of *Muḍārabah* would be valid or not if the *Muḍārib* or the active party subscribed an amount of money (or goods) over and above the subscription of the capitalist. Our view is that the essence of *Qirāḍ* is that the capitalist enters into association with an active partner in an enterprise whereby the first gets a share of the profits (positive or negative) earned by the capital of the first and the work of the second. There is nothing that stands against contributing capital in goods or in precious metals, as long as the value of goods is well determined at the time of concluding the act of *Qirāḍ*. Nor is it against any Islamic rule that the *Muḍārib* would subscribe a fixed amount of capital (again in money or in goods) in which case he would naturally be entitled to a higher stake in the partnership.[25]

There is another important point raised by the different jurists regarding the availability of capital at the time of contracting as a disposable amount. Thus, they do not legalise a *Qirāḍ* act if the capitalist concedes his debt towards the active partner and designates such debt to be his capital share in the prospected enterprise, nor do they consider the act as valid if the capitalist refers the *Muḍārib* to a third person to collect a specified amount before the money is fully collected and materially received. In fact, there is concensus of opinion on this point for the obvious reason that the partnership is an independent act which should not be related to other obligations and that such act does not exist unless its substance exists. However, Ḥanbalites validate the *Qirāḍ* if the capital has been originally deposited with the *Muqāriḍ*, which is more logical than the adverse view.

The Nature of the Partnership

The four Sunnī Imāms have gone as usual into some detail about the nature of the *Muḍārabah* act: is it an act of association or partnership, or is it a sort of proxy or is it a combination of both? Whatever their views may be, there is no doubt that such an act is permissible and valid under the following conditions:

(i) There should be (at least) two persons who, out of their free will, enter into an agreement by which one (or more) would contribute a fixed amount of disposable money to be delivered to the other party who would trade with this subscribed capital for the benefit of the partnership (or association).

(ii) Every party to the act must know for sure and without ambiguity his share in the expected profits and provided that this share is a percentage and not an absolute fixed amount.

In case no profit is realised, the active partner would receive nothing for his efforts. If there is a loss, it would be deducted from the principal (i.e. the contributed capital).

All expenses necessary for implementing the *Qirāḍ* act are deductible before the distribution of any profits, even if such expenses exceed the total of gross profits.

(iii) The active partner must have the absolute freedom to trade in the money given to him and take whatever steps or decisions that he deems appropriate to realise the maximum gain. Any conditions restricting such liberty of action vitiates the validity of the act.

However, the Shāfi'ites elicit the possibility of determining the kind of undertaking which the active partner may trade in. The other Imāms do not agree to this condition, an objection which is entirely unjustifiable in my view. I have taken Al-Jazīrī as reference for the views of the four *Madhhab*.[26]

Strangely enough, Imām Shāfi'ī does not validate *Qirāḍ* if the activity lies outside the domain of strict trading, i.e. buying and selling.[27] Obviously, he took this attitude due to the fact that *Qirāḍ* as approved by the Prophet (peace be upon him) was only for such commercial purposes. But our great Imām allowed himself to go far in analogy and even to set up new rules when there are no precedents regarding many problems, while he denied himself this logical course in such an obvious and important matter. In my opinion, *Qirāḍ* in industrial undertakings is permissible on account of two grounds:

a. If we apply the most rigid analogical rules we find that industry after all is a kind of trade and does not violate any other condition of *Qirāḍ*. Shāfi'ī's plea to forbid *Qirāḍ* in industrial enterprise is based on his view that the result of such an activity is generally controllable and almost predictable, while in commerce the risk is absolutely unknown. If this was the case during his time, it is definitely not so at present, and thus his judgment cannot be accepted, due to fault of reasoning.
b. If we apply the general rule that in origin all transactions and things are permissible unless there is explicit restriction or prohibition, we come to the same conclusion, as there is no restriction or prohibition, tacit or express regarding undertaking industrial activities. After all, if Imām Mālik has opined that the capital can be goods instead of money, then why not a machine?

(iv) The Zahīrīs and the four Imams are of the opinion that the duration of *Qirāḍ* must not be pre-determined or limited. Nevertheless, I am inclined to differ with them all. To start with, they rely on the precedence approved in the Sunnah to which I do entirely agree. Yet, all of them without exception confirmed that either party of *Qirāḍh* will have the right to revoke the act and terminate the partnership on advising the other party of the same (Ibn-Hazm, op cit., p. 249).

I fail to understand the *raison d'etre* of letting such an act so loose, unless that our Imams were aiming at defending the active partner (being the weaker) against the stronger (i.e. the owner). They might have thought that such a limitation of time may let some good opportunities slip from the hands of the *muḍarib* or may upset his plans so that he would not realise the profit he was preparing and working for.

Personally, I feel that by allowing the termination of the act by either side at any time they have actually defeated their own purpose of defending the interest of the active partner, because the owner of capital would have the right to decide at any time even though the active partner would be most unfavourably affected. Logically speaking, there is no valid reason why both parties cannot agree to fix a date for determining their partnership when they are allowed to do so at their full discretion at any time. Cannot any time be 'a determined time'?

Qirāḍ and Banking

Having explained *Qirāḍh* or *Muḍarabah* as stated in Islamic jurisprudence, we come now to the question whether such a system can substitute the actual functions of modern banking in the present free capitalistic economic framework, in a sense that it fits the present banking system and serve the purpose of divesting it from interest.

Qirāḍ Under the Present Banking System

Let us try to figure in which way *Qirāḍ* could be harnessed to eliminate interest in banking operations. Let us assume that this experimental trial will take place in a modern Muslim country whose money in circulation is the usual currency notes issued by its central bank, and that it has commercial and other banks functioning in the manner habitually known in a free competitive economy. Assuming that A is a businessman who realised some profit which he decided not to spend (either in consumption or investment) at the time as his plan is to use the money, say three months later, to meet a certain liability. A would then go to the bank (which would not supposedly be allowed to deal in interest either way) and ask what would the bank give him against a deposit of his dinars for three months. The answer of the bank manager would probably be, "I don't know. Why don't you come back next week and I'll try to find somebody who would be interested in getting this money to invest in his business and pay you a proportion of the profit"?

I suppose that A would not be very happy with such an answer. If A inquires why does not the bank invest it on its own risk, the answer would be: because commercial banks are not allowed to go into business other than purely monetary operations. (We are assuming the present banking system.) Now, let us suppose that the bank has found an entrepreneur (B) who is in need of 1000 dinars for three months and who is ready to pay "something" for getting the money now. The problem would immediately reveal itself in something like the following:

(A) If *Qirāḍ* has to be applied, would the bank be a part of the contract or not? In other words, would the bank accept the money and take the risk of *Muḍārabah*? If yes, then the bank is violating the banking law. If no, then the capitalist is supposed to negotiate directly with the entrepreneur and the role of the bank is confined to introducing both parties to each other – a non-banking function.

(B) If the bank is selling some investment certificates (and there are many capitalistic countries who allow such activity) then it would advise A to buy certificates today at the current price on the market and liquidate them after three months at A's risk and peril. Generally speaking, these certificates represent a portfolio which – under the assumed conditions – would bear no fixed interest and would be entirely invested in shares. It is extremely rare to see companies distributing profits to shareholders every three months, and thus A would not really be entitled to any profit by buying the said certificates. . . . On the other hand, he may collect some capital gain when liquidating his position at the due date, but he may also suffer a loss on his principal.

(C) If an arrangement – somehow – can be made through the bank by means of which A can invest his 1000 dinars in an active enterprise, there would be the difficulty of knowing the equitable share of this additional temporary *capital*. To my mind, it is almost impossible to find a satisfactory answer to this question, especially when the participation is for a short term. A is naturally interested to invest his money with a big reputable firm so as to minimise his risks and inflate his profits. But such firms cannot calculate their profits every day as the production procedures take longer periods than the time allowed by A. There is always a time lag between the date a capital good is purchased and the date the final output is sold out. Over and above, it is almost impossible that every time an investor contributes a certain sum to designate the fair share of profits that sum has added to the net profits (if ever these profits can be ascertained in the short term).

From the above, one can see that it is not practical – if ever possible – to marry *Qirāḍ* with the present banking system. Banks are not allowed to directly engage in commercial or industrial operations or in any speculative transactions, while *Qirāḍ* is based on engaging in all such risky operations. But what if we allow banks to do so? What if we allow banks to accept savings on condition that they would directly invest them in different enterprises? The same question arises again: Who would take the risk? If it is the bank, why should A take any profit at all? If A would take the risk, why go to the bank at all?

Qirāḍ in a Special Banking System

Consequently, it becomes clear that if we want to abolish interest from banks, on borrowing and lending, the prevailing models of banking would not work. In fact, it would be only the minority of savers who would be willing to keep some deposits (without any interest or profit) with banks, and thus, banks would cease to be the main source of credit extension or money supply, or in simple words, what they are at present.

These difficulties and the like made the advocates of *Qirāḍ* suggest changing basically not only the function of banking, but also its philosophy. In my view, they are quite justified in their suggestion because the present system is based entirely on interest transactions. Mawdūdī and Qureshī tend to consider banking as a public service that should best be owned or at least controlled by the State. The main job of banks under such synthesis would be to represent the government in their policies, favouring some categories of productive projects by extending to them the maximum possible credit without interest. They would also function as the main channel of foreign trade settlements and foreign capital movements. In both functions, banks would charge commission for the respective services to cover their expenses but no interest would be required.

It is noticeable that in the case of foreign trade, it is habitual to effect payments over a period of time. For instance, on confirming the order, a certain percentage of the value or a fixed amount is required to be paid, or at least a "credit letter" is supposed to be opened to guarantee to the exporter the collection of his dues against shipment, or in many cases a few months after shipment. In actual practice, banks extend such payment facilities against collaterals furnished by their clients and they do claim interest and charges. The first is against the advance of money to be paid to the exporter and/or against the letter of credit, while the second is for other services such as negotiation of documents and banking guarantees and confirmations.

Qirāḍ and Interest

I should like here to state that *Qirāḍ* can take place whether banks are charging interest or not. Another clearly important point is that *Qirāḍ* by itself does not abrogate or interfere with the actual banking system, nor is it an element that if encouraged to the extreme would by itself put an end to interest dealings. We have to bear in mind that *Qirāḍ* is nothing more than a partnership which cannot be instituted except by the free-will of the partners. Those who are advocating *Qirāḍ* propose legal intervention to prohibit dealing in interest. The question is whether such legal interdiction would really lead to the abolition of interest, even when banks are nationalised and are prohibited to charge or pay interest? I personally very much doubt that for many obvious reasons.

First, let us presume that we are going to apply the prohibition of interest in the usual economic system prevailing at present in the free competitive countries. In other words, interest would be prohibited while "other things being equal". Money holders would most probably seek a "black market" in which they would be able to lend money for a "price" or a hidden interest built into the repayment of the principal. To do this, they would not be willing to deposit their money with banks, thus depriving them of the source of their credit facilities. Capitalists would find scores of tricks to get around the law and would bleed the needy as long as banks were not able to meet the demand for money. It is obvious that if deposits with banks were substantially curtailed, banks would not be able to create the usual credit amounting to four times the money deposits. It would not be commendable that the Government would simply print more currency notes and deposit them with banks in an effort to replace the withdrawn capital as this would conduce to serious inflation that could hit the poor rather than the rich, and would upset the economic norm.

Second, let us presume that interest is legally prohibited, that savers of money find it difficult to charge interest in defiance of the law, and that banks are provided with enough funds to meet the demand for money. In such a hypothetical case, money holders would either spend their "sterile" liquid money on consumption or investment. In either case, *Qirāḍ* would play an insignificant role, or at the most, its role would not exceed by far what it was before introducing the new system. Actually, there are increasing numbers of people who are going to the stock exchange and buying shares as an investment instrument. A share thus obtained is a participation by capital in an enterprise where others undertake the productive work itself; it is a kind of *Muḍārabah*. Most probably these would continue their practice and stick to their stock-exchange market. Those who are accustomed to living on their fixed incomes yielded by interest would have to switch to another less-secure investment. They could go to the stock exchange directly or resort to some investment institutions to place their money for them.

Whatever the behaviour of the money-holder in an economy where interest is prohibited, banks functioning would have to change radically.

(1) Government authorities would have either to run the banking systems themselves or keep them under very vigilant control exercising very restrictive policies. Failing such state control would lead either to a credit crisis or illicit dealings in interest.

(2) A major function of commercial banks would be to study the applications of borrowers and extend credit on the basis of two criteria:

(a) The security of collaterals.
(b) The conformity of the enterprise to the Government's general production planning.

(3) The issue of "Investment Certificates" to be offered to those who

have available surplus funds and who wish to invest in enterprises at minimum risks.

(4) The undertaking of foreign-trade services.

The thorny problem under such terms would be the supply of money. It is quite possible that money-holders would prefer to hoard their money or to hoard gold or any other durable commodity whose "carrying cost" is relatively low. Monetary authorities in such cases would be obliged to provide banks with quantities equivalent to hoarded money plus the would-be-created money, in order to meet the demand for current transactions and new capital goods.

Another subsidiary problem would be the source of borrowing of an entrepreneur whose application was turned down by the government-controlled banks. With the rate of borrowing reduced to zero, one would expect a rush to banks for contracting loans and one can readily accept that demand on money would far exceed its supply. An addition to the total quantity on the market would lead to an inflationary situation, especially as hoarders would be ready to liquidate their stocks whenever it suited them to do so. Inflation would bring down the value of money in terms of goods, and stock-hoarders would greatly benefit from such a situation – a benefit which would be hardly justifiable especially if gold were traded.

In short, by applying *Muḍārabah* alone, and leaving the other economic elements as they are at present, while prohibiting interest, nothing much can be achieved and more harm could perhaps be done than good. In my view, other Islamic rules must simultaneously be applied to reach a reasonably practical solution. But before I submit my suggestions, I should like to give a short resumé to those solutions proposed by some eminent Western economists which are mainly based upon the Islamic theme of prohibiting interest and preserving the exchange value of money at a relatively stable standard. It is futile to prohibit interest without fixing the standard of value.

IV

THE ISLAMIC SOLUTION

I have intentionally entitled this section the Islamic "Solution" and not the Islamic "Theory". A theory would indicate a scientific hypothesis at the base and a logical synthesis which may be developed into a "theory" that can serve as the basis of a "scientific law" once it is proven beyond doubt.

We have no monetary theory in Islam. God in the Qur'ān and Muḥammad (peace be upon him) in the Tradition never analysed the meaning of money or defined its functions. They did not explain to us why interest has been so strictly forbidden that the menace to those who "devour" it is more than any other menace directed to those Muslims who would commit other sins:

> "O ye who believe! Observe your duty to Allah and give what remaineth (due to you) from usury, if you are (in truth) believers. And if you do not, then be warned of war (against you) from Allah and His Messenger. And if ye repent then ye have your principal (without interest). Wrong not, and ye shall not be wronged." (2: 278–279)

Islam gave us some basic rules administering the means of exchange of goods and left it open to us to build on these solid foundations whatever structures we deem fit and appropriate to our ever-changing civilisations and economic conditions. We have always to bear in mind that in the Islamic framework economics is an aspect of the Muslim's life which does not separate the material from the spiritual or the secular from the theological. It is only a means to help the individual within his society to contribute to the eternal process of human-development and welfare.

Basic Rules

Let us now examine these basic rules about our social material behaviour.

(1) *Work and reward.* Every Muslim is under the obligation to work in order to live, and nobody is entitled to any gain or reward without exerting a productive effort and shouldering the subsequent risk. In other words, any gain realised by any person earned without work is not legitimate. Any work, effort or enterprise that insures to its owner a gain without risk or that precludes any loss to him is equally illegitimate.

(2) *Hoarding and monopoly.* Human-beings in a Muslim society are under the obligation not to hoard money or goods required by other members of their society nor to try to monopolise any goods likewise needed. They are expressly required by Qur'ānic injunctions to "spend" without cessation and never to keep money "cornered," hoarded, or even idle. To spend in the "right" way is to spend in legitimate consumption or in productive investment, or in social welfare – all the three aspects are spending in the cause of God. (Qur'ān: IX: 34; LVII: 7; XIV: 31; II: 3, 159 and 282; LXVI: 7; VIII: 6.)

(3) *Depreciation.* Everything in this world is subjected to the natural law of depreciation (Qur'ān LV: 26) it is only God – our *Rabb* – who is Everlasting and Infinite. To ascribe this divine qualification to anything is tantamount to *shirk*, i.e., association with God. This is a denunciation to the essence of belief in God according to Islamic tenets. All monies must

depreciate by lapse of time and it is the duty of the Islamic state to impose and collect the "tax" or rate of depreciation in accordance with Islamic jurisprudence. This tax is *Zakāt* which is one of the five cornerstones of this great Religion.

(4) *Money as a means of exchange.* In as much as money is concerned it is supposed to be a means of exchange and nothing more. It is not a normal commodity which can be bought and sold, even if it is made of gold and silver. It is always recommended in Islam to exchange goods against money and then to buy what is needed for the same money. Buying and selling are two faces of the same coin: the exchange transaction. The two processes are so closely linked that the word (*Bā'a*) – sold – means bought as well. Anybody withholding money is committing a prohibited crime against himself and his community.

(5) *Interest is Ribā.* All sorts of lending money against interest (i.e., increment to be paid to the lender at the due date over and above his principal debt) is prohibited usury. Any state following the Islamic laws must legally prohibit such usurious dealings and must establish an appropriate system for borrowing without interest.

(6) *Social solidarity.* Muslims are ordained to establish solidarity and mutual help in their societies within the framework of their political structure whereby the ruler (the government) have the obligation to provide the citizens directly or indirectly with the essential amenities of life in case of their poverty, incapacity or unemployment. Against this obligation, the ruler has the right to impose more taxes and to assign work to the unemployed who must obey him in this case. Besides, there is the general moral obligation of a Muslim towards his Muslim co-religious members of society. This aspect of voluntary human fraternity which has become the centre of modern radical reformatory doctrines is an integral part of the Islamic faith.

A number of Western scholars stress the point that man's needs are not exclusively material, that the present material civilisation is alienating man, enslaving him and making him a psychopath. They suggest different remedies which fall far behind what Islam suggests in this regard. The Muslim gets the message of human fraternity, co-operation and mutual help since his early childhood through the Qur'ānic versions and the behavioural code of his Islamic society. He is *aware* that all wealth belongs to God and that he must share whatever part thereof bestowed upon and entrusted to him with his fellow men. It is a social system where giving and doing "good" is the criterion for distinction among citizens.

This is an important point though it may not look relevant to the subject of this paper. Its importance derives from the fact that anybody who wants to apply the Islamic "Solution" must apply the whole "Islamic System" if he is serious and keen to achieve success and avoid a shocking failure:

> "Then is it not only a part of the Book (Qur'ān) that ye believe in, and do you reject the rest? But what is the reward of those who behave like this but disgrace in this life?" (2: 85)

The System

(a) *Between Ribā and Zakāt*

I do not intend to explain in detail what is *Ribā* (usury) in Islam, but I believe that all sorts of interest that we meet in our present Western Economic models is usury as previously defined. It is what is technically called in *Fiqh*: "Ribā Al-Nasī'ah" which is categorically forbidden by the Qur'ān and the *Sunnah*. This idea has been expressed by most modern Islamic thinkers: Mawdūdī, Qureshi, Abū Zahrah, Isa Abdou and others who treated the subject. This opinion is in fact derived from the concensus of views of the four Imāms and Zahrīyah corroborated by Shī'ah Imāms. There is also a very clear trend among old and modern jurists that the solution to the problem of interest is engrained in the system of *Zakāt* which is the only specific financial "technique" mentioned in Islamic jurisprudence. However, the meaning of *Zakāt* has never been well defined and one would feel lost in front of the great differences of opinion among jurists about this "corner" of Islam. If the key to the interest-free economic problem is *Zakāt*, then we must be very clear about the meaning and scope of this word.

(b) *What is Zakāt?*

There is unanimity that it is one of the five pillars of Islam, that in the legal sense it means "a right on wealth" or "the specified part of wealth designated by God to be given to certain beneficiaries".[28] A better definition in my view is that given by Al-Shawkānī, he states:

> "Linguistically, *Zakāt* means growth; one says *Zakā az-Zar'* meaning the plant grew up. It can also mean 'purification'. In *Sharī'ah* (Islamic law), it implies both meanings. The first meaning is construed as to cause growth in wealth, or as to cause more reward or as to pertain to increasing wealth, such as is the case in commerce and agriculture. This first meaning is supported by the Tradition. 'No wealth decreases because of *Ṣadaqāt* (*Zakāt*)'; owing to the fact that its reward is multiple. There is also the Tradition: 'God increases (the reward of *Ṣadaqāt*'. The second meaning is construed to imply that *Zakāt* purifies the human soul from the vice of avarice as well as sins."[29]

I am more inclined to agree with Al-Shawkānī's interpretation though I feel that the essence of the meaning is growth of wealth not simply because God would bless such contribution, but because of a more pertinent and important reason. I have already referred to the natural law of depreciation, and the subtle meaning of associating with God an ever-increasing object. I have also referred to the fact that money must continue in circulation as this is the only way to keep production growing without check. Hence, the growth of wealth implied by *Zakāt* is in my opinion a confirmation of the general rule of the inevitability of depreciation and a practical orientation toward the necessity of not hoarding money and goods but keeping them continuously in circulation.

There is no doubt that *Zakāt* has a great role in the domain of social welfare and in exalting the Muslim's religious feelings; but these questions, though of vital importance for any sound society lie outside my present essay. What I should like the reader to consider is: what is that system that Islam prescribes to Muslims to enable them to develop their economy without touching interest which is prohibited usury? To me, the answer is *Zakāt*.

May I emphasise once again that such a system pre-supposes that it is only an integral part of a complete independent philosophy which embraces all aspects of life and that it is only a means to achieve the Islamic idea of a happy life in a welfare state.

(c) *Function of Zakāt*

(i) *Zakāt*, in my opinion, is a tax in that system in which the main economic principles mentioned above are enacted and applied in a state where private ownership and free competition are liberally practised.

(ii) *Zakāt*, being a tax on wealth itself, does not heed the person who is in possession of the taxable wealth. Whether that person is a "minor" or a "fool" or a "slave" is of no import whatsoever. Imāms have unjustifiably raised the point of who is liable to *Zakāt*, a question, which in my view, is irrelevant as it should only be: "which wealth is subject to *Zakāt*?".

(iii) All wealth having market values is subject to *Zakāt* except those goods which are specifically exempted by express injunction. It is illogical to confine *Zakāt* to the well-known eight commodities: Gold, silver, wheat, barley, dates, camels, cows and sheep (including goats) as alleged by Ibn-Ḥazm.[30] Nor is it logical to go with the other four Imāms subjecting some edibles and excluding others, or exacting *Zakāt* from whatever is gold and silver only, etc. The jurists in their attempt to make *Zakāt* look just and fair in their respective ages have resorted to analogy copying 'Umar Ibn al-Khaṭṭāb when he subjected horses to *Zakāt*. They were not applying any specific Qur'ānic injunction or approved *Sunnah*, but following the general rule of introducing what realises the general welfare and social justices in their communities.

I do not see why we, at our present advanced and more civilised age, should not follow their example and adopt the same analogical system to qualify *Zakāt* in a way that culminates in the realisation of our Islamic ideology. I believe that *Zakāt* should be imposed on all goods (with the exception of what was specifically exempted). To do that in the most effective way, and to arrive at the goals of *Zakāt* as mentioned above, I feel that the most practical way, the most fitting and convenient, if not the only possible one, is to tax money in circulation in a way analogous of that suggested by Silvio Gesell and adopted in the Austrian town of Wogel in the early thirties.

I have reached this conclusion, as the nature of our modern economy and the whole set-up of commerce, industry and agriculture has taken entirely new aspects and dimensions which are entirely different from those known to our great Imāms who lived hundreds of years ago. We have already seen that Imām Shāfi'ī disqualified the Act of *Qirāḍ* if the subject of partnership is an industrial activity, on the sole plea that in industry gain is predictable and determinable, while it is not the case in commerce!

(d) *Zakāt against Interest*

If the above interpretation of *Zakāt* is acceptable, and if we apply a system similar to that suggested by Gesell, i.e. impose *Zakāt* on money in the hands of those who are holding it, money in the new sense will be carrying a cost and will lose its supremacy over the genuine goods it represents.

Before elaborating on the new "purified" money, I should like to dispose of a juristic problem that would face any authority intending to apply the Islamic way of life without prejudice to the established texts of jurisprudence. There is no doubt about most of the sayings of the Prophet (peace be upon him) concerning the collection of *Zakāt* and the limits of exemption, the above-mentioned eight commodities. There is also no doubt about the other Qur'ānic verse ". . . and with (agricultural) produce of all kinds . . . eat of their fruit in their season, but render the dues that are proper on the day that harvest is gathered . . . " (6: 141)

The wide difference about what is subject to *Zakāt* among jurists makes me more inclined to interpret *Zakāt* in a way more expedient, logical and just. Nevertheless, even if one sticks to the narrowest interpretation of the word and believes that *Zakāt* is only imposed on the eight commodities, excluding commerce, minerals and all other goods, my answer to this is that there is another obligation or "right" on wealth. This extra tax or "dues" mentioned in the aforementioned verse does not specify the quantity nor the quality of the taxed goods. Bukhārī quoted the *Ḥadīth* of Mu'ādh addressing the Yemenites and his asking them to pay *Zakāt* in cloth rather than in cereals – an indication that *Zakāt* should not necessarily be collected in kind.[31]

If we follow the views of the different schools of Imāms, we may say that most of them accepted the criterion that *Zakāt* should be imposed on any commodity which has a market value, whether it is an agricultural or an industrial product. This is a valid argument if only on the basis of the accepted rule that there is another right on wealth. The Qur'ānic text is rather general covering wealth.

"Of their goods (*Amwāl*) take alms . . . " (9: 103). The word "alms" in this text may be misleading as the Arabic word *Ṣadaqāt* means *Zakāt* in this context, while alms would give the impression of voluntary charity. As well, the Arabic word *Amwāl* means money and goods.

In short, it is my conviction that *Zakāt* is a tax that should be imposed on all sorts of goods. It is not an *income tax*, but a tax on any sort of "capital", once it is realisable. As for the amount of this tax, how to be collected and the numerous details concerning the qualifications of the "taxable capital", such issues cannot be amply dealt with here and, indeed, should be the subject of an independent research.

For the purpose of this paper, I shall treat *Zakāt* and the right on wealth as two sources of public revenue of equal importance in meeting the requirements of the Islamic state. Besides, I take it for granted that such a state will give priority in the course of its budgeting to the poor, the needy and the rest of the eight categories of people who should receive *Zakāt* as stipulated in the Qur'ān (9 : 60).

I would also not object to the idea that *Zakāt* should always be singled out and collected separately in accordance with the Qur'ānic injunctions and in fulfilment of the *Farā'iḍ*. Other taxes should then be distinctly imposed and collected under other names. Such minor points should not detract us from the main economic issue which to my mind constitutes the backbone of the Islamic state.

The system I am suggesting is quite elastic and can fit in the most conservative Islamic schools of thought. There is nothing in our jurisprudence against "stamping" the currency notes, forcing them to circulate without being held or hoarded. The indications are that Muslims are strongly exhorted to spend and invest but not to monopolise or hoard. Anybody who is interested to save is entitled to do so provided he surrenders his savings to the banks which become a part of the government institution (or strictly controlled by it). If he does so, he would be exempt from paying the "stamp" as long as his money is in deposit. The reason for such exemption is that the bank will lend the money to those who may need it, either for their investment or consumption purposes, and thus money will be put back into circulation for the benefit of both producers and consumers.

As we have seen in "The Natural Economic Order" of Gesell, such a system would put an end to interest on all borrowings for investment. I differ from Gesell in that I suggest that even personal loans for consumption should not carry any interest, while Gesell finds it necessary to impose interest on such loans to penalise the prodigal and the lazy. My view is that banks do not entertain unsecured loans, while *Zakāt* takes care of the poor and the needy in the Islamic order. So, extravagance and prodigality will find it difficult to tap lending sources.

Another major point of difference from Gesell is land exploitation. Islamic jurisprudence allows the private ownership of land, whether rural or urban. In my view, agricultural land can be exploited in an Islamic state only in either of the following manners:

(a) When the owner of the land may cultivate it himself and for his own account, he may hire labour, but he is supposed to meet all expenses necessary for cultivation. This entitles him to the full yield of such land, which yield may turn out to be negative if the value of his crops fall too short to cover his expenses.

(b) He may enter in a sort of *Qirāḍ* contract with a farmer who becomes a partner to till the land, while the owner supplies the other elements necessary for cultivation: seeds, manure, machinery, water, etc. In this case, labour is to be assessed in relation to the total value of the other factors contributed by the landlord, and the yield is shared between them according to this relation without including any share to the land itself. In case the farmer contributes anything other than his labour, he gets a share of the total yield in proportion to what he contributed. In no case, rent – i.e. giving the land to the farmer at a fixed amount of money or a fixed share in the output – is permissible.[32]

Urban land also should not be allowed to be a source of unjustifiable unearned income. The increase of capital values of urban sites are rarely the result of the owner's efforts; it is generally speaking, a result of some social demographical agglomeration and the facilities provided by the community or its government. Any benefits stemming from such developments and facilities must be enjoyed by the community represented by its government. Thus, owners of urban sites are not allowed in the Islamic state to earn any more when selling their plots. If such an important measure is not adopted, many may be tempted to withhold land in lieu of depreciating money and to expect a certain unearned income instead of the prohibited interest.

By collecting *Zakāt* and by imposing a carrying cost on money, I believe there will be a new economic system where banks will gladly lend money without charging any interest, where borrowers will be more keen than their lenders to settle their debts, and where money will lose its divinity and sacredness. There will be enough funds for gifted borrowers to innovate and to increase production. Demand will precede supply in most cases, indicating to entrepreneurs the right direction for new investments and cutting risks to the bone. Full employment will be the norm rather than an abstract or the exception, and labour will be the most demanded and scarce element of production.

Zakāt will be collected and thus Social Security will be ascertained for every citizen. Personal loans for the needy and the poor will not occur because such people will automatically be looked after. Entrepreneurs will not find any difficulty to get the necessary capital for their sound projects, without paying interest which used to be a charge on their profit – or, indeed, on the consumer. Competition will bring profit and incomes closer together with the lapse of time, and people will not be distinguished by their wealth and the money in their vaults. Banks will function in a way quite similar to that explained under the Gesellian pattern except that no interest at all will be charged. If the government needs money, it will either borrow from the central bank without interest if the loan is short-term, or it will increase the value of "stamps" on money in circulation, or impose a new tax. In no case should the government resort to deficit financing, and indeed there will be no necessity for such a policy. If money value is stabilised, there will be no recession nor inflation as Harrod put it clearly, and irrespective of the method such stabilisation takes place.

Notes

1 Harold Barger: *Money, Banking and Public Policy* (Rand, McNally and Co., Chicago, 1962), p. 8: Roy Harrod, *Money* (Macmillan, St. Martins Press, 1969), pp. 3, 4.

2 A. C. Day, and S. Peza: *Money and Income* (N.Y.: Oxford University Press, 1968), p. 5.

3 Pau Samuelson: *Economics* (4th ed. 1958). McGraw-Hill, N.Y., p. 50. Italics ours.

4 J. R. Hicks: *The Social Framework* (Oxford, 1971), p. 21.

5 Quotation from Silvio Gesell: *The Natural Economic Order*, translated by Philip Pye (Neo-Verlag, Berlin, Frohman, 1929), p. 7.

6 Roy Harrod: *Money* (Macmillan, St. Martins Press, 1929), p. 4.

7 Irving Fisher: *Money Illusion* (Vail-Ballou Press, N.Y., 3rd ed., 1929), p. 18.

8 P. Samuelson: op. cit., p. 57.

9 James Tobin: "Money and Economic Growth", *Econometrica*, 33 (Oct., 1965), p. 676.

10 Pesek, Boris and Saving, Thomas: *Money, Wealth and Economic Theory* (Macmillan, New York, 1967), p. 77.

11 Don Patinkin: *Studies in Monetary Economics* (Harper and Row, N.Y., 1972), pp. 168 and 809.

12 Samuelson: op. cit., p. 50. Italics ours.

13 Patinkin: op. cit., p. 118. Italics ours.

14 J. M. Keynes: *The General Theory of Employment, Interest and Money*, London, p. 22.

15 J. M. Keynes: op. cit., p. 225. Italics ours.

16 R. Harrod: *Towards a Dynamic Economics* (Macmillan, London, 1969), pp. 65, 66, Italics ours.

17 Ibn Hazm: *Al-Muḥalla* (Al-Maktab Al-Tijārī li'l-Tibā'ah wa an-Nashr, Beirut), Vol. 8, p. 247.

18 Al-Shawkānī: *Nayl al-Awtār* (Dar al-Jeel, Beirut), Vol. 6, p. 394.
19 Ibn al-Qayyim al-Jawziyyah: *I'lām al-Muwaqqi'in* (Dar al-Jeel, Beirut), Vol. I, p. 250.
20 Ibn Hazm: op. cit., p. 247.
21 'Abd al-Rahmān al-Jazīrī: *Al-Fiqh 'Alā al-Madhāhib-Arba'ah* (Al-maktab al-Tijāri, Beirut), Chapter *Muḍārabah*.
22 Al-Shawkānī: op. cit., p. 392.
23 Al-Bukhārī: *Sahīh*, Dār, Iḥyā' al-Turāth al-'Arab, Vol. 3, p. 180.
24 *Ibid*, Vol. 3.
25 'Abd al-Rahmān al-Jazīrī: op. cit., p. 137.
26 *Ibid*. Chapter *Muḍārabah*.
27 Al-Shawkānī: op. cit., p. 44.
28 'Abd al-Rahmān al-Jazīrī: op. cit., Vol. 2, p. 435.
29 Al-Shawkāni: op. cit., Vol. 2, p. 169.
30 Ibn Hazm: op. cit., p. 209.
31 Al-Bukhāri: op. cit., Vol. 2, p. 144.
32 Mahmūd Abū Sa'ūd: *Khutut Ra'īsiyyah fi al-iqtisād al-Islāmi* (Maktabah al-Manār), Kuwait. Second edition, p. 76 and seq.

CHAPTER FIVE

The Relative Efficiency of Interest-Free Monetary Economies: The Fiat Money Case

*Dr. Mabid Ali Muhamed Mahmoud Al-Jarhi**

I

GENERAL

MONETARY theory, like the rest of macroeconomics, suffers from the logical ramifications of being built on a structure of perfect-market models. The assumptions underlying such models, *viz*, perfect information and zero transactions costs, give no reason for anyone to hold money. Nevertheless, economists have proceeded to impose the existence of money on such models as a first step to found an economic theory of money. Obviously, this is untenable. A consequence of such action is the common misconceptions and erroneous policy recommendations in monetary literature.

Naturally, the first step to restore some analytical consistency to monetary theory is to reconstruct the basic price-theoretic structure to include the necessary frictions which make transactions costly and thus make money necessary to hold. This, however, is beyond the scope of this paper and has been undertaken, from different angles and in different ways by some economists.

The purpose of this paper is to challenge the traditional institutional arrangement of paying interest on money as an efficient monetary policy. Having done this already somewhere else, for economies with commodity means of exchange, we will concentrate on fiat means of exchange. Both cases of government and privately-produced fiat money will be considered. Moreover, private borrowing and financial intermediation will be given analytical attention.

---

* Dr. Mabid al-Jarhi has served in the Institute of National Planning, Cairo; and the Islamic Development Bank, Jeddah.

The paper introduces a set of fiat means of exchange into an economy and a few related questions. First, how much money should an individual use in order to spend his income? Second, how much should the government produce in order to provide for the optimal use of money, and how should it distribute its money? Third, given the size of government money, how much would a private producer supply of his own money under conditions of imperfect information? Fourth, how do private concerns and financial intermediaries behave within our theoretical framework? The fifth and last question is how much should the government produce of its own money, how should it distribute it among different individuals, and what regulations should it impose on the banking system and financial intermediaries, in order to provide for the optimal supply of monetary services?

The conclusions of this paper make it obvious that economies with no interest payments on borrowing and no bank multiple creation of money are most optimal between the different institutional arrangements considered. This means that it is most efficient if the government initially provides its own money free, lends it free, and imposes a 100% reserve ratio on banks.

We expect such conclusions to be more of a surprise to economists in Muslim countries than to the young economists of the Western world, who have grown sceptical about accepting the results of models which are devoid of viscosity. Nonetheless, we hope our conclusions will be an inspiration to the economists of the Muslim world to revamp the economies of their own countries and rid them of the traditions of old Western economics. We finally hope that this will be a first step towards constructing an Islamic economic theory.

II

INTRODUCTION

In a free market economy, interest is the price of money. It is the price at which the "producers" of money sell their "output". Since this price depends on the quantities of money supplied, its determination raises the question of the optimum supply of money.

The treatment of the optimal supply of money in the literature has been mostly traditional in nature, and we are using the word "traditional" in a special sense. The basic fault with the traditional approach is that it ignores the issue of the *raison d'etre* of money, namely, the existence of transactions costs. One class of the traditional approach contains no explicit treatment of transactions costs.[1] The other class, while it accounts for transactions costs in a fashion, presumes the existence of money from the very outset. This lends no particular usefulness to the treatment of those costs.[2]

Some economists have attempted to remedy the inadequacies of the traditional approach by introducing frictions explicitly in the standard perfect-market model. Those non-traditionalists have taken various approaches.

One group incorporated transactions costs in the standard Walrasian model while keeping exchange centralised.[3] These models throw light on the existence of monetary equilibrium as well as the function of money as a substitute for a central transactions authority. However, some economists believe that only in a framework of decentralised exchange can the role of money be understood.[4]

Another group of non-traditionalists introduce imperfect information into their models as a vehicle of studying monetary exchange.[5] However, they disagree about what kind of information should be considered imperfect.

In order to introduce explicitly transactions costs into the classical model we have constructed elsewhere[6] a class of transactions cost functions for exchanges (each containing the sale of one item and the *quid pro quo* purchase of another) carried out by an individual. This class is based upon several postulates related to costly information.

The first postulate is that the information available to each individual about a particular exchange can be represented by a price quotation. The second postulate is that the distribution of such prices is sufficiently well-behaved to be adequately presented by a standard deviation. The two postulates imply a *price conjecturing process* which takes place as a part of the exchange process.

The distribution of conjectured prices represents the "true" opinion of all traders; its standard deviation represents the true variability of information, or TVI for short. The perception of any individual of those prices represents a different distribution whose standard deviation is called the reflected variability of information; or RVI for short.

The third postulate is that transactors are not equally informed about prices, i.e., their RVIs are different. In other words, information differentials exist between people about each exchange. The fourth postulate is that each individual is not equally informed about different goods, i.e., he has a different RVI for each exchange.

As price searching takes place, the fifth postulate says that sampling traders for this purpose is costly.

Let $t^v_{i,j}$ refer to the transactions costs of an exchange carried out by an individual v and involving the sale of the quantity x_i for the quantity x_j, where $i \neq j$. We can, therefore, write the transactions cost function of that exchange as

$$t^v_{i,j} = t^v_{i,j}(\sigma_{i,j}, \sigma^v_{i,j}, \ell^v_{i,j}, x^v_i, x^v_j); i \neq j \tag{1}$$

where $\sigma_{i,j}$ is the TVI and $\sigma^v_{i,j}$ is the RVI, and

$$\ell^v_{i,j} = 1/(\sigma^v_{i,j} - \sigma^v_{i,j}) \tag{2}$$

The behaviour of $t^v_{i,j}$ is determined by:

$$(\delta t^v_{i,j}/\delta \sigma_{i,j}) < 0 \tag{3}$$

$$(\delta t^v_{i,j}/\delta \sigma^v_{i,j}) < 0 \tag{4}$$

$$(\delta t^v_{i,j}/\delta \ell^v_{i,j}) > 0 \tag{5}$$

$$(\delta t^v_{i,j}/\delta x^v_i) > 0 \text{ and}$$

$$(\delta^2 t^v_{i,j}/\delta x^{v2}_i) > 0 \tag{6}$$

$$(\delta t^v_{i,j}/\delta x^v_j) > 0 \text{ and}$$

$$(\delta^2 t^v_{i,j}/\delta x^{v2}_j) > 0 \tag{7}$$

The above class of transactions cost functions is suited to exchanges involving real goods. This implies that they must also be suited for describing exchanges involving commodity means of exchange, or CME.

III

THE NATURE AND CREATION OF FIAT MEANS OF EXCHANGE

1. The Nature of Fiat Means of Exchange

Fiat assets are defined to be those assets whose holding draws no real rate of return of their own. They are used either for transactions services, or for the (interest) payments their seller may provide. They could be fully or partly convertible into another class of fiat assets. But, they may not be convertible at all into any other kind of assets while the transactions services they render qualify them to be treated as net wealth.

The fiat nature of FME calls for certain measures to entice traders to use them. Because these assets have no real services of their own, their owner, barring other payments, must use them for exchange in order to get any transactions yield. In order to do so, he must himself persuade prospective buyers of the usefulness of FME in transactions. The producer of FME will therefore find it insufficient for his assets to yield transactions services in order that they may be accepted by households as a means of exchange. He must use additional incentives.

One possible incentive is to stand ready to convert these assets, fully or partially, into other, already generally acceptable, FME. Convertibility then would cause people to consider the use of FME in the light of the quality and value of the assets into which they can be converted. When the producer of FME is the government, and when such an institution has a sufficiently high volume of transactions, the mere acceptance of the producer of his own FME as a payment for government services can be sufficient to provide for their general acceptance. Otherwise, when the volume of government transactions is insufficient, coercion should work, when its FME are declared legal tender. One last alternative is to pay the holders of FME a rate of return compensating them for whatever they would earn on alternative assets.

One thing we must stress is that it is possible to do away with the above incentives after the particular FME has been in use for a while. Once FME are used on a large scale in exchange, traders will accumulate sufficient information about their transactions servicces, and will continue to use them as before. Another thing we must stress, and which will become clear below, is the relationship between those incentives and the process of creating FME.

2. Transactions Cost Functions and Fiat Means of Exchange

The class of transactions cost functions introduced above was designed for exchanges involving real goods. In order to make this class applicable to exchanges involving fiat assets, one variable must be added: the price level in terms of the respective fiat asset. Since such an addition implies some relationship between that variable and the transactions costs of related exchanges, an additional postulate must be provided.

Let us assume that a certain fiat means of exchange, ${}_f\Phi_i$, is already in circulation. Let us also assume the relative prices of all goods in the economy can be calculated in terms of ${}_f\Phi_i$. With the assignment of the proper weights, a price level can be calculated from those prices, which we will call the asset-price level of ${}_f\Phi_i$ and referred to symbolically as ${}_f\Gamma_i$. Naturally, when an individual v makes an exchange involving ${}_f\Phi_i$, he must have some conception about its asset-price level. His conception will be termed ${}_f\Gamma_i^v$.

Given any relative price for a certain exchange involving ${}_f\Phi_i$ the higher the asset-price level as perceived by v, ${}_f\Gamma_i^v$, the lower is his perception of the real value of the quantity of ${}_f\Phi_i$ involved. Since this real value represents his total expenditures, if he is a seller of ${}_f\Phi_i$, or receipts, if he is buying it, the lower his perception of this real value, the less he will search and the less vigorously he will negotiate. Conversely, the lower ${}_f\Gamma_i^v$, the higher will be his perception of the real value of his expenditures or receipts of ${}_f\Phi_i$ from that particular exchange, given any relative price involved. The higher his perception of that real value, the more he will search and the more vigorously he will negotiate.

Therefore, an additional postulate, which is applicable only in the case of exchanges involving fiat assets, can be made. The transactions costs of an exchange involving a fiat asset varies inversely with individual's perception of its asset-price level.

3. The Creation of Fiat Means of Exchange

A FME is primarily a source of transactions services. Hence, its ability to produce such services, and to qualify as a means of exchange must depend on the nature of its transactions cost functions of the different exchanges in which it may be involved. The production of a certain FME asset is therefore tantamount to the creation of a set of transactions cost functions with certain characteristics. Keeping in mind the postulates provided about the relationships between the total and the marginal transactions cost of an exchange and the different arguments entering its transactions cost function, those characteristics must produce a state of transactions cost differentials that would justify the use of the fiat asset in question as a means of exchange. In other words, the *quality* of a FME asset must depend on the characteristics of the set of the transactions cost functions of the exchanges it enters; such a quality represents the effectiveness of that asset as a means of exchange.

The quality of a FME depends upon the size of its exchange fields as well as the range of quantities at which it can be traded. Both factors are influential in determining the transactions cost saving from the use of such an asset as a means of exchange. This implies that, when two FME assets are compared, the one with the larger exchange field or wider range of traded quantities, or both, has a superior quality to the other.

An important question is what can the producer do in order to *create* a fiat means of exchange? The answer to that is *not* to provide the buyers of such an asset the *actual* relative prices of that asset in its different exchanges. Such a method is impossible to use because the producer, whether a private concern or government, is subject to imperfect information like anyone else. The only difference in this respect is that the money producer is an information specialist, which makes his perception of the exchange ratios of the FME he produces closer to reality than that of non-specialists.[7]

The producer can, instead of providing exchange ratios, manipulate the asset-price level of the FME he produces. This manipulation can be done through the control of the quantity sold. This should be, in our world of imperfect information in which producers are price searchers, available to all producers.

In addition to regulating output, the producer sometimes will have to trade his asset in order to align its current stock with the current (stock) demand. Yet, the producer cannot guarantee the real value of his asset in terms of real goods. This prohibition is made out of theoretical necessity, for such an action would bring about commodity bonds. In addition, there are some peculiarities which depend on whether the producer is a private concern or a government, which are discussed below.

All such activities that the producer undertakes to make the characteristics of his FME prominent will be called the *information characterisation* of an asset or, in short, asset characterisation.

(a) Production of Government Fiat Means of Exchange, GFME

Starting with a pure CME economy, government production of fiat means of exchange, GFME, even when accompanied by the process of asset characterisation, may not earn exchange circulation of an intensity equal to that of CME. In the absence of coercion, GFME will be capable of gaining the trust of traders as a source of transactions services only after a period (perhaps extended) of initially cautious and hesitant use. It might appear paradoxical that "general acceptability" of money is self-generating, for the more people use and accept GFME, the more other individuals will join the bandwagon. However, once the information-generating aspect of exchange is recognised, the paradox disappears. The more often a FME is exchanged, and the wider the participation in that exchange, the more information is generated about its characteristics as a means of exchange. To overcome initial mistrust and hesitation, and to avoid costly and more intensive asset characterisation, the government may use a mixture of enticement and coercion to establish general acceptability for its own GFME.

In a multiple CME economy the government cannot circulate GFME whose quality is lower than that of the existing CME without either paying holders for the difference in quality to compensate them for the loss in transactions services resulting from the substitution of CME with inferior GFME, or using coercion. Such action on the part of the government will be ruled out, for it would cause the whole society a dead-weight loss. The government will thus be left with two choices. The first is to produce GFME each of which has quality equal to that of a corresponding CME in circulation. The second is to produce GFME of superior quality to some or all CME. The first action will have effects similar to those of issuing bonds against CME, and such effects have already been discussed elsewhere. The second option is to replace those CME whose transactions services are dominated by GFME, and if all CME were replaced, the economy would become a pure fiat money economy. Examples of such an economy are considered below.

(b) Production of Private (Secondary) Fiat Means of Exchange, SFME

Private production of FME is, in contrast with public production, hindered by two obstacles. On the one hand, private producers do not have sufficient resources to enable them to carry out the asset characterisation process on a scale wide enough to bring about general acceptability. On the other hand, private producers do not have the coercive power available to the government which would allow them to gain general acceptability for their own FME. Private producers can attempt to enforce their asset characterisation effort by offering to pay rates of return on their fiat asset comparable to those on CME. Such offers would make privately issued assets equivalent to commodity bonds, for each asset would be a claim to a stream of returns equal to that of some CME. In such a case, they would not be *fiat* assets.

The only way to overcome their resource and coercive power limitations is for private producers to make their assets convertible into GFME. A scheme of this sort allows them to benefit from the government asset characterisation efforts while giving them the liberty of differentiating their own products. Therefore, privately produced FME cannot exist without the existence of GFME; the latter will thus be considered as *primary* or *base* assets while the former will be termed *secondary* fiat means of exchange, or SFME. A pure inside (privately produced) money economy can therefore exist only in a commodity-money world, where such assets would be claims against the future delivery of CME.

IV

PURE GOVERNMENT FIAT MEANS OF EXCHANGE ECONOMY

In this section we consider an economy in which the government issues a collection of GFME whose quality dominates that of the existing CME, so that they effectively replace all the existing commodity money. Under such an arrangement, the government can give away its own GFME, it can sell them, or it can rent them; all three possibilities will be investigated. Then, the questions of the optimality of the stock of GFME and of government policy will be examined.

1. Some Basic Concepts

Now let us introduce a vector of GFME containing elements each of which is a fiat asset whose transactions cost function is superior to a corresponding CME asset; such a vector is

$$_f\Phi = ({_f\Phi_1}, \ldots, {_f\Phi_h}), \text{ and} \tag{8}$$

$$_f\pi = (\pi_1, \ldots, \pi_h) \tag{9}$$

are their corresponding accounting prices.

It is now possible to calculate, in terms of each one of these GFME, a set of relative prices, of all goods and construct some weighted average of them that represents the price level in terms of a particular GFME. In other words, there will be as many price levels calculatable as there are GFME assets. Let us define such a set of *asset-price levels* as:

$${}_{f}\Gamma = ({}_{f}\Gamma_{1}, \ldots, {}_{f}\Gamma_{h}) \tag{10}$$

It is clear from above that the production of GFME is not costless, because of the needed process of asset characterisation. When a particular GFME is issued and used in exchange, it will cause a change in its corresponding price level. Such a price level must be considered at this stage to be one of the information characteristics, which is one of the arguments in the price-conjecturing function of that asset. A change in that argument would necessitate a revision of the price conjecturing process. To counteract this revision, the government will have to incur extra asset characterisation costs. In other words, the marginal cost of asset characterisation, mcac, of any GFME must be rising with the rate of issuing such an asset.

2. The Supply of Real GFME

Given that the government will issue a set of GFME with transactions cost functions producing superior qualities to those of the initially existing CME, the sale of GFME, if and when it is done at the proper price, will cause CME to fall into disuse as it is replaced by GFME.[8] How much should be produced and at what price will depend on the demand for, as well as the marginal cost of producing GFME.

The cost of producing one extra real unit of a fiat asset through changing its nominal size depends on two elements: the marginal cost of asset characterisation and the change in the price level in terms of that asset, due to a change in the number of its nominal units. As pointed out above, the creation of one real unit of GFME, through a change in the supply of its nominal units, must be accompanied by utilising resources. Those resources are expended in providing information about the asset-price level of the GFME in question as well as the amount of trading necessary to bring such information as close as possible to reality. The real value of those resources may be less than, equal to, or greater than the value of the extra real unit created depending, in part, on the change in the asset-price level which may result from such an action.

In addition, the resulting change in the price level in terms of that asset, or equivalently the change in the relative price of the fiat asset, will have to be compensated for in order to effectively increase its *real* stock by one unit. This implies that the creation of one real unit of GFME could be accomplished by utilising resources which might cost up to, or more than, the value of that unit depending on the resulting change in the corresponding price level as well as the extra asset characterisation costs caused by that change.

It is therefore possible, as in figure 1, to plot the marginal cost of creating an extra unit of a real GFME asset as a proportion of the real

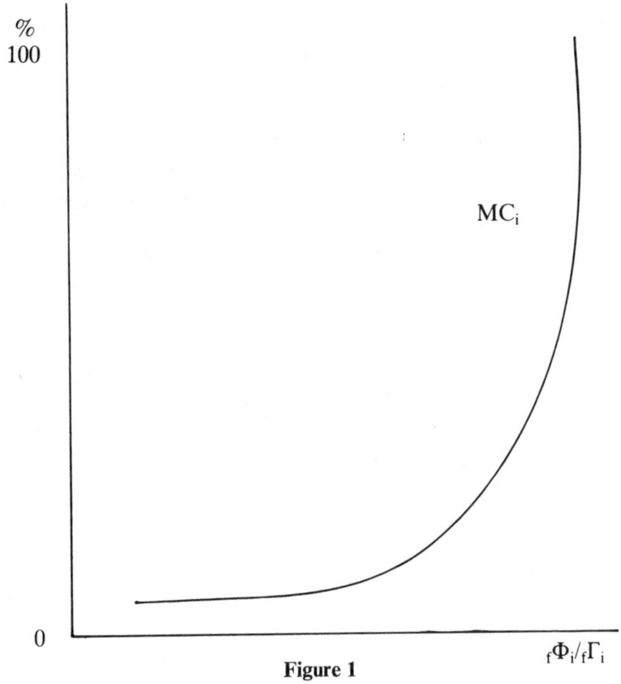

Figure 1

value of that unit; this proportion would rise with the real value created of that asset until, the rise in the corresponding price level reaches a certain limit, and becomes unity. At that limit, no real fiat units can be added by increasing the nominal quantity. It is quite possible that further increases in the nominal quantity could lead to an erosion of the real stock, which would cause the MC_i curve to bend backwards; such a possibility, however, is not shown on the graph.

Another aspect of the above supply relationship is how it is influenced by the change in the flow of information available to the traders of the GFME asset in question. An increase in this flow resulting, e.g., from a greater incentive for traders to trade the asset, reduces the marginal cost of asset characterisation. Consequently, the MC_i curve shifts to the right. The opposite is also true.

3. The Demand for Real GFME

Given the information characteristics of the GFME ${}_f\Phi_i$, traders will hold real quantities of that asset until its rate of transactions services, at the margin, deflated by its asset-price level is equal to its net rate of return.[9] Due to the postulate advanced about increasing marginal transactions costs of exchanges, the rate of transactions services will decline with the quantities of the real FME held. Therefore, we obtain a negatively sloped demand curve for real GFME, depicted in figure 2 as ${}_f\rho_i({}_f\Phi_i/{}_f\Gamma_i)$. However, as the quantity of real GFME increases, more transactions services become available. This increase in transactions services reduces the aggregate transactions of the whole community, and increases real income, which in turn increases the demand for real GFME and shifts the ${}_f\rho_i$ curve upward.

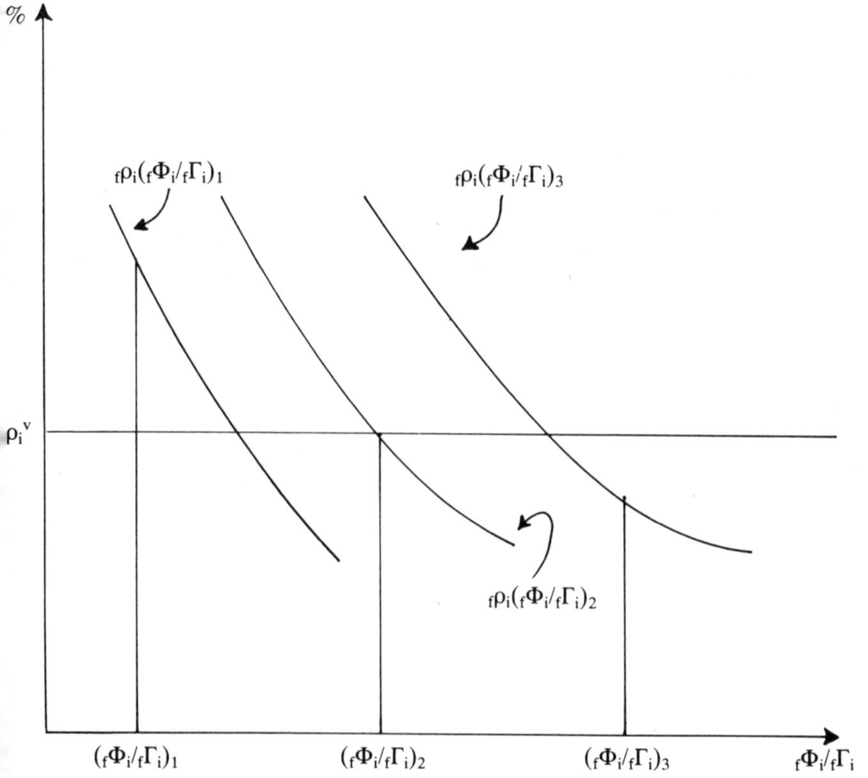

Figure 2

An increase in real income, resulting from a decrease in real transactions outlays, increases the demand for real GFME. This implies that when more real GFME is created, people's wealth rises by the present value of the transactions services stream created by that increase, which in turn, given the proper rate of discount, is reflected as an increase in real income. That latter increase leads to a rise in the demand for real GFME by an amount that depends upon the wealth elasticity of demand for real money. Therefore, we can postulate that for each level of real GFME there corresponds a level of income, and consequently, a level of demand for real GFME. Figure 2 shows this relationship by depicting three demand curves for the real balances associated with ${}_f\Phi_i$, each associated with a certain level of real balances. Given any net rate of return, say ${}_f\rho_i^v$, the increase in demand for real balances measured at this rate must be smaller than the increase in real GFME, measured on the horizontal axis, which caused such an increase in demand.

4. Providing GFME for a Price

Using the demand and supply functions introduced above can provide us with some guidelines in the case of the government wishing to produce the market clearing quantity of a certain GFME asset, while charging a price equalling marginal cost. Figure 3 shows one of the family of the demand curves introduced above and the supply curve MC_i. Remembering that each demand curve is associated with a certain level of real money, there is only one demand curve which would intersect MC_i at a point indicating exactly its related level of real balances. Such a point is Q, where the equilibrium level of the real GFME asset produced is 0a.

The government can sell its real GFME at a payment equal to ${}_f\rho_i$ per fatrah, as *rent*. Alternatively, it can charge the equivalent relative price per

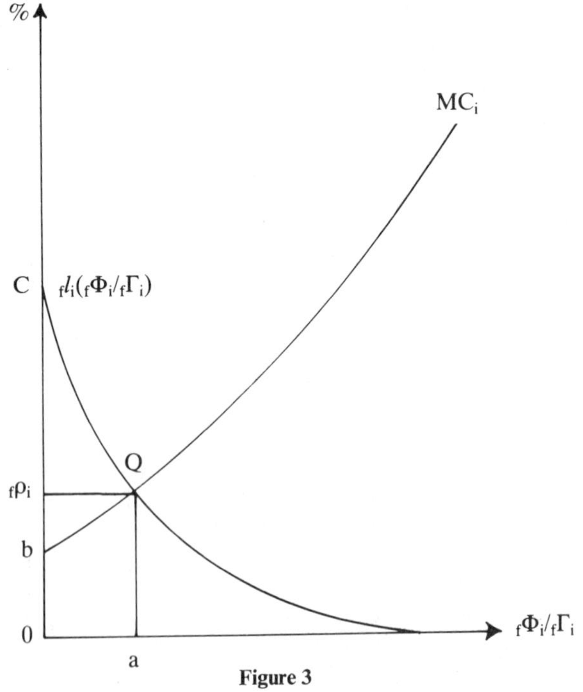

Figure 3

unit of real GFME. This affords it some net earning. Assuming such earnings are given back to the consumers as lump-sum subsidies, the total social welfare gained from the production of real money associated with ${}_f\Phi_i$ is equal to the area bQc.

5. Free Provisions of GFME

In order to distribute GFME free, a mechanism must be developed to do so without causing any redistribution effects.[10] Some may suggest, as a means of doing so, that such a distribution should be done in the same proportion to everyone's wealth. This method, however, has redistribution effects of its own. An individual's benefit from GFME will be the transactions services he can derive from them, which depends on the difference between his current portfolio and that which enables him to reach his optimal consumption. Such a difference determines the volume of exchanges a person desires to undertake. When one gets an amount of GFME, albeit it stands at the same proportion to his wealth as that of any other individual, it may exceed or fall short of his optimal exchange requirements; this causes him to gain transactions services at a proportion to his income which is rarely equal to that of others. It is therefore better to distribute GFME at the same ratio to the absolute value of the difference between the individual's current and desirable portfolio, in order to eliminate such redistributive effects.

Referring back to figure 3, the government can provide the amount 0a free of charge, or provide the satiation level of real GFME free of charge. In both cases we will assume it continues financing the costs of production through lump-sum taxation and distributing its net earnings in lump-sum subsidies.

(a) Limited Free Provision

Suppose that the government distributes the quantity 0a, shown in figure 4, for free. The reduction in the price of GFME leads to an excess demand, which can be satisfied only through purchases of the same asset, either from the government or from other individuals. As real balances increase, due to the resulting decrease in the asset-price level, the demand curve shifts outward. Meanwhile, the larger volume of trading in the same GFME provides a greater flow of information to traders, decreasing the marginal cost of asset characterisation, and thus shifting the MC_i curve to the right.

A new equilibrium point will be established at Q′ where, in addition to the free provision of 0a, traders will buy aa′. The increase in social welfare is equal to the difference between the area b′Q′c′ and the area bQc. The increase in social costs is equal to the area aa′Q′g. Obviously, the net benefit to society from this policy is positive. This policy is thus superior to the provision of 0a at a price.

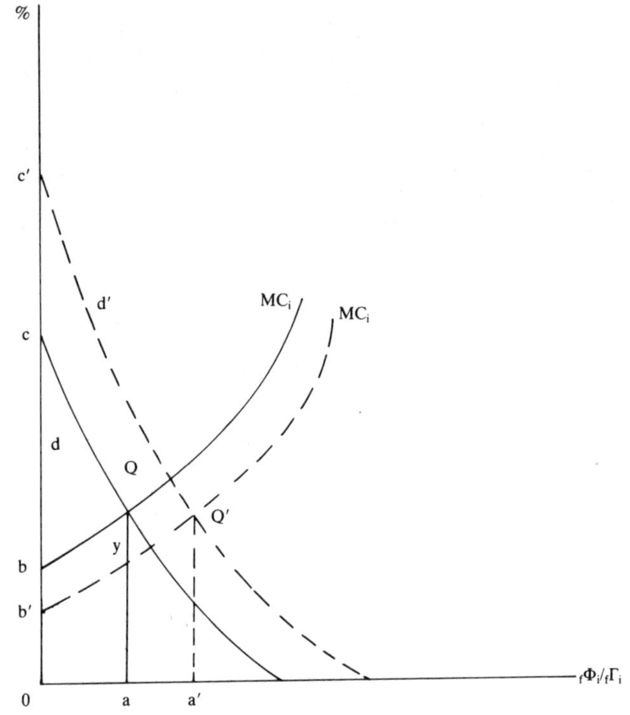

Figure 4

where

$$d = {}_f\rho_i({}_f\Phi_i/{}_f\Gamma_i)$$
$$d' = {}_f\rho_i({}_f\Phi_i/{}_f\Gamma_i)'$$

(b) Unlimited Free Provision

(i) *Providing the satiation level of GFME.* Suppose the government distributes sufficient amounts of GFME in order to effectively keep its price at zero, that is to give away the quantity 0e in figure 5. The initial increase in real balances by the amount of ae will increase traders' wealth and shifts the demand curve outward. More exchanges using ${}_f\Phi_i$ will result, increasing the flow of information about its asset-price level and thereby shifting the supply curve to the right. To fulfill its policy, the government must finally provide oe″. While the level of social welfare increases, there is a dead-weight-loss to society equal to the area e″Q″d″.

The social loss resulting from such a policy makes it inferior to the policy of providing a limited free provision of GFME.

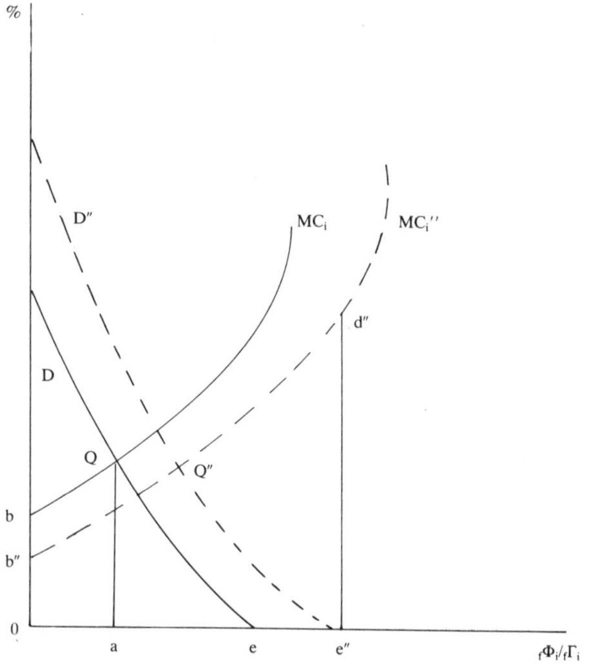

Figure 5

where

$$D = {}_f\rho_i({}_f\Phi_i/{}_f\Gamma_i)$$
$$D'' = {}_f\rho_i({}_f\Phi_i/{}_f\Gamma_i)''$$

(ii) *Tracing equilibrium levels.* In this case, the government uses the policy of "limited free provision" repeatedly for the purpose of expanding the existing stock of real GFME to its maximum, while increasing social welfare and costing the community no deadweight loss. First, as shown in figure 6, the government distributes the quantity 0a free which, as shown in figure 4 will cause the stock of real GFME to expand to 0a′. Then the government offers an amount equal to aa′ for free. This creates a wealth effect which pushes the demand curve to the right by an amount which is less than that caused by the initial gift of 0a. This is because, given the wealth elasticity of demand for real GFME, aa′ is smaller than 0a.

The latter gift aa′ causes the exchange in the GFME to increase, by an amount which is less than that caused by the gift 0a, leading to a new flow of information about the asset-price level and shifting the supply curve to the right. The economy finally settles at the level 0a″ ′ of real GFME. The government can then proceed to distribute a further gift of a′a′ ″, expanding the volume of real balances further.

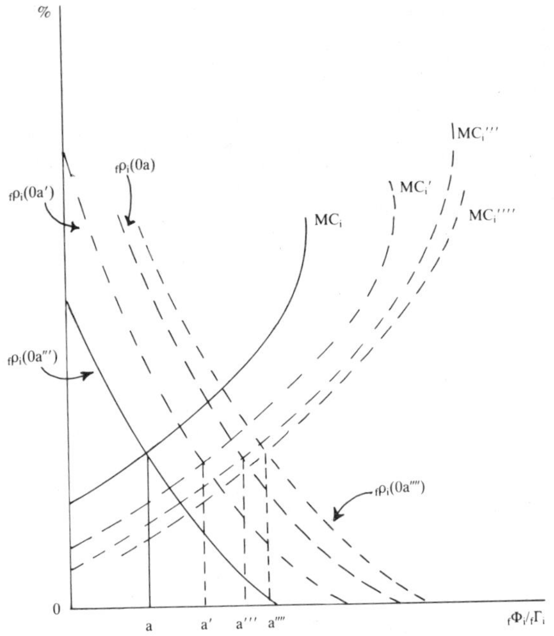

Figure 6

The repetition of such a policy expands the total supply of real balances by decreasing amounts. This is because the amounts of gifts are decreasing which causes their effects on the supply and the demand schedules to get successively weaker. The total supply of real balances will ultimately reach a level, say 0a″ ″ beyond which no further expansion is possible.

This policy expands the total supply of real GFME beyond what the other policies mentioned above can. Moreover, despite the fact that the government has provided all the existing stock of real GFME for free, the marginal unit of that stock brings forth a positive net rate of return.

The sale or rent policy reaches an equilibrium where the marginal return from an extra unit of real balances is equated with its marginal cost. The equilibrium quantity of each nominal GFME asset will be associated with an equilibrium price level and an equilibrium rate of return. Under such circumstances, social and private costs are equated with no trace of Friedman-type inefficiency. Non-convexity inefficiencies do not exist either.

Such is also the case with the policy of free provision. Nevertheless, there are two basic and important differences between them. The free provision policy produces a larger quantity of real balances, and in addition, it is associated with a higher level of real income. The rules of Pareto optimality suggest that such a policy would be optimal because of its capability of placing the whole community on a higher level of social welfare.

V

MIXED GFME AND SFME ECONOMIES

1. Secondary Fiat Means of Exchange

It may be recalled from above that the private producer of SFME must incorporate in his contract some provision for convertibility into GFME in order to be able to sell his assets. Yet, even if the private producer could persuade his customers that his SFME provides services identical to those of some GFME, they would not buy it without some additional enticement. The reason is that since the private producer's portfolio is one of the information characteristics considered in the formation of the transactions cost function of his SFME, the GFME asset will always be better because its producer is always solvent. Such enticement may include product differentiation and cheaper prices.[11]

The first kind of enticement is perhaps the most important, for it provides the SFME producer with a chance to improve upon the quality of the aggregate stock of means of exchange. As our economy initially, in a pure GFME world, contains exchange fields each of which is dominated by a GFME asset, the SFME producer can manipulate the quality of his asset in order to have an exchange field of its own. Within such an exchange field, the SFME asset can afford its user services which he cannot derive from any other GFME asset except at higher transactions costs. In order to do so, the transactions cost function of the SFME asset need not be superior to that of any GFME asset; it need just be sufficiently different.

The second kind of enticement, namely lower prices, is related to the question of convertibility. In order that the private producer can save himself a good part of the asset characterisation costs he issues his SFME promising the instant delivery on demand of some GFME asset. Keeping reserves on hand is therefore necessary for the producer to meet his obligation, when encashment is demanded. However, depending on the relative desirability of holding SFME to that of holding the GFME they promise to deliver, the instant encashment clause will not always be fully exercised, which necessitates the holding of only fractional reserves. This means that for every quantity of a GFME asset used as a *base asset*, a multiple of its value of SFME assets can be created. It also means that the SFME producer can offer prices for his SFME assets which are lower than the corresponding GFME assets they promise to deliver. It must be noted though that this is possible only when the government does not require 100 per cent reserves.

The private producer will find that his marginal cost of asset characterisation (mcac) rises with his rate of output, for changing that rate will change the relative price of his SFME asset and will require the supply of additional information to its holders. For instance, when the supply of a SFME asset increases and its relative price goes down, its holders may suffer a wealth loss which can be avoided by either resorting to instant encashment into the GFME base asset or by the producer compensating them for that loss. The higher the rate of SFME output the greater will be the tendency to resort to instant encashment and the consequent necessity to compensate holders, and then reassure them that the current value of the asset still warrants its continued use. All these costs are parts of the mcac, and thus it should rise with the rate of output.

The marginal cost of acquiring reserves, mcar, depends on the cost of changing the producer's portfolio in order to contain higher proportions of base assets. The latter cost is basically the transactions cost of exchanging assets currently held for reserves. The higher the rate of output, the more reserves are needed, and the more reserves a portfolio contains, the greater the difficulty of adjusting it to include even more reserves. Therefore, the mcar must rise with the rate of output.

The marginal cost of producing SFME must therefore rise with the volume produced, because of the similar behaviour of its components: mcar and mcac. Moreover, the production of SFME must be related to that of GFME because of the fact that the former requires the use of the latter as reserves. When SFME producers are left on their own, they will choose some reserve ratio between the base asset they hold and the SFME asset they produce. However, the government may interfere, forcing them to hold reserves at a proportion to their SFME production that is higher than the one they desire to hold. Of particular interest is the case when the government forces a 100 per cent reserve ratio.

In order to account for different conditions of GFME and SFME production, we will consider the economy on hand under conditions of free as well as non-free GFME assets. Each of those cases will be considered when reserves are fractional and when they are 100 per cent. To do so, we will assume that private producers will attempt to produce SFME each of which promises the instantaneous delivery of one of the GFME assets listed in (6.1). The corresponding vector of SFME assets and their asset-price levels will be:

$${}_f\varphi = ({}_f\varphi_1, {}_f\varphi_2, \ldots, {}_f\varphi_h), \text{ and} \tag{13}$$

$${}_f\Upsilon = ({}_f\Upsilon_1, {}_f\Upsilon_2, \ldots \, {}_f\Upsilon_h) \tag{14}$$

Before dealing with each of those cases, we must outline the relationships between the demand and supply schedules of each SFME and the same schedules of each corresponding GFME. First, taking ${}_f\varphi_i$ and ${}_f\Phi_i$ as examples, since they are not the same assets, they must have different demand schedules. However, since there are no *a priori* reasons for one schedule to be higher than the other, we will treat them as if they had the same schedule. Such a simplification will make the diagrammatic treatment below easier to manage. Second, because of the higher mcac to the private producer, the supply curve of the real balances resulting from the issue of ${}_f\varphi_i$ will always be higher than that of ${}_f\Phi_i$. However, since the creation of the real money associated with ${}_f\varphi_i$ involves the issue of more of its nominal units, its asset-price level as well as the asset-price level of ${}_f\Phi_i$ will be affected. The increase in the real amount of the SFME asset will thus cause a spillover on the real value of the GFME asset. Such a spillover increases the cost of producing the real GFME and shifts its supply curve to the left. Needless to say, the extent of the shift depends upon the amount of the nominal SFME issued.

2. The Case of Government Sale of GFME

(a) 100 per cent reserve ratio

Starting with the equilibrium in figure 3, the supply curve of real SFME can be drawn as mc_i which lies above MC_i. The introduction of SFME causes MC_i to shift to the left. Such a shift, however, will not be large because of the institutional restraint imposed upon the issue of nominal SFME by the imposition of a 100 per cent required reserve ratio. The final equilibrium as shown in figure 7a, includes the amount $0a_1$ of real GFME which is smaller than that appearing in figure 3.

The producer of real SFME, behaving as a price searcher,[12] will, by consulting his marginal revenue schedule, produce the amount $0b_1$ of real SFME. If the government forces marginal cost pricing upon the producer, the real SFME produced will increase to $0b_2$. In either case, the introduction of SFME assets increases the wealth of the community as it increases real SFME more than it reduces real GFME.

(b) The Fractional Reserve Case

Figure 7b shows the fractional reserve case. Because of the relative ease with which the nominal units of ${}_f\varphi_i$ are produced, two differences distinguish this case from the previous one. First, the cost of asset characterisation of the real units of ${}_f\varphi_i$ is higher. Second, the amount of spillover on the marginal cost of the real GFME asset is also greater. This causes the equilibrium quantity of real GFMA, oa_2, and the equilibrium quantity of real SFME, $0b_3$, to be smaller than $0a_1$ and $0b_1$ respectively. Even with marginal cost pricing enforced, we get $0b_4$ of real SFME which is less than $0b_2$. Therefore, under the assumption of the government sale of its FME, the case of 100 per cent reserve ratio is superior to the case of fractional reserves.

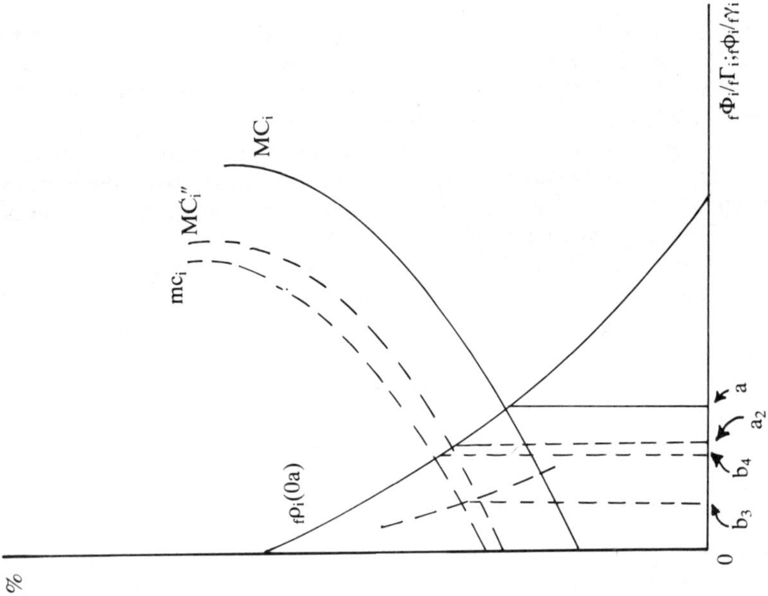

Figure 7b

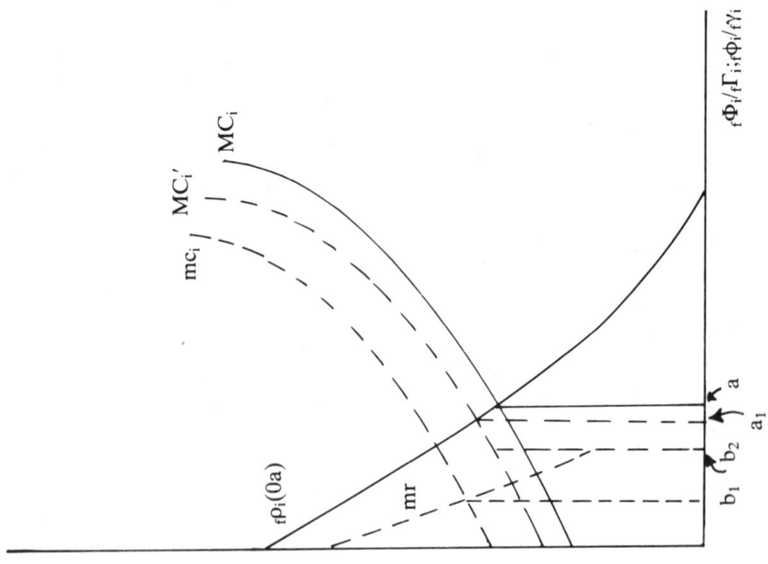

Figure 7a

3. The Case of Free GFME

When we discussed the pure GFME economy, it was found that the policy of providing free GFME through the tracing of equilibrium levels was the optimal policy. Since our discussion is motivated here by the objective of finding the optimal monetary policy within this new institutional arrangement, we will assume that the government has already reached the objective of free GFME provision through the tracing of equilibrium levels. Given the optimal supply of real GFME produced by such a policy, we will compare the cases of 100 per cent reserve ratio and of fractional reserves to see which provides a higher level of real balances.

(a) 100 Per Cent Reserve Ratio

Figure 8a duplicates the final equilibrium resulting from a free GFME distribution through the tracing of equilibrium levels, from figure 6. The introduction of SFME causes MC_i to shift to MC_i' because of the accompanying spillover. Besides, the supply curve of real SFME, mc_i will lie to the left of MC_i'. The final equilibrium brings forth the quantity $0a_5$ of real GFME and either $0b_5$ or $0b_6$ of real SFME, depending on whether marginal cost pricing will or will not be enforced.

(b) The Fractional Reserve Case

Starting from the same final equilibrium plotted in figure 6, the introduction of SFME will cause a greater amount of spillover on the cost of producing real GFME because of the relative ease of creating nominal units under fractional reserve rules. The shift in MC_i is thus greater than in the case of 100 per cent reserves. The same relative ease of producing nominal units of SFME causes its supply curve to lie further to the left from the supply curve of GFME than in the 100 per cent reserve ratio case. Therefore, while the total amount of real balances produced increases by the introduction of the SFME asset, the net gain in the case of fractional reserves is smaller than in the case of 100 per cent reserve ratio.

VI

FINANCIAL INTERMEDIATION

Elsewhere, we presented a model in which, borrowing was done in a CME economy by issuing private bonds promising the future delivery of CME.[13] That process of borrowing was found to have been enhanced in efficiency when the process of financial intermediation was introduced. In this section, we attempt to consider how borrowing and intermediation will evolve in a fiat-means-of exchange world. Two new classes of fiat assets will be introduced: household fiat assets, HFA, and intermediate

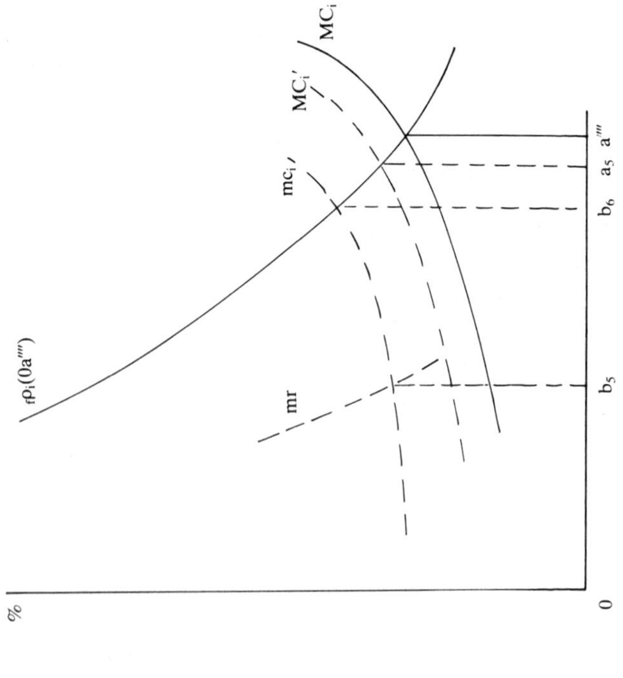

Figure 8a

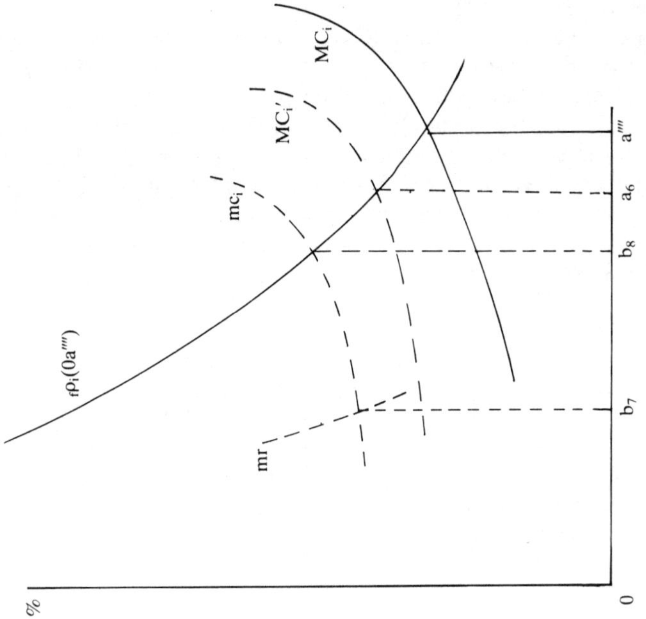

Figure 8b

fiat assets, IFA. Then, the economic effects of intermediation will be considered.

1. Household Fiat Assets

When a trader intends to conduct some exchange involving the purchase of some item, it is generally true in this economy that this can be done with lower transactions costs when the purchase of a certain FME asset is involved than when that of any other item is. Nonetheless, the trader may not have on hand sufficient balances of that means of exchange, in which case he can offer instead a bond promising the future delivery of that asset. The use of this bond will sometimes cause him to incur less transactions costs than the spot or the future trading of any other item.

The borrowing process will therefore be conducted within a FME economy and through the exchange of household fiat assets, which promise the future dęlivery of some GFME or SFME. Let us consider, as an example, the issue of an HFA by a particular household, v, promising the delivery of some quantity of ${}_f\Phi_i^v$ in the beginning of the next fatrah. The bond units of such issue will be denoted by ${}_f\bar{b}_i^v$ whose present value is equal to ${}_f\Gamma_i\,{}_f\Phi_i/(1 + {}_f\rho_i^v)$, where the v superscript used on ${}_f\rho_i^v$ is used to distinguish it from the rate of return on ${}_f\Phi_i$ itself. Such present value is equal to ${}_f\bar{a}_i^v\,{}_f\bar{b}_i^v$ where the first term is the price per unit of the bond.

In order to be able to sell his bonds, the individual will have to pay to the buyer (the lender) the rate of return of the FME promised as well as the cost of information the latter must incur in order to make sure that the borrower is within his budget constraint and his portfolio assets of value are sufficient to pay back the debt. This extra cost of information which we will call *lending costs*, increases at the margin with the size of the debt issue, for the larger the amount of borrowing, the harder it becomes to persuade a lender that the borrower is still within his budget constraint, i.e., that his asset holdings are sufficient to repay his lenders. This must be added to the fact that the demand curve for such a bond issue must be upward sloped, for more borrowing can be done only at higher rates of return.

On the other side of the picture, the bond issuer (the borrower) would be willing to sell more of his bonds as the rate of return, that he must pay, decreases, so that he moves along a negatively sloped supply curve. Yet, the more he borrows, the more adjustment is needed in his portfolio in order to increase its contents of those assets which can be transformed into the borrowed FME with the least possible transactions costs. Most probably, those assets will be some other FME. The cost of such an adjustment is similar to the cost of acquiring reserves which the producer of SFME has to incur. Such a cost, when accounted for, shifts his supply curve to the left.

Since borrowing a certain FME depends upon the current supply of that asset as well as its rate of return, it will make a difference whether it is

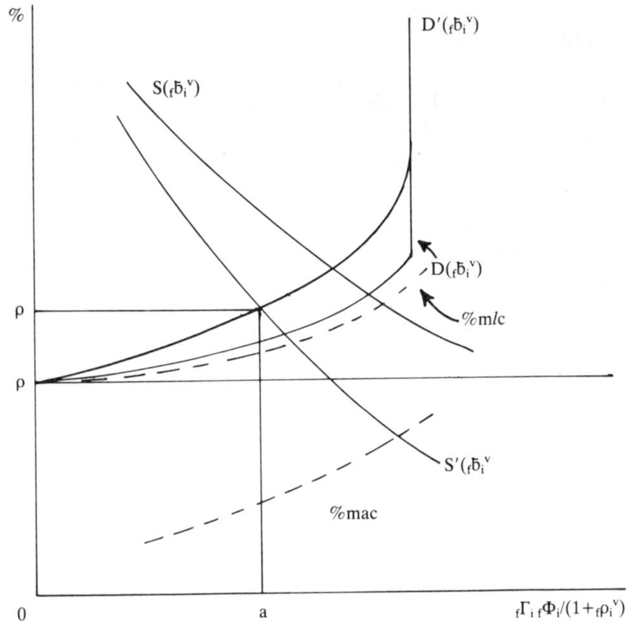

Figure 9

presently sold by its producer or provided free up to the satiation point by the government.

(a) Household Borrowing with Costly FME

When the FME borrowed is already being sold at the market rate $_f\rho_i$, shown in figure 9, lenders will buy the individual's FME bonds only at rates higher than $_f\rho_i$. The demand curve of those bonds will thus take the shape of D($_f\bar{b}_i^v$), when the marginal lending costs, mlc, are not included. At some level of borrowing, beyond which the individual will be exceeding his budget constraint, he can borrow only at infinite rates, which causes the demand curve for his debt to become vertical. The addition of the rising marginal lending costs, mlc, as a proportion of the present value of the marginal debt unit, causes the demand curve to take the position D′($_f\bar{b}_i^v$).

The individual's supply curve for his own debt, not considering the cost of adjusting his portfolio, S($_f\bar{b}_i^v$), slopes downward to show his willingness to borrow at lower rates. However, when the increasing marginal cost of adjusting his portfolio, mac, as a proportion of the present value of the marginal debt unit is considered, the supply curve takes the position

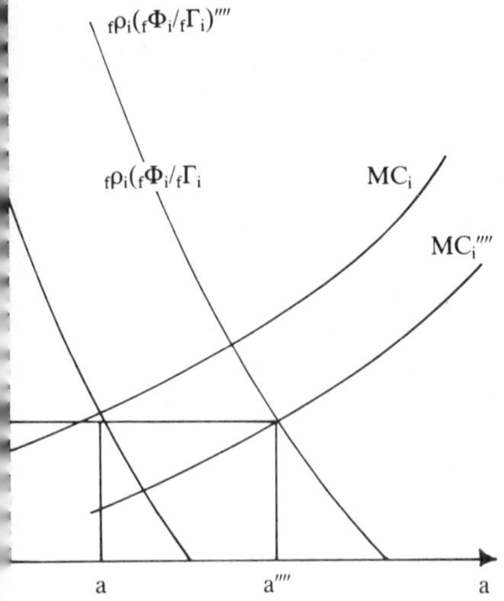

Figure 10a

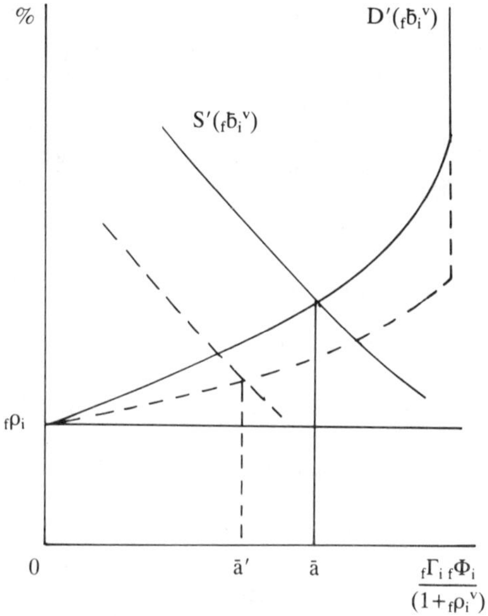

Figure 10b

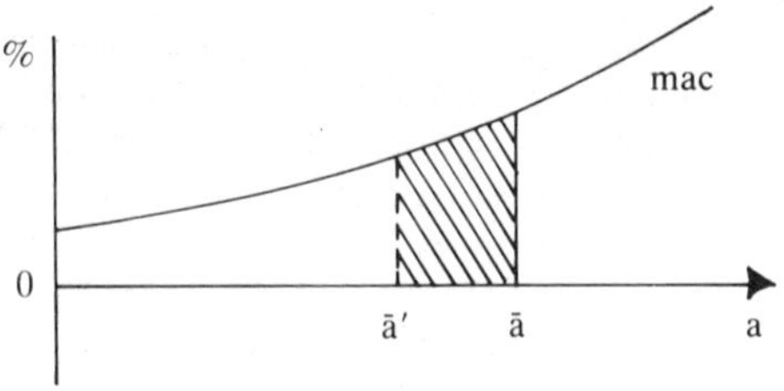

Figure 10c

where
$a = {_f\Gamma_i}\,{_f\Phi_i}/(1 + {_f\rho_i^v})$

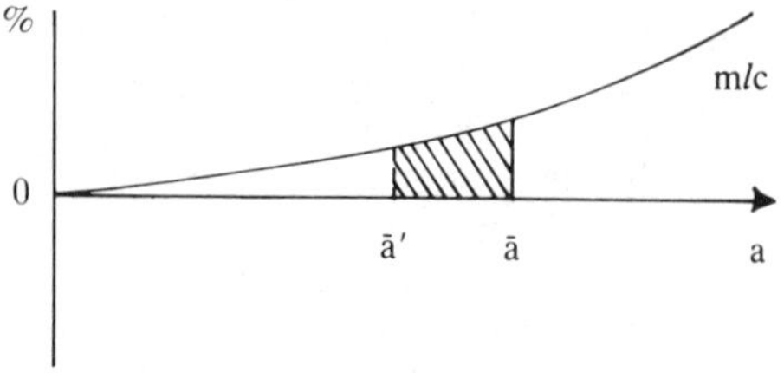

Figure 10d

$S'({}_f\bar{b}_i^v)$ which stands at an increasing distance from the former curve because of the increasing mac.

The equilibrium amount borrowed by v of the asset ${}_f\Phi_i$ is 0a and the rate paid is ${}_f\rho_i^v$. This rate is higher than the rate paid for spot trading of the borrowed FME because of the additional costs of borrowing incurred by both the borrower and the lenders.

(b) Household Borrowing and Free GFME

In this section we will discuss the effects of two government monetary policies on private borrowing. First, the discussion of the policy of giving free GFME through the tracing of equilibrium points will enable us to see the effects of an increase in the quantity of real GFME on the volume as well as the social costs of borrowing. Second, we will discuss the effects of providing a satiation level of real GFME on the same variables.

(i) *Tracing equilibrium levels.* Figure 10a shows the initial equilibrium level of real GFME 0a and the corresponding level of borrowing 0ā in figure 10b. When government policy of free distribution of GFME through the tracing of equilibrium levels produces the greater volume of real GFME 0a″ ′, the demand and supply schedules must change.[14] The demand for bonds will go down, signifying that, because of the relative abundance of real GFME, lenders are willing to lend greater amounts at the same rate of return. Meanwhile, the supply curve will shift down, showing that the borrower will borrow less at each rate of return. This causes the amount of borrowing to go down from 0ā to 0ā′. Figures 10c and 10d show the marginal costs of adjusting portfolios and the marginal lending costs respectively. The sum of the areas under the two curves, up to the amount of borrowing, represents the resources expended in the process of borrowing. The reduction of the amount of borrowing, because of free GFME, reduces this social cost by the sum of the two shaded areas in the latter diagrams.

(ii) *Providing the satiation level of GFME.* Figure 11a reproduces the case of free government provision of GFME up to satiation level plotted in figure 5 above. The production of 0e″ of real GFME costs the society a deadweight loss equal to the striped area Q″e″d″, and brings the rate of return on the marginal unit of real GFME down to zero. Since real GFME is freely available, lenders are willing to buy bonds at any rate above zero, but high enough to cover the marginal lending costs. This brings the demand curve to $D''({}_f\bar{b}_i^v)$, in figure 11b, which exactly traces the mlc curve. Moreover, the demand for borrowing at rates of return higher than zero disappears. Because people can satisfy their demands for means of exchange without cost, and because borrowing itself causes borrowers to incur portfolio adjustment costs, borrowers would sell their bonds only at

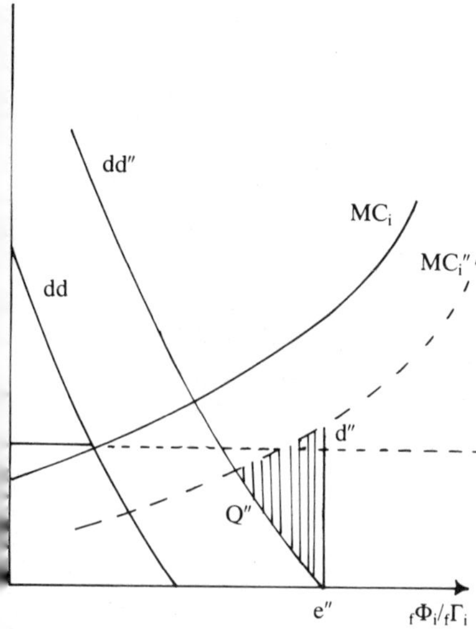

Figure 11a

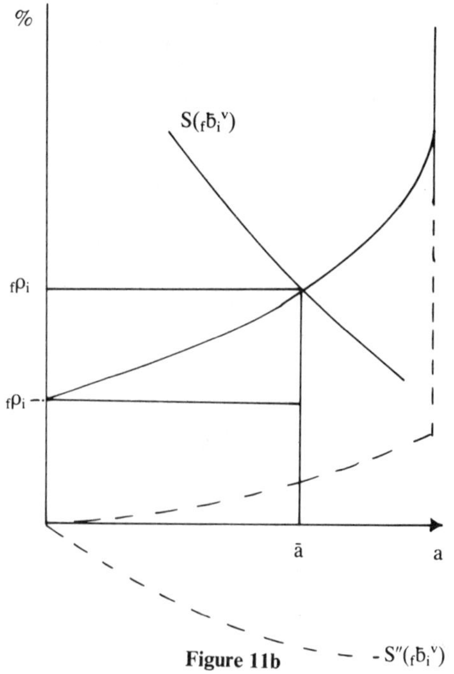

Figure 11b

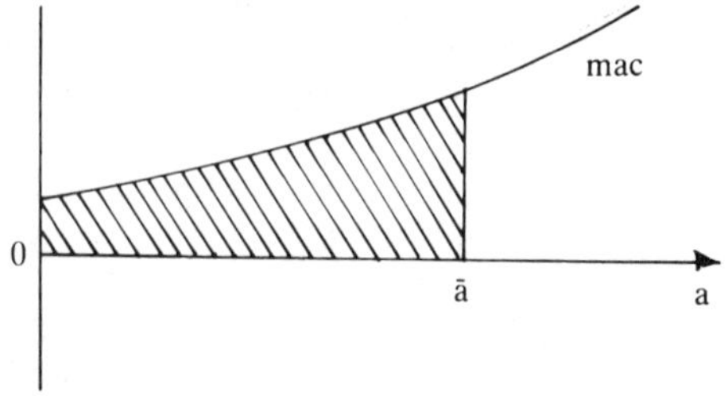

Figure 11c

where

$$dd = {}_f\rho_i({}_f\Phi_i/{}_f\Gamma_i)$$
$$dd'' = {}_f\rho_i({}_f\Phi_i/{}_f\Gamma_i)''$$
$$a = {}_f\Gamma_i\,{}_f\Phi_i/(1 + {}_f\rho_i^v)$$

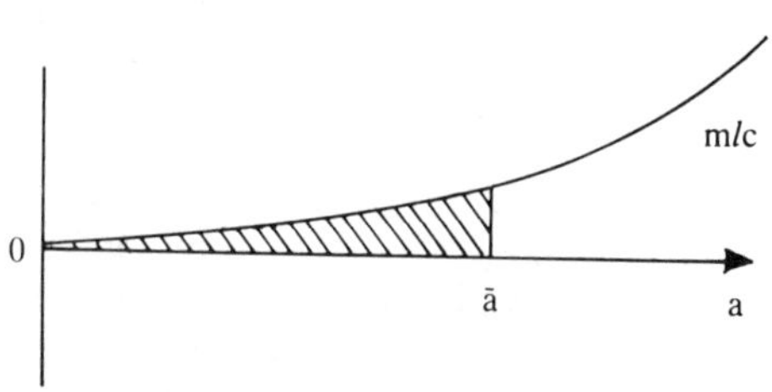

Figure 11d

negative rates of return, This means that they would demand compensation for the cost of borrowing in order to do so. This causes the supply curve for bonds to appear in the fourth quadrant, where it indicates at each quantity lent the corresponding (negative) values on the mac curve.

The sum of the shaded areas under the mac and mlc curves in figures 11c and 11d respectively measure the social costs associated with the volume 0ā of private lending. When that lending disappears because of free GFME provision, that cost disappears too. However, such a saving in resources is associated with a welfare cost measured by the area of Q″e″d″. The merit of the policy of free GFME up to satiation levels must therefore be judged through the comparison of the saving on lending costs and the welfare costs indicated in figure 11a. This, at the moment, is an empirical question.

2. Intermediate Fiat Assets

(a) Financial Intermediation

The reason for the existence of financial intermediation in this theoretical framework is information imperfection coupled with the ability to gain from specialising in the collection of information. No individual in this model can perceive the vector of prevailing prices perfectly. The set of each individual's conjectured prices, which determines the composition of his portfolio, will always fail to be the same as his vector of trading prices. Therefore, such a composition will always fail to minimise the transactions costs of fulfilling his obligations, when the bonds he has issued come to maturity. He must therefore continue to adjust the composition of his portfolio, which causes him to incur the portfolio adjustment costs mentioned above.

As a borrower, when the individual specialises in the information about the optimal portfolio composition, i.e., that which minimises his transactions costs at the time of the maturity of his debt, he can reduce his mac below the level reached by non-specialists. Such an intermediary can thus issue intermediate fiat assets, IFA, of quality superior to the household fiat assets, HFA, issued by non-specialists. The IFA are superior in the sense that they are issued at a lower mac than the HFA. The supply of IFA, at the same rates of return, is thus higher than that of HFA.

As a lender, the individual must collect information about the composition of the portfolios of his borrowers. Doing so costs him the mlc. If he is an information specialist, his mlc will be below that of a non-specialist. Being able to lend more cheaply causes the intermediary's demand for HFA to be higher than that of non-specialists for the same assets, at the same rates of return.

Figures 12a and 12b plot the markets of IFA and HFA, respectively. In the first diagram, the SIA schedule represents the supply of IFA. In the second diagram, the SHA schedule represents the supply of HFA.

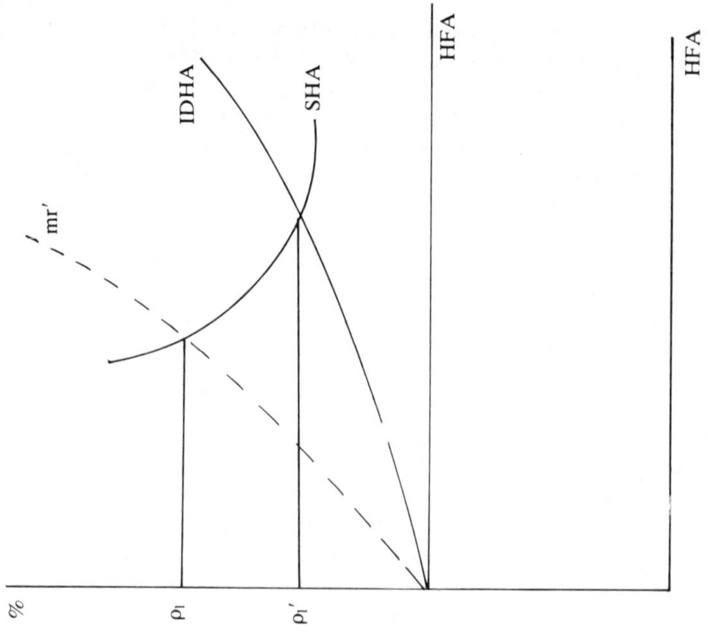

Figure 12b

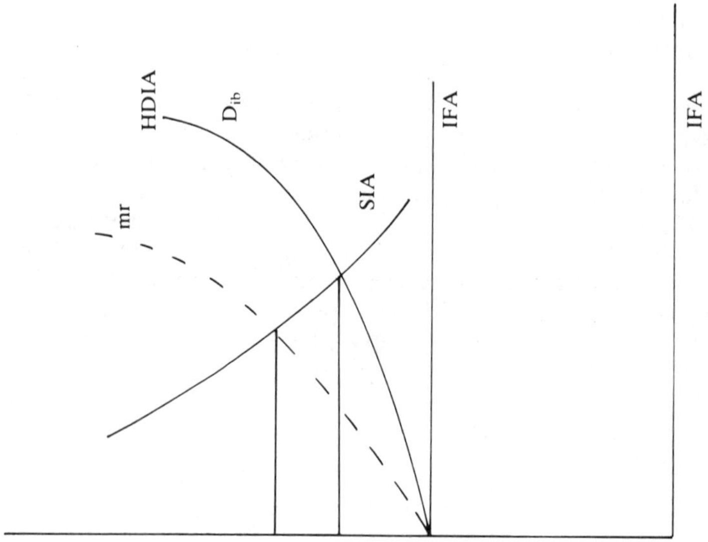

Figure 12a

Their relative positions are such that, if they were on the same diagram, the former would be closer to the ordinate than the latter, reflecting the lower level of mac associated with intermediate borrowing. Similarly, the schedule of households' demand for IFA, appearing in figure 12a, would be to the left of the schedule of intermediaries' demand for HFA, appearing in 12b, were they drawn on the same graph. This reflects the lower mlc associated with the latter.

In our model of imperfect information, all sellers behave as price searchers. The consideration of the marginal revenue curve associated with each demand curve in the above diagrams yields ρ_b and $\rho\ell$ as the borrowing and lending rates, respectively paid and received by intermediaries. The difference between both rates represents the margin of profit.

(b) Intermediation and Pricing Control

The government can undertake a policy of forcing non-monopolistic pricing in both the IFA and HFA markets. This reduces the borrowing and the lending rates to ρ_b' and $\rho\ell'$ respectively, but still keeps a profit margin for intermediaries to operate with. Moreover, the volume of lending through intermediaries expands. However, while the enforcement of marginal cost pricing on intermediaries may be easy for they would be small in number, its enforcement on issuers of household fiat assets may be very costly, for they would be rather numerous. An enforcement of marginal cost pricing on intermediaries only will force them out of business, because it reduces their borrowing rate.

(c) Intermediation and Free GFME

While intermediaries reduce the costs of borrowing and lending, they must borrow and lend at rates equal to or below the rates which are available to households directly. The reasons are that the intermediary lending rate must be no greater than the household's rate, and, that the intermediary borrowing rate must be below their lending rate.

The government's successive offers of free GFME through the tracing of equilibrium points will greatly reduce the cost of borrowing to households, but will not eliminate them. The resulting reduction of the household lending rate will necessarily reduce the margin of profit obtained by intermediaries, and, consequently, curtail their operations.

The provision of free GFME up to the satiation level reduces the costs of household borrowing to zero. This totally eliminates all intermediation.

VII

THE OPTIMAL SUPPLY OF FIAT MEANS OF EXCHANGE AND GOVERNMENT POLICY

In a world of only GFME, it was found that the optimal monetary policy would be to expand the stock of real balances through successively decreasing gifts of means of exchange, keeping all the time the rate of return on the marginal unit of real GFME equal to its marginal cost of production. The advantage of this policy is that it allows the stock of real balances to expand to the maximum possible amount without violating the efficiency rules.

In a world containing both GFME and SFME, the conditions under which SFME are produced become important. While the policy of successively tracing equilibrium points in the market of GFME remained optimal, it must be coupled with 100 per cent reserve ratio and an enforcement of marginal cost pricing in the SFME market.

The policy of providing GFME free of charge up to the satiation level was initially discarded because of a deadweight loss associated with its inefficiency. Nonetheless, when private borrowing was considered, the merits of discarding such a policy became less apparent. The reason is that such a policy would completely eliminate any need for private borrowing, thus saving the community the resources expended in marketing household fiat assets. The possibility that the real value of those resources could offset, and might exceed, the deadweight loss associated with the satiation level of GFME must therefore be considered. We could not, however, provide a theoretical support that the former gain will outweigh the latter loss. Such support can only come from an empirical evaluation.

While efficiency in the debt market requires the imposition of marginal cost pricing on household as well as intermediate issuers of fiat assets, there are reasons to believe that costs of this imposition on households could exceed the benefits. The imposition of pricing regulations on intermediaries alone will force them out of the debt market, causing the community to lose their services.

This dilemma can be solved by the policy of free GFME up to the satiation level. The abundance of GFME in this case eliminates the need for a debt market, and the existence of intermediation will therefore be unnecessary. This must be considered as an extra advantage of the GFME satiation policy.

Notes

1 10, 15, 18, 19, 24, 25, 28, 29, 33, 34, 35, 36, 37.
2 1, 4, 7, 14, 34.
3 11, 16, 17, 20, 21, 30, 31, 38.

4 8, 23.
5 3, 5, 6, 9, 12, 13, 22, 23, 26, 27.
6 Mabid A. M. M. Al-Jarhi, "The Optimal Supply of Money and Optimal Monetary Policies", Ph.D. Dissertation, University of Southern California, 1975, Ch. III.
7 A producer with a profit motive will find it hard to sell such information because of the characteristics of information which makes it resemble public goods.
8 This should not be construed as "good" money driving "bad" money out of circulation in violation of *Gresham's Law*. It would be confusing the "superiority" of an asset in the sense of costing its user less transactions costs with its "superiority" as a store of value.
9 The net rate of return of an asset, η_i when multiplied by the nominal value of the asset Φ_i, gives the net value of services $\eta_i \Phi_i$. That net value must be generally equal to the value of real services which is, for fiat assets, equal to zero, plus the value of transactions services. If the rate of transactions services obtained from Φ_i is equal to l_i, then:

$${}_f\ell_i \, {}_f\Phi_i / {}_f\Gamma_i = {}_f\ell_i \, {}_f\Phi_i, \qquad (11)$$

which implies that

$${}_f\ell_i / {}_f\Gamma_i = {}_f\ell_i' \qquad (12)$$

where ${}_f$ refers to the *fatrah* during which the exchanges are made.
10 The attempt to exclude such effects is not due to their undesirability, but rather to the analytical problems their existence may cause. For a free doubling of initial GFME, see, for example, D. Patinkin, *Money, Interest, and Prices*, 2nd ed. (New York: Harper and Row, 1965), ch. II. Another case is the famous Friedman's helicopter which, with an Arabian-Night magic, doubles the initial money holdings of everyone; see M. Friedman, "The Optimum Quantity of Money," in *The Optimum Quantity of Money and Other Essays* (Chicago: Aldine, 1969), pp. 4–7. Doubling initial holdings of GFME cannot be done here, for we are introducing them into an initially CME economy where such holdings are zero at the outset.
11 For a parallel treatment of this point see B. P. Pesek and T. R. Saving, *The Foundations of Money and Banking* (New York: Macmillan & Co., 1968).
12 It would be inconceivable, under the present assumption of information costs, and with costly transactions, to have a perfectly competitive market anywhere in the economy.
13 Mabid Ali Al-Jarhi, "The Optimal Supply of Money".
14 Although this policy may change the rate of return at equilibrium in any direction, we have, for diagrammatic simplicity, assumed it unchanged.

References

1. Akerlof, G. A., "The Demand for Money: A General Equilibrium Inventory-Theoretic Approach", *Review of Economic Studies*, 40 (January 1973), pp. 115–130.
2. Al-Jarhi, Mabid A. M. M., "The Optimal Supply of Money and Optimal Monetary Policies", Ph.D. Dissertation, University of Southern California, 1975.
3. Arrow, K. J., "The Role of Securities in the Optimal Allocation of Risk Bearing", *Review of Economic Studies*, 31 (April 1964), pp. 91–96.
4. ——, "Transactions Demand for Cash, an Inventory Approach", *Quarterly Journal of Economics*, 66 (November 1952), pp. 545–556.
5. Brunner, K., and Meltzer, A. H., "Some Further Investigations of Demand and Supply Functions of Money", *Journal of Finance*, 19 (May 1964), pp. 240–283.
6. ——, "The Uses of Money: Money in the Theory of an Exchange Economy", *American Economic Review*, 61 (December 1971), pp. 784–805.
7. Clower, R. W., "Is There an Optimal Money Supply?", *Journal of Finance*, 25 (May 1970), pp. 425–433.

8. ——, "Theoretical Foundations of Monetary Policy", in Clayton, G., et. al., eds., *Monetary Theory and Monetary Policy in the 1970s*, London: Oxford University Press, 1971.
9. Debreu, G., *Theory of Value*, New York: John Wiley and Sons, 1959.
10. Friedman, M., "The Optimum Quantity of Money", in *The Optimum Quantity of Money and Other Essays*, Chicago: Aldine, 1959, pp. 1–50.
11. Hahn, F. H., "Equilibrium with Transactions Costs", *Econometrica*, 39 (May 1971), pp. 417–439.
12. Howitt, P. A., "Stability and the Quantity Theory", *Journal of Political Economy*, 82 (January/February 1974), pp. 133–151.
13. ——, "Walras and Monetary Theory", *Western Economic Journal*, 11 (December 1973), pp. 487–499.
14. Johnson, H. G., "Is There an Optimal Money Supply?", *Journal of Finance*, 25 (May 1970), pp. 433–442.
15. ——, "Money in a Neoclassical One-Sector Growth Model", in *Essays in Monetary Economics*, Cambridge, Mass., Harvard University Press, 1967, pp. 143–178.
16. Kurz, M., "Equilibrium in a Finite Sequence of Markets with Transactions Costs", *Econometrica*, 42 (January 1974), pp. 1–20.
17. ——, "Equilibrium with Transactions Costs and Money in a Single-Market Exchange Economy", *Journal of Economic Theory*, 7 (August 1974), pp. 333–368.
18. Levhari, D. and Patinkin, D., "The Role of Money in a Simple Growth Model", *American Economic Review*, 58 (September 1968), pp. 713–753.
19. Marty, A. L., "Gurley and Shaw on Money in a Theory of Finance", *Journal of Political Economy*, 69 (February 1961), pp. 56–62.
20. Niehans, J., "Money and Barter in General Equilibrium with Transactions Costs", *American Economic Review*, 61 (December 1971), pp. 773–783.
21. ——, "Money in a Static Theory of Optimal Payment Arrangements", *Journal of Money, Credit, and Banking*, 1 (November 1969), pp. 706–726.
22. Ostrey, J. M., "The Informational Efficiency of Monetary Exchange", *American Economic Review*, 63 (September 1973), pp. 597–610.
23. ——, "The Informational Efficiency of Monetary Exchange", UCLA Dept. of Economics discussion paper no. 15, November 1971.
24. Patinkin, D., *Money, Interest, and Prices*, 2nd ed., New York: Harper and Row, 1965.
25. Phelps, E. S., "Anticipated Inflation and Economic Welfare", *Journal Political Economy*, 73 (February 1965), pp. 8–12.
26. Radner, R., "Competitive Equilibrium Under Uncertainty", *Econometrica*, 36 (January 1968), pp. 31–58.
27. ——, "Problems in the Theory of Markets Under Uncertainty", *American Economic Review*, 60 (May 1970), pp. 454–460.
28. Samuelson, P. A., "Nonoptimality of Money Holdings Under Laissez-Faire", *Canadian Journal of Economics*, 2 (May 1969), pp. 303–308.
29. Sidrauski, M., "Inflation and Economic Growth", *Journal of Political Economy*, 75 (December 1967), pp. 796–810.
30. Sontheimer, K., "On the Determination of Money Prices", *Journal of Money, Credit, and Banking*, 4 (August 1972), pp. 489–508.
31. Starr, R. M., "Equilibrium and the Demand for Media of Exchange in a Pure Exchange Economy with Transactions Costs", Cowles Foundation Discussion Paper no. 300, October 1970.
32. ——, "Exchange in Barter and Monetary Economics", *Quarterly Journal of Economics*, 70 (May 1972), pp. 290–302.
33. Stein, J. L., "Neoclassical and Keynes-Wicksell Monetary Growth Models", *Journal of Money, Credit, and Banking*, 1 (May 1969), pp. 153–171.

34. Tobin, J., "Liquidity Preference and Behaviour Toward Risk", *Review of Economic Studies*, 25 (February 1958), pp. 65–86.
35. ——, "Notes on Optimal Monetary Growth", *Journal of Political Economy*, 76 (July/August 1968), pp. 833–873.
36. Tolly, G. S., "Providing for the Growth of the Money Supply", *Journal of Political Economy*, 65 (December 1957), pp. 465–485.
37. Tsiang, S. C., "A Critical Note on the Optimum Supply of Money", *Journal of Money, Credit, and Banking*, 1 (May 1969), pp. 266–280.
38. Wallace, N., "An Approach to the Study of Money and Non-money Exchange Structures", *Journal of Money, Credit, and Banking*, 4 (November 1972), pp. 828–837.

CHAPTER SIX

Zakāt and Fiscal Policy

*Dr. F. R. Faridi**

The present paper is an attempt to analyse *Zakāt* as the irreducible minimum ingredient of the fiscal policy of an Islamic State. At the very outset it rejects the popular stipulation that fiscal management in an Islamic State is coterminous with *Zakāt*: on the contrary, it assumes the permissibility and also occasional desirability of additional mobilisation of resources for state production of "social goods" in an Islamic Society. It attempts to incorporate *Zakāt* in the overall framework of fiscal policy and studies it as the "leading sector" of the broader complex of revenue-expenditure pattern of public authorities. *Zakāt* is treated here only as an "economic variable", though its religious importance cannot be minimised, and will be occasionally referred to during the course of this study. The general economic significance of *Zakāt* happens to be directional, and normative. It defines the norms of economic activity, also of fiscal activity as a subsection thereof and determines, through its effects on economic variables, flows and magnitudes, the direction along which the economy is desired to move.

Assumptions and Limitations

(a) The study assumes a socio-cultural milieu based on Islamic precepts and values. The Islamic fiscal policy can operate only as a complement to other facets of socio-economic policy: its success or failure depends on their availability. Like its counterpart elsewhere its objectives are derived from the aspirations and goals of the people where it operates and its *modus operandi* is subject to their value-orientations and behavioural pattern. There is nothing like "pure fiscal theory" comparable to "pure science". Hence, we assume an Islamic society. It must be noted, however, that this assumption is not "idealistic" referring to some highly abstract set of concepts. It refers to an institutional organisation based on Islamic teachings, some important features of which are as follows:

(1) Prohibition of interest (*ribā*).
(2) Prohibition of gambling, hoarding and fraudulent trade practices.
(3) Imposition of *Zakāt*.

* Dr. F. R. Faridi, Reader, Economics Department, Aligarh University, Aligarh (India).

(b) In addition to the above, the present analysis assumes minimum mobility of capital and labour as between the interest-free and interest-based societies. This assumption is particularly meaningful in view of the absence of interest and prohibition of a number of investment avenues in the Islamic economy which are highly lucrative in the modern "interest laden" and capitalist societies. Free mobility of capital as between an "interest-free" and "interest-laden" society may, other things remaining equal, encourage flight of capital from the former to the latter, and thereby vitiate the "investment effect" of *Zakāt* analysed in the following section. It may be contended that such an assumption is unnecessary for it assumes an inherent repulsion to "risk taking" in the richer classes of the society. But that is not true for it overlooks the fact that prohibition of interest is only one ingredient of the Islamic economic policy. This assumption, however, does not rule out state-to-state international capital transactions for obvious reasons.

Limitations

One major limitation of the subsequent analysis is the absence of any empirical base to support its conclusions. This is as it should be, on account of the present conditions of Muslim societies which do not provide the institutional framework in which the Islamic fiscal policy based on *Zakāt* has to operate. Hence, the present analysis has been attempted more or less on the pattern of scientific conjecture. The present socio-economic system of the developing countries modified in essentials of Islamic cultural milieu has been assumed for this analysis. This writer is aware of the implications of this severe limitation but believes that the present analysis is still essentially not wide of the mark and serves to provide necessary insights into *Zakāt* and its relationship with Islamic fiscal policy.

Zakāt is the positive component of Islamic economics while the prohibition of interest is its negative ingredient. Together they draw the landscape of the Islamic economy and represent, as it were, the two facets of the same policy. The description of *Zakāt* (or *Ṣadaqah*) in the Qur'ān, its exposition by the Holy Prophet through his words and actual implementation, and its subsequent elaboration by *Ṣahābah* (Companions of the Prophet) and Islamic jurists give the student of economic theory substantial insight into the economic and fiscal orientation of an Islamic economy.

Fiscal Norms of an Islamic Society

The basic orientation of an Islamic economy[1] is mutual sharing of the community's income between the affluent and have-nots. The rich are encouraged to transfer a part of their earnings through *Zakāt* and *Ṣadaqāt* to the poor. While *Zakāt* is a compulsory levy, the *Ṣadaqah* is a voluntary transfer of one's savings. This objective may be described as that of social insurance which is an obligation of both the state and the individual. We have avoided the use of the word egaliterianism to describe the said objective for reasons to be stated later. An important corollary of Islamic economic teachings is the productive use of investment of *al-Amwāl*, the economic resources, for the economic betterment of the society. Hence the promotion of productive use of economic resources happens to be another norm of an Islamic economy.[2] Since the objectives of fiscal policy are derivatives from the overall goals and orientations of the socio-economic policy of a society, we can state its two objectives as follows:

(1) To ensure minimum means of livelihood to each and every individual in the community.
(2) To ensure productive use of economic resources for the material well-being of the community.

Zakāt as the Determinant of the Nature of Fiscal Policy

In terms of the current phraseology the two objectives may be described as growth with "social justice". In the attainment of these objectives the Islamic fiscal theory does not preclude the use of modern techniques of raising revenue *per se*. Nor does it consider the state allocation of economic resources as required by the socio-economic priorities in contemporary developing economies as inherently incompatible with its own system. But *Zakāt* occupies a central place in Islamic fiscal policy and operations. Since its rate is given it lends an element of stability to public revenues which is particularly useful in maintaining budget stability.[3] A set *Zakāt* rate however does not involve a fixed collection since a rise or fall in individual incomes would be automatically reflected in corresponding changes in the total *Zakāt* collections. The revenue collection from *Zakāt* would, however, provide the stable minimum quantum of revenues required for the promotion of the above objectives of fiscal policy. But *Zakāt* also lays down certain imperatives of the tax system of an Islamic economy. These may be enumerated as hereunder:

(1) No additional levies on personal or collective incomes can be imposed on assessees whose incomes fall below the *Niṣāb* stipulated in *Zakāt*.
(2) In the calculation of assessable income "expense" items shall have to be deducted as are done under *Zakāt* law. The deductible items have been examined in detail in the *Sharī'ah* in different cases, such as the owners of cattle wealth, the producers of agricultural goods, the traders, and other affluent groups. These have to be taken account of and strictly adhered to, not only in *Zakāt* but additional levies as well.
(3) Double or multiple assessment of the same base is not possible in one stipulated period in *Zakāt*. Hence such a policy is to be avoided in case of other direct taxes. The fiscal implication of this principle

should be fully understood. It involves the exclusion of such levies as wealth tax if assessed on the base of the *Zakāt*, that is, net wealth of the *Zakāt* assessee and are yearly recurrent. As far as those taxes which are leviable once, such as inheritance tax, or estate duties they are a separate category, and are assessed on a base different from the *Zakāt* base. Hence these do not fall under the purview of this principle.

Given these principles the Islamic State is free to impose additional levies to meet its ordinary and welfare or growth expenditures. Before we proceed to consider the economic implications of *Zakāt*, let us study this aspect of the matter a little more closely.

Additional Levies

We have maintained above that an Islamic State can impose additional direct levies to raise its revenues. The most important of modern fiscal devices in this sphere are taxes on personal or corporate incomes. Income tax is assessed on a base different from *Zakāt* – it is levied on current incomes and not savings, although it allows certain specific deductions, but it takes into account neither the net savings of the assessee nor the period for which he holds them intact. Consequently the third principle stated above does not cover it. But the exemption limit allowed under income tax laws shall not fall below *Niṣāb*. This tax is also not subject to principle No. 2 above since it takes into account the flow and not the magnitude. The second important tax is inheritance and/or estate duty which is also permissible as pointed out above.* Similarly taxes on professions, etc., whose base is different from *Zakāt* are all legitimate. Taxes on consumption expenditure may sometimes become necessary to discourage deliberate evasion of *Zakāt* and wilful obstruction in the fulfilment of its secondary function, namely, the promotion of productive investment of one's savings. Capital gains tax has also a different base and is levied only at one particular point of time. Thus quite a number of currently operative direct levies are permissible in an Islamic State.

All of these and similar direct taxes are subject to variations both in respect of the exemption limits and rates, depending upon economic and equity considerations in a society. A steeply progressive rate of income tax with a low or moderately high exemption limit is popular in most of the developing economies these days. But this is not a universally valid policy measure, for general economic sluggishness may call for an entirely different order of things. Indications in the developing economies point to a relaxation in this policy on account of what is popularly described in

* This is the view of the author. Other Muslim scholars and jurists hold a different view and they do not accept the view that estate duty or death duty can fit into the Islamic fiscal framework. Editor.

current economic literature as "stagflation". The harmful effects of steeply progressive taxes on incentive and the drastic erosion of the real value of money have forced new thinking in both the affluent and poor economies.

Income Elasticity of *Zakāt*

The element of flexibility noticeable in the fiscal devices other than *Zakāt* has led some of our friends to question the authenticity and universality of a given rate of *Zakāt* and to recommend a change thereof.[4] In our opinion such a recommendation is contrary to *Sharī'ah* and is born of a misunderstanding of both the nature of *Zakāt* and also its alleged "inflexibility". In the first instance, it must be clearly understood that *Zakāt* is not a "tax" only. It is an *'Ibādah* as well. No change in it is permissible. In the second place *Zakāt* is not an "inflexible" fiscal measure. Its base is the net savings, or net wealth of an assessee. These bases are variable in size and are likely to grow or decline in response to variations in income. In addition, the deductions allowed on account of trade or consumption expenditure do not vary in magnitude proportionately to fluctuations in the scale of economic activity or incomes. The marginal propensity to consume bears a stable relationship to income in the short period and may decline, other things being equal, after a certain level of individual income. Thus deductions allowed on account of consumption expenditure have little likelihood of substantial growth to the detriment of *Zakāt* collections. The case of trade expenses is not so clear. But certain items of costs are subject to economies of scale. Hence every change in the scale of economic activity may not cause a proportional rise (or fall) of such costs. These considerations lend "built-in flexibility" to the statutory rate of *Zakāt* although its degree of sensitivity of yield in response to changes in income may not be so high as that of some other taxes.

Stability and Countercyclical Use of *Zakāt*

The statutory rate of *Zakāt* and fixed *Niṣāb* (or exemption limit) accords to fiscal policy the much needed stability core. In the first place, a fiscal system based on *Zakāt*, involves an automatic fluctuation in state revenues in response to changes in the size of its base in response to changes in income. Together with appropriate combinations and permutations of other taxes, it may work for an automatic stabilisation of total income (and employment). In addition it may also lead to a stable budget. The latter point may be understood more accurately in terms of the specific items of *Zakāt* disbursements. Quite a few of these are intended as transfer payments to the poor (or unemployed). As economic prosperity increases the required volume of such expenses may decline, thereby causing an accumulation of budget surpluses. These accumulated budgetary surpluses on account of *Zakāt*, may be held over during these years[5] and used when recession or depression sets in and causes hardship to people. Of course, under *Zakāt*, all unemployed people will not benefit, for only such would be entitled to benefit as do not own *Niṣāb*. Nevertheless the budgetary surpluses or deficits, arising out of *Zakāt* collections may be disbursed in a countercyclical manner, or more appropriately, as an element of compensatory fiscal policy.

In deflationary conditions, the total *Zakāt* collections would decline, in spite of its fixed rate. While during the period of rising incomes, and thriving business, *Zakāt* levies may be paid out of the current flows of income, during the downward swing of the economy they may constitute a charge on hoarded wealth and/or net savings. This is likely to reduce the assessable wealth and hence *Zakāt* collections. Together with this development, greater deductions on expense account may be allowed in view of the falling individual incomes. Thus the number of people assessable and the total *Zakāt*-able wealth would tend to decline.

The stable tax rate combined with a variable volume of disbursement of *Zakāt* funds in response to rise or decline in total employment in an advanced economy serves as an automatic regulator of government expenditure. This characteristic of *Zakāt* tax, if judiciously combined with similar fiscal devices, is likely to work for stability without major dislocations in the economy.

The Developing Economies and *Zakāt*-Based Fiscal Policy

Nearer home is the question of *Zakāt*'s impact on a developing economy. Most of the Muslim countries fall into this category. Let us, therefore, consider and analyse the impact and utility of *Zakāt* as a fiscal measure in an Islamic developing economy. Such an economy shares a number of characteristics commonly associated with a developing economy. But in addition to these, its distinctive features are the prohibition of interest, exclusion of speculative purchase and sale of stocks, hoarding and stockpiling of goods with the express design to create scarcity, merchandising of prohibited goods and services such as wines, etc. In such an economy the most urgent problems are development and social justice. Fiscal policies in Islamic developing economies would be geared towards increase in private and public savings to release real resources for productive investment and to allocate public expenditure in such a way that it serves the twin purpose of growth and social welfare. In what respects, and to what extent, can *Zakāt* collections and disbursement be of use in the implementation of these objectives?

A: Savings and Investment

Zakāt levies may have two opposite effects on private savings and investment. An annual *Zakāt* levy on net savings (or net wealth) above the *Niṣāb* limit is likely to strengthen the propensity to consume. An individual saver may derive greater satisfaction from extravagant expenditure to avoid the yearly *Zakāt* levy which threatens to eat away his net savings. Thus the consumption function has an upward shift. But it may produce an entirely different reaction in him. In order to protect his wealth from gradual erosion, he may turn his idle wealth into active real or financial resources. His willingness to invest may be intensified.[6] Both these tendencies would, in the ultimate analysis, cause an upward shift in the demand for goods and services produced in the economy. Hoarded wealth would be turned into an active agent of demand, while investment would increase in response to, and almost in proportionate measure to, the power of *Zakāt* to erode idle resources. Increased demand for consumer and capital goods would contribute to greater production.

Considered from another angle, the power of *Zakāt* to erode idle wealth, and its punitive imposition on hoarded precious metals, would tend to increase the supply of savings (in an economic sense) in comparison to its demand.

B: Decline in Expected Rate of Return on Savings

This effect of *Zakāt* would be beneficial in as much as it would reduce the expected rate of returns, thereby pushing investment in economically less profitable, yet socially productive and urgent directions. In the absence of interest-yielding transactions, the reduced profit expectations, are likely to induce private capital to venture into those fields which, in normal circumstances, it would leave for public authorities. Of course, there would be a minimum profitability limit of such investments. Its rate of return must not be below the *Zakāt* rate but must be above it measured by the cost of inconvenience involved in such investments. The unduly long gestation period of such investment may work as another constraint. Thus even though the *Zakāt* levy is likely to reduce the price of savings (or to use our own expression, the expected rate of return on savings) it would still leave a large area for the state expenditure programme.

C: Willingness to Work

Looked at from another angle, the punitive nature of *Zakāt*, would exercise a healthy and positive impact on people's willingness to work – one of the parameters of economic development pointed out by Lewis.[7] The natural desire to protect one's net savings, in the absence of the effortless accretion to it through interest, would strengthen the desire of the individual to work harder, or to enable others to work harder with the help of his resources. In this way idleness would be discouraged and work rewarded.

Public Expenditure and *Zakāt*

So much then about the impact of *Zakāt* levies on private savings and investment. Turning now to public consumption and investment, we may visualise a positive relationship conducive to increased production and greater justice between *Zakāt* and the fiscal policy. *Zakāt* levies are likely to provide substantial funds to the state exchequer in a developing economy for three reasons. Firstly it would make accessible to the tax authorities such items as are ordinarily beyond their purview. One of the features of a backward economy is substantial investment in precious metals and landed property as a savings avenue. This preference for non-economic investment in precious metals renders a sizeable quantity of national wealth non-available for productive use and inaccessible to the state fiscal machinery in ordinary circumstances. The *Zakāt* levies on such "hoardings" would discourage such unproductive investment, and provide incentive for economic investment. On the other hand it would enable the state to lay its fiscal hands on these items of "net wealth". This would provide substantial funds to the state. Secondly the low exemption limit of *Zakāt* (*Niṣāb*) would enable the state to throw its fiscal net quite wide. Thirdly, the incentive effect of *Zakāt* would be likely to increase productive investment, and hence net savings in the economy. As this happens the base of the *Zakāt* levy would widen, bringing in more resources.

But more important is the disbursement of *Zakāt* funds. In this connection we will consider the avenues of expenditure and their *modus operandi*. The Qur'ān [8] has specified clearly the categories of people, and the avenues, on which *Zakāt* collections can be expended. The categories of people entitled to benefit from *Zakāt* are the poor, the pauper, the indebted, the wayfarer, the new converts and the avenues have been enumerated as the liberation of slaves, maintenance of *Zakāt* administration, and last but not least "in the path of Allah". Without going into the details of the minute interpretative analyses of each of these categories and avenues by the leaders of Islamic jurisprudence, we may rest satisfied, for the present, with their apparent meanings and consensus regarding the last-mentioned avenue.

It may be noted that this detailed specification of the items on which the *Zakāt* fund can be expended is eminently useful in the context of the experience of many developing economies in the modern world. As pointed out by a host of economists, such as Myrdal, Bauer, Ursula Hicks, Nurkse, Chelliah, an economically appropriate allocation of public expenditure between competing needs of growth and equity has been one of the major headaches of the developing economies in recent times. Swayed by short term political considerations or ideological indoctrination, the governments in the developing countries have tended to ignore long term growth needs and have wasted scarce resources on wrong notions of social justice or short term schemes of welfare. On the other hand, we have noticed excessive emphasis on production planning weighted in favour of schemes with long gestation periods and increased investment in capital goods industries, at the expense of improvements in the standard of living of the masses. The Islamic fiscal policy based on *Zakāt* would provide the state with a reasonable minimum of resources intended for social welfare. No exogenous considerations, economic or political, and no fiscal contingency except that related to *Zakāt* objectives, would be allowed to curtail the social welfare expenditure below the quantity raised through *Zakāt*, except of course, that specified in *Zakāt* law itself. In the second place, the delineation of items of *Zakāt* disbursement, would also serve to protect its allocation against the economic, fiscal or political whims of the administration.

In the context of the developing economies of today, this characteristic of *Zakāt* collection and disbursement would be of immense utility.

Investment of *Zakāt* for the Benefit of the Poor

The most important aspect of the matter is the mode of disbursement of *Zakāt* funds. The simplest method is to expend these funds through transfer payments to those entitled to receive them. But a deeper understanding of the objectives of *Zakāt*, in the light of modern economic analysis, makes its utilisation possible in such a manner as to produce a cumulative effect on poverty and as an instrument of active fiscal policy designed to promote the welfare function of public expenditure. These funds or a part thereof may be earmarked for productive investment intended for the benefit of eligible recipients in firms or industries owned by them. Such investments may be dovetailed with overall investment priorities of the economy. Thus these funds would serve two purposes at the same time. On the one hand, they would minimise the non-investment or consumption expenditure arising out of substantial and regular transfer payments of *Zakāt* in an economy. Since the marginal propensity to consume at low levels of income is not usually more than unity, and since in a developing economy it is fairly high all round, the two would together further depress the ratio of savings to GNP. While at high levels of employment the upward shift of the consumption function may be desirable in certain conditions, the developing economies are confronted with an unusually low ratio of savings to current incomes and would very much like to restrict consumption. If *Zakāt* funds flow into investment channels, it would reduce its negative effects on savings and add to gross national product. On the other hand, investment-oriented disbursement of these funds would have a cumulative effect on poverty.

Multiplier Effect

A certain amount of *Zakāt* funds, invested according to the overall production priorities of an economy, would benefit the poor, in particular, and the economy, in general, through its multiplier effect on employment and incomes. Let us for the sake of illustration, assume that Rs.100 are spent as transfer payments in one year. If the marginal propensity to consume is 1, which is most likely to be the case for people below the poverty line, all this amount would be expended on the purchase of consumer goods. These resources would thus be lost for ever in so far as the recipients are concerned, with the exception of such cases, and such parts thereof, as are spent on the improvement of the productive efficiency of the spender. The economy may benefit in so far as the additional demand for consumer goods increases production and employment. The resultant multiplier effect however is likely to be low on account of the strong probability that such funds would, for the most part, be spent on non-durable consumer goods. If however, the same amount was invested in productive activity, a regular flow of income would accrue to the recipients, while the said amount would not only remain intact but may progressively increase, depending upon the rate of profit and the immediate expenditure needs of the recipients. At the same time assuming income multiplier equal to 3, which is the value usually assigned to it in the developing economies, the said amount would benefit the economy three times its original value.

The periodical net profits from such enterprises would accrue to the shareholders, the recipients of *Zakāt* who have agreed to invest therein. But such of these as opt for employment in these undertakings would benefit on two counts, both as shareholders receiving dividends and as wage-earners. With the lapse of time, many one-time recipients of *Zakāt*, may not remain eligible for it. Yet they would continue to receive incomes from these undertakings. The savings from such enterprises may either be ploughed back into the same, or elsewhere. It must be noted, however, that such corporate net wealth would be assessable for *Zakāt* in the period subsequent to the payment (or investment). There is every likelihood that individual's net wealth built up through these investments would also attain the *Niṣāb* limit after a few years and become assessable for *Zakāt*. In this way the expenditure of *Zakāt* funds would have a multiple effect on the economy. It would gradually eliminate poverty instead of providing recurring financial support to the same set of people. It would increase employment and income in the economy, thereby raising the standard of living in the economy. And lastly it would enhance the aggregate volume of *Zakāt* collections.

Investment in Welfare Services

Zakāt funds may also be allocated to those avenues of public expenditure which improve the working conditions and the efficiency of the eligible recipients. Improved housing facilities, health services, training programmes, educational institutions and a number of similar services may be initiated for this purpose. In this fashion, the welfare function of public expenditure would be promoted. A survey of the poor economies of today reveals the alarmingly low ratio of such expenditure to GNP in many of them. If even 1 per cent of net national wealth, not current national income, is earmarked yearly for such services, it would account for a reasonably high level of welfare expenditure in the state budget.[9]

If the foregoing stipulation is legitimate *Zakāt* can be used as an effective instrument in the fulfilment of the allocative as well as the distributive functions of fiscal policy. As stated earlier this allocation can be woven into the overall investment priorities of the economy in such a way as to serve both purposes. In addition, it can be handled as an element of compensatory fiscal policy and can bring about adjustments in consumption, savings, and investments.

The Ratio of Transfer Payments

It must be pointed out however, that we are not advocating the complete elimination of transfer payments from *Zakāt* revenue. In the first place such a policy may lead to a deliberate misuse of *Zakāt* funds by the state. Secondly, transfer payments are the best mode of *Zakāt* disbursements in certain cases, such as debts, accidents, starvation, old age, support etc. Thirdly the time lag involved between investment and current flow of income may require transfer payments. Fourthly, failures of business and industry launched through *Zakāt* funds may necessitate transfer payments to those affected.

The best alternative would be to devise a reasonable distribution of *Zakāt* revenues into the alternative uses pointed out above. The ratio of these uses to each other may not be rigidly fixed. But we can safely assume that the Qur'ānic enumeration of eight uses does serve as an indicator that not less than 12.5 per cent of the total should be earmarked for each use. Yet it does not stipulate that the disbursing authority shall not be competent to transfer funds from one alternative use to the other in the interest of the eligible recipients themselves and to serve its objectives better.

Notes

1 Cf. Hassanein, M., "Towards a Model of the Economics of Islam" in MSA: *Contemporary Aspects of Economic and Social Thinking in Islam* (Proceedings of the III East Coast Regional Conference), N.Y. 1970.

2 For a penetrating analysis of the norms of an Islamic Economy see Mawdudi: *Economic Problem of Man and its Islamic Solution.* Maktabah Jamā't-i-Islāmī Delhi; Al-Qarḍawī, Y.: *Fiqh al-Zakāt*, p. 43, Vol. I and p. 851, Vol. II: 1969. Ibn-'Āshūr, M. T., *Principles of Social Organisation in Islam* (Arabic), pp. 190–197; Maktabah al-Rasmiyeh, Tunis, 1964; Qutb, Syed: *Social Justice in Islam* (Arabic); Ghazali, M., *Islam and Economic Organisation* (Arabic), Cairo; Abū Zahra: *Tanzīm al-Islām-li-'lmujtama'*; Abu Saud, M., *Main Features of Islamic Economy* (Arabic); Ziauddin Rees, M., *Al-Kharāj* in *An Islamic State* (Arabic); Nahdha Misr and Abu Yusuf, *Al-Kharāj*, *Al-Matba' al-Salafiya.*

3 See CED, "Taxes and Budget", a programme for prosperity in a free economy, in *Readings in Fiscal Policy*, A.E.A. London: 1965, p. 360.

4 See for instance, Zadi, A. M., "The Role of *Zakāt* in the Islamic System of

Economics of Curing the Poverty Dilemma" (p. 14) in AMSS: *Proceedings of the Third Seminar*, Gary, Indiana, 1974.

5 It may be noted here that, contrary to the opinion of some Islamic jurists, there is no compulsive direction in the Qur'ān or the *Sunnah* to disburse the *Zakāt* collections immediately. If *Zakāt* is intended for the benefit of its poor recipients, it may require both its immediate transfer, and/or its retention depending upon what serves their interest better.

6 Cf: Kahf Monzer, "A Model of the Household Decision in the Islamic Economy" in AMSS: Proceedings, op cit. (p. 21).

7 See Lewis, W. A., *The Theory of Economic Growth*, London: 1963 (low priced edition), p. 33.

8 The Qur'ān IX: 60.

9 It would be highly illuminating to attempt a calculation of the ratio of *Zakāt* revenues to total public revenues in an Islamic economy. But an empirical investigation is not possible for various reasons. Yet a scientific conjecture can be made, keeping in view the following features of *Zakāt* levy: (a) It is a tax (say, at a constant rate of 2.5%) on net national wealth (that is investible goods). (b) Most of this amount is specifically earmarked for expenditure on the welfare of the poor. It would be very difficult to attempt such a calculation in the present study. For the sake of tentative illustration, let us assume that GNP is equivalent to net national wealth (minus those owned by authorities). Suppose further that public revenues constitute about 25% of GNP. In that case about 10% of total public revenues would be spent on the welfare of the poorer sections of an economy. This estimate is, however, only illustrative and open to substantial corrections in the light of both an accurate assessment of the ratio between *Zakāt* assessable non-state net wealth of the economy and GNP, on the one hand, and GNP and public revenues, on the other, and future empirical investigation.

CHAPTER SEVEN

The Political Context of Islamic Economics: High and Low Road Strategies

*Dr. Ijaz Shafi Gilani**

ONE of the primary functions of any science is classification. Whether in natural or social sciences, the task of an analyst is to classify disparate events under formal classes. By definition, therefore, such classes or categories are formal and artificial. Nevertheless, they help in: (a) comprehension of the problem, and (b) projection of non-existing futures.[1] The act of *formalisation* becomes especially important for a discussion about desirable but non-existing (one could also say utopian) situations. The subject of our discussion falls into this class of problems. We are carrying out discussion about a system of economic relationships which does not exist. Nevertheless, we have certain notions about a desirable future system. What should be a relevant classification for our discussion? One could conceive of several classifications depending on one's interests and the level of discussion. For the purposes of a discussion on the Political Context of Islamic Economics, I have preferred to categorise the discussion under three classes: THEORY, POLICY and PRACTICE.

Theory, Policy and Practice

By Theory, I refer to the abstract principles of economic activity: principles related to consumer behaviour, the nature of money, distribution of wealth, etc.

By Policy, I refer to a strategy for the realisation of certain objectives in a given time and horizon. Policy comprises guidelines based on certain theoretical beliefs.

By Practice, I refer to the concrete steps for carrying out a policy in a specific operation. Social philosophers of different ages and areas of the world have conceived of social planning under similar categories. One finds

---

* Dr. Ijaz Shafi Gilani is Chairman, Department of International Relations, Quaid-e-Azam University, Islamabad. Educated at the Universities of Karachi and MIT Massachussets, his specialisation is in International Relations and Economics.

a reference to these categories in a wide spectrum of writings sufficiently diverse to include Ibn-Khaldun, the American literature on the so-called Policy Sciences and the works of Communist strategists such as Mao and Lenin.[2] There are grey areas in between Theory, Policy and Practice. And that aspect of it is most crucial. It is the task of any leadership to have a clear vision of what falls in which category. A choice of this nature requires both technical competence and an artful intuition about the political environment.

This paper is an attempt to perform a two-fold task of:

(a) Clarifying the distinction between Theory, Policy and Practice.
(b) Focussing on the Policy aspect of Islamic Economics.

A Framework for Policy Formulation

Policy Formulation is usually for a middle range time-period, let us say for a period from five to fifteen years. It is our hypothesis that for this time range, the objectives of political leaders play a decisive role in the determination of economic relationships. In this statement, we are making an explicit disagreement with the orthodox Marxist and Liberal conceptions about economic determinism.[3] At any stage of human history and means of production, political leaderships are faced with a number of choices regarding economic relationships. We argue that within the parameters which are provided by long range forces, political leaderships make the decisive choices. Therefore, a discussion on economic policy or strategy, must contain a discussion of the objectives of political leaders.[4]

Political leaderships can be divided into several types. We have chosen two types that we think are most inclusive and explanatory for our purposes:

(a) Goal-Oriented Leadership.
(b) Value-Oriented Leadership.

This division is based on the categories of human motivation provided by Max Weber.[5] Max Weber has two other categories: effective or sentimental and traditional motivations. The difference between these and the earlier two categories is that these (the latter two) are not based on calculation, and hence are in a way not rational. We assume that all political leaderships in our times are rational. However, one type of rationality is based on the pursuit of values and principles, the other type of rationality is based on the pursuit of goals only.

The political leaderships in the Islamic community of our time can be divided into goal-oriented leadership and value-oriented leadership. As we shall explain below each leadership has elements of the other category. However, the driving force in each case is represented by one motivation. To repeat, our division into ideal types is formal and not based on evidence from the empirical world.

Let us call the value-oriented policy the *High Road Strategy* and the goal-oriented policy the *Low Road Strategy*.

Value-Orientation and Goal-Orientation

As Muslims, we adhere to certain values dealing with economic issues and relations. These values are related to production, distribution and consumption of wealth. The pursuit of these values is supposed to achieve two goals: prosperity in our individual and group lives and prosperity in the world hereafter.[6] The goal of prosperity in this world is broken down into sub-goals such as group-solidarity as a means to achieve the goal of prosperity. Similarly there are other sub-goals such as higher rate of economic growth, higher standard of living, etc.

It is imperative that in due course of time, certain groups of a community should become more concerned with goals than with values that originally inspired those goals. This can happen for several reasons. Firstly, the distinction between values and goals and the link between the two is never very clear and definitive. Secondly, there is a tendency among most individuals and groups to be concerned with the immediate and concrete rather than with the distant and abstract. Thirdly, the pursuit of certain goals develops a dynamism of its own. Conscious and unconscious interests develop which obstruct such changes in goals which may be desirable under changed circumstances. The rigidity on goals means a negation of the primacy of values. On the other hand, it is also imperative that in a community, certain groups should rise with a renewed enthusiasm about the primacy of values. We believe that the history of any dynamic community is shaped by an ongoing struggle between these two groups: groups to whom values are primary and groups to whom goals are primary. The fate of a community is largely determined by the nature and the shape of this struggle. This struggle can be productive or unproductive in terms of the development of the community. Therefore, we should try to understand and perhaps shape this struggle.

Since Islamic Economics is one aspect of the multi-faceted Muslim community, it is subject to the kind of struggle mentioned above. To repeat our earlier terminology, Islamic Economics is subject to an implicit and explicit struggle between the High Road (value-oriented) and Low Road (goal-oriented) strategies. Below we turn to a rather tentative analysis of these two strategies. In each case we shall ask the following questions:

(a) Who are the prominent proponents of the strategy?
(b) What is the nature of their objectives?
(c) What is the nature of their own motivations, and the nature of their appeals to the Muslim community?

Since the method of this paper is not empirical but primarily theoretical, our use of empirical examples may be lacking in accuracy. Nevertheless, our purpose of laying out a theoretical framework for further analysis will be served.

High Road Strategy

(A) The proponents of this strategy comprise of the revivalist movements which have operated in almost all Muslim countries in this century. In almost all cases their organisation was established during the period of the struggle of Muslim peoples against their colonial masters. The immense humiliation of foreign rule inspired a devotion to the forgotten values of Islam. In most cases the Revivalists provided the ideological seed for independence movements. The treasured Muslim value "sovereignty of none other than Allah" was invoked with great intensity. The "Sovereignty of Allah" was a value; national independence was a goal. Gradually the goal took precedence over the value. And in almost all cases, the Revivalist groups were pushed to the back seat during the final stages of independence movements, or very soon afterwards.

Consequently the High Road Strategy groups of today are very clearly non-governmental groups. They, generally, constitute the sentiments or the organisation of opposition to the ruling regimes in the Muslim countries. *To summarise, their first characteristic is that they are non-governmental, often opposition groups.*

Secondly, they are organised on a national basis. Since in each case they emerged during a period of struggle against colonial rule and were important members of independence movements, the locus of their organisation was coterminous with that of the independence struggle. *The second characteristic of the proponents of the High Road Strategy is that they are national in organisation.*

Thirdly, in almost all cases these groups were involved in bitter conflict with the post-independence regimes, which resulted in a substantial out-migration of their prominent members. An unanticipated result of this out-migration is the creation of certain transnational links among them.[7] *The third characteristic of the High Road strategies is that they seem to be acquiring a transnational organisation.*

(B) By our definition, the objectives of High Road Strategies are value-oriented. In the realm of Economics, these values are related to questions, such as, production, distribution and consumption of wealth. Since the relevant unit for the attainment of these objectives happens to be nation-state, their activities are focussed around the domestic politics of nation-state. The tendency to concentrate on domestic politics is further reinforced by the national form of their organisation.

To summarise, the objectives of High Road strategists are value-oriented and related to domestic politics of nation states.

(C) The question of motivations is highly speculative, nevertheless extremely central to a discussion about the creation of a new world order or a new system (such as Islamic Economics). There are two aspects to motivations: motivations of the leadership of change itself and motivations which underlie the appeal of this leadership to the community in general. The second aspect of motivations reveals the perception of the leadership about the behaviour of the community, i.e., their perception of what inspires or can inspire the community.

Following our method of constructing ideal-types, we divide motivations into two types:

(a) self-interest;
(b) altruism (non-self-interest)

While self-interested behaviour is predicated on the assumption that one can increase one's utility by an increase in one's own pleasures, altruistic behaviour is predicated on the assumption that one can increase one's utility without reference to personal pleasure. In simpler words, for altruistic behaviour social interest takes precedence over individual interest.[8]

Altruistic behaviour can be crucial for the creation of a new social system. The irony of a movement of change is that those whose interest lies in change are often too weak to organise change, and those who have the strength to bring about change have an interest in status quo. It is precisely some form of altruistic behaviour that breaks this vicious circle. A movement for social change aims at creating a social good, in the form of a better society. While the benefits of the new society are enjoyed by a large group of people, the cost incurred in bringing about the change is borne by a much smaller group.[9] The motivation for bearing this cost often comes from the altruistic instinct of man.

Returning to the question of motivations in a Strategy for Islamic Economics, we argue that the High Road strategists operate under motivations of altruism. This is in conformity with their objectives which aim at bringing about a fundamental change in the existing social structures. While their personal activity is motivated by altruism, their appeals to the community comprise of a combination of self-interest and altruism. It comprises a promise of better life here and hereafter. Such a combination is perfectly suitable to the logic of collective action for change. It contains an appeal to two audiences: to those whose interest lies in change and who can be motivated by self-interest, and to those whose interest lies in status quo and who can be motivated for change by an appeal to altruism. However, the correct combination of this duality of appeal is not an easy job. As a result of this complexity, some groups have accused the Revivalist movements of supporting radical change, while others have accused them of supporting the status quo.

To summarise, we can say that the motivations of High Road strategists are basically altruistic.

Low Road Strategy

(A) The proponents of this strategy belong mainly to the Modernist movements. The Modernist movements, like the Revivalist movements arose in response to the colonial domination of the West. They, like the Revivalists, chose to fight the colonial West. But, unlike the Revivalists, they were markedly influenced by the secular philosophy of Western political thought. While they did not renounce their identification with Islam, their concern was not the revival of Islamic principles. Their activities became focussed around the establishment of independent and modern nation-states. Their identification was with the community of Islam but not necessarily with the principles of Islam. In most cases they did not express explicit disinterest in the introduction of Islamic principles. On the contrary, the need for such an effort was given some approval. Nevertheless, the main drive behind their activities was national development and modernisation.

Since the leaderships of the independence movements in the Muslim countries were largely composed of modernist elements, they constituted the national governments after independence, as political leaders or civil servants. *Therefore, the first characteristic of the Low Road strategists is that they are composed largely of governmental or semi-governmental groups.*

What is the scope of their operation regarding Islamic Economics? This is rather interesting because of a paradox. The scope of the activities of national governments regarding Islamic Economics is international. Various national governments of Muslim countries have sought co-operation with other Muslim countries on the basis of Islamic solidarity. This is paradoxical because the Revivalists, who tend to be more universalistic in their ideas tend to operate nationally, and the national governments, who by definition are particularistic, tend to operate internationally. But, despite this apparent paradox, the international focus of the Low Road Strategy is understandable. The domestic application of Islamic Economics requires a structural change in conformity with Islamic Principles. This is not the primary concern of the Low Road Strategy.

On the other hand, the international application of Islamic Economics primarily demands solidarity in the international Muslim community. And since the latter interests the Low Road Strategy, its activities tend to be in the international field. *The second characteristic of the Low Road Strategy is that the focus of its activity is international.*

(B) By our definition, the objectives of the Low Road strategists are goal-oriented. These goals can be generally described as economic growth, industrial development and higher standard of living. In order to achieve these objectives, the Low Road strategists lay emphasis on certain principles of Islam, such as, solidarity among the community, hard work and discipline, etc. But to them, the more salient aspect of Islamic solidarity is in the international field. Here they seek to make economic agreements and treaties with other Muslim countries for mutual development and growth.[10]

To summarise, the objectives of the Low Road strategists are goal-oriented and focussed around international co-operation.

(C) On the question of motivations, we shall repeat our earlier statement about the composition of the Low Road strategists. They are largely composed of governmental groups. Since most governmental activity is carried out on non-altruistic considerations, altruism is not a prominent motivation in this group. Social theorists tell us that organisation leads to a decline in utopian visions.[11] This seems more true for organisation of governments. Governments operate on the basis of individual or group self-interest.[12] Consequently, their appeals to the community are also based largely on self-interest. The objectives of the Low Road Strategy do not include a radical change in the social structure. Instead, the objective is to concentrate on the total capabilities of the society, with some neglect of relative group capabilities within the society. The orientation is toward reform rather than radical change. The philosophy of reform is not inconsistent with the logic of self-interest. Each individual and group can theoretically perform a countervailing influence on the power of other individuals and groups by simply taking care of their own self-interest.

To summarise, we can say that the Low Road strategists operate on the motivations of self-interest.

Summary

Up to this point, we have argued that an analysis of the objectives of political leaderships is crucial to a correct understanding of economic relationships. We classified objectives of political leaders into two categories: value-oriented and goal-oriented. We then proceeded to draw up two classes of strategies: High Road and Low Road strategies. We analysed the Actors, the Objectives and the Motives involved in each strategy. All of the above is part of our effort to set up a framework for the formulation of a Policy for Islamic Economics. Up until this point, our discussion has been focussed around the *Actors* in the process. We shall now give a brief analysis of the *Environment* in which the Actors play their roles.

The Environment of Action

Historians have a habit of labelling every period of history by a distinctive characteristic. We find titles such as the Age of Reason, the Age of Enlightenment, the Age of Crisis, the Age of Democracy, etc. Historians do this retrospectively. Their observations of a certain period shows the predominance and the frequency of the occurrence of a certain characteristic. Why do we find this phenomenon in history? Different social scientists have suggested that human actions have a tendency towards disequilibrium. The path of human endeavours is not from one equilibrium to another disequilibrium.[13] Societal action, they would argue, is generated by an interplay of surpluses and deficits, to use the jargon of economics. It is precisely this characteristic of human action which brings about the predominance of a certain quality in every age. The task of a prudent and creative leadership is to make a correct judgement about what is most required in its age. A correct judgement on this would enable the leadership to shape the future according to its vision, rather than react to circumstances casted by others. He who has a correct judgement of his *environment* can exert great influence in shaping it. Regarding the subject of this paper, we can argue that *a successful Islamic Economic Strategy must be based on a correct assessment of the socio-philosophical environment of our age.*

What is the predominant characteristic of our environment? By its very nature, this question needs extensive discussion on the one hand, and can be answered only in speculative terms on the other hand. To the author of this paper, it appears that future historians will remember our age as the Age of Justice. Our age has witnessed an intense interest in justice within nations and justice among the larger community of nations. To say that ours is an Age of Justice does not imply that justice prevails in our age. This would be as wrong as, for example, assuming that reason prevailed in the so-called Age of Reason. Reason was not prevalent but the ideal of Reason was the most appealing and affective ideal in that age. So may be our case: justice is certainly not prevailing today, but it appears to be most needed. As an ideal, it has and, perhaps, will continue to warm the hearts of those living in our Age. A Strategy for Islamic Economics should, in my opinion, give a special place to the notion of economic and socio-political justice.

Depending on their judgement of the environment, and as a function of their objectives and motivations, different groups in an Islamic community are bound to come up with different strategies for Islamic Economics. A study of policy formulation must include the process of interaction among these competing strategies.

In reference to the earlier sections of this paper, we shall now look into the process of interaction between High Road and Low Road Strategies.

Interaction Among Competing Strategies

The two strategies have certain similarities and differences. In terms of the scope of its desired activities, the High Road is inclusive of the activities of the Low Road. In other words, the High Road includes the objective of creating a Muslim community but goes beyond that in insisting that the organisation of such a community should be strictly according to the principles of Islam. In the past, this difference has led to a bitter conflict. Muslim governments (who would be generally placed under our Low Road category) sought to acquire their legitimacy from their association with Islam. But on this, they were challenged by the proponents of the High Road Strategy, who believed that the Low Road Strategy was not inclusive enough to be titled as an Islamic Strategy. Since governments or regimes, are extremely sensitive on the question of their legitimacy, the High Road Strategy was bitterly resented by them. Gradually the conflict between the two strategies became a dispute on each other's legitimacy. Conflicts in which the contending parties deny the legitimacy of each other's existence are always bitter and often irrational (a good example would be conflict among certain sects of a religion). In such a conflict, the parties do not make a genuine effort to understand the true objectives and motivations of each other. Such conflicts are not productive in terms of the community. In conventional terms, they are negative-sum conflicts.

However, not all conflicts have to be negative sum. Conflictual process can very well be a positive-sum process. This is not to forget that a positive-sum conflict is not always desirable. This question should be decided by one's relationship to the community under consideration. Suppose A and B are in conflict over C. The ultimate objective of A is the elimination of the total community C. The ultimate objective of B is to maintain status quo as obtains in C. In this situation, negative-sum conflict may not be undesirable for the purposes of A. In effect, for A they might be desirable, because each negative-sum conflict diminishes the total capabilities of C. Let us see another situation in which A and B have mutual interest in enhancing the capabilities of the total community C. Nevertheless A and B have conflict regarding their relative capability within C. In this situation a positive-sum conflict may be more desirable.

The lesson we draw from the above discussion, is that in determining his strategy, a strategist should understand his relationship to the opposing party as well as his own attitude and the attitude of the opposing party to the space in which the conflict is taking place.

Let us return to the issue of interaction between High Road and Low Road strategies. It is the understanding of this author that there is a logic for conflict between the two, for reasons of difference on their composition, objectives and motives, as explained earlier. Nevertheless, this conflict can be positive-sum, let us call that *un-antagonistic conflict*, rather than negative-sum, let us call that *antagonistic conflict*. In the past the conflict has been largely on the antagonistic pattern. One reason for that was that each did not recognise the legitimacy of the other. For transforming the conflict to an un-antagonistic pattern, the two will have to extend greater legitimacy to each other.

This was our third and final step towards setting-up a framework for formulating a Policy for Islamic Economics. The first step was related to the *Actors*, the second to the *Environment*, the third to the *Interaction*.

In the third step, we underscored the need for a strategist to determine whether his interaction with competing strategies will be based on an antagonistic or un-antagonistic pattern.

Interaction Among Muslim Economists

Towards the end of this paper, I shall make a diversion from the discussion on interaction among competing strategies to interaction among economists. Muslim Economists are making an effort to work out a Theory and a Policy for Islamic Economics. In their effort to do this, how should they communicate among themselves and with the larger community of Muslims? In order to answer this question, we should say a little about the functions of an economist in general. Of the several functions they perform, the following come readily to mind:

(1) Explanation of the existing economic relations in a society.
(2) Make projections into the future, based on a knowledge of the "anatomy" of the existing economic system.
(3) Help in economic planning, based on an understanding of the above two.
(4) Lay out a framework for basic transformation of existing economic relationships.

The last of the above functions is performed by unconventional economists. This activity goes beyond conventional economics to the borders of philosophy and covers all areas of social sciences. The system transformation function requires a holistic understanding and a vision into the future. Since it deals with a non-existing system, it is less concerned with qualities required for the implementation of an existing system. Because of their lack of interest in conventional techniques, system-transformation economists are sometimes relegated to a low status within the dominant academic tradition.[14] In his study of economic philosophers, Robert Heilbroner introduces us to a system-transforming caste of economic philosophers who formed an "Underworld of Economics".[15] The dominant tradition, then, comprised of the early mathematical economists like Edgeworth, Walras and Jevons. Mathematical Economics, as Heilbroner explains, develops during a period of basic agreement on a system.

I take the opportunity to indicate this subject for discussion because I feel there should be greater clarity in our mind about:

(a) The relevant techniques for a group of economists interested in system-transformation.
(b) Our relationship with the dominant academic tradition of our times.

I would not hesitate to point out a contradiction inherent in the above argument. The techniques required for system-transformation are different from the techniques required for system-implementation. But if system-transformation efforts are serious and purposive then they must contain a formula for a post-transformation system. This is an inherent dilemma: how to reconcile the utopian character of system-transformation with the pragmatic character of a post-transformation society.

Instead of creating confusion by an unreal effort to make consistency out of real dilemmas, we should squarely face this contradiction. In other words, our policy formulation should focus on:

HOW TO ACHIEVE UTOPIAN (AND ALTRUISTICALLY MOTIVATED) GOALS BY PRAGMATIC MEANS?

Notes

1 Arthur L. Strincho, MBE, *Constructing Social Theories*, 1968.
Abraham Kaplan, *The Conduct of Inquiry*, Chandler Publishing Company, 1968.

2 Muhsin Mahdi, *Ibn Khaldūn's Philosophy of History*, The University of Chicago Press, 1957.
Daniel Lerner and Harold D. Lanwell, eds., *The Policy Sciences: Recent Developments in Scope and Method*, Stanford, Stanford University Press, 1971.

3 On this similarity between the Marxist and the Liberal positions see Raymond Aron, *Main Currents of Sociological Thought*, Vol. I (1970).

4 On the political nature of economic decision-making see Robert Dahl and Charles Lindbloom, *Politics, Economics, and Welfare*, New York, Harpers and Brothers, 1953. Also see:
Richard M. Cyert and James G. March, *A Behavioural Theory of the Firm*, Prentice Hall, 1963.

5 Max Weber, *The Theory of Social and Economic Organization*, ed. with Introduction by Talcot Parsons, The Free Press of Glencoe, 1964.

6 فى الدنيا حسنة وفى الآخرة حسنة .

7 By "transnational" we refer to groups of individuals from different national backgrounds who do not represent their national governments. On the definition of "transnational", see Robert Keohane and Joseph Nye, eds., *Transnational Relations*, Harvard University Press, 1972.

8 For an interesting discussion on self-interest and altruism as two different but equally rational modes of action, see Norman Frohlic, *Self-interest and Altruism, What Difference?*, Journal for Conflict Resolution, Vol. 18. No. 1, March 1974, pp. 55–73.

9 Mancur Olson, *The Logic of Collective Action*, Harvard University Press, 1965.
Thomas C. Schelling, *On the Ecology of Micromotives*, The Public Interest, No. 25, Fall 1971, pp. 59–98.

10 For example, a resolution on economic matters presented at the Lahore Summit of Islamic countries was based on the theme of mutual co-operation for prosperity, development and control over natural resources.

11 Robert Michels, *Political Parties*, The Free Press, New York, 1972.
Karl Mannheim, *Ideology and Utopia*, Harcourt, Brace and World Inc., New York, 1936.

12 For a systematic treatment of different explanations of government behaviour, see Graham T. Allison, *Essence of Decision*, Little Brown and Company, Boston, 1971.

13 Most notably see:
Albert Hirschman, *A Bias for Hope*, Yale University Press, New Haven and London, 1971.
——, *The Strategy of Economic Planning*, Yale University Press, New Haven, 1958.
Gunar Myrdal, *Economic Theory and Underdeveloped Regions*, Harper Torchbooks, Harper and Row Publishers, 1957.

14 For interesting insights into the sociology of knowledge, particularly on the creation of new paradigms, see:
Thomas Kuhn, *The Structure of Scientific Revolutions*, The University of Chicago Press, 1970.

15 Robert Heilbroner, *The Wordly Philosophers*, Simon and Schuster, New York, 1972.

Selected Bibliography

Allison, Graham T., *Essence of Decision*, Little Brown and Company, Boston, 1971.

Aron, Raymond, *Main Currents of Sociological Thought*, Vol. 1, Anchor Books, Doubleday and Company, Inc., N.Y., 1970.

Cyert, Richard and James G. March, *A Behavioral Theory of the Firm*, Prentice Hall, 1963.

Earle, Edward E., ed., *Makers of Modern Strategy*, Princeton University Press, 1971.

Frohlic, Norman, *Self-Interest and Altruism, What Difference?* Journal of Conflict Resolution, Vol. 18, No. 1, March 1974.

Hirschman, Albert, *A Bias For Hope*, Yale University Press, New Haven and London, 1971.

——, *The Strategy of Economic Planning*, Yale University Press, New Haven, 1958.

Heilbroner, Robert, *Wordly Philosophers*, Simon and Schuster, New York, 1972.

Kaplan, Abraham, *The Conduct of Inquiry*, Chandler Publishing Company, 1964.

Keohane, Robert and Joseph Nye, eds., *Transnational Relations*, Harvard University Press, Cambridge, Massachusetts, 1972.

Kuhn, Thomas, *The Structure of Scientific Resolutions*, The University of Chicago Press, Chicago, 1970.

Lerner, Daniel and Harold L. Lasswell, eds., *The Policy Science: Recent Developments in Scope and Method*, Stanford University Press, 1951.

Mahdi, Muhsin, *Ibn Khaldūn's Philosophy of History*, University of Chicago Press, 1957.

Mannheim, Karl, *Ideology and Utopia*, Harcourt Brace and World Inc., New York, 1956.

Michels, Robert, *Political Parties*, The Free Press, New York, 1962.

Myrdal, Gunnar, *Economic Theory and Underdeveloped Regions*, Harper Torchbooks, Harper and Row Publishers, 1957.

Dahl, Robert and Charles Lindbloom, *Politics, Economics and Welfare*, Harper and Brothers, New York, 1953.

Olson, Mancur, *The Logic of Collective Action*, Harvard University Press, Cambridge, Massachusetts, 1965.

Schelling, Thomas, *On the Ecology of Micromotives*, The Public Interest, No. 25, Fall 1971.

Stinchombe, Arthur L., *Constructing Social Theories*, 1968.

Weber, Max, *Theory of Social and Economic Organization*, ed., with introduction by Talcot Parsons, The Free Press of Glencoe, 1964.

CHAPTER EIGHT

The Islamic Welfare State and its Role in the Economy

*Dr. M. Umar Chapra**

ISLAM has a set of goals and values encompassing all aspects of human life including social, economic and political. Since all aspects of life are interdependent and the Islamic way of life is a consistent whole, its goals and values in one field determine the goals and values in the other fields as well. This paper seeks to examine the interrelationship between the economic and political content of the Islamic way of life and discusses the functions and nature of the Islamic state in the light of its basic imperatives within the framework of financial constraints.

a. The Basic Imperatives

The Islamic way of life, being goal-oriented, is inconceivable without an organised community governed in accordance with the tenets of Islam. The Qur'ān unequivocally condemns disorder and anarchy (2: 205) and the Prophet (peace be on him) stressed the need for organisation and authority in Muslim society. This stress is also vividly reflected in several statements as well as the actual behaviour of his Companions and in the thinking of Muslim jurists. 'Umar, the second Caliph, emphasised that there could be no organised society without an *imām* (sovereign) and that there could be no *imām* without obedience.[1] The famous jurist Shāfi'ī recorded the mood of his age (A.H. 150–204) by stating that there is *ijmā'* (consensus) among Muslims that there must be a caliph.[2] Likewise, Ibn Ḥanbal stressed that the absence of an *imām* could only result in disorder.[3]

This teaching of Islam with respect to authority and organisation has continually influenced all Muslim political thinking except perhaps that of the Khawārij. Abū Ya'lā and Māwardī, both contemporaries in Baghdad during the first half of the fifth century of the *Hijrah* (eleventh century C.E.), and both writing on the characteristics of an ideal state, stressed that the exercise of *imāmah* (sovereignty) is an absolute necessity.[4] Māwardī went even further, stating that the existence of an *imām* was as

*Dr. Umar Chapra is Economic Adviser, Saudi Monetary Agency, Riyadh.
This chapter was also incorporated in "*Islamic Perspectives*," Islamic Foundation, 1979.

necessary as the striving for truth and the acquisition of knowledge.[5] Ibn Khaldūn emphasised that the institution of caliphate is a *shar'ī* obligation and that Muslims are obliged to establish and maintain it.[6] Similar ideas were expressed by Ibn Taymīyah,[7] Shāh Walī-Allāh[8] and a number of other scholars. Such an attitude toward the state is quite natural since Islam advocates certain goals and ideals which would be difficult of realisation without a value- and goal-oriented state. This idea was expressed beautifully by the famous Muslim poet-thinker Muḥammad Iqbāl (d. 1938) when he stated that "the state according to Islam is only an effort to realise the spiritual in human organisation".[9]

Thus the state is viewed by Islam as an instrument for the realisation of the ultimate goals, both spiritual and material, of the Islamic society. However, the authority exercised by the state is not absolute. It is a trust from God and is to be exercised in accordance with the terms of the trust as laid down in the *Sharī'ah*. Two of the most important terms of this trust are that the state should be democratic and welfare-oriented.

Democratic Orientation

Sovereignty, according to Islam, vests in God. It is only His Will that should prevail in this world. Says the Qur'ān:

> Is it not His to create and to govern? (7: 54)
> Sovereignty is for none but God. (12: 40)
> Follow the Revelation sent to you from your Lord, and follow not, as friends or protectors, other than Him (7: 3).

The sovereignty of God implies the rule of the Divine Law as revealed by Him in the Qur'ān to the Holy Prophet and as elaborated in the Prophet's *sunnah* during the course of his mission. Man as vicegerent of God on earth (2: 30, 6: 165) can neither make nor abrogate the Divine Law. Man must necessarily submit to it if he realises that the All-knowing God in His Great Wisdom is the best guide of man in all his affairs. Given the Divine Law, all individuals who submit to it must be partners in its implementation. Hence, once the sovereignty of God is recognised, the authority for its establishment is vested in the whole *ummah* and is to be exercised in the light of the Qur'ān and *Sunnah* through the democratic process of consultation with the *ummah*,[10] (or its rightful representatives) as the Qur'ān enjoins:

> And consult them in affairs. (3: 159)
> And they conduct their affairs by mutual consultation. (42: 38)

Welfare Commitment

The mission of the Holy Prophet is defined by the Qur'ān to be a merciful blessing (*raḥmah*) for all mankind (2: 107). Some manifestations of this merciful blessing are stated explicitly in the Qur'ān. These include, among others, the fostering of "good life" (*ḥayāt ṭayyibah*) and "welfare" (*falāḥ*),[11] provision of ease and alleviation of hardship,[12] generation of prosperity,[13] nurturing a climate of love and affection,[14] and ensuring freedom from moral corruption,[15] hunger, fear[16] and mental tensions.[17] Hence, all organisations and institutions, including the state, should reflect the character of merciful blessing, and cater to the "welfare" of all people.

The welfare function of the Islamic state was particularly stressed by the Prophet when he stated: "Any ruler who is responsible for the affairs of Muslims but does not strive sincerely for their well-being will not enter Paradise with them."[18] The Companions of the Prophet clearly appreciated this welfare role of the Islamic state as is evidenced by numerous utterances of the early caliphs and their instructions to their governors. 'Umar, the second Caliph, wrote to Abū Mūsā, the governor of a province: "The best of men in authority is he under whom people prosper and the worst of them is he under whom people encounter hardships".[19] Muslim jurists have unanimously held that catering to the welfare of the people and relieving them of hardships is the basic objective of the *Sharī'ah* and hence of the Islamic state.[20] The letter addressed to Caliph Hārūn al-Rashīd by his Chief Justice, Abū Yūsuf, vividly clarifies the welfare character of the Islamic state,[21] and the same stress is evident in the writings of medieval Muslim thinkers like Māwardī, Abū Ya'lā, al-Ghazālī, Ibn Khaldūn, Ibn al-Qayyim and Ibn Taymīyah. The evidence in the Qur'ān and *Sunnah* and the writings of Islamic scholars for the welfare function of the Islamic state is so overwhelming that it would be absolutely unjustified not to term the Islamic state as a "welfare state".

Strategy of Welfare

But there are other political systems which also claim to be welfare-oriented. The difference lies essentially in their basic philosophy of what constitutes human welfare. Islam distinguishes itself by its own unique philosophy of welfare which is comprehensive and consistent with its concept of human nature. Man has been created from matter[22] but has been infused with a part of the Divine spirit.[23] The matter and the spirit together constitute the indivisible human self which is free but responsible before God for all its actions within the frame of reference of Divine guidance. He is intelligent and capable of differentiating between right and wrong and acting on his own initiative. His mission is to fulfil his obligations as the vicegerent of God on earth. He is not only a member of the brotherhood of Islam but also a part of mankind, the family of God.[24] Only that philosophy of welfare is best suited to man which enables him, firstly, to attain a fuller realisation of his complete indivisible self (spiritual as well as material) in keeping with his status as vicegerent of God and, secondly, to make the optimum all-round contribution to his *ummah* and to mankind.

The concept of welfare in Islam can hence be neither exclusively "other-worldly" nor purely "this-worldly". While urging Muslims to gain mastery over nature and utilising the resources provided by God for the service and betterment of mankind, Islam warns Muslims against single-minded concentration on material acquisitions as the highest measure of human achievement and ignoring the indispensable spiritual content of the human self. Islam rather provides a spiritual orientation to all material effort and creates a harmony between the innate spiritual and material urges of individuals and groups. Islam has so firmly and exquisitely dovetailed the spiritual and material aspects of life that they may serve as a source of mutual strength and together serve as the foundation of true human welfare and happiness. According to Islam, negligence of either of the two aspects of life will prevent mankind from achieving true welfare. In fact there is no division between material and spiritual aspects of life in Islam. All human effort whether for "material", "social", "educational", or "scientific" goals is spiritual in character as long as it conforms to the value system of Islam. Working hard for the material well-being of one's own self, family and society is as spiritual as the offering of prayers, provided that the material effort is guided by spiritual values. This synthesis of the material and the spiritual is what is missing in the welfare concept of the other two systems, capitalism and socialism, as they are morally neutral.

This teaching has infiltrated all Muslim thinking throughout the ages. Ghazālī defines the objective of the *Sharī'ah* to be the promotion of welfare of people which lies in safeguarding their faith, their life, their intellect, their posterity, and their property, and concludes that whatever ensures the safeguard of these five serves public interest and is desirable.[25] Ibn al-Qayyim emphasised that the "basis of the *Sharī'ah* is wisdom and welfare of the people in this world as well as the Hereafter. This welfare lies in complete justice, mercy, welfare, and wisdom; anything that departs from justice to injustice, from mercy to harshness, from welfare to misery and from wisdom to folly has nothing to do with the *Sharī'ah*".[26]

This is, of course, a general indication of what is implied by welfare in Islam. More specific positions have been taken by the *Sharī'ah* on many issues, which need not be elaborated here. In brief it may be stated that the welfare of individuals in an Islamic society may be realised if there is a proper environment for:

(a) a fuller realisation of Islamic spiritual values in the individual as well as in society,
(b) an adequate fulfilment of all basic needs of life.

These are briefly discussed below under the spiritual and material roles of the state. This dichotomy is only for the convenience of discussion and does not imply a separate identity for the two roles which are closely integrated.

Spiritual Uplift

Since Islam lays a preponderant stress on moral values, the Islamic state cannot be a passive observer of the ethical scene in society. It is the responsibility of the Islamic welfare state to look after the spiritual health of its people. Hence the need of taking practical measures by the state to bring to a living reality the moral code of Islam has been stressed by all Muslim political thinkers and jurists. This does not necessarily imply that the Islamic state is a police state forcing people into certain channels of behaviour by use of its coercive power. There is some kind of built-in indoctrination in all systems, including the capitalist, and the Islamic system is no exception. The Islamic system, however, in compliance with the spirit of the Qur'ānic verse: "There is no compulsion in religion" (2: 256), shuns the extreme course of regimentation of thought and action, as it gives significant value to individual freedom. It is for this reason that Islam lays stress on education and creation of conditions conducive to the practice of the moral norms on which the edifice of the whole Islamic way of life is raised.

The realisation of the spiritual values of Islam in the individual and society demands that the Islamic state should strive in three major directions. First, it must foster conditions conducive to the creation of homes which would inculcate respect for and adherence to Islamic moral teachings in the rising generation. Islam has provided a blueprint for fostering love and affection, and mutual help and co-operation among the members of the family (nuclear as well as extended), and for generating a suitable environment for the proper upbringing of children. Second, the Islamic state must cast the educational system in the mould of Islam so that educational institutions produce young men and women imbued with the ideals of Islam. Third, the state should enforce those norms and values of Islam which are amenable to legal enforcement and should inflict the prescribed penalties for violations so that they serve as a deterrent to prospective violators.

Material Well-being

Adequate fulfilment of basic material needs, is, in the Islamic frame of reference, as necessary for human welfare as spiritual uplift. Therefore, while arranging for the spiritual guidance of men by a chain of prophets to all people through space and time, God has also provided all necessary resources for his material well-being. Says the Qur'ān: "He it is Who has created for you everything on earth" (2: 29) and "has made subservient to you whatever is in the heavens and the earth and granted you His bounties, manifest and hidden" (31: 20, see also 4: 32–3, 16: 12–14, 22: 65 and 45: 12). Two fundamental principles may be derived from these verses. One, that God-given resources are for "you", which is addressed to all people and not to any privileged group or class; and two, that they are meant for general human welfare, and at least, for eradicating poverty and fulfilling the basic material needs of all people.

There can be little dispute that some of the basic material needs of individuals that must be satisfied are:

(i) training and education to develop the innate abilities of the individual and to enable him to cater for his well-being independently without becoming a burden on others;
(ii) a suitable job, profession, or trade in keeping with his aptitude, ability, ambition, and needs of society so that he and society both benefit from his ability and training;
(iii) adequate food and clothing;
(iv) comfortable housing;
(v) a generally healthy environment combined with appropriate medical facilities, and
(vi) adequate transport facilities to enable a worker to commute to his place of work without unreasonable discomfort and to convey his product to appropriate markets at reasonable cost.

These material needs of the individual and their fulfilment have been so explicitly recognised by the *Sharī'ah* that quotations from the Qur'ān and the *Sunnah* and Islamic writings would be tantamount to elaborating the obvious.[27]

The fulfilment of these spiritual and material needs of individuals and society would naturally necessitate the playing of a vital role by the state in the economic system of Islam. Nevertheless, it may be stressed here for the sake of clarity, that it is basically the moral responsibility of the individual to cater for his own needs through his own volition and effort. Islam categorically condemns begging and sloth and places great stress on hard work. The Prophet enjoined: "Beg not anything from people"[28] and that: "A man has not earned better income than that which is from his own labour".[29] 'Umar, the second Caliph, symbolised this Islamic teaching for earning one's own livelihood through hard work by saying: "No one of you should stay away from seeking livelihood and say: 'O God! Give me sustenance', for the sky will not rain gold and silver";[30] and that: "Seek of the bounty of God and be not a burden on others".[31]

The individual is not only expected to work for his own livelihood and welfare but is also expected to do his best on every job or mission he undertakes. "God desires that whenever anyone of you performs a job he does it perfectly."[32] In fact the spiritual and material goals of the Islamic society cannot be fully realised until all Muslims, men or women, put forth their best in keeping with the optimum potential of their God-given talents.

Although it is essentially the responsibility of the individual to depend on himself and to try to do his best, the market forces need not always automatically be conducive to this. And even if the individual does his best it is a well-recognised fact that the blind operation of market forces may not always reward him optimally for his socially-productive effort. It would hence be the responsibility of the state to play a positive role in guiding and regulating the economy to ensure that the objectives of the *Sharī'ah* are fulfilled. This positive role of the Islamic state cannot be equated with the term "intervention" of the state under capitalism. The term "intervention", in addition to carrying an opprobrious connotation, smacks of commitment to *laissez faire* capitalism under which the best state is the one which plays the least role.

The question is: what specific role should the Islamic state play in the economy and how much regulation or control should it exercise? In principle it may be stated that the state should play an adequate role to bring to fulfilment the goals of the Islamic system without unduly sacrificing individual freedom or compromising social welfare. An important measure would be to contain the self-interest of individuals within moral restraints so as to prevent the individual from exploiting society to gratify his self-interest, and to safeguard against society exploiting the individual by curbing his inherent rights or preventing him from enjoying the lawful fruits of his labour and skill. The goal should be to bring about a healthy balance between the interests of the individual and of society in harmony with one of the fundamental teachings of the Prophet: "The individual should not inflict harm [on others] nor should any harm be inflicted on him [by others]". This brings all instruments of direct and indirect controls, including wage-price controls and nationalisation, to the extent considered necessary in the overall interest of the Muslim society, within the tool-kit of the Islamic state. What instruments are to be used and to what extent, would be determined essentially by circumstances, given the guiding principles of the *Sharī'ah* and particularly the commitment of the Islamic state to social welfare in a manner that would not destroy individual freedom.

Specification of certain essential elements of the positive role, or the essential economic functions of the Islamic welfare state hence becomes necessary. The following section of this paper briefly specifies these functions.

b. Economic Functions

Some of the essential functions of the Islamic welfare state with respect to the economy may be stated to be:

(1) to eradicate poverty and create conditions for full employment and a high rate of growth;
(2) to promote stability in the real value of money;
(3) to maintain law and order;
(4) to ensure social and economic justice;

(5) to arrange social security and foster equitable distribution of income and wealth;
(6) to harmonise international relations and ensure national defence.

There is no specific significance in the order in which the above functions have been stated. All the functions are important and none may be ignored. Each of these functions is briefly discussed below.

(1) Eradication of Poverty, Full Employment and Optimum Rate of Growth

Since economic resources are a trust from God, it is the moral obligation of the trustee to employ these resources efficiently to realise the purpose of the trust which is the welfare of all the vicegerents of God. This naturally implies: firstly, eradication of poverty and satisfaction of all basic human needs; secondly, full and efficient employment of all human and material resources to attain an optimum rate of economic growth and improve the standard of living of all people; and, thirdly, avoidance of conditions generating deficient or excess demand and leading to unemployment or inflation. The word "optimum" has been preferred here in place of "maximum" or "high" to allow for a margin for harmony with the goals of spiritual uplift and social welfare. This is because economic growth is not an isolated phenomenon and is to be viewed against its impact on the moral fabric of Muslim society, the goal of social and economic justice, and the overall "welfare" of *all* people.

For a realisation of this objective it would be incumbent upon the Islamic state not to leave the essential function of allocation of resources, particularly scarce resources, or the determination of aggregate demand to the unhindered operation of blind market forces. It should itself play a positive role and consciously contribute towards the attainment of desired goals through (i) rational planning, and (ii) building the necessary physical and social infra-structure.

(i) *Planning.* It is now widely recognised that undisciplined self-interest and unguided play of market forces may not always work out for the best of all strata of society and may not necessarily lead to optimum efficiency in the use of resources because of limitations of individual horizon, lack of awareness or appreciation of social costs, and unbalanced growth in different sectors of the economy unrelated to the welfare needs of the people. The Islamic state should, therefore, resort to planning and play an active role in the implementation of its plans.

The need for planning does not imply that the Islamic state can resort to regimentation or unscrupulous control of the private sector. What it does imply is that instead of leaving the allocation of resources and the management of aggregate demand primarily to the blind interplay of market forces, the state should play an active and conscious role in not only determining priorities and guiding or channelling the scarce resources in the light of those priorities, but also regulating demand so that occurrence of recession or inflation is avoided.

Priorities should, of course, be determined in accordance with, firstly, the terms of the trust as laid down in the *Sharī'ah* by the Creator of all resources, and secondly, the needs and general overall welfare of God's vicegerents. The basic teachings of the *Sharī'ah* are eternal and universal but the needs of man might differ with changes in time, geographical environment, stages of economic and social development and progress of technology. It may be stated that in general the efficient use of resources for the satisfaction of fundamental needs of *all* trustees should receive the utmost priority.

(ii) *Physical and social infrastructure.* For the growth of an economy and the development of a healthy and prosperous society, the existence of a basic physical and social infrastructure is generally recognised to be an absolute necessity. Much as investment in necessary physical capital leads to the development of an economy, the provision of such capital does not appeal to private entrepreneurs because direct monetary returns for investors are small and the amount of capital required is generally beyond their capacity. But since social benefits are so much in excess of private benefits, investment in these sectors must rank high in the development plans of an Islamic state as it should in the development plans of any developing economy.

The Qur'ān enjoins upon Muslims to gather whatever strength they are capable of (8: 60). The significance of "strength" here need not be confined to military strength. It could also be implied to refer to the economic strength which, among others, lies at the root of military strength. An essential part of this latter strength is the provision of an infrastructure through the improvement and extension of roads and highways, building of dams and bridges, provision of irrigation networks, construction of ports, airports and telecommunication services, and furnishing of facilities essential for providing external economies to different sectors of the economy. The role of the state here is obviously of primary importance. Therefore, whenever the Prophet appointed a governor, he instructed him to strive for creating ease rather than hardship for the people.[33] One of the means by which the state could generate prosperity is to provide the necessary infrastructure. Public works programmes, therefore, received significant attention during the days of 'Umar and other caliphs.

The provision of social capital (education, public health, etc.) should also be an undisputed area of the activity of an Islamic state. The general case for education is obvious. Since according to the Prophet, "acquisition of knowledge is obligatory for every Muslim",[34] public investment in education is necessary. Educational efforts must, however, go beyond attempts to increase the degree of literacy, for literacy is only a means to real education and not an end in itself. The general aim of education in Muslim society must be to raise Muslims who would conform to the ideals laid down in the Qur'ān and the *Sunnah*, to introduce the process of change that would bring about the Islamic environment, to teach ever-new skills, and to stimulate the incentive for research and invention of new techniques of production and distribution so as to utilise God-given resources more efficiently. The education system, in addition to building upright moral character, should also inculcate in the student the spirit of hard work and efficiency, economy and frugality, avoiding waste and extravagance, and making productive investment of savings so that in addition to the individual, it benefits society in general as well.

If education is one sphere of social capital towards which the government should take positive steps, another is public health. The Prophet declared that "a strong Muslim is better and more beloved before God than a weak one",[35] and that "cleanliness is half of faith".[36] Therefore, it may be inferred that it is the responsibility of the Islamic state to provide a healthy environment combined with adequate medical facilities so as to improve the health and efficiency of people and to reduce suffering from sickness and disease. With respect to a clean and healthy environment one may also argue in favour of better sanitation facilities, curbing of pollution, provision of clean and safe water supplies, hygienic and comfortable housing, and clearance of slums.

(2) Stability in the Real Value of Money

One of the most serious problems of contemporary society is persistent inflation with accompanying decline in the real value of money and monetary assets. This is not because inflation and growth are necessary counterparts of each other but because of a number of inflation-prone post-War phenomena which it is not necessary to delve into in this paper. In fact stability in the real value of money is vitally important not only for the continued long-term growth of an economy but also for social justice and economic welfare.

Honesty and justice in all measures of value has been unequivocally stressed in the Qur'ān:

> And give full measure and weight with justice (6: 152).
> So give full measure and weight without defrauding men in their belongings and do not corrupt the world after its reform. This is better for you, if you are believers (7: 85; see also, 11: 84–85, 17: 35, and 26: 181).

These verses should be considered to apply not only to individuals but also to society and the state and should not be confined merely to conventional weights and measures but should also encompass all measures of value.

Money also being a measure of value, any continuous and significant erosion in its real value may be interpreted in the light of the Qur'ān to be tantamount to corrupting the world because of the adverse effect this erosion has on social justice and general welfare which are among the central goals of the Islamic system. This implies that any activity or behaviour of individuals, groups, or institutions in an Islamic state which significantly erodes the real value of money should be considered to be a national issue of paramount importance and treated with a sense of concern. Nevertheless, there are other goals which are of equal, or greater, importance. If there is an unavoidable conflict between the realisation of these goals and a compromise becomes inevitable then the goal of stable real value for money may be somewhat relaxed provided that the damage done by such relaxing is more than offset by the realisation of other indispensable national goals.

It may hence be considered obligatory for the Islamic state to resort to healthy monetary, fiscal and incomes policies and appropriate direct controls when necessary, including wage-price controls, to minimise erosion in the real value of money, thus preventing one group of society from knowingly or unknowingly shortchanging others and violating the Islamic norms of honesty and justice in measures.

This does not imply that Muslim countries, individually or collectively, would be able to stabilise the value of their currencies by their own effort. In a world where all countries are mutually interdependent and where the monetary and fiscal policies of some major industrial countries are responsible for a substantial degree of price instability, it may not be possible for the small and open economy of an individual Muslim country to achieve the desired stability unless the major industrial countries follow saner policies. However, what it does imply is that an Islamic state should itself be clear about its role with respect to price stability and should be determined to contribute whatever it can for the attainment of that goal.

(3) Law and Order

The importance of this universally recognised function of the state cannot be overstressed. This is because the degree of law and order in a society and the extent of security of life and property are one of the prime determinants of growth and stability of an economy and the inner happiness of individuals. In his remarkably terse but powerful farewell pilgrimage address, in which the Holy Prophet forcefully enunciated a number of principles for the socio-politico-economic system of Islam, he declared: "Your lives and your properties are as sacred as this day of *Ḥajj*".[37] On another occasion he emphasised: "Whatever a Muslim possesses is unlawful for another Muslim, his wealth and property and his life".[38]

On the basis of this, Muslim jurists have unanimously stressed the duty of the Islamic state to safeguard the life and property of all individuals within its boundaries[39] so that, in the words of the Prophet, "a woman travelling alone from Ḥīra' to the Ka'bah feels such security that she has fear of none but God".[40]

(4) Social and Economic Justice

Since Islam considers mankind as one family, all members of this family are alike in the eyes of God and before the Law revealed by Him. There is no difference between the rich and the poor, the high and the low, or the white and the black. There is to be no discrimination due to race, colour or position. The only criterion for a man's worth is character, ability, and service to Islam and humanity. Said the Holy Prophet: "Certainly God does not look at your faces or your wealth; He looks at your heart and your deeds".[41] "The noblest of you are the best in character."[42] To be even more emphatic the Prophet warned of the disastrous consequences of discrimination and inequality before the Law for an individual or a nation:

> Communities before you strayed because when the high committed theft they were set free, but when the low committed theft the Law was enforced on them. By God, even if my daughter, Fāṭimah, committed theft I will certainly cut her hand.[43]
>
> Whoever humiliates or despises a Muslim, male or female, for his poverty or paucity of resources, will be disgraced by God on the Day of Judgment.[44]

'Umar, the second Caliph, wrote to Abū Mūsā al-Ash'arī, one of his governors, asking him to treat everyone before him alike in respect so that the weak did not despair of justice from him and the high did not crave for undue advantage.[45] This spirit of social justice thoroughly permeated the Muslim society during the period of the first four caliphs, and even in the later period, though a little subdued, did not fail to find its manifestation on several occasions. It may be pertinent to quote what the renowned jurist Abū Yūsuf wrote in a letter addressed to Caliph Hārūn al-Rashīd: "Treat alike all individuals irrespective of whether they are near you or remote from you", and that "the welfare of your subjects depends on establishing the Divine Law and eliminating injustice".[46]

The Islamic teaching of brotherhood and equal treatment of all individuals in society and before the Law would not be meaningful unless accompanied by economic justice so that everyone gets his due for his contribution to society or to the social product and that there is no exploitation of one individual by another. This point is also very well stressed in Islamic writings. The Qur'ān urges Muslims to "withhold not what is justly due to others" (26: 183),[47] implying thereby that every individual must get what is really due to him, and not more by depriving others of their share. The

Prophet aptly warned: "Beware of injustice for injustice will be equivalent to darkness on the Day of Judgment".[48] This warning against injustice and exploitation is designed to protect the rights of all individuals in society (whether consumers or producers and distributors, and whether employers or employees) and to promote general welfare, the ultimate goal of Islam.

Of special significance here is the relationship between the employer and the employee which Islam places in a proper setting, specifying norms for the mutual treatment of both so as to establish justice between them. An employee is entitled to a "just" wage for his contribution to output and it is unlawful for a Muslim employer to exploit his employee. Three persons, declared the Prophet, who will certainly face God's displeasure on the Day of Judgment are: he who does not fulfil his covenant with God; he who sells a free person and enjoys the price; and he who engages a labourer, receives due work from him, but does not pay him his wage.[49] This *ḥadīth*, by placing exploitation of labour on an equal footing with contravention of the covenant with God and enslaving of a free person suggests how repugnant exploitation of labour is to the spirit of Islam. Besides being paid the "just" wage, Islam requires that labourers should not be made to work so hard or in such miserable conditions that their efficiency declines, their health deteriorates, or their ability to enjoy income or participate in family life gets impaired. If they are made to perform a task which is beyond their capacity they should be provided with sufficient help (manual or technical) to enable them to do the job without undue hardship. Said the Holy Prophet:

> "Your employees are your brethren whom God has made your subordinates. So he who has his brother under him, let him feed him with what he feeds himself and clothe him with what he clothes himself and not burden him with what overpowers him. If you do so then help him".[50]

On the basis of these teachings, fixation of minimum wages and maximum working hours, creation of appropriate working conditions, enforcement of precautionary measures against industrial hazards, and adoption of technological innovations to reduce hardships would be fully in conformity with the spirit of Islamic teachings.

While this is the treatment expected of an employer to his employees, Islam, because of its commitment to justice, protects the employers by placing certain moral obligations on the employee as well. These include, among others, honesty, diligence and efficiency in the performance of the function for which the employee has been hired. "An employee who excels in his devotion to God and also renders to his employer the duty, sincerity and obedience that he owes him, for him there is double reward [with God]."[51] In this field, the Islamic state could play an important role through inculcation of Islamic work ethics in employees and imparting of appropriate vocational education.

(5) Social Security and Equitable Distribution of Income and Wealth

Given the commitment of Islam to human brotherhood and to social and economic justice, gross inequalities of income and wealth could only be repugnant to its spirit. Such inequalities could only destroy rather than foster the feelings of brotherhood that Islam wishes to create. Besides, since all resources are gifts of God to all human beings (al-Qur'ān, 2: 29), there is no reason why they should remain concentrated in a few hands. Hence, Islam emphasises distributive justice and incorporates in its system a programme for redistribution of income and wealth so that every individual is guaranteed a standard of living that is humane and respectable and in harmony with the dignity of man inherent in his being the vicegerent of God on earth. A Muslim society that fails to guarantee such a humane standard is really not worthy of the name as the Prophet declared: "He is not a true Muslim who eats his fill when his next-door neighbour is hungry".[52]

Hence, Islam emphasises distributive justice and incorporates in its system a programme which seems to contain the following five essential elements: one, as discussed earlier, making arrangements for training, and then rendering assistance in finding gainful employment to those unemployed and looking for work in accordance with their ability; two, enforcing a system of "just" remuneration for those working; three, making compulsory arrangements for insurance against unemployment and occupational hazards, old-age pensions and survivors benefits for those who can afford to provide for this; four, providing assistance to those who, because of disability, physical or mental handicaps, or adolescence are unable to support themselves or to attain a respectable standard of living by their own effort; and five, collecting and distributing *Zakāt* and enforcing Islamic teachings related to the division of the estate of a deceased person to accelerate the distribution of income and wealth in Muslim society so that, in the words of the Qur'ān: "wealth does not continue to circulate merely among your rich" (59: 7).

It is the duty of the Islamic state to ensure a respectable standard of living for every individual, who is unable to take care of his own needs and hence requires assistance. The Prophet clearly declared that: "He whom God has made an administrator over the affairs of Muslims but remains indifferent to their needs and their poverty, God will also be indifferent to his needs and poverty".[53] He also said that: "He who leaves behind him dependants, they are our responsibility,[54] and that "the ruler [state] is the supporter of him who has no supporter".[55] These and other similar *ḥadīths* lay down the gist of Islamic teachings in the realm of social security.

'Umar, the second Caliph, explaining redistributive justice in Islam, emphasised in one of his public addresses that everyone had an equal right in the wealth of the community, that none, not even he himself, enjoyed a greater right in it than anyone else, and that if he were to live longer, he would see to it that even a shepherd on Mount Sinai received his share from this wealth.[56] Caliph 'Alī is reported to have stressed that "God has made it obligatory on the rich to provide the poor with what is adequate for them; if the poor are hungry or naked or troubled, it is because the rich have deprived them [of their right], and it will be proper for God to hold them responsible for this deprivation and to punish them".[57] The jurists have almost unanimously held the position that it is the duty of the whole Muslim society in general, and of its rich in particular, to take care of the basic needs of the poor, and if the well-to-do do not fulfil their responsibility in spite of their ability to do so, the state should compel them.

The Islamic concept of justice in the distribution of income and wealth does not require equal reward for everyone irrespective of his contribution to society. Islam tolerates some inequalities of income because all men are not equal in their character, ability, and service to society (6: 165, 61: 71, and 43: 32). Therefore, distributive justice in the Islamic society, after (i) guaranteeing a humane standard of living to all members through proper training, suitable job, "just" wages, social security and financial assistance to the needy through the institution of *Zakāt*, and (ii) intensifying the distribution of wealth through its system of dispersal of the estate of a deceased person, allows such differentials in earning as are in keeping with the differences in the value of the contribution made or services rendered to society.

The Islamic stress on distributive justice is so emphatic that there have been some Muslims who have been led to believe in absolute equality of wealth. Abū Dharr, a companion of the Prophet, was of the opinion that it is unlawful for a Muslim to possess wealth beyond the essential needs of his family. However, most of the Prophet's companions did not agree with him in this extreme view and tried to prevail upon him to change his position.[58] But even Abū Dharr was not a protagonist of equality of flows (income). He was in favour of equality of stocks (wealth accumulations). This, he asserted, could be attained if the entire surplus of income over "genuine" expenses (*al-'afw*) was spent by the individual in improving the lot of his less fortunate brothers in particular and society in general. The consensus of Muslim scholars in spite of being intensely in favour of distributive justice, has, however, always been that if a Muslim earns by rightful means and from his own income and wealth fulfils his obligations toward the welfare of the society by paying *Zakāt* and other compulsory and voluntary contributions, there is nothing wrong in his possessing more wealth than other fellow Muslims.[59]

In reality, however, if the Islamic teachings of *ḥalāl* and *ḥarām* about income and acquisition of wealth are sincerely followed, if the norm of justice to employees and consumers is applied, if provisions for redistribution of income and wealth are implemented, and if the Islamic law of inheritance is enforced, there will remain no gross inequalities of income and wealth in Muslim society.

(6) International Relations and National Defence

With respect to the wider sphere of mankind and the Muslim *ummah*, it is the responsibility of the Islamic state to try to make as rich a contribution as it can toward the spiritual and material uplift of mankind. If resources permit, it should provide assistance to relieve hardship and promote growth and accelerated development in deserving countries. The guiding principles of its policies in international economic relations may in the light of Islamic teachings be briefly stated to be: one, to co-operate in all matters contributing to "righteousness" and "piety" and to refrain from co-operating in "aggression" and "sin",[60] and two, to work positively for the welfare of mankind because it is the family of God.[61]

These principles, of course, relate to all countries and all people to whom the Islamic state is linked by bonds of universal human brotherhood as propounded by Islam. However, with Muslim countries to which the Islamic state is also united by bonds of common ideology, it should manifest greater solidarity and co-operation in all fields of life to enhance the unity and dignity of the *ummah* and the glory of Islam.

The Islamic state should also promote international understanding and peace in keeping with the teachings of Islam which by its very name stands for peace. It should encourage and support any constructive move towards peace, and should honour all treaties and agreements to which it is a partner. Nevertheless, while working for peace as a basic objective, the Islamic state should do its utmost to strengthen its defences so as to prevent or frustrate any aggression against its faith, territory, freedom and resources since the Qur'ān enjoins: "And prepare against them whatever force you can" (8: 60). This may be understood to imply preparedness in terms of both men and hardware, including compulsory military service, efficient training, high morale, and diversification of sources of supplies if these cannot be produced locally or in collaboration with other Muslim countries. Nevertheless, in compliance with Islamic teachings, the military strength of the Islamic state should be used only for a "just" cause in a "just" manner against those who nurture, or resort to, aggressive designs:

> And fight in the way of God against those who fight against you, but do not transgress limits for God loves not the transgressors (2: 190).

c. The Wherewithal

To live up to all the above obligations, the Islamic state would naturally stand in need of adequate financial resources. This is not the subject of this paper but without its review, even though it might have to be confined to a consideration of some of its basic principles, the paper would remain incomplete.

One principle which is clearly recognised by all jurists is that the state has no right to acquire resources by *confiscating* property duly possessed by individuals or groups.[62] However, if income or property has been wrongfully acquired, then the state not only has the right to confiscate it, rather it is its moral responsibility to rectify this state of affairs.

As for the means of income of the Islamic state, they are the following:

The Primary Sources

If the acquisition of resources through either confiscation or nationalisation without just compensation is to be ruled out then the primary sources left would be the following *in addition to the sale of revelant services.*

(i) *Zakāt*;
(ii) Income from natural resources;
(iii) Taxation; and
(iv) Borrowing.

In this paper these different heads cannot be treated in detail. What we are attempting to do below is merely to state some broad principles.

(i) *Zakāt*

To enable Muslims to bring to fulfilment a society which is like a single nuclear family, where wealth is equitably distributed and where the essential needs of all deserving individuals are met primarily by mutual help with the planning and organisational assistance of the state, Islam has instituted a powerful social security system giving it a religious sanctity which it enjoys nowhere else in the world. It is a part of the religious obligations of a Muslim to pay *Zakāt* at a prescribed rate on his net worth or specified income flows to the *Zakāt* fund.[63] Of such great significance is the institution of *Zakāt* in Islam that whenever the Qur'ān speaks of the obligation to establish prayers it also simultaneously stresses the obligation of Muslims to pay *Zakāt*. The Prophet went so far as to declare that "whoever offers prayers but does not pay *Zakāt*, his prayers are in vain".[64]

There is a general consensus among jurists that collection and disbursement of *Zakāt* is essentially the responsibility of the Islamic state.[65] This was the practice during the days of the Prophet and of the first two Caliphs, Abū Bakr and 'Umar. Abū Bakr even used coercion against those who refused to pay *Zakāt* to the state. It was 'Uthmān, the third caliph, who allowed the payment of *Zakāt* directly to the needy. Abū Bakr al-Jaṣṣāṣ, the renowned commentator of Qur'ānic legal injunctions, argues on the basis of the Qur'ānic verse: "Take alms out of their assets to cleanse and purify them thereby" (9: 103), that it is the duty of the state to institute a system for the collection of *Zakāt*.[66]

However, even if the state collects *Zakāt*, the proceeds are likely to be limited. Moreover, the expenditure heads for *Zakāt* are clearly enumerated in the Qur'ān.[67] Even though some jurists have widened somewhat the coverage of the expression *fī sabīl Allāh* (in the way of Allah), it can hardly be made to include all expenditure heads of the Islamic state. Thus, if the Islamic state is to live up to its obligations it must have access to resources beyond the *Zakāt* collection. In view of this the contention of some jurists that the state has no claims on the wealth of individuals beyond the *Zakāt* is simply not tenable. Revenues would have to be raised through other means.

(ii) *Income from Natural Resources*

It has already been established that natural resources have been provided by God for the welfare of all people. The monetary benefit derived from these resources should, therefore, permeate to all people and should not under any circumstances be allowed to be diverted solely to certain individuals or groups. The acceptance of this principle does not necessarily restrict the management of these resources to the state alone. Whether the state or private enterprise should manage the exploitation of these resources should be determined by the criterion of efficiency. However, even if private enterprise is to manage and operate these resources the profit derived by it should not be more than what is justified by the services rendered and the efficiency attained.

In countries with abundant natural resources to contribute an adequate income to the state treasury to finance public expenditure (as is the case in some major oil-producing Muslim countries) there may be little need for additional sources of revenues. However, countries where income from this source is either not available, or if available, is not sufficient, the state would have to supplement its income by resorting to taxation and/or borrowing if necessary.

(iii) *Taxation*

The right of the Islamic state to raise resources through taxes cannot be challenged provided that taxes are raised in a just manner and are within a certain "bearable" limit. This right is defended on the basis of the Prophetic saying that "in your wealth there are also obligations beyond the *Zakāt*"[68], and one of the fundamental principles of Islamic jurisprudence that "a small benefit may be sacrificed to attain a larger benefit and a smaller sacrifice may be imposed in order to avoid a larger sacrifice".

Most jurists have upheld the right of the state to tax. According to Marghīnānī, if the resources of the state are not sufficient, the state should collect funds from the people to serve the public interest because if the benefit accrues to the people it is their obligation to bear the cost.[69] Abū Yūsuf also supports the right of the ruler to increase or decrease taxes depending on the ability of the people to bear the burden.[70] However, only a just tax system has been held to be in harmony with the spirit of Islam. A tax system which is oppressive and too onerous as compared with the ability of the people to bear has been unanimously condemned. All rightly-guided caliphs, particularly 'Umar, 'Alī, and 'Umar ibn 'Abd al-'Azīz are reported to have stressed that taxes should be collected with justice and kindness, that they should not be beyond the ability of the people to bear, and should not deprive the people of the basic necessities of life.[71] Abū Yūsuf indicated that a just tax system could only lead to an increase in tax receipts and the development of the country.[72] Māwardī emphasised that taking more is iniquitous with respect to the rights of the people, whereas taking less is unfair with respect to the rights of the public treasury.[73]

Ibn Khaldūn genuinely reflects the trend of thinking during his time on the question of justice in the distribution of the tax burden by quoting from the letter of Ṭāhir ibn al-Ḥusain to his son who was the Governor of a province:

> So distribute [taxes] among all people with justice and equity, making them general and not exempting anyone because of his nobility or wealth, and not exempting even your own officials or courtiers or followers. And do not levy on anyone a tax which is beyond his capacity to pay.[74]

In view of the goals of social justice and equitable distribution of income a progressive tax system seems to be perfectly in harmony with the goals of Islam. It must, however, be emphasised that from the discussion of the jurists what is relevant from the point of view of modern times is the right of the Islamic state to tax with justice. It would not be proper to conclude that taxation should be strictly confined to the items mentioned by the jurists. Circumstances have changed and there seems to be the need for devising a tax system which is in harmony with the goals of Islam and yields sufficient revenue to allow a modern Islamic state to discharge its functions as a welfare state.

(iv) *Borrowing*

If total revenue from all the above sources (including sale of services) is not sufficient, the Islamic state would stand in need of borrowing. In this case because of the Islamic injunction against interest, the borrowing would need to be free of interest.

For certain sound income-yielding projects amenable to sale of services and distribution of dividends it may be possible to raise funds on the basis of profit-sharing. However, the scope for this is limited in the case of most public projects. In case profit-sharing is not possible or feasible, the

Islamic state may have to borrow funds and this would be possible only if the private sector of the Muslim society is so highly inspired by the ideals of Islam that it is willing to forego the return. In modern acquisitive Muslim societies imbued perhaps more with hedonistic ideals of the economic man as conceived by Adam Smith rather than by the altruistic teachings of Islam, and with continuous erosion of the real value of savings because of the high rate of inflation, it may be expected that borrowing without any return may tend to be unproductive unless it is made compulsory.

Expenditures financed by borrowing from the central bank tend to be inflationary, unless accompanied by a corresponding increase in the supply of goods and services, thus violating the norm of monetary stability as already discussed. Therefore, under normal circumstances borrowing from the central bank may be resorted to when a corresponding increase in output can be more or less ensured. Borrowing from the central bank may also be defended under certain special circumstances even if there is no corresponding rise in output provided it is felt that damage done by a small degree of inflationary financing is more than offset by other economic or non-economic gains that are likely to be realised. This seems to conform to the principle that a smaller sacrifice may be imposed to avoid a larger sacrifice and that the smaller of two evils may be tolerated.

"Richest" or "Ideal"

It may be contended here that all Islamic states may not have access to "adequate" resources to finance the functions discussed above and could not hence become "ideal". Here it is important to clarify that the "ideal" Islamic state should not be confused with the "richest" one. The ideal is to be construed in the light of general spiritual and material welfare attained for God's vicegerents within the framework of resources. Hence an Islamic state may be considered to have attained the position of "ideal" if it has at least (i) elevated the spiritual level of the Muslim society and minimised moral laxity and corruption; (ii) fulfilled its obligations for general economic welfare within the limits of its resources; and (iii) ensured distributive justice and has weeded out exploitation. Adequacy of resources is a relative term and is to be judged against attainable standards in the light of the stage of economic development.

It is, of course, the duty of the Islamic state to make a concerted effort to muster the maximum feasible level of resources and to harness them as efficiently as possible for fulfilling the widest possible range of responsibilities. Resources at the disposal of any society, rich or poor, may generally be expected to be scarce compared with the demands on them and every Islamic state would have to establish a schedule of priorities in the light of the *Sharī'ah* and the welfare needs of the people. Planning would hence be an essential function of every state. Since planning could be misdirected to satisfy certain vested interests, decision-making in planning should be through the Islamic process of consultation so that different viewpoints and interests are given due consideration.

Raising an optimum level of resources and utilising it efficiently within the framework of a "just" plan demands unscrupulous honesty on the part of the common man as well as government employees. This demands that, on the one hand, the common man should be willing to provide honestly to the treasury the resources needed for attaining general social welfare, and, that on the other hand, corruption, including offering of gifts, let alone undisguised bribery, for obtaining an undue advantage in money, position, jobs or contracts is to be completely eliminated:

> And swallow not your wealth among yourselves by false means, nor seek to gain access thereby to judges to swallow other people's property wrongfully with knowledge thereof (2: 188).

The Prophet (peace be on him) is reported to have said:

> "How can a governor I have appointed say, this is for you [the treasury] and this is a gift for me! Why doesn't he sit in his parent's home and see if he gets those gifts? By God, in Whose Hand is Muḥammad's life, anyone of you who takes [unduly] anything from this [what belongs to the treasury] will have it around his neck on the Day of Judgment." The Prophet then raised his hands and said twice: "O God! Have I conveyed?"[75]

While this honesty is expected in both the public and the private sectors, there are certain additional demands which public sector employees must fulfil. A Muslim public servant would be failing in his duty to God and society if he takes his remuneration but does not render his due in terms of diligence, efficiency and conscientiousness:

> Any Muslim ruler entrusted with the affairs of Muslims who dies while he was cheating the people will find Paradise foreclosed for him.[76]

Unless this level of honesty is attained and every individual works diligently and conscientiously for the implementation of Islamic teachings, the Islamic ideal of a morally-orientated welfare state cannot be fully realised. The ruler and the ruled must work hand in hand for the realisation of these goals. While the state stands duty-bound to make an honest effort to create the ideal conditions which Islam visualises, it is also obligatory for the public to render to the state their best in terms of co-operation and goodwill to crown the state efforts with success. It must be fully realised that the extent of movement towards the "ideal" Islamic state would necessarily depend on the quality and character of the people and the power *elite* in Muslim society.

d. Nature and Identity

The above discussion indicates that the Islamic state is essentially a welfare state and is duty-bound to play an important role in the economy for the fulfilment of the goals of the *Shārī'ah* in the economic field as briefly specified above. This welfare role is, however, to be played within the framework of individual freedom which Islam values greatly. The most important pillar of the Islamic faith is the belief that man has been created by God and is subservient to none but Him (13: 36) and that one of the primary objectives of the prophetic mission of Muḥammad (peace be on him) is to release mankind from all burdens and chains enslaving it (7: 157). This provides not only the essence of the Islamic charter for individual freedom from all bondage but also subjects man to the sovereignty of God in all aspects of life which essentially implies subordination of man to the moral law as specified in the Qur'ān and the *Sunnah*.

Because man is born free, no one, not even the state, has the right to abrogate this freedom and to subject him to regimentation. It is this respect for freedom which prompted 'Umar, the second caliph, to declare: "Since when have you begun to enslave people although their mothers bore them as free men?"[77] This commitment of Islam to individual freedom has led to a consensus among Muslim jurists that in normal circumstances restrictions may not be imposed on a free and sane adult. Thus freedom of expression, occupation and movement are assured in an Islamic state.

It is to realise this norm of individual freedom that Islam has incorporated in its economic system the essential elements of free enterprise after conditioning it to its own norms and values. The institution of private property along with the market mechanism has been integrated into the Islamic system in such a manner that an "appropriate" part of the production and distribution of goods and services is left to individuals and voluntarily-constituted groups enjoying freedom in their dealings and transactions.[78] The profit motive has also been upheld as, besides being consistent with human nature, it provides the necessary incentive for efficiency in the use of resources which God has provided to mankind.

However, since social welfare has a place of absolute importance in Islam, individual freedom – though of considerable significance – does not enjoy a place independent of its social consequences. It is sacred only as long as it does not conflict with the larger social interest or the overall spiritual and material goals of Muslim society, or as long as the individual does not transgress the rights of others. Property can be owned privately but is to be considered a *trust* from God and is to be acquired and spent in accordance with the terms of the trust. The profit motive has also been subjected to certain moral constraints so that it serves individual interest within a social context and does not lead to economic and social ills or violate the Islamic goals of social justice and equitable distribution of income and wealth.

Mixed Capitalism? Socialism?

All these various considerations make the Islamic state completely distinct from both the socialist and the capitalist systems. First of all, socialism, as conceived by Marx, is basically amoral and based on the concept of dialectical materialism; while capitalism, being a secular ideology is, at best, morally neutral. In contrast Islam lays emphasis on both the moral and the material aspects of life and erects the edifice of economic well-being on the foundation of moral values. The foundation being different, the superstructure is bound to be different too.

Moreover, Islam is also fully committed to human brotherhood with social and economic justice, to equitable distribution of income, and to individual freedom within the context of social welfare. Although both socialism and mixed capitalism also claim to pay allegiance to social justice, the concept of justice in socialism or mixed capitalism is not based on human brotherhood reinforced by inviolable spiritual criteria for social and economic justice. In fact Marxist socialism under the influence of dialectics condones injustice done by one group to the other and even the annihilation of one group by the other. In *laissez faire* capitalism with its slogan of "Don't interfere, the world will take care of itself" there was no innate ideal of social justice to be attained through conscious state effort, while in mixed capitalism the roots of social justice lie in group pressures rather than in an intrinsic belief in human brotherhood.

Although capitalism also recognises freedom of the individual there are no spiritual constraints on this freedom. The constraints that do exist are determined primarily by the pressures of competition or the coercive power of the state, and secondarily by changing social norms without any spiritual sanctity. In the Islamic system, however, the individual is subject to inviolable spiritual values in all aspects of life, including the acquisition, spending and distribution of wealth. Islam normally recognises, like capitalism, the freedom of enterprise with the institution of private property, the market system and the profit motive, but it differs from capitalism because, as already indicated, property in Islam is a trust from God and man as trustee and vicegerent of God is responsible to Him and subject to His guiding principles.

Although both socialism and capitalism recognise equitable distribution of income, in capitalism this recognition is again an outcome of group pressure while in socialism it is accompanied by negation of individual freedom. Islam achieves this equitable distribution within the framework of individual freedom but with spiritual and legal imperatives to safeguard public interest, moral constraints against unearned income, and social obligations to ensure a just distribution of income and wealth.

The Islamic welfare state is hence neither capitalist nor socialist. It is based on its own values and guided by its own goals. It has its own identity and bears no resemblance to any other form of state.

Notes and Sources

1 Yūsuf ibn 'Abd al-Barr al-Qurṭubī, *Jāmi' Bayān al-'Ilm wa Fadluh* (Madina: al-Maktabah al-'Ilmiyyah, n.d.), vol. 1, p. 62.
2 Muḥammad ibn Idrīs al-Shāfi'ī, *al-Risālah* (Cairo: Muṣṭafā al-Bābī al-Ḥalabī, 1940), ed. Aḥmad M. Shākir, p. 419: 1154.
3 Abū Ya'lā Muḥammad ibn al-Ḥusayn, *al-Aḥkām al-Sulṭāniyyah* (Cairo: 'Īsā al-Bābī al-Ḥalabī, 1938), p. 3.
4 Abū Ya'lā, op. cit., p. 3.
5 Abū al-Ḥasan 'Alī ibn Muḥammad al-Māwardī, *al-Aḥkām al-Sulṭāniyyah* (Cairo: 'Īsā al-Bābī al-Ḥalabī, 1960), p. 5.
6 'Abd al-Raḥmān ibn Khaldūn, *Muqaddimah* (Cairo: al-Maktabah al-Tijāriyyah al-Kubrā, n.d.), pp. 191–96.
7 'Abd al-Salām ibn Taymiyyah, *al-Siyāsah al-Shar'iyyah fī Iṣlāḥ al-Rā'ī wa al-Ra'iyyah*, ed. Muḥammad al-Mubārak (Beirut, Dār-al-Kutub al-'Arabiyyah, 1961), pp. 138–44.
8 Shāh Walī-Allāh al-Dihlawī, *Ḥujjat-Allāh al-Bālighah*, Urdu translation by 'Abdul Raḥīm (Lahore: Qawmī Kutubkhānā, 1953), vol. 2, p. 601.
9 Muhammad Iqbal, *The Reconstruction of Religious Thought in Islam* (Lahore: Shaikh Muhammad Ashraf, 1954), p. 155.
10 For a discussion of the essential difference between Islam, democracy and theocracy, the significance of man's vicegerency and the implication of this for the political system of Islam, see Abul A'lā Mawdūdī: "Economic and Political Teachings of the Qur'ān" in M. M. Sharif (ed.), *A History of Muslim Philosophy* (Wiesbaden: Otto Harrassowitz, 1963), vol. 1, pp. 193–4 and 197, and *Khilāfat wa Mulūkiyyat* (Lahore, Islamic Publications, 1966), pp. 31–36 and 69–70, *The Political Theory of Islam* (Lahore, 1960), and *Islamic Law and Constitution* (Karachi, 1955).
11 "Whoever, male or female, does good and is a believer, We shall certainly make him live a good life and give him his reward for the best of what he did" (16: 97). "Serve your Lord and do good that you may have welfare (*falāḥ*)" (22: 77).
12 "God desires ease and not hardship for you" (2: 185).
13 "And if the people of the towns had believed and kept their duty, We would certainly have opened for them blessings from the heavens and the earth" (7: 96). "And the good land – its vegetation comes forth abundantly by the permission of its Lord. And the bad land, its vegetation comes forth but scantily. Thus do We repeat the messages for a people who give thanks" (7: 58).
14 "Those who believe and do good deeds for them the Beneficent will surely bring about love" (19: 97).
15 "If you do it not there will be discord and great mischief" (8: 73). "Corruption has appeared in the land and sea on account of what people have done to make them taste a part of their doing so that they may return" (30: 41).
16 "And Allah sets forth a parable: A town safe and secure to which its provisions come in abundance from every quarter; but it was ungrateful for Allah's favours, so Allah made it taste a pall of hunger and fear because of what they did" (16: 112). "So let them serve the Lord of this House who feeds them against hunger and gives them security against fear" (106: 4).
17 "Those who believe and whose hearts find peace in the remembrance of Allah. Surely it is in the remembrance of Allah that hearts find peace" (13: 28).
18 Abū al-Ḥusayn Muslim al-Nīsābūrī, *Ṣaḥīḥ Muslim* (Cairo: 'Īsā al-Bābī al-Ḥalabī, 1955), vol. 1, p. 126.
19 Abū Yusuf Ya'qūb ibn Ibrāhim, *Kitāb al-Kharāj*, 2nd ed. (Cairo: al-Maṭba'ah al-Salafīyah, A.H. 1352), pp. 14–15.
20 Muḥammad Abū Zahrah, *Uṣūl al-Fiqh* (Damascus: Dār al-Fikr al-'Arabī, 1957), p. 355.

21 Abū Yūsuf, op. cit., pp. 3–17.
22 "He it is Who created you from clay" (al-Qur'ān, 6: 2).
23 "And when thy Lord said to the angels: 'I am going to create a mortal of sounding clay, of black mud fashioned into shape; so when I have made him complete and breathed into him of My Spirit, fall down making obeisance to him'" (15: 28–29).
24 "But if they repent and keep up prayer and pay the *zakāt* they are your brothers-in-faith" (9: 11).
"The believers are nothing but brethren; so make peace between your brethren and keep your duty to Allah that you may be treated mercifully" (49: 10).
"Mankind is the family of God and the most beloved of them before Him is he who is best to His family", Walī al-Dīn al-Tabrīzī, *Mishkāt al-Maṣābiḥ* (Damascus: al-Maktab al-Islāmī, A.H. 1381), ed. M. Nāṣir al-Dīn al-Albānī, vol. 2, p. 613: 4998.
25 Abū Ḥāmid Muḥammad al-Ghazālī, *al-Mustaṣfā* (Cairo: al-Maktabah al-Tijārīyah al-Kubrā, 1937), vol. 1, pp. 139–40.
26 Ibn al-Qayyim al-Jawziyyah, *I'lām al-Muwaqqi'īn* (Cairo: al-Maktabah al-Tijārīyah al-Kubrā, 1955), vol. 3, p. 14.
27 By way of example it may be pointed out here that Ibn Ḥazm, on the basis of the Qur'ānic verse: "Then if one of them does wrong to the other, fight the one who does wrong until he returns to the command of God" (49: 9), argues that it is proper to fight with those who deprive others of basic necessities of life because the one who has denied his brother his due right has in essence wronged him. He also argues that it is the responsibility of the rich in every country to fulfil the needs of the poor and the ruler [state] should compel them to provide the necessary sustenance, protective clothing, and housing that ensures protection and privacy. He also quotes the following *ḥadīth* of the Prophet narrated by Abū Sa'īd al-Khuḍri: "He who has a surplus animal to ride on should give it to one who has none, and he who has surplus provisions should give them to him who has none, and the Prophet mentioned so many items of wealth that we felt none of us has any right over his surplus wealth" (Ibn Ḥazm, *al-Muḥallā*, vol. 6, pp. 156–59: 725). See also p. 200 ff. above.
28 Abū Dāwūd al-Sijistānī, *Sunan Abū Dāwūd* (Cairo: 'Īsā al-Bābī al-Ḥalabī, 1952), vol. 1, p. 382.
29 Muḥammad ibn Yazid ibn Mājah al-Qazwīnī, *Sunan Ibn Mājah* (Cairo: 'Īsā al-Bābī al-Ḥalabī, 1952), vol. 2, p. 723: 2138; and Abū 'Abd al-Raḥmān ibn Shu'ayb al-Nisā'ī, *Sunan al-Nisā'ī* (Cairo: Muṣṭafā al-Bābī al-Ḥalabī, 1964), vol. 7, p. 212.
30 'Alī al-Ṭanṭāwī and Nājī al-Ṭanṭāwī, *Akhbāru 'Umar* (Damascus: Dār al-Fikr, 1959), p. 268.
31 Qurṭubī, op. cit., vol. 2, p. 15.
32 Cited on the authority of Bayhaqī, *Shu'ab al-Īmān* by Jalāl al-Dīn al-Suyūṭī, *al-Jāmi' al-Ṣaghīr* (Cairo: 'Abd al-Ḥamīd Aḥmad Ḥanafī, n.d.), vol. 1, p. 15.
33 Muslim, op. cit., vol. 3, p. 1358; and Abū Dāwūd, op. cit., vol. 2, p. 559.
34 Muḥammad ibn Yazīd ibn Mājah al-Qazwīnī, *Sunan Ibn Mājah* (Cairo: 'Īsā al-Bābī al-Ḥalabī, 1952), vol. 1, pp. 81–224; see also, Qurṭubī, op. cit., vol. 1, pp. 3–13.
35 Ibn Mājah, op. cit., vol. 1, p. 31: 79.
36 Muslim, op. cit., vol. 1, p. 203: 1.
37 Muslim, op. cit., vol. 2, p. 889: 147; and Ibn Mājah, op. cit., vol. 2, p. 1297: 393.
38 Abū Dāwūd, op. cit., vol. 2, p. 568.
39 Abū Ya'lā, op. cit., p. 11; Māwardī, op. cit., p. 16; and Abū al-Ḥasan 'Alī al-Marghīnānī, *al-Hidāyah* (Cairo: 'Īsā al-Bābī al-Ḥalabī, 1965), vol. 2, pp. 98 and 132.
40 Muḥammad ibn Isma'īl al-Bukhārī, *al-Jāmi' al-Ṣaḥīḥ* (Cairo: Muḥammad 'Alī Ṣubayḥ, n.d.), vol. 4, p. 239.
41 Muslim, op. cit., vol. 4, p. 1987: 34.
42 Bukhārī, op. cit., vol. 8, p. 15.
43 *Ibid.*, p. 199.

44 *Musnad al-Imām Zayd wa 'Alī al-Riḍā ibn Mūsā al-Kāẓim* (Beirut: Maktabah al-Ḥayāt, 1966), p. 478.
45 Abū Yūsūf, op. cit., p. 117.
46 *Ibid.*, pp. 4 and 6.
47 See also 83: 1–3: "Woe to the cheaters; who when they take the measure [of their due] from men, take it fully. And when they measure out to others or weigh out for them, they give less than is due".
48 Reported on the authority of *Musnad* of Aḥmad and Bayhaqī, *Shu'ab al-Īman* by Suyuṭī, op. cit., vol. 1, p. 8.
49 Bukhārī, vol. 3, p. 112.
50 *Ibid.*, vol. 1, pp. 15–16. The word used in the *ḥadīth* is "slaves" and not "employees" as in the translation. If a humane treatment is expected to be meted out to slaves, then employees are certainly entitled to an even better treatment.
51 *Ibid.*, vol. 3, p. 186. See also footnote 50.
52 Abū 'Abd-Allāh Muḥammad ibn Ismā'īl al-Bukhārī, *al-Adab al-Mufrad*, 2nd ed. (Cairo: Quṣayy Muḥibb al-Dīn al-Khaṭīb, A.H. 1379), p. 52: 112.
53 Abū Dāwūd, op. cit., vol. 2, p. 122.
54 *Ibid.*, p. 124.
55 *Ibid.*, vol. 1, p. 481.
56 Muḥammad Ḥusayn Haykal, *al-Fārūq 'Umar* (Cairo: Maktabah al-Nahdah al-Miṣrīyah, 1964), vol. 2, p. 233.
57 Abū 'Ubayd Qāsim ibn Sallām, *Kitāb al-Amwāl* (Cairo: at-Maktabah al-Tijārīyah al-Kubrā, A.H. 1353).
58 See the comments on verse 34 of *sūrah* 9 of the Qur'ān in the commentaries of Abū al-Fidā' Ismā'īl ibn Kathīr, *Tafsīr al-Qur'ān al-'Aẓim* (Cairo: 'Īsā al-Bābī al-Ḥalabī, n.d.), vol. 2, p. 352; and Abū Bakr al-Jaṣṣāṣ, *Aḥkām al-Qur'ān* (Cairo: Maṭba'ah al-Bahiyyah al-Miṣriyyah, A.H. 1347), vol. 3, p. 130. See also Mawdūdī, "Economic Teachings of the Qur'ān" op. cit., p. 179, for a critical discussion of the effort by some writers to establish "equal" distribution from verse 10 of *Sūrah* 41 of the Qur'ān: "And He made in it [the earth] mountains above its surface, blessed it, and placed therein provisions in due proportion, in four days, alike for [all] seekers". The implication here is that provisions are equally accessible to all seekers.
59 See the commentary of Ibn Kathīr, op. cit., vol. 2, pp. 350–3.
60 Help one another in righteousness and piety but help not one another in sin and aggression (5: 3).
61 Mankind is the family of God and the most beloved of them before Him is the one who is best to His family (*Mishkāt*, op. cit., vol. 2, p. 613: 4998).
Be kind to those on earth and He who is in the Heavens will be kind to you (*ibid.*, p. 608: 4669).
62 For example, Abū Yūsuf expressly voices this feeling by stating that "the state has no right to acquire forcibly the property that rightly belongs to an individual except by duly established methods". (Abū Yūsuf, op. cit., p. 117.)
63 For a comprehensive treatment of the subject, see, Yūsuf al-Qarḍāwī, *Fiqh al-Zakāt* (Beirut, Dār al-Irshād, 1969), 2 vols.
64 Abū 'Ubayd, op. cit., p. 354: 919.
65 Qarḍāwī, op. cit., vol. 2, pp. 747–91.
66 Jaṣṣāṣ, op. cit., see the commentary on verse 103 of *Sūrah* 9, vol. 3, pp. 190–92.
67 "The *zakāt* is for the poor, the needy, those employed to administer it, those whose hearts are desired to incline (to the Truth), freeing the slaves, those in debt, the way of Allah and the wayfarer – an injunction from Allah. And Allah is Knowing, Wise" (9: 60).
68 'Abd-Allāh ibn 'Abd al-Raḥmān al-Dārimī, *Sunan al-Dārimī* (Damascus: Maṭba'ah al-I'tidāl, A.H. 1349), vol. 1, p. 385. For a detailed discussion of this subject see Qarḍāwī, op. cit., pp. 963–92.

69 *al-Hidāyah*, op. cit., vol. 4, p. 105.
70 Abū Yūsuf, op. cit., p. 85.
71 *Ibid.*, pp. 14, 16 and 86.
72 *Ibid.*, p. 111.
73 Māwardī, op. cit., p. 209.
74 Ibn Khaldūn, op. cit., p. 308.
75 Muslim, op. cit., vol. 3, p. 1463: 26.
76 Mishkāt, op. cit., vol. 2, p. 321: 3686.
77 Ṭanṭāwī and Ṭanṭāwī, op. cit., p. 268.
78 The word "appropriate" may appear to be in contrast with "every" used by Mawlānā Mawdūdī: "The economic scheme presented in the Qur'ān is based entirely on the scheme of individual ownership in every field" – "Economic Teachings of the Qur'ān", op. cit., p. 179. It is, however, not because he qualifies his statement on p. 180 by indicating that "there is nothing in the Qur'ān to prevent a certain thing being taken over from individual control and placed under collective control, if necessary". Thus the choice of which sectors should be in private ownership and which should be nationalised would be made essentially on the basis of public interest.

CHAPTER NINE

Economic Development in an Islamic Framework

*Khurshid Ahmad**

A MAJOR challenge confronts the world of Islam: the challenge of reconstructing its economy in a way that is commensurate with its world role, ideological, political and economical. What does this demand: economic development with a view to "catch up" with the industrialised countries of the West, Capitalist or Socialist, according to one's inclination and sympathy, or politico-economic dependence? Or does it demand total socio-economic reconstruction in the light of a basically different model, with its own set of assumptions, ideals and growth-path, something that would be unique and value-specific? Whether the Muslim world is clear about this fundamental question or not, we will try to see in a moment. It is, however, clear from the topic we propose to discuss that our primary concern is not with the "catching up" ideology. Instead, our objective is to discern the nature and ethos of economic development in an Islamic framework.

The subject can, however, be approached in a number of ways. One may try to explore the nature and processes of economic development as they may unfold themselves in a society that is Islamic in actuality, or at least where some approximation with the norm has been achieved. This approach has a number of merits but its immediate relevance to the Muslim world situation is somewhat limited. What is more relevant and pressing is the need to clearly identify the Islamic ideal of economic development, to measure the distance between this ideal and the present-day reality of the Muslim world and to formulate appropriate strategy/strategies for pursuing developmental efforts in such a way that an Islamic framework of life may ultimately be evolved. This formulation of the problem has immediate relevance for the Muslim economist and planner. It would be naïve to think that correct answers to this problem have already been found or can be developed in one or a few papers, or even in one or a few conferences. It

* Professor Khurshid Ahmad, Chairman, Institute of Policy Studies, Islamabad. Professor Ahmad has taught at the University of Karachi and is a former Federal Minister on Planning and Development and Deputy Chairman, Planning Commission, Pakistan.

This chapter was incorporated in "*Islamic Perspectives*," Islamic Foundation, 1979.

would be only through sustained research by a team of economists, by unceasing original thinking and, above all, by a great deal of practical experimentation that we might be able to discover an Islamic road to economic development.

We must not rule out the possibility of the appearance of a number of approaches within an Islamic framework and we should be prepared to examine them carefully and even experiment if they merit such a response. It may be worthwhile to distinguish between an *Islamic economy* and an *Islamising economy* and to admit the possibility of a multiplicity of approaches/models, although with a strong central core of unity and uniformity. What follows is just one person's reflection on the problem under discussion. It is being presented as tentative formulations primarily in order to provide a basis for discussion and further exploration.

The Starting-point

Muslim countries suffer from widespread economic underdevelopment, i.e., non-utilisation and/or underutilisation of human and physical resources with consequent poverty, stagnation and backwardness. Even those countries which are resource-rich, the state of their economies remains predominantly underdeveloped. The standard of living of the common man is generally low. Some Muslim countries have over the last two decades maintained an above average rate of growth (i.e., average rate of growth of all the less developed countries), nonetheless, there has been little real economic development.[1]

There are gross structural deformities within the economies of the Muslim countries. Whatever development is taking place is contributing, *inter alia*, to the aggravation of these deformities, viz. gross inequalities in distribution of income and wealth, severe imbalances between different geographic regions, between economic and social sectors, between sectors within the economy, particularly agriculture and industry, and a number of imbalances and iniquities within the industrial and agricultural complexes.

Most of the Muslim countries have been unable to internalise the engine of growth. Their economies are dependent on the Western countries in a number of ways – for the import of foodstuffs, manufactured goods, technology, etc. on the one hand, and for the export of their primary products on the other. Some of them are suffering from the effect of lingering legacies of colonial economic relationships and appear as perfect examples of a "centre-periphery" relationship.[2]

The paradox of the Muslim world is that it is resource-rich, but economically poor and weak. Development planning has been introduced in a number of Muslim countries. In some, the art is now at a fairly advanced level. Nigeria, Egypt, Syria, Algeria, Iran, Pakistan, Malaysia, Indonesia are some of the instances. But in almost all these countries developmental effort is modelled after the prototypes of growth developed by the Western theorists and practitioners of planning and "sold" to the planners in the Muslim countries via international diplomacy, economic pressurisation, intellectual infiltration and a number of other overt and covert means. Whatever be the source of inspiration – the Capitalist economies of the West or the Socialist models of Russia and China – no effort worth the name seems to have been made to rethink the basic issues of development economies in the light of the ideals and values of Islam and its world strategy. A very simplified version of economic development has been adopted as policy ideal: industrialisation. This is believed to depend, primarily and predominantly, on capital formation. Industry is regarded as the leading sector and expanding investment in it is believed to be the royal road to development Utopia. A rather quick way to achieve this objective is import substitution. This approach is based on extensions and variations of the Harrod-Domar model of macroeconomic planning.[3] Under this approach growth prospects are constrained by the operation of two "gaps" (deficiencies): the domestic "savings gap" and the "balance of payments gap"; and these gaps can be filled by one talisman – foreign aid.

It is interesting to note that even those countries which have not formally subscribed to the Western growth models and have claimed to follow some kind of a socialist path to development have pursued a similar capital- and aid-centred strategy. Kalecki and Lange models both assign a central role to investment in development. Russia's international economic policy has broadly pursued this very approach.[4]

A comparative study of the development policy and of actual economic performance of the Muslim countries shows that the strategy of imitation has failed to deliver the goods.

How do this policy and the actual developments stand in relation to Islam? It would be correct to say that developmental policies have been more or less Islam-neutral. It is our submission that as far as Islam is concerned it cannot be neutral *vis-à-vis* economic development. But there is no evidence to support that generally speaking the policy makers derived any inspiration worth the name from Islam and tried to translate its economic deals into development policies, some lip-service here and there notwithstanding. Actual policies have had little or no relation to Islam with the result that the economies of the Muslim world have failed to be transformed towards Islam and the deformities and iniquities inherited from the colonial period and beyond have generally aggravated.[5]

A survey of the literature dealing with Islam and development shows that even at the academic level discussion has hovered around a few points of general significance only. Western writers[6] have mostly dwelled upon the alleged "fatalism" in Muslim society and on lack of "achievement-motivation". Muslim writers have tried to show that Islam provides for all those factors which are needed for economic development. Some work has been done to suggest the broad objectives of economic effort and enterprise that Islam wants to be pursued by the individual and society.[7]

Excepting one or two tentative yet pioneering works no serious effort has been made to spell out the implications of these goals for development strategies and policies.[8] Moreover, the effect of the work that has been done so far is hardly discernible at all on the actual development processes. All the evidence suggests that the actual movement towards development is altogether bereft of Islamic inspiration. If Islam comes into the picture, it is at a later stage, and mostly in either of the following two forms:

(a) Some people bring it into the debate to legitimise certain policies;
(b) Others use it as a point of reference for criticising certain policies and actual developments.

There is, however, one point which came out prominently in this debate and discussion: Islam's main concern is in *encouraging* economic development *with* social justice and not in disregard of the demands of social justice.

Our Approach: Assumptions and Commitments

The primary task of any theory of development is to examine and explain the nature of the processes of development and factors responsible for it, to identify and analyse principal obstacles to development in a given situation, and to try to prescribe the most desirable and the most efficient ways and means to remove those obstacles and achieve various dimensions of economic development.

It can hardly be overemphasised that such an effort must be made with academic rigour and scholarly detachment. Nonetheless, it would be idle to assume that this theorising can take place in a climate of positivistic objectivity and of complete value-neutrality. Most of the economic thinking that masquerades as value-neutral turns out, on closer scrutiny, to be otherwise. The result of this approach, however, is that its value-assumptions remain apparently hidden. They remain implicit, and as such, are not susceptible to evaluation in an ordinary way.[9]

This is unfair and improper. We agree with Myrdal that "efforts to run away from the valuations are misdirected and foredoomed to be fruitless and damaging" and that "the only way in which we can strive for objectivity in theoretical analysis is to lift up the valuations into the full light, make them conscious and explicit, and permit them to determine the viewpoints, the approaches and the concepts used. In the practical phases of a study the stated value premises should then, together with the data established by theoretical analysis with the utilisation of those same value premises – form the premises for all policy conclusions".[10]

The major contribution of Islam lies in making human life and effort purposive and value-oriented. The transformation it seeks to bring about in human attitudes and *pari passu* in that of the social sciences is to move them from a stance of pseudo-value-neutrality towards open and manifest value-commitment and value-fulfilment. The first premise which we want to establish is that economic development in an Islamic framework and Islamic development economics are rooted in the value-pattern embodied in the Qur'ān and the *Sunnah*.[11] This is our basic frame of reference.

Our second premise is that this approach clearly rules out imitativeness. The Capitalist and the Socialist models can have no place as our ideal-types, although we would like to avail from all those experiences of mankind which can be gainfully assimilated and integrated within the Islamic framework and can serve our own purposes without in any way impairing our values and norms. But we must reject the archetype of capitalism and socialism.[12] Both these models of development are incompatible with our value system; both are exploitative and unjust and fail to treat man as man, as God's vicegerent (*khalīfa*) on earth. Both have been unable to meet in their own realms the basis economic, social, political and moral challenges of our time and the real needs of a humane society and a just economy. Both are irrelevant to our situation, not merely because of the differences in ideological and moral attitudes and in socio-political frameworks, but also for a host of more mundane and economic reasons: differences in resource bases, changed international economic situations, bench-mark differences in the levels of the respective economies, socio-economic costs of development, and above all, for the fundamental fact that the crucial developmental strategy of both the systems – industrialisation through maximisation of investible surplus – is unsuited to the conditions of the Muslim world and the demands of the Islamic social ideals.[13]

The body of knowledge and experience developed and structured in the form of development economics is important and useful but its real relevance and applicability to our situation is rather limited. Although literature on development economics is burgeoning, it fails to come to grips with real complex problems of the less developed countries in general, and of the Muslim world in particular. Development theory as it has developed in the West (both in the Capitalist and Socialist countries) has been conditioned by the unique characteristics, specific problems, and explicit and implicit values and socio-political infra-structure of the Western economies. This theory cannot be indiscriminately applied to Muslim countries. Moreover, a major part of the Western development theory remains an outgrowth of the capital theory.[14] Because of this fundamental weakness, it fails to tackle adequately the multi-dimensional problems of development.

Two major areas of development in recent development theory relate to the realisation that investment in man – education, health, etc. – is a strategic factor in the economic development of a society, and that socio-political factors play an important part in growth and non-growth alike. It is interesting to observe that the "investment in man" approach is leading to some widening of the "capital theory" as it has thrown new light on a somewhat neglected aspect of capital – the human capital.[15] Consequently, a more comprehensive and integrated view of capital is being developed,[16] as such a promising opportunity to rethink the basic premises of economics and the place of man in the total framework has almost been lost. The socio-economic factors, despite an increasing awareness of them still continue to be treated outside the mainstream of the theory of development and may perhaps remain so unless an interdisciplinary theory of development is evolved.[17]

It is instructive to observe that despite all differences in emphasis on a socio-political framework, the socialistic theory of growth also treats the problem of capital-formation and investment as the real key to growth. Both the Kalecki and Lange models assign a central role to investment.[18]

Development economics is presently passing through a period of crisis and re-evaluation. It is coming under attack from a number of directions. An increasing number of economists and planners are becoming sceptical about the whole approach of contemporary development economics.[19] There are others who consider the application of a theory based on Western experience to a different socio-economic situation, as is being done in the less developed countries, inappropriate and injurious to the prospects of development.[20] There are others who are critical of the tools and instruments of development planning and regard the alleged sophistications and mathematical refinements as pseudo-scientific inasmuch as they contain elements of simplification, abstraction and even falsification.[21] There are still some others who are becoming disenchanted with the very idea of growth – some because of its socio-economic and ecological costs[22] and others because they have begun to see the limits of growth.[23] In the light of this and other considerations it can realistically be suggested that the state of development economics today is not a very healthy one.[24] We, therefore, suggest that the central ideas of development economics and its suggested remedies deserve to be re-examined. A much more critical approach deserves to be adopted towards the panaceas that have been "sold" to the Muslim countries.

The above submissions spell out some of the negative aspects of our approach, that is, what an Islamic approach to development should not be. On the positive side we submit that our approach should be frankly ideological and value-oriented. In development economics, as in economics or in any branch of human activity, there is an area which deals with technological relationships. But such technological relationships *per se* are not the be-all and end-all of a social discipline. Technological relationships are important and they should be decided according to their own rules. But technological decisions are made in the context of value-relations. One effort is to weld these two areas and to make our values explicit and to assign to them the role of effective guide and controller. This means that as against an imitative stance, our approach must be original and creative. It is only through a thorough understanding of the social ideals and values of the Qur'ān and the *Sunnah* and a realistic assessment of our socio-economic situation – resources, problems and constraints – that we can adopt a creative, innovative strategy for change. As such our approach would be ideological as well as empirical and somewhat pragmatic – pragmatic not in the sense that ideals and values can be trimmed to suit the exigencies of the situation, but pragmatic in the sense that ideals and values are to be translated into reality in a practical and realistic way.

Islam stands for effort, struggle, movement and reconstruction – elements of social change. It is not merely a set of beliefs. It also provides a definite outlook on life and a programme for action, in a word, a comprehensive milieu for social reconstruction. We would, therefore, conclude this section by submitting some basic propositions about the dynamics of social change as they reveal themselves by reflection on the Qur'ān and the *Sunnah*. They also provide some indicators for purposes of policy.

(a) Social change is not a result of totally pre-determined historical forces. The existence of a number of obstacles and constraints is a fact of life and history, but there is no historical determinism. Change has to be planned and engineered. And this change should be purposive – that is, a movement towards the norm.
(b) Man is the active agent of change. All other forces have been subordinated to him in his capacity as God's vicegerent (*khalīfa*). Within the framework of the divine arrangement for this universe and its laws, it is man himself who is responsible for making or marring his destiny.
(c) Change consists in environmental change and change within the heart and soul of man – his attitudes, his motivation, his commitment, his resolve to mobilise all that is within him and around him for the fulfilment of his objectives.
(d) Life is a network of inter-relationships. Change means some disruption in some relationships somewhere, as there is a danger of change becoming an instrument of disequilibrium within man and in society. Islamically-oriented social change would involve least friction and disequilibria, and planned and co-ordinated movement from one state of equilibrium to a higher one, or from a state of disequilibrium towards equilibrium. As such change has to be balanced and gradual and evolutionary. Innovation is to be coupled with integration. It is this unique Islamic approach which leads to revolutionary changes through an evolutionary trajectory.

These are some of the major elements of healthy social change through which Islam wants man and society to move from one height to another.

The task before the Islamic leadership, intellectual as well as politico-economic, is to clearly formulate the objectives and strategy of change and the ways of achieving it and also to establish institutions and inaugurate processes through which these policies could be actually implemented.

Islamic Concept of Development

Now we would like to elaborate on some of the essential elements of the Islamic concept of development.

Economic development, according to the current literature on development, consists of a "series of economic activities causing an increase in the productivity of the economy as a whole and of the average worker, and also an increase in the ratio of earners to total population".[25] It is looked upon as a dynamic process, involving structural changes, which produce a significant and sustained improvement in the performance of the economy, actual as well as potential, measured usually in real per capita terms and which is spread over a fairly long period of time. Its substance lies in enabling a people to meaningfully control their economic environment so as to improve the quality of life.[26]

Islam is deeply concerned with the problem of economic development, but treats this as an important part of a wider problem, that of human development. The primary function of Islam is to guide human development on correct lines and in the right direction. It deals with all aspects of economic development but always in the framework of total human development and never in a form divorced from this perspective. This is why the focus, even in the economic sector, is on human development with the result that economic development remains an integrated and indivisible element of the moral and socio-economic development of human society.

The philosophic foundations of the Islamic approach to development, discussed by us in detail elsewhere,[27] are as follows:

(1) *Tawḥīd* (God's unity and sovereignty). This lays the rules of God-man and man-man relationship.

(2) *Rubūbiyyah* (divine arrangements for nourishment, sustenance and directing things towards their perfection). This is the fundamental law of the universe which throws light on the divine model for the useful development of resources and their mutual support and sharing. It is in the context of this divine arrangement that human efforts take place.

(3) *Khilāfah* (man's role as God's vicegerent on earth). This defines man's status and role, specifying the responsibilities of man as such, of a Muslim, and of the Muslim *ummah* as the repository of this *khilāfah*. From this follows the unique Islamic concept of man's

trusteeship, moral, political and economic, and the principles of social organisation.

(4) *Tazkiyah* (purification *plus* growth). The mission of all the prophets of God was to perform the *tazkiyah* of man in all his relationships – with God, with man, with the natural environment, and with society and the state.

We would submit that the Islamic concept of development is to be derived from its concept of *tazkiyah*, as it addresses itself to the problem of human development in all its dimensions and is concerned with growth and expansion towards perfection through purification of attitudes and relationships. The result of *tazkiyah* is *falāḥ* – prosperity in this world and the hereafter.

In the light of these foundational principles, different elements of the concept of development can be derived. We would submit the following as its essential features:

(a) The Islamic concept of development has a comprehensive character and includes moral, spiritual and material aspects. Development becomes a goal- and value-oriented activity, devoted to the optimisation of human well-being in all these dimensions. The moral and the material, the economic and the social, the spiritual and the physical are inseparable. It is not merely welfare in this world that is the objective. The welfare that Islam seeks extends to the life hereafter and there is no conflict between the two. This dimension is missing in the contemporary concept of development.

(b) The focus for development effort and the heart of the development process is man. Development, therefore, means development of man and his physical and socio-cultural environment. According to the contemporary concept it is the physical environment – natural and institutional – that provides the real area for developmental activities. Islam insists that the area of operation relates to man, within *and* without.[28] As such human attitudes, incentives, tastes and aspirations are as much policy variables as physical resources, capital, labour, education, skill, organisation, etc. Thus, on the one hand, Islam shifts the focus of effort from the physical environment to man in his social setting and on the other enlarges the scope of development policy, with the consequent enlargement of the number of target and instrument variables in any model of the economy. Another consequence of this shift in emphasis would be that maximum participation of the people at all levels of decision-making and plan-implementation would be stipulated.

(c) Economic development is a multi-dimensional activity,[29] more so in an Islamic framework. As efforts would have to be made simultaneously in a number of directions, the methodology of isolating one key factor and almost exclusive concentration on that would be theoretically untenable. Islam seeks to establish a balance between the different factors and forces.

(d) Economic development involves a number of changes, quantitative as well as qualitative. Involvement with the quantitative, justified and necessary in its own right, has unfortunately led to the neglect of the qualitative aspects of development in particular and of life in general. Islam would try to rectify this imbalance.

(e) Among the dynamic principles of social life Islam has particularly emphasised two: First, the optimal utilisation of resources that God has endowed to man and his physical environment, and secondly, their equitable use and distribution and promotion of all human relationships on the basis of Right and Justice. Islam commends the value of *shukr* (thankfulness to God by availing of His blessings) and *'adl* (justice) and condemns the disvalues of *kufr* (denial of God and His blessings) and *ẓulm* (injustice).

In the light of this analysis the development process is mobilised and activated through *shukr* and *'adl* and is disrupted and distorted by *kufr* and *ẓulm*.[30]

This is basically different from the approach of those who look upon production and distribution in either/or relationship with the development process and is a much wider and more dynamic concept than that of the role of production and distribution in development. The developmental effort, in an Islamic framework, is directed towards the development of a God-conscious human being, a balanced personality committed to and capable of acting as the witness of Truth to mankind.

We may, therefore, submit that in an Islamic framework economic development is a goal-oriented and value-realising activity, involving a confident and all-pervading participation of man and directed towards the maximisation of human well-being in all its aspects and building the strength of the *ummah* so as to discharge in the world its role as God's vicegerent on earth and as "the mid-most people". Development would mean moral, spiritual and material development of the individual and society leading to maximum socio-economic welfare and the ultimate good of mankind.

Goals of Development Policy

In the light of this concept we can formulate in some detail the general goals of development policy and the more specific targets for a developmental plan for a Muslim society.

(A) *Human resource development* should be the first objective of our developmental policy. This would include the inculcation of correct attitudes and aspirations, development of character and personality, education and training producing skills needed for different activities, promotion of knowledge and research, and evolution of mechanisms for responsible and creative participation by the common people in key developmental activities, in decision-making at all levels and finally in sharing the fruits of development. This would call for a high priority for the expansion and Islamisation of education and for the general moral orientation of the people and for evolving a new structure of relationships based on co-operation, co-sharing and co-participation. This would also entail a highly efficient machinery for the mobilisation of human resources and the inculcation of a spirit of self-sacrifice and the individual's maximum contribution towards the achievement of social goals.

(B) *Expansion of useful production.* Continuous and sustained increase in the national produce would be an important objective, but our concern would be on the one hand, with the quantum and efficiency of production, and on the other with the achievement of a correct product-mix. Production would not mean production of anything and everything which may have a demand or which the rich may be able to buy; production would be concerned with things which are useful for man in the light of the value-pattern of Islam and the general experience of mankind. The production of all those things whose use is forbidden in Islam would not be allowed; those whose use is discouraged, their production would be discouraged, and all that is essential and useful would be given priority and encouragement. In the light of this policy, the pattern of production and investment would be moulded according to the priorities of Islam and the needs of the *ummah*. We feel that three priority areas would be:

(i) Abundant production and supply of food and basic items of necessity (including construction material for building houses and roads and basic raw materials) at reasonably cheap prices.
(ii) Defence requirements of the Muslim world.
(iii) Self-sufficiency in the production of basic capital goods.

(C) *Improvement of the quality of life.* Efforts should be made towards improving the real levels of living of *all* people and towards the achievement of their moral, economic and social welfare. This would call for a high priority for at least the following:

(i) Employment creation, with all its consequent structural, technological, investmental, regional and educational adjustments.
(ii) An effective and broad-based system of social security, assuring the basic necessities of life for all those who are unable to undertake gainful employment or otherwise deserve society's help and assistance. *Zakāt* should be the nucleus of this system.
(iii) Equitable distribution of income and wealth. There would be an

active income policy directed towards raising the income level of the lowest income groups, reducing the ratio of inequality concentration in society, and leading to a greater diffusion of wealth and power in society in general. A reduction in the extent of income differentials would also be one of the indicators of developmental performance. To serve this purpose the tax system will also have to be reorganised.

(D) *Balanced development*, that is balanced and harmonious development of different regions within a country and of the different sectors of society and the economy. Decentralisation of the economy and proper development of all parts and sectors is not only a demand of justice, but is also essential for maximum progress. This would also remedy economic dualism from which most of the Muslim countries suffer and would lead to greater integration within each country. This is an area in which principles of regional analysis and use of developments in the fields of econometric techniques and input-output analysis can be immensely useful.

(E) *New technology*, that is evolution of indigenous technology, suited to the conditions, needs and aspirations of the Muslim countries. The development process would become self-sustained only when we become not only independent of foreign aid, but when after mastering the technology that has grown in a different economic and cultural environment we are able to internalise the process of technological creativity and begin to produce technology that bears the stamp of our distinctness. This would call for a high priority for research and a new spirit to face the challenges of our times.

(F) *Reduction of national dependency on the outside world and greater integration within the Muslim world.* It is a direct demand of the *ummah's* position as *khalīfah* that its dependence upon the non-Muslim world in all essentials must be changed to a state of economic independence, self-respect and gradual building-up of strength and power[31]. The defence and independence of the Muslim world and the peace and serenity of mankind are objectives that reign prominently in our developmental planning.

If these are to be the objectives of our developmental policy then we will have to make some major changes in the content and methodology of our developmental planning. Some areas where new approaches and new techniques will have to be evolved are as follows:

(a) We will have to abandon the use of all those simplified aggregative growth models which concentrate on the maximisation of the growth-rate as the sole index of development as basis for planning. The limitations of these models and of exclusive concentration on the growth-rates are being increasingly realised by development economists.[32] But we will have to undertake a much more fundamental and thorough re-examination of the entire apparatus of planometrics.[33] Our problem is extensive development of technical capacity to formulate operational plans to achieve our socio-economic objectives and to evolve new techniques through which we may arrive at more realistic decisions in the fields of investment planning, incomes and wages policy, location and regional development, reconstruction of tax structure and policy and in the evaluation of developmental performance. The writer feels that in the first phase we may avoid using growth-models for purposes of actual decision-making, although we may continue to experiment with them at a more theoretical level and further intensify our search for more appropriate techniques. In the meanwhile, on an experimental basis, techniques of system analysis and of input-output analysis (with a much widened matrix which may include a number of social inputs and outputs, as is also being suggested by some planners),[34] may be tried and further developed. Similarly efforts may be made to develop a series of composite indexes to measure the effects of developmental effort on different social and economic indicators (each given certain weight in the light of its position in our priority matrix), which should include indicators that may reveal aspects of the moral health of the nation (e.g., crime rate, divorce rate, level of corruption, litigation rate in selected areas, participation rate, industrial disputes, etc.). A number of efforts are being made in this direction[35] and there is no reason why we cannot give these techniques a more useful and meaningful twist.

(b) We have to adopt a multi-objective approach to development. Instead of being bogged down in econometric approaches whose usefulness is doubtful, it may be advisable to develop a more problem-oriented approach and evaluate the success of planning and development efforts on the basis of improvements in specific problem areas.

(c) Given the conditions of international instabilities and exploitation, of internal imperfections and market deformities and the tremendous demands of developmental efforts, it is suggested that the Muslim countries and a number of new social institutions and organisations specially established for specific objectives should play a much more positive role. At the moment governments are ill-equipped to perform this role as are private individuals. But it is easier for a government to remedy its weaknesses and establish institutions which can rectify the situation. Since one of the objectives of policy would be decentralisation, we would submit that local government authorities should be developed with a more powerful base in the local population, with greater participation from the people and with a system of checks and balances and national vigilance and guidance to make them unique agencies for multi-purpose development. Even though comprehensive planning should be resorted to, it would be inadvisable to proceed in that direction without achieving efficient decentralisation of power and control and without reducing the bureaucratisation of society. We believe that small- and medium-scale private enterprise should be encouraged and developed. Local and regional authorities should not become substitutes for small and medium private enterprise; they should create the proper environment for work and development and undertake all that is needed for purposes of efficient and equitable growth of this type of enterprise. They should, however, undertake the enterprises which call for larger investment and organisation and should act as national-service institutions and not degenerate into profit-making public corporations. Profit should not be the purpose of these agencies. They should be genuine instruments for value-oriented economic development and the distribution of the benefits of development to the people.

(d) Research and Planning. Another very important area is the organisation of short-period and long-period (more basic) research to think out problems and ways to seek creative solutions, reorganisation and development of statistics, and planned growth of research organisations in areas where they are needed to prepare more realistic plans for the future. We need a new strategy for research to serve the ideological demands of the future.

Notes and Sources

1 See Pearson, Lester B., *Partners in Development*, London: Pall Mall, 1969, pp. 27–72, and annex 1, pp. 231–353; Amin, Galal A., *The Modernisation of Poverty: A Study in the Political Economy of Growth in Nine Arab Countries*, 1945–1970, Leiden: E. J. Brill, 1974.

2 See Prebisch, R., *Towards a New Trade Policy for Development*, New York: United Nations, 1964. For a review of the overall situation of the Muslim countries see Cook, M. A. (ed), *Studies in the Economic History of the Middle East from the Rise of Islam to the Present Day*, London: Oxford University Press, 1970, pp. 373–427; Baster, James, *The Introduction of Western Economic Institutions into the Middle East*, *Chatham House Memoranda*, London: Oxford University Press, 1960; Hershlag, Z. Y., *Introduction of the Modern Economic History of the Middle East*, London: Oxford University Press, 1964; World Muslim Congress, *Some Economic Resources of the Muslim Countries*, Karachi: Umma Publications, 1961. For overall background, see also Cook, M. A. "Economic Developments", in Schacht, Joseph and Bosworth, C. E. (ed.), *The Legacy of Islam*, Oxford, 1974, pp. 210–43.

3 See Hershlag, Z. Y., "Growth Models for the Middle East", in Cook, M. A. (ed.), *Studies in the Economic History of the Middle East*, op. cit., pp. 373–96; Myrdal, Gunnar, *Asian Drama, An Inquiry into the Poverty of Nations*, London: Allen Lane, 1968, vol. III, Appendix 3, pp. 1843–2003.

4 Egypt (1958–70) and Syria represent this category. See Lange, Oscar, *Economic Development Planning and International Co-operation*, Cairo: Central Bank of Egypt, 1961; Falkowski, Meczslaw, "Socialist Economists and the Developing Countries", *Polish Perspective*, Warsaw, vol. X (March 1967) reprinted in Shaffer, H. G., and Pryble, Jan, S. (eds.), *From Under-development to Affluence: Western, Soviet and Chinese Views*, New York: Appleton-Century Crofts, 1968.

5 See Amin, Galal, A., *The Modernisation of Poverty*, op. cit.; Jamā'at-i Islāmī, *Economy Committee Report*, Karachi, 1964 (mimeo).

6 See Waardenburg, J. D. J., "Notes on Islam and Development", *Exchange* (Netherlands), 1973, pp. 3–45; Alfian, "Religion and the Problem of Economic Development in Indonesia", *Indonesia* Magazine, no. 9 (1971), pp. 16–26; Geertz, Clifford, "Modernisation in a Muslim Society: The Indonesian Case", in Bellah, Robert N., *Religion and Progress in Modern Asia*, New York: The Free Press, 1965, pp. 93–108; Rodinson, Maxime, *Islam and Capitalism*, London: Allen Lane, 1974. For a recent empirical study evaluating the relationship of religion and economic and social development see Adelman, Irma and Morris, Cynthia Taft, *Economic Growth and Social Equity in Developing Countries*, Stanford University Press, 1973, pp. 38–39. Cf. the views of some Muslim scholars, e.g., Rahman, Fazlur, "The Impact of Modernity on Islam" in Jurji, Edward J. (ed.), *Religious Pluralism and World Communications*, Leiden: E. J. Brill, 1969, pp. 248–262; and Arkun, Muhammad, "Islam Facing Development", mimeographed paper circulated at JCM European Conference on East-West Relations (November 1974).

7 See Mawdūdī, Abul A'lā, "Islāmī Niẓām-i Ma'īshat kē Uṣūl awr Maqāṣid" (Principles and Objectives of the Islamic Economic Order) in Mawdūdī: *Ma'āshiyāt-i Islām*, Lahore: Islamic Publications, 1969, pp. 141–164; Siddiqi, M. N., *Some Aspects of the Islamic Economy*, Lahore: Islamic Publications Ltd., 1970 (Ch. III: "The Quranic Norm", pp. 27–40); Chapra, M. Umar, *Economic System of Islam*, London: Islamic Cultural Centre, 1970. For a brief but candid review of this aspect of literature on Islamic economics see Siddiqi, M. N., "A Survey of Contemporary Literature on Islamic Economics", mimeographed paper presented to the International Conference on Islamic Economy held at Makka (February 1976), pp. 20–21 and 70–73.

8 The *Jamā'at-i Islāmī* Pakistan tried to suggest an alternative strategy in its *Manifesto for the 1970 Elections*. It is brief but succinct and thoughtful. The Economic Programme Committee of the *Jamā'at-i Islāmī* Pakistan tried to prepare a more comprehensive statement of Islam's economic strategy. See *Mawjūdah Ma'āshī Buḥrān awr Islāmī Ḥikmat-i Ma'īshat* (The Contemporary Economic Crisis and Islam's Economic Strategy), Lahore: *Jamā'at-i Islāmī* Pakistan, n.d. (1970). A recent doctoral dissertation makes a similar effort in the context of the problems of environmental engineering. See Hussaini, S. Waqar Ahmad, *Principles of Environmental Engineering System Planning in Islamic Culture: Law, Politics, Economics, Education and Sociology of Science and Culture*, presented to Stanford University, California, 1971. See particularly ch. VI. See also Ṣiddīqī, Na'īm, "Islām kā Mīzānī Naẓarīyah-i Ma'īshat" (Islam's Balanced Ideology of Economics) in *Chirāgh-i Rāh: Socialism Number*, Karachi, 1967, pp. 496–525.

9 Gunnar Myrdal writes in *Asian Drama* (op. cit., vol. I, pp. 31–32): "The problem of objectivity in research cannot be solved simply by attempting to eradicate valuations . . . every study of a social problem, however limited in scope, is and must be determined by valuations. A 'disinterested' social science has never existed and never will exist. Research like every other rationally pursued activity, must have a direction. The viewpoint and the direction are determined by one's interest in a matter. Valuations enter into the choice of approach, the selection of problems, the definition of concepts, and the gathering of data, and are by no means confined to the practical or political inferences drawn from theoretical findings. The value

premises that actually and of necessity determine approaches in the social sciences can be hidden. In fact, most writings, particularly in economics, remain in large part simply ideological . . . Throughout the history of social studies, the hiding of valuations has served to conceal the inquirer's wish to avoid facing real issues" . . . See also Myrdal, G., *Value in Social Theory: A Selection of Essays on Methodology*, London [c. 1958].

10 Myrdal, G., *Asian Drama*, op. cit., p. 33.

11 A number of development economists have confessed that development planning cannot be ideologically neutral and that development economics is a "normative" discipline. Dudley Seers says that development is "inevitably a normative term" (Seers, D. "The Meaning of Development", *International Development Review*, December, 1969, p. 2). Galbraith asserts that "Economic development is an intrinsically normative subject" (Galbraith, John K., *The Underdeveloped Country*, Toronto: Canadian Broadcasting Corpn., 1965, p. 20); Lauchlin Currie says that in the field of development "a non-normative approach is especially sterile". (Currie, L. *Obstacles to Development*, East Lansing: Michigan State University Press, 1967), p. 45.

12 For a more detailed discussion, see Ahmad, Khurshid, *Socialism yā Islām* (Socialism or Islam), Karachi: Chirāgh-i Rāh Publications, 1969.

13 See Ahmad, Khurshid, "The Third World's Dilemma of Development", *Non-aligned Third World Annual*, edited by Andrew Carvely, St. Louis, Missouri: Books International, 1970, pp. 3–18. See also Myrdal, *Asian Drama*, op. cit., particularly vol. I, pp. 5–35, vol. II, pp. 709–955, vol. III, pp. 1843–2003. See also Viner, Jacob, "The Economics of Development", in Agarwala and Singh, *The Economics of Underdevelopment*, Bombay: Oxford University Press, 1958; Kuznets, Simon, "Underdeveloped Countries and the Pre-Industrial Phase in the Advanced Countries", in Agarwala and Singh, *ibid.*, pp. 135–153; Welch, Claude E., "The Challenge of Change: Japan and Africa", in Spiro, Herbert, J., *Patterns of African Development: Five Comparisons*, Englewood Cliffs, N. J.: Prentice Hall Inc., 1967, pp. 63–90.

14 "Post-Keynsian capitalist growth theory for the mature economy generically has insisted in placing capital accumulation at centre stage and focussing on the resultant secular increases in labour productivity. It has consistently emphasised the twin conditions governing such increases; the willingness of a society to refrain from consumption and the fact that the investment into which savings may be channelled will result in increased productive capacity along with increased flows of income. In the language of the Harrod-Domar tradition, it is the propensity to save and the marginal capital output ratio which determine the growth rate. One hardly needs to be reminded that the body of contemporary capitalist growth theory consists of a series of extensions and modifications of this basic Harrod-Domar relationship." Gustav Ranis, "Theories of Economic Growth in Capitalist Countries", *Problems in Economic Development*, ed. E. A. G. Robinson, London: Macmillan, 1965, p. 4. For a brief but precise review of contemporary growth theory see Ranis, loc. cit.; also idem, "Economic Growth: Theory", *International Encyclopaedia of Social Sciences*, vol. IV, London: Macmillan, 1968, pp. 408–17; Hahn and Matthew, "Theories of Economic Growth: A Survey", *Surveys of Economic Theory*, vol. II, London: Macmillan, 1965; Kregel, J. A., *The Theory of Economic Growth*, London: Macmillan, 1972.

15 Schultz, Theodore W., "Investment in Human Capital", *American Economic Review*, vol. 51 (March 1961), pp. 1–17; idem, *The Economic Value of Education*, New York: Columbia University Press, 1963; Schultz, *et al.*, "On Investment in Human Beings" *Journal of Political Economy*, vol. 20, no. 4 (1962); Morgan, Theodore, "Investment versus Economic Growth", *Economic Development and Cultural Change*, vol. 17 (April 1969), pp. 392–414.

16 Johnson, Harry G., "Comments on Mr. John Vaizey's paper", *The Residual Factor and Economic Growth*, ed., John Vaizey, Paris: OECD, 1964.

17 For a critical appraisal of the economic and other social sciences from the viewpoint of their contribution to development theory see Hetzler, Stanley A., *Technological Growth and Social Change*, London: Routledge and Kegan Paul, 1969, ch. 5, "Other Social Science Hypotheses on Development". For a thorough critique of the development theory, see Myrdal, *Asian Drama*, op. cit., Appendix 3 and Currie, Lauchlin, *Accelerating Development*, New York: McGraw-Hill [c. 1966], chs. 2 and 3.

18 For a review of the major socialistic theories of growth, see Lange, Oscar, *Economic Development Planning and International Co-operation*, Cairo: Central Bank of Egypt, 1961, p. 10; Brus, W. and Laski, K., "Problems in the Theory of Growth under Socialism", in Robinson (ed.), *Problems in Economic Development*, op. cit., pp. 21–54; Brenner, Y. S., *Theories of Economic Development and Growth*, London: George Allen and Unwin, 1966, pp. 223–47.

19 See Martin, Kurt and Knapp, John (eds.), *The Teaching of Development Economics*, Chicago: Aldine, 1967, Part IA and Part IIA; Myrdal, *Asian Drama*, op. cit.; Streeton, Paul, *The Frontiers of Development Studies*, London: Macmillan, 1973. Schumacher, E. F., *Small is Beautiful: A Study of Economics as if People Mattered*, London: Blond Briggs, 1973.

20 See Baur, P. T., *Dissent on Development*, London: Weidenfeld and Nicolson, 1971; Seers, Dudley, "The Limitations of the Special Case", in Martin and Knapp, op. cit.

21 Mynt, H., "Economic Theory and Development Policy", *Economics*, May 1967, pp. 117–30; Vernon, Raymond, "Comprehensive Model-Building in the Planning Process: The Less Developed Economics", *The Economical Journal*, March, 1966, pp. 57–69.

22 See Mishan, E. J., *The Costs of Economic Growth*, London: Staple Press, 1967; Hodson, H. V., *The Diseconomics of Growth*, London: Earth Island, 1972.

23 Meadows, Dennis, *et al.*, *The Limits to Growth*, New York: A Potomac Associate Book, Universe Books, 1972; Mesarovic, Mahajli and Pestel, Edward, *Mankind at the Turning Point: The Second Report to the Club of Rome*, New York: E. P. Dutton, rev., 1974. The debate on this issue is vast and proliferating. For a critique of this line of attack see Beckerman, Wilfred, *In Defence of Economic Growth*, London: Jonathan Cape, 1974.

24 For a more detailed discussion of this issue by this writer see "The Third World's Dilemma of Development", *Non-aligned Third World Annual*, St. Louis: Books International of DHTE International Inc., 1970, pp. 3–18. For a recent brief but succinct statement see Adelman, Irma, "On the State of Development Economics", *Journal of Development Economics*, 1974, pp. 3–5.

25 Bonné, Alfred, *Studies in Economic Development*, London: Routledge and Kegan Paul, 1960, p. 250.

26 See Burton, Henry J., *Principles of Development Economics*, Englewood Cliffs: Prentice-Hall Inc., 1965, pp. 2–3; Kindleburger, Charles P., *Economic Development*, New York: McGraw-Hill 1965, ch. I; Hagen, Everil, *The Economics of Development*, Homewood, Illinois: Richard D. Irwin, 1968, ch. 2; Lewis, Arthur, *The Theory of Economic Growth*, London: George Allen and Unwin, 1955, pp. 420–35; Kuznets, Simon, *Six Lectures on Economical Growth*, Glencoe, Ia: The Free Press of Glencoe, 1959, ch. 1.

27 See this writer's *Islam and the Contemporary Economic Challenge*, mimeographed paper presented to the International Youth Seminar, Riyadh, December, 1973.

28 "God does not change the condition of a people unless they first change that which is in themselves" (The Qur'ān, 13: 11).

29 This is being increasingly realised by development economists. One of the lessons, insists Max F. Millikan, we must learn from the developmental experiences of

mankind is to see development "as a systematic interaction of a large number of elements". See Millikan, Max F., "A Strategy of Development", in U.N., *The Case for Development*, New York: Praeger Special Studies, 1973, p. 25.

30 The Qur'ān says: "It is God who has created the heaven and the earth. He sends down rain from the skies, and with it brings out fruits to feed you. It is He who has made the ships subject to you, that you may sail through the sea by His command. He has also harnessed the rivers for you. And also the sun and the moon, both diligently pursuing their courses. He has subdued for you the day and the night and has given you of all that you ask for. If you try to count God's favours to you, you would never be able to count them all. But man is given up to injustice and ingratitude" (14: 33–34). In the context of this divine policy for human sustenance and development, it is very important to say *inna al-insāna la-ẓalūmun kaffār*. This refers to things that disrupt and destroy the process of human development. Reference as to the disvalues of ingratitude, i.e., non-utilisation of what God has given, and injustice, i.e., their misuse in the social sense, see al-Ṣadr, M. Bāqar, *Iqtiṣāadunā* (Beirut, 1968).

31 See the Qur'ānic injunction: "Against them make ready your strength to the utmost of your power, including steeds of war, to strike terror into (the hearts of) the enemies of God and your enemies and others besides whom you may not know" (8: 61).

32 See U.N., *The Case for Development*, op. cit., particularly chs. 1 to 3. A joint study by the World Bank Research Centre and the Institute of Development Studies, Sussex, *Redistribution with Growth* (Hollis Chenery, Montex Ahluwalia, C. Bell, John Dulcy and Richard Jolly), London: Oxford University Press, 1974, breathes some fresh air into the debate although the canvas still remains very limited.

33 We owe this term to a UNESCO study on recent developments in Social Sciences: *Main Trends in Human and Social Sciences*, Netherlands: Mouton, 1970.

34 See Pajestkr, Joseph, "Social Dimensions of Development", in U.N., *The Case for Development*, op. cit.

35 See Adelman, Irma and Morris, C. T., *Economic Growth and Social Equity in Developing Countries*, op. cit.; Hakamori, H. and Yamashita, S., "Measuring Socio-Economic Development Indicators, Development Paths and International Comparisons", *The Developing Economics*, Japan, vol. XI, no. 2 (July, 1973), pp. 111–45; Drewnowsky, J., *Studies in the Measurement of Levels and Welfare*, Geneva: UN Research Institute for Social Development, 1970.

PART II

Surveys on Islamic Economics

CHAPTER TEN

Muslim Economic Thinking: A Survey of Contemporary Literature

*Dr. Muhammad Nejatullah Siddiqi**

Introduction

ALTHOUGH Muslim thinkers have discussed the economic principles of Islam earlier, exclusive attention to the subject is a twentieth century phenomenon. It started in the third decade and specialised works appeared in the fourth. Part of the provocation was provided by the worldwide economic crisis during the thirties and forties and the increasing exposure of the Muslim mind to the Socialist doctrines, and the impact of the Russian Revolution. There was a great spurt in these writings during the fifties and the sixties which is related to the emergence of a number of independent Muslim countries, and the rise of a powerful Islamic Movement which raised hopes of serious attention to the application of the Islamic teachings in the practical affairs of the new states. At this stage general discussion on the economic philosophy of Islam is supplemented by efforts at system formulation and discussions on specific issues relevant to modern life. Analytical study of the economic injunctions of Islam and an analytical approach to the criticism of modern institutions from the Islamic viewpoint is comparatively recent in origin, though it is receiving more and more attention.

The modern institutions of banking, insurance, joint stock companies, stock exchange and progressive taxation called for a response from Muslim thinkers and jurists (i.e. ulema specialising in *fiqh*) as they appeared in these Muslim countries and started involving the religious masses. A review of these institutions in the light of the *Sharī'ah*, a search for alternatives in case some of them were found repugnant to Islam, and for arguments for the legitimacy of those which could be accommodated, led to

*Dr. Nejatullah Siddiqi is Professor of Economics and Head of Department of Islamic Studies, Aligarh Muslim University, Aligarh. Dr. Siddiqi is amongst the pioneers of Islamic Economics and has authored over half a dozen works on different aspects of Islamic Economics. Presently he is on sabbatical leave working with the International Centre for Research in Islamic Economics, King Abdul Aziz University, Jeddah.

many works on the subject. By the very nature of this background, the discussions were more juridical than economic.

Most of these writers were ulema or journalists with little knowledge of economics. The system of education the Muslim countries had inherited from Imperial Powers had scrupulously segregated Islamic education from modern education and there were no arrangements for producing a trained economist who had direct access to the Islamic sources. This inhibited professional economists from making any significant contributions to the subject. It also accounts for the fact that the ulema who found themselves constrained to discuss the subject failed to do justice to it. The first works on the subject by professional economists appeared in English in the late forties of this century, but these writers had to rely on secondary sources so far as Islamic injunctions are concerned. Even now when we have quite a number of economists fully equipped to draw upon the original sources of Islam, the subject lacks the most crucial support required for its proper growth – teaching in Universities. Modern economics, as we now understand the term, is largely the handiwork of University teachers in Economics. But Islamic Economics is not a subject being taught at the post-graduate level anywhere in the wide world – with the sole exception of a few universities in Egypt and Pakistan, where both the syllabus and the teaching facilities leave much to be desired.

The institutional framework of a society has a direct bearing on research in Social Sciences, particularly in Economics. The institutions that developed in the Imperialist regimes were alien to the Islamic framework of the society and the economy, and therefore no serious thinking by the professional economist could be directed towards Islamic Economics. The ulema also discussed the economic problems without the actual framework operating on the tenets of Islam. Islamic Economics lacked the live relationship with real life which was a prerequisite to its growth. There was no testing ground for the various hypotheses being formulated and no empirical evidence upon which to draw while making formulations.

In this historical situation it would have made a big difference if a clear commitment to the economic philosophy of Islam had come from some of the new independent Muslim countries. But even this has been lacking till now, and many writers on the subject aimed at soliciting such a commitment from their people and governments, through their writings. They took on themselves the task of convincing their readers of the desirability and viability of the Islamic economic system. They have yet to be called upon to manage the economy and solve its actual problems in the light of Islamic injunctions.

These are some of the important facts to be kept in mind while surveying the literature on Islamic Economics as they explain many of its important features, and the relative emphasis placed on the various issues under discussion. There are indications of some change in the situation described above as evidenced by the increasing attention paid to Islamic economics, both at the popular and the official level. This too is reflected in the recent contributions on such subjects as interest-free banking, *Zakāt* and social security. Analytical study conscious of its relevance to practical affairs is gradually replacing philosophical dissertations on the comparative virtues of the Islamic system, which augurs well for the future growth of the literature.

This survey covers the three principal languages in which the bulk of the literature on our subject has appeared in the last half century – Arabic, Urdu and English. Some contributions were made in the Persian, Turkish, French and Indonesian languages, which are planned to be surveyed separately. Multiplicity of languages coupled with deficient communications has also affected the growth of thinking on the subject. No efficient translation and abstraction services have been available. We do not have a single journal exclusively devoted to our subject. Very few review articles are published on the contributions that are made. There have been no across-the-table discussions at seminars and academic conferences. As a result our writers have had few opportunities of knowing each other's views and of benefiting from scholarly criticism. One finds the same points being made again and again in different languages at different times, while a promising idea suggested by one thinker has to wait for quite a long time before it is taken up by some other writer to develop further. There is controversy but little criticism, there are many opinions but few conclusions arrived at after systematic discussion. The implications of such a state of affairs for the "survey" are obvious.

Constraints of time and space make it necessary to keep this study brief. It has not been possible to go into the details of the subjects discussed in the survey. It was considered specially desirable to avoid details where these details were more juridical in nature than economic. For the sake of brevity we had also to exclude from this survey works on economic history and those relating to the economic problems of the present-day Muslim countries.

A survey of contributions relating to the entire area of economics raises serious methodological problems. One is always left with a feeling that a more suitable scheme could be evolved. It is hoped that in future the different topics covered in this study will be surveyed separately and more critically by some economists.

As a glance at the table of contents would reveal, we begin with a brief consideration of the economic philosophy of Islam, followed by the general outlines of the economic system of Islam. Specific aspects of the economic system which might attract greater attention from economists have been treated separately at some length in the third section. We have tried to focus attention on analytical discussions by dealing with them in two separate sections: Islamic critique of contemporary economic theories and systems, and development of economic analysis in an Islamic framework. The last section notes contributions on the history of economic thought in Islam.

An economist reading the first two sections may feel that undue importance is being attached to views relating to ownership, ends of economic enterprise and the code of conduct for various economic agents. These subjects do not figure very prominently in modern economics as certain views have been accepted long since and nobody feels like questioning them. The concern of Islamic economists with these basic issues is borne of their feeling that the divergence of Islamic economic thinking from the other schools of thought is rooted in this area. They also think that these are the foundation stones for the development of the institutions favourable for the growth of the society and the economy according to Islamic values.

This survey covers books as well as the periodical literature. In the circumstances it is not possible to claim that one knows about each and every contribution to the subject. This is especially true of the papers contributed to the numerous popular journals in the three languages. Yet, I do hope that I have not missed many of them, as a glance at the bibliography will show.

We have generally avoided mention of particular authors when recording a view that is held unanimously. Specific contributions are noted when a subject is controversial or because of their originality.

This survey was completed in December, 1974 for presentation at the First International Conference on Islamic Economics scheduled for March, 1975. The Conference was eventually held in February, 1976 and more than sixty papers were presented on various aspects of Islamic Economics. In revising this survey for publication due notice has been taken of these contributions, along with such other recent works as were available to the writer.

The Bibliography originally appended to this survey has now been replaced by its improved version published separately by the U.K. Islamic Foundation.[1] All numbers appearing in parenthesis in the text of the survey refer to this printed bibliography. The figure following the colon indicates the page number of the reference cited. Other references appear as footnotes. The bibliography is being appended to this survey for ready reference.

I

ECONOMIC PHILOSOPHY OF ISLAM

The key to economic philosophy of Islam lies in man's relationship with God, His universe and His people, i.e. other human beings, and the nature and purpose of man's life on earth. Man–God relationship is defined by *Tawḥīd*. The essence of *Tawḥīd* is a total commitment to the will of Allah, involving both submission and a mission to pattern human life in accordance with His will. The will of Allah constitutes the source of value and becomes the end of human endeavour. Life on earth is a test, and its purpose should be to prove successful in the test by doing Allah's will. The entire Universe with all the natural resources and powers is made amenable to exploitation by man, though it is owned by Allah and Allah alone. Life on earth being a test and all the provisions available to man being in the nature of a trust, man is accountable to Allah and his success in the life hereafter depends on his performance in this life on earth. This adds a new dimension to the valuation of things and deeds in this life.

With every human being sharing the same relationship with God and His Universe, a definite relationship between man and man is also prescribed. This is a relationship of brotherhood and equality. "*Tawḥīd* is a coin with two faces: one implies that Allah is the Creator and the other that men are equal partners or that each man is brother to another man." (7: 35).

While the writers on the subject agree on this basic philosophy, one finds variety of emphasis in their elaboration of the last-mentioned point: the relationship between man and man in sharing the bounties of Allah. It is agreed that for the test life is to be conducted in fair circumstances and no one should go without an adequate share of resources that are needed for survival and a good life. Equality of opportunity and social care of the disabled is the minimum that this calls for. They differ, however, regarding the mode of equal or equitable sharing of these resources by individuals, and the degree of social control necessary – a subject we take up later on.

It is also agreed that Islam rejects asceticism and a good life means, among other things, a materially well provisioned life. Basing his argument on two clear verses of the Qur'ān,[2] another writer declares that sufficiency (*Kifāyāh*) and peace (*amn*) are the two inalienable features of the good life envisaged by Allah (77, 1: 6–9), a point that finds the widest support in the literature on the subject (73: 24).

Economic Enterprise

The above philosophy provides the proper perspective to man's economic activities. No inhibitions attach to economic enterprise. Men are encouraged to avail themselves of the vast opportunities of productive enterprise afforded by the almost limitless bounties of Allah:

> "And if ye would count the bounty of Allah ye can not reckon it."
> (XIV: 34)

Every writer on the subject cites verses from the Qur'ān and traditions from the Prophet to show that agriculture, trade, commerce and industry and the various forms of productive enterprise known in the early days of Islam have been explicitly mentioned in this context. What is crucial, however, is the motivation, the ends of economic activity. Given the right motivation all economic activity assumes the character of worship (*'Ibādah*).

Many writers discuss the proper ends of economic enterprise in detail. These ends may be individual or social. Legitimate individual ends include the fulfilment of personal needs and those of the family. Saving to provide for the future and the desire to leave an inheritance are also recognised as proper ends of productive effort. The minimum necessary for survival is in fact a duty to earn. While no maxima are fixed in quantitative terms, moderation in fulfilment of these needs is emphasised and greed, avarice and the unsatiable yearning for more and more comforts and luxuries is decried.

Moderation is generally defined with reference to the negative concepts of extravagance (*isrāf*) and expenditure on goods and services prohibited by Islam (*tabdhīr*). Indulgence in luxurious living and the desire to show off is condemned (29: 438–453; 120: 68–73). Islam cannot tolerate conspicuous consumption of the leisure class (62: 141–144).

Recent writings on economic enterprise attach great importance to the social ends, which are summed up by the phrase "striving in the cause of Allah". Eradication of hunger and poverty, disease and illiteracy and mobilisation of resources for strengthening the Islamic state and spreading the message of Allah are stated to be the laudible aims of individual economic activities. One who engages in productive activities for these purposes is doing God's will, and is promised adequate rewards here and hereafter (77, 1: 130–138; 24; 619: 25–30; 477). The authors of the *Jamā'at-i-Islāmī* Pakistan Economic Committee Report regard it an end of economic enterprise "to make the Islamic society economically strong so that it develops and is able to compete successfully with other economies the world over" (125: 26).

It is pointed out that in view of the limitless nature of the social ends of enterprise, as against the limited nature of the individual ends, economic enterprise as such is afforded limitless scope and utmost encouragement.

Ownership

The nature and scope of ownership has been one of the most discussed subjects in the literature on Islamic Economics, works exclusively devoted to the subject being available in a number of languages. Every important writer has touched on the subject and all the different approaches to an Islamic reorganisation of the modern economy show themselves in their treatment of property rights in Islam. Below we shall try first to state what is generally agreed upon and then to differentiate between specific contributions.

Real ownership belongs to Allah, man holds property in trust for which he is accountable to Him, in accordance with rules clearly laid down in the *Sharī'ah* and the economic philosophy underlined above. Acquisition of property as well as its uses and disposal are subject to limits set and should be guided by the norms laid down by Allah. Absolute ownership of man is a concept alien to Islam, as it belongs to Allah alone. There are definite obligations towards others attending upon the individual rights of ownership. Besides private property, public ownership is a central concept in Islam. The respective scopes of the two are not rigidly defined but left to be determined in the light of certain principles, depending on the needs and circumstances (3: 8; 62: 111–119, 160–162; 70: 80; 134; 158: 41–90; 171: 150).

Differences centre around three main points:

(a) the central position of private ownership;
(b) the relative scopes of public and private ownership;
(c) the degree of social control on private ownership rights and the circumstances justifying abrogation or abridgement of such rights.

Some writers assert that the Real Owner has bestowed ownership rights to the whole of human society, in the first place and it is wrong to give individual ownership a central position in the Islamic economic system. They stand for social ownership of land and other natural resources, confining private property to articles of consumption, living quarters and the like. Perwez (60) and Nasir A. Sheikh (154: 139–225) in Pakistan and some Arab socialists take that position.

While this extreme socialistic position does not find sizable support in the literature, and is generally rejected as an unsuccessful attempt to mould Islam according to socialism, there are eminent authorities denying a central place to individual ownership rights. The martyr, 'Abd al-Qādir 'Audah deserves quoting at length in this context:

> "The society (*Jamā'ah*) through its functionaries such as rulers and counsellors has the authority to organise the ways and means of utilising wealth. All wealth belongs to Allah but Allah has made it for the good of the society. The rule in Islam is that all rights belonging to Allah are for the good of the society which sits in authority over them, and not the individuals.
>
> "The society, through the rulers representing it, can, when the public interest demands, abrogate the individual ownership of benefits of a property, subject to the condition that a suitable compensation is paid to the owner of the benefits involved.
>
> "Though Islam allows ownership without limit, it authorises society, as the entity for ensuring the rights of God and for organising utilisation of wealth, to subject the individual ownership of par-

ticular kinds of property to limits, when this is necessitated by public good. This it can do through its representatives. This may apply to ceilings on agricultural holdings or to urban property." (214: 48–49).

This approach gives priority to social good and makes representatives of the society the sole arbiters in determining the demands of social good.

Abdul Hamid Abu Sulaiman recognises the individual's right to own the fruits of his labour, but so far as the natural resources, natural powers, and general circumstances of the society are concerned every individual has an equal share in them. As all individuals do not have equal capacity to put these resources to proper use, the more capable are allowed to use more than their due share. They cannot, however, claim the whole of their produce from this extra use of resources, only the share of labour belongs to them while the part of produce ascribable to natural resources belongs to the society as the representative of those who use less than their due share of these resources (7: 17–19; 8: 69–70). Private ownership of land, capital or other natural powers cannot be allowed to become a means of exploiting other individuals and subjugating them (8: 43). The rationale of allowing inequality in the private ownership of means of production is stated by him in these words:

> "A strict equality in the ownership of natural resources would require very frequent redistribution of those resources among members of society. This would be disruptive to economic activity and social relations. A reasonable alternative is, first, to avoid frequent redistribution and permit private ownership of resources, thus achieving stability; and second, to redistribute equally among members of society that part of income which is due to natural resources, thus achieving equality and justice" (8: 70).

Equal sharing of the "income from natural resources" is basic to Abu Sulaiman's understanding of *ribā* and his views on land rent, share cropping and profit-sharing, subjects which we discuss below at appropriate places. Though he cites specific texts in support of specific views they are basically results of an analytical system rooted in his conception of *Tawḥīd*.

Most of the writers approach the subject in an eclectic manner as their basic source material is the vast *fiqh* literature on the subject. As a position midway between *fiqh*-based eclecticism and a system derived from one basic principle can be mentioned Siddiqi's effort to derive the basic tenets relating to ownership rights from Islam's world view, its social outlook and its philosophy at law (158: 41–90), concluding that "the individual, the state and the society each have claim on property rights in view of the principle that the Islamic State has a jurisdiction over individual rights, being the embodiment of God's vicegerency on earth and representative of the people. This jurisdiction is however, functional, depending upon the values and objectives cherished by Islam" (158: 74). These principles are followed up by a detailed discussion of the circumstances justifying abrogation or abridgement of individual property rights by such measures as nationalisation, ceilings, control on prices, profits and rents and compulsory purchase or borrowing, etc. (221, II: 155–282).

Bāqir al Ṣadr is also critical of the view that in Islam individual ownership is the rule and public ownership the exception. He regards individual ownership, state ownership and communal ownership as three forms existing parallel to one another in Islamic Law (171: 257). Though Tahāwī's eclecticism makes him assign the central position to individual rights of ownership, he puts the state representing the society on an almost equal footing as regards vicegerency of the Real Owner (77: I: 174). This gives the state "the right to intervene in private property by regulating it, putting ceilings or confiscating after due compensation when the owner deviates from the basic role of property – that it should be an instrument of service to the society" (77, I: 217).

The early writings of Mawdūdī lean heavily towards assigning the central place to individual ownership (51: 32). His later views are nearer to the middle position that admits social control whenever social interest calls for it. But he would still like to keep state intervention at the minimum (51: 116). Far from the position taken by Abu Sulaiman, his views on specific issues like land reforms are shaped by this approach, for which he finds support in the *fiqh* literature. A similar position is taken by the martyr Sayyid Quṭb who declares the right of individual ownership basic to the Islamic system. Both of them emphasise, however, the need of ensuring the fulfilment of the basic needs of each and every individual and justify such social action as may be necessary for that purpose (Mawdūdī 51: 404–407; Quṭb 62: 162). This, however, is one of the points on which there is a complete consensus. What distinguishes some of them is their insistence on specific provisions in the *fiqh* literature relating to individual rights that sometimes stand in the way of radical reforms that modern life calls for. One is inclined to agree with Ali Abdul Qadir (224: 11) that the economic philosophy of Islam relating to right of ownership "did not change the ordinary juristic attitude to the practical relations of people and property" which finds expression in *fiqh* literature.

Notwithstanding individual stances, some of the powerful collective movements for Islamic reorientation of modern life have tended towards the approach closer to the "economic philosophy of Islam". Both the *Ikhwān al-Muslimūn* and the *Jamā'at-i-Islāmī* have, on occasions, issued manifestoes recommending ceilings on rural and urban property and other measures of social control (125; 168).

One tends to conclude that the more our thinkers attend to the actual conditions prevailing in their societies the more realistic their approach becomes. Policy recommendations directed at the Islamic transformation of a society moulded over a long period by feudalism and capitalism draw more and more inspiration from the ultimate Goals of the Islamic system rather than being governed by specific legal rulings given in normal circumstances.

Relations of Production: Co-operation

With a positive attitude to economic enterprise and socially-oriented purposive rights of ownership, individuals and groups in the brotherhood of man are enjoined to co-operate with one another in patterning life on earth in accordance with the Will of Allah. Economic relations, especially those in production and exchange of wealth, should be co-operative in nature. "Rivalry and cut-throat competition make no sense in this context" (73: 27). Co-operation is seen as the basic value in Islam's economic philosophy (8: 36; 77, II: 199; 10: 27). Besides being required by human brotherhood and equality, unity of purpose and common ultimate interests, and also besides being explicitly enjoined by the Qur'ān and the *Sunnah* it is the attitude that suits the practical interests of mankind today and can save it from the ravages of capitalistic competition. 'Ali 'Abd al-Rasul calls, in this context, for "constructive competition" aiming at what is best for the society and high quality production, while avoiding all activities injurious to other producers and the consumers.[3]

As regards the institutionalisation of the co-operative attitude, and how far the new institutions will be different from those prevalent in the fields of production, exchange and distribution, detailed studies are still awaited. Siddiqi's study of entrepreneurial behaviour is only a beginning (619: 139–152). Despite the great attention paid to the subject by Kahf (612: Chapter IV) no progress is made along these lines.

The Islamic view of co-operation does not rule out free and fair competition in the market, provided all economic agents adhere to Islamic morality. Competition is emphasised in contrast to monopoly whose elimination is regarded as a prerequisite to ensuring justice and growth (51: 152; 619; 181).

This makes it still more necessary to visualise how the co-operative spirit will translate itself into action where millions of individual units are involved, knowledge is imperfect and communications involve costs.

Development and Growth

Islam's economic philosophy does not stop at teaching men to co-operate after having encouraged them in productive enterprise. It creates a powerful drive for development. A true Muslim looks upon developmental efforts as striving in the cause of Allah (*jihād fī sabīl Allāh*) (595: 128; 477: 36; 484). The Muslim society orients its policies in order to ensure sufficiency and peace for all and any relaxation in this regard is looked upon as rejection of the bounties of Allah (77: I: 6–9). Economic development has become a necessary condition to be fulfilled to enable the Muslim peoples to perform their mission with the humanity that the Qur'ān declares to be their *raison d'etre*. This mission is related to the well-being of all human beings. It cannot be performed while Muslim countries continue to be politically and economically subservient to the powers which stand for alien cultures (158: 130, 484). A narrow nationalistic approach to economic development does not harmonise with the Islamic spirit which calls for a global approach ensuring co-operation between the rich and poor nations to usher in an era of universal prosperity and banish hunger and fear from human society.

As to the Islamic strategy for economic development its chief distinguishing feature is that social justice and growth go together (177: 593). This is ensured by the motivation that Islam provides for economic development (56: 45). Individual profit motive is not the chief propelling force in Islam. Developmental efforts are mainly social and the individuals willingly co-operate in this venture (475: 43, 96–113).

Seen in the context of the Islamic world view, developmental efforts cannot become an end in themselves, nor a rising GNP the only index of "growth" in the Islamic sense. The aim is a good life with all its dimensions, the economic aspect being only one of them. Emphasising this point Ṭaḥāwī (77, II: 229–232) goes on to state how Islam's emphasis on work, on the fullest exploitation of natural resources, and on an active role for the state will ensure growth with justice.

II

ECONOMIC SYSTEM OF ISLAM

While economic philosophy states the overall approach, the economic system comprises ways and means of securing human welfare in general and economic welfare in particular. Economic literature on the subject discusses "alternative methods of determining the bill of goods to be produced, the allocation of resources to produce it, and the distribution of the resulting income".[4] The ownership of means of production and the extent to which the market mechanism or central authority is relied upon for decision making have been the chief criteria for distinguishing one economic system from the other.

Emphasis in Islamic literature on the subject has been somewhat different. The ends of the economic system are discussed, followed by a discussion of those behaviour patterns on the part of economic agents which are expected to go a long way in securing these ends.

The state enters the scene to guide and regulate voluntary actions and ensure the achievement of goals. Allocation of resources, organisation of production and exchange and distribution of the resulting income is effected by the twin forces of morally-oriented free individual action and state regulation. Islam's strategy in organising its economic system rests, therefore, on three main flanks: clearly specified goals, well defined moral attitudes and behaviour patterns on the part of economic agents, and specific laws, rules and regulations enforceable by the state.

Goals of the System

Economic well-being is one of the goals emphasised by every writer, though each one of them proceeds to mention a number of other, non-economic, goals too. We shall first consider the contents of this goal, according to various writers, before we pass on to examine their views on non-economic goals.

We have already referred to Ṭaḥāwī's twin goals of sufficiency and peace which can come about by eradicating hunger and fear from society and ensuring the fulfilment of the basic needs of each and every human being. His list of basic needs includes food, clothing and shelter; medical aid for the sick and domestic services for the invalid, education for those who need it, marriage in some cases and "all that is regarded necessary according to the custom of the society" (77, I: 394). This is a point that finds universal support in the literature and the list of basic needs given by Mawdūdī (51: 406), Sayyid Quṭb (62: 240–241), Musṭafā Sibā'ī (70: 203) and Siddiqi (221, II: 92) does not differ materially from the above.

Bāqir al Ṣadr emphasises provision of ease and convenience in life, consequent upon growth and development and maximum utilisation of natural resources (171: 595). Kahf makes "maximisation of the rate of utilisation of resources" the first goal of economic policy in Islam (612: 93) along with minimisation of the distribution gap and observance of the Islamic code of conduct by the various economic agents.

In view of the exhaustible nature of the natural resources it would, however, be more appropriate to replace the concept of maximum utilisation by optimisation. The *Jamā'at-i-Islāmī* Pakistan Economic Committee Report comes closer to this view when it states the same principle as "the best utilisation of the maximum amount of natural resources" (126: 25). Abu Aiman (Dr. Said Ramazan) also regards discovering sources of wealth and their exploitation as an obligatory duty (3: 21).

Turning to non-economic goals, it is emphasised that fulfilment of "spiritual needs" must take place besides the fulfilment of material needs (5: 13). Mawdūdī gives priority of place to "safeguarding the freedom of man" followed by his "moral growth" which requires freedom of choice for the individual. Social justice, equality of opportunity and co-operation come next in Mawdūdī's list of basic objectives of Islam's economic system (51: 145). Chapra's list gives priority to "economic well-being" followed by "universal brotherhood and justice, equitable distribution of income and freedom of the individual within the context of social welfare" (115: 5).[5]

Siddiqi discusses the rationale of including these non-economic goals in the ends of economic system and points out the impact their inclusion has on the ways and means adopted for achievement of the ends of economic system in Islam (73: 28). Morally-orientated individual action is expected to ensure the achievement of socially desired results to a large extent. Law and social control are to guide, regulate and supplement individual actions and compensate the deficiencies that still remain. To quote Mawdūdī:

> "For establishing economic justice, Islam does not rely on law alone. Great importance is attached for this purpose to reforming the inner man through faith, prayers, education and moral training, to changing his preferences and ways of thinking and inculcating in him a strong moral sense that keeps him just. If and when these means fail, Muslim society should be strong enough to exert pressure to make individuals adhere to the 'limits'. When even this does not deliver the goods, Islam is for the use of the coercive powers of law to establish justice by force." (51: 145).

Even though recent thinking is far more positive regarding the role of the state in securing the goals mentioned above the emphasis placed by Mawdūdī on morally-oriented voluntary action represents a tendency deeply rooted in the Islamic mind and exemplified by the vast literature on the code of conduct of various economic agents. A distinction is always made in this connection between what is obligatory and what is desirable. The obligatory is legally enforced, the desirable is ensured through education. Any deficiency in the attainment of goals is then made up by the state enforcing the desirable part of the code as well as taking other compensatory and positive measures. It is in this manner that the desired allocation of resources and distribution of incomes is effected. The respective roles of the market mechanism and planned action are determined accordingly. We shall therefore proceed first to study the various codes of conduct for economic agents: the owner, the consumer, the entrepreneur; producer, employer, trader etc. and the labourer. This will be followed by an examination of the role envisaged for the market mechanism and the role visualised for the state.

The Owner

Behavioural norms for the owner have been discussed by a number of writers including Hifẓur Rahman (120: 68–77, 299–302), Mawdūdī (51: 81–96), Sayyid Quṭb (62: 111–112), Siddiqi (221, I: 205–288), Manna' Qattān[6] and A. Mannan (132: 77–85). The owner has no right to destroy useful property. Wasteful use and extravagance is prohibited. He has to avoid using it in a manner injurious to others or detrimental to public interest. Other individuals and the society have a claim on the owner's property. This includes the obligation to support dependents in the nuclear family and other members of the extended family when they are in need (336; 221, I: 252–259).

Besides obligatory *Zakāt* the owner owes help to those in dire need, and should not refuse a loan in cash or kind when a request comes from one who is in real need. Several writers stress the significance of the provision that the presence of a pressing need obliges those with a surplus to surrender such part of their surplus as will fulfil that need (77, II: 214; 221, I: 272–280).

While there is a consensus on illegitimacy of "interest" charged on money loans, the owner's right to income from his property in forms of rent and profit has been a matter of controversy in the literature. The right of the owner to cultivate his own land or employ his own capital in productive enterprise or profitable business is not disputed. In that case he is the owner of the accruing surplus over cost. The legally binding *Zakāt* is of course to be realised from him. Abu Sulaiman advocates a larger share for society in the produce of land where the land holding of the owner is more than his "equal share", as explained above. Controversy centres round giving the land to another person for cultivation on money rent or on the basis of share cropping, or giving capital on a profit sharing basis, i.e. *muḍārabah*.

Abu Sulaiman allows profit sharing but "the share of the capital owner is only to compensate him for probable loss" (8: 59). He is not entitled to a net pure profit. Other writers on the subject endorse the unanimous verdict of all the four principal schools of Islamic law that the two parties to the *muḍārabah* contract are free to agree on any formula of sharing the profits provided these shares are fixed percentage-wise and not in the form of given amounts (176: 30). Abu Sulaiman's opinion is derived from his basic stand relating to the equal sharing of gifts of God (other than the fruits of personal ingenuity and labour). But he fails to counter the obvious argument that an entrepreneurial decision is involved in selecting the right party in *muḍārabah* (221, I: 167–171). He does not support his view by any precedents from the *Sunnah* and gives no argument against the unanimous verdict of *fiqh*. Contemporary writers on Islamic banking, who make *muḍārabah* the basis of its operations, do not stipulate any ceilings on the percentage share of capital in profits.

In discussing money rent on cultivable land a distinction must be made between plain land in its natural form in which the owner has not invested any labour or capital to effect improvements, and improved land. There is no dispute that money rent is valid in the case of the latter variety in lieu of "depreciation".

As regards the first-mentioned variety Abu Sulaiman regards charging money rent by the owner as illegal (8: 30–31 and 41–42). This is the position that can be inferred from Mawdūdī's statement on the subject (232: 60). Abu Sa'ūd also equates such rent to interest charged on money capital (5: 93).

There is no denying the fact that money rent (on agricultural land) usually stands at a level higher than depreciation. A question is raised regarding the legitimacy of such (higher) rent. One asks what would be the rationale behind the capital, time and effort invested in the improvement on land if money rent is allowed only to the extent of depreciation.

The question can be answered after a close look at the nature of the return to these improvements in terms of value. These are uncertain as they involve the uncertain market price of the produce. Should the investor in land improvements himself cultivate the land, the returns shall legitimately accrue to him. Share cropping should also be allowed as it is the physical product that is shared and the share of the investor-owner remains uncertain. To allow him to charge a certain fixed sum, in lieu of investments in improvements, as part of its rent would be tantamount to *ribā* whose essence is charging a certain fixed sum against uncertain value returns.

Ṭāhāwī finds that there are authentic traditions from the Prophet both allowing and prohibiting money rent on land. He thinks the two verdicts relate to two different situations. Money rent on land is to be declared illegal if there is undue attention of people towards agriculture at the cost of industry and trade (77, I: 268–269). He also notes that the jurists who have allowed money rent do so on the basis of "necessity", otherwise they agree that it is against the principles of analogy (77, I: 271). Whatever one's judgment on Taḥāwi's historical account, he fails to provide an economic rationale for his solution.

Nasir A. Sheikh (154: 181) opposes both land rent and share cropping, laying down that "a person can possess only that much land which he can himself cultivate. The surplus he has to surrender to the state". A. Mannan also disfavours leasing of land on rent or on the basis of share cropping (132: 106–108).

Such a dogmatic position is hardly tenable, economically speaking, as Akram points out (613: 34–36). A. Mannan also refutes, like Akram, the view that rent should be prohibited as it is similar to interest (132: 135–154).

S. M. Yusuf discerns "in early Islam a definite tendency to ordain the future development of agriculture in such a way that there is no charge for the use of what Ricardo in his own definition of rent called original and indestructible powers of land". Quoting Iqbal's *Bāl-e-jibrīl* he ascribes the same view to him (242: 34).

Share Cropping

Share cropping is considered valid by most of the contemporary writers such as Mawdūdī (232: 60), Bāqir al Ṣadr (171: 531), Hifzur Raḥmān (120:

236), Ḥāmid (229), Ṭaḥāwī (77, I: 271), Siddiqi (221, I: 184–192) and Taqī Amīnī (226).

Those who regard it as illegal include: S. M. Yusuf (242), Mazharuddin Siddiqi (72: 70), Abu Sulaiman (8: 43–44) and Ḥyder Zamān Ṣiddīqī (244). We shall not enter the controversy in so far as it is based on the various traditions involved and their legal interpretation. As regards the points of economic philosophy involved, we have clarified Abu Sulaiman's position above. Those who allow share cropping compare it to profit sharing and argue that all owners do not have the capacity to cultivate their land directly, and it should therefore be open to them to benefit from it in co-operation with others, as in the case of profit sharing. The crucial question therefore is: in so far as the owner of a piece of land is entitled to the whole net produce of his land when he is the cultivator, his claim is established both on the part of the net produce that is due to his labour, and the part that is due to land. Shall he be allowed to give it to another person and *share* with him the part of the net product that is due to land? It is this question that Abu Sulaiman answers in the negative and others answer in the affirmative. It is clear that a negative answer amounts to the negation of ownership *per se*. If the owner of cultivable land is allowed to hire labourers to get his land cultivated and appropriate the net produce why should he be disallowed from entering into a "partnership" with the same labourer and share the whole of the produce with him? Abu Sulaiman might say that the "owner" is entitled to this much of land – as his proportionate share in the free natural resource that is land – and no more. This provides a case for a ceiling on ownership of agricultural land and not a case against share cropping. So far as the question of supplying the seeds etc., is concerned different schools of Islamic law lay down different formulas and one is free to recommend one that is just to both the parties, but to disallow share cropping as such is not understandable. The share cropping labourer is likely to do his job with greater interest than the hired labourers and may well end up with a higher reward. Those who disallow share cropping seem to disregard both its needs and advantages in their urge to ensure justice for which alternative means may be available.

The Consumer

The list of articles whose consumption is prohibited in Islam is well known and non-controversial. There is no limit to what one might consume to lead a good life, so increasing efficiency and playing the role Islam envisages for a true Muslim in the service of society. But indulgence in luxurious living is undesirable. Some writers recommend a ban on certain luxury items or subjecting them to heavy taxes in order to discourage their consumption, especially when the economic conditions of the society do not permit expenditure of scarce resources on their production (221, II: 172–173, 219).

Bāqir al Ṣadr suggests that resources should not be allowed to be diverted to the production of luxuries until the production of necessaries is ensured in sufficient quantities (171: 611). The consumer must abstain from extravagance defined as expenditure in excess of what is necessary to fulfil a need. Extravagance is related to the average standards of consumption obtaining in a society, the idea being that big departures from these standards should not be permissible. Several writers have discussed the concept of extravagance, including Naiem Siddiqi (74).

The Entrepreneur: Producer and Trader

The code of conduct for a Muslim entrepreneur has been discussed in detail by Mawdūdi (51: 83–89), Siddiqi (619: 35–64), Chapra (115: 27–33) Ali Abdur Rasul[7] and Kahf (612: 15–20), among others. Dishonesty, fraud and deception, coercive practices, and gamblesome or usurious dealings are prohibited. He should not do anything injurious to others. This rules out hoarding, speculation and collusion among producers and traders against the interests of the consumers. Monopoly is also regarded as injurious to the interests of society. He is charged with justice and truthfulness in all his dealings. On the positive side he should serve the interests of the society. Social good should guide him in his decisions, besides his own profit. As to the question how a care for the good of the society would influence entrepreneurial decisions, no deep study is available besides Siddiqi's preliminary discussion in *Economic Enterprise in Islam*. This question raises basic issues such as the role of information in the translation of good intentions into socially desirable concrete results, and the way individual good intentions can be organised and institutionalised. No serious attention has been paid to these sociological aspects of the behaviour of the producer and trader in Islamic society. Some writers have paid special attention to the obligation of the employer towards his employees (425; 426; 438; 444; 165). These discussions also suffer from the limitations indicated above, in so far as they fail to translate the cherished norms into operational programmes of action. A notable exception, however, is Abdul Majeed Qureshi (439; 440; 441) whose views we discuss below, under labour and industrial relations.

This leads us to the question of evaluating the market system. Everyone will agree with Chapra that "although the market system has been recognised by Islam because of the freedom it offers to individuals, it is not to be considered sacred and inalterable. It is the goals of the Muslim society which are more important. . . ."

The market system must therefore be modified as necessary to make it conform to the ideals of Islam as much as possible (115: 23–24). Examine however the following statement by the same author: "In Islam the allocation of resources is optimum if it is first in conformity with the norms of Islam and then in accordance with consumers' preferences. In a truly Islamic society there is no likelihood of any divergence between the two" (115: 82). The meaning of the second sentence is not entirely clear. Does it mean that if all economic agents behave in accordance with the Islamic code of conduct and the distribution of income and wealth is according to the Islamic ideals, the functioning of the market system would result in optimum allocation of resources, in the Islamic sense? An affirmative answer raises questions relating to knowledge, wisdom, power and organisation which have not been discussed so far.

Kahf's discussion on the market structure (612: 29–45) focuses its attention on co-operation and emphasises the role of the government in the market. Both the supervisory and control functions of the government and its social insurance role are seen as permanent features of the market in Islam. He neither poses nor answers the question raised above.

The market system as a means of distributing incomes in society is rated very low by our writers. There is a greater need of modification, through state action, of the market solution in this case than in the case of allocation of resources. As the basic reason calling for such a modification is advanced the argument that in Islam there are two grounds for entitlement to income: work and need. The market may reward work but it cannot possibly provide for need. The final distribution of income must conform to the Islamic ideals of social justice which involves fulfilment of the basic needs of every individual as well as a levelling of the glaring disparities.

Bāqir al Ṣadr regards work to be the chief basis of distribution (171: 309–312). But this results in one class of people earning more than they need and another class earning less than they need. This solution has to be modified by transferring some income from the former class to the latter (171: 313).

Property, which is based in Islam primarily on work, becomes a secondary basis for distribution next to work and need (171: 321). Ṭahāwī also endorses the same theory (77, II: 227–28).

Commenting on distribution, Abu Sulaiman puts great reliance on properly functioning markets. Intervention by public administration is, however, likely to become necessary (8: 71).

Role of the State

Without prejudice to the emphasis on freedom of the individual, the state's role in economic life has come to be emphasised more and more in the literature. This role mainly comprises four types of action.

(1) Ensuring compliance with the Islamic code of conduct by individuals through education and, whenever necessary, through coercion.
(2) Maintaining healthy conditions in the market to ensure its proper functioning.
(3) Modifying the allocation of resources and distribution of income

effected by the market mechanism by guiding and regulating it as well as by direct intervention and participation in the process.

(4) Taking positive steps in the field of production and capital formation to accelerate growth and ensure social justice.

It is agreed that the state enjoys the widest powers for performing these functions, subject to the constraint that it functions in a democratic manner and decisions are taken after due consultation, by true representatives of the people.

Bāqir al Ṣadr has discussed the role of the state in Islam's economic system at some length. Besides enforcing the relevant laws the state guarantees social security, ensuring fulfilment of needs to each individual, and maintains a balance in the standards of living in the society (171: 615–636). The state's direct responsibility as regards social security is based on the general claim of the entire society on natural resources, and on the fact that those individuals of the society who do not have the capacity to work also have this claim (171: 621). Bāqir then proceeds to show how the creation of a "public sector" is the means to discharge this responsibility. As regards maintaining the Social Balance he stresses the point that it refers not to the levels of income but to the standards of living (171: 626). The balance does admit, however, of moderate differences. Besides enforcing the *Sharī'ah* laws, guaranteeing fulfilment of needs and maintaining the social balance, the state has the important function of undertaking fresh legislation to regulate and guide the economic life in affairs left unregulated by the *Sharī'ah*. This "sphere open to fresh legislation" mainly related to relations between man and the world of nature as distinct from the relations between man and man. These relations change with changing knowledge, discovery of new resources, powers of production, etc. They have to be properly regulated in order to ensure justice and protect the interests of the society. Such regulations could not be a part of the permanent law, the *Sharī'ah*, as their need arises *denovo* due to changed conditions of life. Islam authorises the properly constituted government to fill this gap. The government can prohibit something hitherto regarded as "permissible", or make some "permissible" act an obligatory one: "When the Ruler prohibits something by nature permissible it becomes *ḥarām*, when he orders that it be done, it becomes *wājib*" (171: 643). (This power does not extend to what is already prohibited or obligatory in law.) This discussion (171: 637–643) is the clearest one gets in the literature, when read in the light of what the writer has written on the same subject in the earlier part of the book. While the state cannot legalise what is explicitly illegal in *Sharī'ah* or absolve individuals of duties *Sharī'ah* has explicitly charged them with, it can always issue a fresh list of dos and don'ts, to regulate the economy and guide it towards the cherished goals (171: 612).

In his discussions on the role of the state in the economy Muhammad al Mubārak declares the state to be one of the three pillars of the Islamic economic system, along with faith and commitment to moral values and certain principles of organisation. Its function is to establish justice and ensure fulfilment of needs by organising the public utilities and the social security system (134: 106–127).

In his doctoral dissertation on the "Political Economy of the Islamic State", Awsaf Ali (114) concludes that the social philosophy of Islam envisions an economic society based on a wide-ranging state direction of, and participation in, the economic, commercial and financial spheres.

Fazlur Rahman (27: 5) says that "in the basic interest of socio-economic justice, the state shall interfere with private wealth to the extent that socio-economic justice demands". He thinks that "if it is found that the condition of the society is economically irremediable in the visible future without the state taking over direct management of industry, Islam would not only not forbid this but would obviously enjoin this upon the state as a most imperative duty".

Chapra also regards an active economic role by the state to be an inalienable feature of the Islamic economic system (115: 41–42); providing physical and social overhead capital and arranging social security are listed among the necessary functions of a modern Islamic state (115: 40). In a more recent paper on the subject, this list includes maintaining stability in the value of money and harmonising international economic relations, besides the eradication of poverty and the creation of conditions favourable for full employment and a high rate of growth.[8] As a general principle, its sphere of activity is determined by the goals of the Islamic system (115: 50). But he also insists that "the procedure it should adopt is education and not coercion . . ." (115: 50), which indicates a strong influence of Mawdūdī's views on the subject. Nobody will deny the principle that where education serves coercion should be eschewed. But we must be very clear on the point that the goals of the Islamic system have got to be achieved and coercion is allowed where education fails (221, II: 156–165). Among such measures of coercion permitted in certain circumstances have been listed restrictions on individual freedom of action, regulation of business activities, fixation of prices, wages, rents and rates of profit, taxation, taxing away the entire surplus wealth, use of coercion in purchase or hire, nationalisation, ceilings on property, economic planning and financial penalties (221, II: 166–283).

Among close associates of Mawdūdī, Naiem Siddiqi has also spelled out many positive actions by the state which are called for in the circumstances prevailing in some of the Muslim countries (584: 514–522). Chapra is more positive in his recent paper when he lays down that "For a realisation of this objective it would be incumbent upon the Islamic State not to leave the essential function of allocation of resources, particularly scarce resources, or the determination of aggregate demand to the unhindered operation of blind market forces. It should itself play a positive role and consciously contribute towards the attainment of desired goals through (i) rational planning, and (ii) building the necessary physical and social infrastructure".[9]

A very active role for the state is envisaged in the report of the economic committee of *Jamā'at-i-Islāmī* Pakistan, written by Khurshid Ahmad and Naiem Siddiqi (126: 40–52). A trend which is fully reflected in the *Jamā'at* manifesto for the 1970 elections (125: 22–32). Having these very conditions in mind Kalim Siddiqi (494) makes a plea for a very active role by the state, which is to "exercise, on behalf of God, proprietary rights over surplus value or capital and manage and direct further investment" (494: 28).

We have already mentioned Mawdūdī's cautious approach regarding the intervention of the state in economic life. There are several writers who regard the expanding economic role of the state in modern times as unhealthy and want the Islamic system to check this tendency, e.g. Mahmud Abū Saūd (5: 70–71). The increasing emphasis on a more positive role for the state in the Islamic economy, as exemplified by the writers mentioned above, seems to indicate an irreversible trend reflecting the changing conditions of modern economic life which is becoming more complex and interdependent.

III

ECONOMIC SYSTEM OF ISLAM: SOME SPECIFIC ASPECTS

Within the basic framework outlined above our writers have discussed such specific aspects of the system as public finance, money and banking, social security and insurance, industrial relations and development and growth.

Public Finance

A vast literature is available on public finance in Islam in view of the explicit provisions in the *Sharī'ah* in this regard and the historical material available on the subject. Besides Aghnides' *Mohammedan Theories of Finance* a number of specialised works are available, though mostly historical and descriptive in nature (333; 293; 298)[10].

This is also true of the chapters on public finance found in almost every work on the economic system of Islam. Our interest lies in the way the operation of Islamic institutions like *Zakāt* and the application of general principles of policy derived from public finance in early Islamic history is visualised in modern circumstances.

Zakāt

The centre piece of Islamic Public Finance being *Zakāt*, its coverage, rates, beneficiaries and administration have been discussed in detail. The most comprehensive work in Qarḍāwī's *Fiqh al Zakāt* (313). In English "The Law and Philosophy of *Zakāt*" is less original yet comprehensive on points of law (319). Among economists A. Mannan's book (132) has a good chapter on Public Finance and Fiscal Policy, and some of the younger economists have offered analytical pieces on the subject (623; 624; 615).[11]

(a) Coverage

It is generally agreed that the coverage of *Zakāt* has to be extended to forms of wealth not known in the early days of Islam. Shares and securities, savings in the form of insurance premia and provident funds, rented buildings and vehicles on hire, machinery and other capital goods. Qarḍāwī (313, I: 139, 466–486, 581–573), Abu Zahra (300: 181–186) and Mawdūdī (51: 339–342, 351–363) discuss the application of *Zakāt* to these assets and the rates applicable to them.

Many issues continue to be controversial, one of them being the *Zakāt* on machinery and capital goods. Mawdūdī regards only the marketable produce of industrial units to be subject to 2.5% annual tax, like all other merchandise (51: 339) exempting capital goods and machinery installed in these units from *Zakāt*. Akram finds this view to be inconsistent with Mawdūdī's opinion on *Zakāt* of shares in industrial concerns (613: 102). Abu Zuhra advocates a 10 per cent tax on the net income (profits) of these concerns (300: 184). Qarḍāwī endorses his view subject to two important modifications. Firstly, he categorises rented buildings and vehicles on hire and also such enterprises as poultry farms and dairy farms along with industrial units. Secondly, in all these cases he advocates a 10 per cent levy on profits *net of depreciation costs* (313, I: 476–482). A. Mannan also stresses the need of making due allowance for depreciation and adds that "the question of the rate of *Zakāt* is linked up with productivity which varies from industry to industry". He pleads for a flexible rate "so that the element of progression may be introduced in fixing the rate of *Zakāt*" (132: 291).

Similar controversies surround some of the other forms of wealth mentioned above. The number of opinions, arguments and counter arguments in each case being too many to be recorded here. Our interest lies in the economic aspect of the discussion rather than in the points of law involved and their interpretations. Analogical reasoning is often supplemented by a reference to the public interest, equity and incidence, etc. The entire issue awaits a thorough re-examination in which the new taxes are seen as part of the whole structure of *Zakāt* taxes, paying careful attention to their functions in the economy.

(b) Rates

The ulema are unanimous in regarding the rates of *Zakāt* as permanently fixed by Islamic law, but a number of recent writers, mostly economists, argue in favour of making these rates amenable to modification by the state. Afazuddin (621: 10), Izadi (613: 14), Husaini (121: 200–205), Salih Tug[12] and Mahmud Ahmad take this stand. Mahmud Ahmad (168: 133) quotes Maulana Abul Kalam Azad's letter to him in support of his view. The economic arguments in favour of flexible rates are met, however, by the ulema when they point out that the state is empowered to levy additional taxes, over and above the prescribed *Zakāt*. It is, therefore, in case of the "new forms of wealth", for which no explicit provisions are found in the *Sharī'ah* that the arguments in favour of flexible rates have practical significance.

The arguments in favour of valuation of the *niṣāb*, i.e. the exemption limits prescribed by the *Sharī'ah* are, however, more formidable, economically speaking. Akram refers to the anomalies existing in the present structure of *niṣāb* (613: 103) and a change in *niṣāb* has been advocated by Rafiullah (314), Zayas (321: 74–76), Uthman (79) and Fanjari.[13] Hasanuzzaman also pleads for rethinking on the subject with a view to having a uniform *niṣāb*.[14]

Waqar Husaini takes the position that "the exact types and rates of taxes used by the Prophet Muḥammad need not be applied in contemporary times" (121: 204). The main economic reason is stated as follows:

> "Logically and practically it is impossible to treat as watertight compartments the three branches of fiscal planning: resource allocation, economic stabilization and income and wealth distribution. . . . In a smoothly running Islamic economic system, the 'redistribution' function through progressive taxation would wither away, leaving it the task of merely maintaining the egalitarian economic system with proportional taxation. To achieve and maintain such an egalitarian system, except for minor direct transfer payments mainly to those mentally and physically deprived of the capacity to earn, the main heads of expenditure of *Zakāt/Ṣadaqah/Infaq* tax revenues would be in the resource allocation and stabilisation branches. This would be consistent with the multiple goals of the Islamic economic system, spending on all the beneficiaries enumerated in the Qur'ān by maintaining full employment and enabling everybody to acquire earned income and wealth in a manner that preserves human dignity".[15]

Husaini's stand is contrary to the consensus on the juristic principle involved. There has been unanimity as to the sanctity of the rates explicitly fixed by the Prophet. This permanence has been regarded as a virtue as it rules out tampering with the law of *Zakāt* by the rulers with a view to reducing the share of the have-nots in the wealth of the haves. As regards the need for increasing this share, the state is allowed to levy additional taxes. This coupled with the flexibility in disbursement of *Zakāt* funds, introduces sufficient flexibility in the system to enable it to meet the changing requirements of fiscal planning. One of the major roles of progressive taxation in a modern economy is an equitable sharing of the burden of raising income for the state. Progressive taxation ensures equitable sharing of this burden. As the need for such income is likely to go on increasing, there is no possibility of doing away with progressive taxation.

(c) Disbursement of *Zakāt* Revenue

Among other issues on which there is a difference of opinion is the way *Zakāt* benefits should flow to the various groups of the beneficiaries listed in the Qur'ān. Some ulema insist on direct transfer payments to the beneficiaries. These include Mufti Muhammad Shafi of Pakistan (317: 59–62). Most writers, however, permit the *Zakāt* benefits to flow to the beneficiaries indirectly through institutions providing needed services. These include Mawdūdī (51: 350), Amin Ahsan Islāhī (309) and Ya'qūb Shah (318: 48). According to Qarḍāwī the beneficiaries fall into two groups. To the first, which includes the needy, the officers in *Zakāt* administration and "those whose hearts are to be won over" the *Zakāt* revenue must be transferred directly. The rest can receive the benefits indirectly (313, II: 612–614, 633). But Islāhī argues that the insistence on direct transfer to certain beneficiaries has no basis in the text of the law (309).

Some writers tend to interpret the category "in the cause of Allah" too broadly to include all social services, but Qarḍāwī's thorough discussion on the subject limiting it to the promotion of the cause of Islam in general, in all its possible forms, appears to be balanced and decisive (313, II: 635–669). Most of the specific suggestions made by Muhammad bin Jamāl (625) can be accommodated in the broad framework provided by those who do not insist on *tamlīk* in every case. Such is the stance taken by the *Jamā'at-i-Islāmī* Pakistan Economic Committee Report (126: 93–96).

Akram sees a useful instrument of fiscal policy in the discretionary use of the principle of *tamlīk* by the Islamic State (613: 107).

(d) *Zakāt* on Agricultural Produce and Mineral Wealth

The *Zakāt* levy covers the agricultural produce in the form of '*Ushr* and its half depending on whether the land is irrigated by Nature or by man. This levy applies to every Muslim. But some lands are subject to *Kharāj*, or land tax (i.e. rent payable to the state), irrespective of who owns them. According to majority opinion a Muslim owner-cultivator of such lands will pay *Kharāj* as well as '*Ushr* (or its half), as Qarḍāwī has explained (313, I: 415).

The majority opinion levies '*Ushr* (or its half) on the gross produce of land, but Qarḍāwī has convincingly argued the desirability of making an allowance for the costs incurred on fertilizers, seed, etc. (313, I: 394–397). The same view is taken by 'Abd al-Salam.[16]

On mineral wealth contemporary opinion tends to gravitate towards making the state own all such resources and assuming the responsibility of exploring and exploiting them (Syed Quṭb (62: 121) and Siddiqi (221, II: 19–22)). Individuals who discover any mines may be awarded prizes or given concessional contracts for their exploration.

Several writers, including Qarḍāwī discuss the principles underlying Islamic taxation which are shown to be in conformity with the criteria laid down for just and efficient policies by the modern economists (313, II: 1038–1052). Atif al-Sayyid[17] explains how *Zakāt* surpasses all civic taxes in having three virtues: the *Zakāt* payer has a deep sense of duty towards the Law-Giver, he has a genuine dedication to the aims and objects of this levy and he is aware of his ability to pay it. Mabid Mahmood finds in *Zakāt* a powerful means of redistributing political power which he regards to be a function of wealth (624: 43). Several writers discuss the economics of *Zakāt* in relation to savings and investment to which we shall turn later in the chapter on economic analysis.

Inheritance

The Islamic laws of inheritance are invariably mentioned by our writers along with *Zakāt* in view of their redistributive function, and their role in removing concentrations of wealth is highlighted by almost every writer. Whereas *Zakāt* redistributes wealth in the present generation, the Islamic laws of inheritance do so between the outgoing generation and the present one, so that the wealth accumulated at one point, despite *Zakāt*, is further dispersed.

Social Security and Insurance

Social security is generally discussed in the context of *Zakāt*. Historical material on how the early Islamic State arranged social security is presented by almost every writer on the subject. It is affirmed that new institutional arrangements can always be devised and the various institutions in modern welfare states are referred to approvingly. The principles involved have been discussed, among others, by Bāqir al Ṣadr (171: 615–623). The subject has also been discussed at the International Islamic Conference at Cairo, Kuala Lumpur and other places and practical suggestions mooted (300; 405).

Besides *Zakāt* which provides the Islamic State with funds to finance social security measures, Islam lays great stress on voluntary assistance to the needy. An elaborate concept of mutual responsibility has been presented by Sayyid Quṭb (62), among others. Kashif[18] conceives of a social security scheme in which the state collects *Zakāt* from the haves and transfers it to the have-nots; the employers contribute towards the pensions and Provident Funds of their workers; and the individual with a capacity to pay, contributes in the form of insurance premia. While *Zakāt* caters to the poor and the needy, insurance takes care of the risks to which life and property are exposed.

Insurance

Insurance continues to be one of the most controversial subjects in the literature. Opinion is sharply divided both on the principle of insurance and the forms of its organisation.

Several writers see nothing wrong in insurance, in so far as the basic principles underlying insurance are concerned. It is free from gambling, can be freed from interest which is involved in its present practice, and the ignorance (*jahl*) and uncertainty (*gharar*) involved are not of a degree large enough to call for its prohibition. These writers include Zarqa (380)[19], Yousuf Moosa (256: 101, 181), Ali al Khafeef (361), Mohammad al Bahy (351), Sanousi (373), Roohani (372), Ṭaḥāwī (77, I: 441–470), Taqi Amini (556: 231–232), Sheikh Mahmud Ahmad (168: 201–203), A. Mannan (132: 353–360), Siddiqi (374), Shaheedi and Awad.[20]

Some writers agree with this view so far as general insurance is concerned, but they find life insurance unacceptable as it involves gambling and uncertainty and militates against the Islamic conception of *taqdīr*. Abu Zuhra (376; 365), Ahmad Ibrahim (357) and Shaukat Ali Khan[21] take this stand.

There are some *ulema* (Scholars of Islamic Law), who find an element of gambling in all kinds of insurance as a matter of principle. They also find some other objectionable features, such as *ribā* and uncertainty (*gharar*) inalienably associated with insurance. Some of them, finding that it does not conform to any one of the various contracts validated by Islamic jurisprudence, regard it to be an unnecessary innovation. Sheikh Bakheet (355: 72), Abdullah al Qalqeeli (365), Mustafa Zaid (597; 376), Mufti Mohammad Shafi (531), Jalal Mustafa al Sayyad[22] and Shaukat Ali Kahn[23] take this stand.

Those who find insurance acceptable in principle generally prefer mutual insurance which is organised on a co-operative basis and does not lead to exploitation. The same is true if insurance is organised by the state. But commercial insurance involves exploitation and certain other objectionable features, and is therefore ultravirus of Islam. Abu Zuhra (355; 376; 365), Issa Abdouh (350), Muslehuddin (369), Dasooqi (355) and Ahmad Fahmi Abu Sunnah[24] who otherwise find the principle of insurance acceptable, have offered this opinion. Aṭṭar[25] refutes the view that insurance is gambling but he finds it unacceptable as most of its present forms involve a high degree of uncertainty and the possibility of fraud. He allows mutual insurance schemes but prescribes a number of measures directed at purging commercial insurance of its undesirable features (pp. 41–42). He envisages a system of insurance which is based on *Zakāt*.

Several writers, including Sheikh Ali al Khafeef, Zarqā[26] (380), Siddiqi (374) and Ṭaḥāwī (77, I: 441–470) argue, however, that the same principle underlies all forms of organised insurance. It is possible to regulate commercial insurance in such a manner that it functions without exploitation.

Mawdūdī has opined that insurancc, which presently involves interest, gambling and a violation of Islamic laws of inheritance can be reorganised free of these evils (51: 408–411). But he has not spelled out the details. The same is true of Yūsufuddīn (165, II: 452–454).

Insurance has been discussed at a number of Islamic conferences but a favourable verdict on commercial insurance has been withheld in view of the objections of the above-mentioned eminent scholars. This is brought out by the resolutions passed at the 1965 Islamic Research Congress at Cairo (211) and those adopted in 1969 at Kuala Lumpur (405: 202). As recently as 1976 the First International Conference on Islamic Economics held at Makka resolved that: "The Conference feels that commercial insurance as presently practised does not realise the *Sharī'ah* aims of co-operation and solidarity because it does not satisfy the Islamic conditions for it to become acceptable.

"The Conference recommends the establishment of a committee consisting of specialists in *Sharī'ah* and Economics to recommend a system of insurance which is free from *ribā* and speculation, promotes co-operation in accordance with the *Sharī'ah*, and helps replace the current form of commercial insurance."[27] Most of the *ulema* in India and Pakistan responding to a questionnaire issued by *Majlis Tahqīqāt Sharī'ah*, Lucknow (366) also regarded insurance as legitimate in principle.

The most important issue in the controversy is whether insurance involves gambling. Those who insist that it does quote the relevant definitions given by early jurists. But several writers including Zarqa (380), Ali al Khafeef (361), Aṭṭar, Awad[28] and Ṭaḥāwī (55, I: 451) have pointed out the difference between insurance and gambling. Siddiqi has shown the difference between the risk taken by the gambler, which he creates for himself, and those involved in the ordinary business of life that the insurers try to meet, utilising the law of large numbers, at a cost (374). He has also discussed the economic roles of gambling and insurance. Gambling upsets the normal system based on work and reward and is inimical to equitable distribution of income and wealth, whereas insurance protects the disruption of the system by accidents and events beyond human control. Sayyad[29] has failed to take these points into consideration and dismisses some other dissimilarities between gambling and insurance on insufficient reason.

Next to gambling the commercial organisation of insurance has been the target of attack. The recent trend has been in favour of nationalisation of insurance. Most writers make a plea for a comprehensive system comprising *Zakāt*-based social security and insurance administered by the state. Mutual insurance should be allowed in matters not covered by the state system. As regards commercial insurance it may be allowed to function in certain areas where great importance is attached to innovation and initiative (374).

Most of the contributors on the subject have been *ulema* who have little knowledge of Economics. As a result there is little economic analysis in most of the works on the subject. Very few have referred to the law of large numbers which lies at the basis of insurance and little effort has been made to assess the economic significance of insurance in modern life. Some writers seem to be under the misconception that a comprehensive social security system will do away with the need for insurance. They fail to distinguish between the fulfilment of needs and arrangements designed to increase efficiency and ensure the smooth functioning of large-scale business and industry.

They ignore the obvious point that individuals should be encouraged to provide for themselves, as far as they can, and protect themselves against insurable risks. The state should be called in for helping only those who do not have the capacity to do so, or fail to do so.

As ably argued by Fanjari in a recent paper,[30] there are separate roles for *Zakāt*-based social security and insurance organised on the basis of contributions made by the individuals involved (pp. 7–8). This point is increasingly being appreciated and one tends to agree with Fanjari that the area of consensus is widening and that of controversy shrinking in respect of commercial insurance also (p. 35).

Money and Banking

It is the privilege of the state to issue money and control its supply, that much is above controversy. The introduction of paper currency raised some new issues for the jurists but it was soon agreed that it made no difference.

Bāqir al Ṣadr (171: 325–331), Mahmud Abu Saud (5), Mahmud Ahmad[31] and Kahf (612: 65–68) have paid special attention to money and its role. Bāqir and Saud conclude that the use of money as a store of value is a source of many troubles. While Bāqir regards *Zakāt*, which discourages idle cash balances, and abolition of interest, which frustrates the desire to earn guaranteed profits by using such money, as sufficient remedies for the troubles in the Islamic system, Abu Saud does not stop at that. "It is necessary to issue a new kind of money and subject it to a tax other than *Zakāt* to check hoarding and ensure its continuous circulation and stop all usurious earnings arising from it" (5: 47). As a practical measure he favours the idea of stamped money,[32] suggested by Gessel and briefly tried in the municipality of Woergl, Switzerland in 1922 (5: 40–45). The idea has failed, so far, to find support in the literature.[33] One tends to agree with Kahf when he says that "Abū Saud's proposal discriminates between money assets and non-money assets" and "involves injustice by not taking into account the change of hands during the period and leaving the whole burden of the stamp on the last holder" (612: 67). Kahf thinks that, generally speaking, Islamic writers have overlooked the inter-temperal use of money, i.e. its function as a store of value, which is a boon and not a bane.

Of special interest in the context of money in an Islamic economy is the contribution of Mabid al Jarhi[34] who pleads for the creation of a "fiat means of exchange" by the state and their supply free of cost (i.e. interest) to the public. This method, adopted along with abolition of interest will raise real income.

Akram has discussed money in the international context. An "Islamic solution" to the present international monetary crisis lies in prohibiting interest, speculation, hoarding of gold and suspension of the foreign exchange market, the central banks becoming the only dealers of foreign exchange. Private use of gold may be banned and all the gold mined should flow directly to the monetary authorities (558). Such sweeping reforms cannot be considered, much less accepted, unless they are supplemented by a detailed discussion on the pros and cons, which Akram fails to provide.

Banking

The Islamic evaluation of modern banking centred around the evils of the institution of interest. Very soon it developed into an exploration which bears great promise of giving modern man a new and just institution, of banking without interest.

In discussing modern banking some writers attack the institution of credit and its creation by commercial banks. Mawdūdī's otherwise brilliant study is a case in point (521: 117–133). Issa Abdouh also thinks that credit creation by banks is prejudicial to the interest of people with small incomes (382). Muhammad Uzair blames wide fluctuations in money supply and credit creation for trade cycles (422). This trend culminates in the suggestion made by the Economic Committee of *Jamā'at-i-Islāmī* Pakistan that the power to create credit be taken away from Commercial Banks (126: 80–82). Kahf also deprives private sector banking of the power to create credit, which should be the privilege of the state, the sole creator of money (612: 65–68). Naseer A. Sheikh also regards the power of banks to create money or to extend credit to be the cause of money ills (154: 78), and so do Assal and Fathi.[35]

A: Banking Without Interest

The earliest references to the reorganisation of banking on the basis of profit sharing rather than interest are found in Qureshi (526), Naiem Siddiqi (419) and Mahmud Ahmad (168) in the late forties, followed by a more elaborate exposition by Mawdūdī in 1950 (521). We are not aware of any work on the subject in Arabic during the forties. Three early works on Islam's economic system in Urdu by Hifzur Rahman (120), Gilani (28) and Yousufuddin (165) do not mention the subject.

Qureshi's reference to the subject is brief (526: 156–160) and it is based on a wrong notion of *muḍārabah*. Naiem Siddiqi is more elaborate, having separately discussed the depositor-bank and bank-businessman relations. He suggests a larger share of profit on long-term deposits, as compared to that on short term ones. Despite originality, his scheme also suffers from a misconception about *muḍārarbah* (419). Mahmud Ahmad bases his scheme on partnership. It is not entirely clear whether he distinguishes *muḍārabah* from *Shirkah* (168: 190–224). In Mawdūdī's scheme deposits will be accepted from the public on the basis of partnership, profits being distributed on these "shares". Deposits will also be accepted as "loans" repayable on demand and "*amānāt*" repayable on demand. The "loan" deposit funds will be utilised by the bank for making advances to businessmen on the basis of *muḍārabah*, a facility against which they will be obliged to give short-term interest-free loans from out of the same funds.

Mawdūdī has expressed himself against collection and disbursement of *Zakāt* funds by Islamic banks (133: 304–305).

Though a small booklet of 21 pages, Muhammad Uzair's "An Outline of Interestless Banking" has the distinction of being the first published work exclusively devoted to the subject by a professional economist (422). It contains the core of all the future proposals on the subject, basing depositor-banker and banker-businessmen relations on *muḍārabah*, which is defined correctly. It does not discuss central banking and takes the unrealistic stand that there should be no credit creation. It contains a good, though brief, discussion on international financial relations. In a later study (423) Uzair suggests centralised management of all foreign transactions in the banks of the state.

Ahmad Irshad's work (400) is also devoted exclusively to the subject and contains useful suggestions on the creation of reserve funds to absorb losses. It discusses Industrial Development banks, building corporations and consumption loans. The scheme suffers from a wrong notion about *muḍārabah* as sharing of both profits and losses by the business partners.

Abdul Hadi Ghanameh's 1968 paper on the subject (392) takes a line different from the one along which further thinking on the subject has developed. He relies on issue of common stock for long-term financing and the use of mutual funds for short-term financing. "A mutual fund is an investment company that buys the common stock of other industrial or commercial companies" (392: 96). Unfortunately, the comprehensive book which Ghanameh promises in this paper is not available to us to enable a detailed comparison between his scheme and the one that seems to have now found general acceptance.

Muslehuddin's[36] rejection of *muḍārabah* as the basis of interest-free banking is largely a product of his narrow legalistic approach to *muḍārabah* and of his failure to realise that the very concept of banking is bound to undergo a change once it is organised on a basis other than interest – a point ably argued by Tawfiq Shawi.[37] One such change is a sharp decline in the banks' lending activity and an increase in investment proper.[38] As a matter of fact, an interest-free bank cannot function as a purely commercial bank.

Muslehuddin's contention that the "Islamic bank will not be able to make advances to the concerns which have already invested capital of their own . . . for it will be quite against the principle of *muḍārabah*,[39] has no basis in Islamic jurisprudence and ignores the evidence cited in favour of the contrary from all the four schools of Islamic Law" (176: 72–85).

Another argument against the feasibility of *muḍārabah* is fear of fraudulent practices by banks' business partners who may understate their profits. This view has been controverted by pointing out the possibility of financial and management audit taking care of such practices. It has also been argued that firms failing to report good profits will lose the chances of getting more bank advances and this would serve as a deterrent to such practices.[40]

As regards the supply of short-term credit in an interest-free system it is recognised by almost every writer on the subject that *muḍārabah* can be a basis of such credit only to a limited extent. This does not, however, preclude other solutions as discussed below.

Having rejected *muḍārabah*, Muslehuddin fails to provide an alternative basis for interest-free banking. As banking for him means commercial banking, he ends up with a plea for allowing the banks to realise "service charges" on loans.[41] The main issue of intermediation between savers and investors on a basis other than fixed-interest payment remains unresolved.

The view that *muḍārabah* cannot provide an alternative to interest in the reorganisation of banking has also been expressed by Dr Mahmud Abu Saud on a different ground.[42] He thinks such a reorganisation will lead to the emergence of a "black market" in which interest will reappear.[43] Should the authorities succeed in enforcing the legal prohibition of interest successfully, savers will prefer the stock market and buy shares rather than deposit in *muḍārabah* banks.[44] Hoarding will increase and the monetary authority will be constrained to create more and more cash.[45] This, coupled with the increased demand for interest-free loans and the possibility of the sudden release of the hoarded cash on the stock exchange will pose a constant threat of inflation to the system.[46]

His own solution to these dangers lies in *Zakāt* which can be best applied by taxing money in circulation in a way similar to that suggested by Silvio Gessel.[47] We have already examined this suggestion above. It is obvious that Abu Saud has not cared to examine in detail the recent elaborations of the *muḍārabah*-based model of banking, briefly discussed below. His reference to this model as the "Mawdūdī-Qureshi School"[48] and his failure to take notice of the more systemic works appearing in the sixties and seventies bears this out.

A mature and comprehensive model of interest-free banking has resulted from works appearing in the late sixties by the late Dr. Abdullah al Araby (384), Siddiqi (417), Bāqir al Ṣadr (387) and Najjār (411). Followed by the Egyptian study in 1972 and the deliberation at the Karachi Conference of the Finance Ministers of the Islamic Countries in 1970, they lead us to the adoption of the charter of the Islamic Development Bank in 1974, which is the first major institution of its kind in history. In between we have the "Kuwaiti Investment House" project (405) and some periodical literature contributed by Shalbi (415), Mahmud Ahmad (628), Huda (397), Mannan (407), Muhammad Uzair (420; 421) and Ibrahim Dasooqi Abaza (381).

A. Mannan's textbook on Islamic Economics (132) has a separate chapter on the subject and Dr. Issa Abdouh has also written on the subject (382; 505).

More contributions have been made during the early seventies, including fairly comprehensive studies by Gharib al-Gammal (391), Mustafa Abdullah al-Hamshari (396) and Sami Hamūd,[49] besides the papers presented at the Makka Conference on Islamic Economics.

With the exception of Najjār's scheme, the first mentioned works conceive the bank mainly as a financial intermediary mobilising savings from the public on the basis of profit-sharing (*muḍārabah*) and making advances to entrepreneurs on the same basis. Profits of enterprise are shared by the bank according to a mutually agreed percentage. The bank shares these profits with depositors in the *muḍārabah* accounts according to a percentage announced by the bank in advance. Liability to loss in capital in the bank-entrepreneur deal attaches to the bank, though the bank is not likely to incur losses on the totality of its advances due to diversification of investments. Depositors in *muḍārabah* accounts can be absolved of the risk of loss, attaching to them in principle, by a number of practical devices. A different position is taken by Bāqir which is noted below. The banks shall also accept deposits in current accounts with the promise to pay on demand. No profits are to be paid to such depositors from whom a service charge may or may not be collected. The bank shall be obliged to grant short-term interest-free loans on a limited scale.

This being the essential core of the model, individual contributions have special features to which we turn now.

Najjār's banks are institutions designed to promote savings and effect their useful employment in the rural sector. They would be actively involved in developmental projects resorting to partnership, instead of *muḍārabah*. They have a "Social Service Fund" attracting *Zakāt* donations from the public and organising social services in the locality. They are a decentralised chain of institutions sharing the features of a local bank, a co-operative society and a social service organisation. Najjār does not discuss the other issues involved in commercial banking and central banking. He regards the reorganisation of banks without interest as part of the larger issue restructuring the backward economies of the Islamic countries so that stagnation is ended, dynamism introduced and the process of development started, utilising Islamic values and traditions. The model of interest-free banking he presents is incidental to this larger theme.

Bāqir's work is a response to a questionnaire by a group of people in Kuwait who wanted to know how they could launch a banking company without interest. He presumed that he had to take as given the actual reality obtaining in Kuwait and elsewhere, that the rest of the system continues on un-Islamic lines, and the other banks and financial institutions with which the proposed bank would have to interact and compete continue to function on the basis of interest (387: 57). Accordingly his work does not answer the theoretical but larger question: how banks would function in an interest-free Islamic society. His frame of reference also excluded any discussion on credit control, consumer finance and finance for the government. Credit creation and financial papers are discussed in the very limited context of the operation of a single interest-free bank surrounded by a sea of interest-based institutions.

Unlike Najjār's banks, Bāqir's bank is a financial intermediary not directly participating in productive enterprise. Another significant feature of his bank is that depositors are absolved of the liability to loss, even in principle (387: 72, 187). He is mostly concerned, however, with the juristic justification of this guarantee and does not go into its economic rationale. This preoccupation with the legality rather than economics of the various provisions he has suggested has a deep impact on his entire work. For example, he discusses the various "valid" ways of the bank charging a fee (*Ji'āla*), which appear to be devious methods of ensuring a reasonable income to the bank itself – something to which a straightforward approach is also possible. He has even suggested that the bank make a deposit with some other (interest-based) bank in order to earn interest to meet a particular need (387: 104). Such a suggestion may not be morally repugnant to some people, but what is important for this study is its irrelevance for Islamic economics where what matters are viable alternatives to the present arrangements that have universal validity.

As exemplified by Bāqir's Appendices three and five, his keenness to absolve the depositors of even the theoretical liability to losses has given rise to serious difficulties relating to the legal status of the bank and justification of its share in profits. It is no longer the working partner (*'Āmil*) in relation to the depositors and the capitalist partner in relation to the businessmen, in *muḍārabah* contracts – a position it enjoys in the models suggested by Siddiqi and Abdullah al-Araby. He seeks to resolve this difficulty by relying on particular juristic opinions whose general acceptability is very doubtful. Kahf rightly notes "the suggested application of the principle of the prize, *Ji'āla* as called in Islamic jurisprudence, as percentage of the time deposit bears only a formal difference from interest and I could not find any difference between them as far as content is concerned", and that "to have a workable set up in the long run being built on legal tricks as part of its structure does not seem to me logically sound" (612: 91–92).

Though the major part of Abdullah al-Araby's paper deals with the evils of contemporary banking, his brief discussion on interest-free banking contains the essential core of the model stated above. Besides, he has also discussed international banking, agricultural banks, industrial banks and savings banks.

Siddiqi is mainly concerned with the economics of interest-free banking, having disposed of the juristic issues in a separate work (249). He has full length discussion on the creation and control of credit, consumer finance and finance for the government and, provision of short-term interest-free loans to business. He introduces certain financial papers to replace bonds and securities. His main contribution lies in a number of novel suggestions relating to central banking.

> "The central bank will offer refinance facilities against interest-free loans made by the commercial banks, in case these banks need additional cash to maintain their liquidity. The extent of accommodation provided by the central bank will be fixed as a ratio to loans made by commercial banks" (158: 105).

It is pointed out that the "refinance ratio" would serve as a means for contracting credit in inflationary situations and as an instrument of selective credit control, as different refinance ratios could be fixed with respect to loans given to different sectors of the economy (158: 105).

Siddiqi suggests the use of "shares" issued by the government for financing public sector enterprises as a means of open market operations by the central banks (417: 123–129). Loan Certificates of various denominations and different maturities, to be issued by the government, are suggested as a means of providing short-term finance for it. He suggests tax concessions as an incentive to the "buyer" of these certificates (417: 149–182). He has also suggested how incentives could be built into the system in order to make the banks provide short-term interest-free loans for business (417: 44–60). The problem how to ensure an equilibrium between the demand for interest-free loans and their supply has been discussed by Siddiqi in his recent paper.[50] Much of the demand for call money and very short-term loans emanates from within the financial sector itself and is likely to be eliminated as that sector shrinks in consequence of the abolition of interest. In the production sector, the total demand for short-term credit depends on the volume of long-term investment and the extent of trade credit (credit by one firm to another). Credit needs for the week or the month can be estimated at the macro-level. This could be done by the central bank – which would then ensure a supply commensurate with the demand by manipulating the "refinance ratio" and the "lending ratio". The task of allocating these loanable funds at the micro-level would then be performed by individual banks on the following criteria:

(1) Specific credit needs of a firm.
(2) Social priority attaching to the enterprise.
(3) Nature of the security offered against the loan.
(4) Whether the credit seeker has also obtained long-term advances from the bank for the same enterprise.
(5) Annual, monthly or weekly average of the applicants balance in current account with the bank.

It is within the competence of the Central Bank to exercise direct and indirect influence on banks' decisions on the second ground. Discriminatory use of the refinance ratio is a case in point. Banks are expected to prefer good securities over the not so good and patronise client firms over enterprises in which they have no stakes. A credit seeker's average balances in the current account may provide a basis for overdraft facilities – one form in which short-term credit is granted.

"The Egyptian Study on the Establishment of the Islamic Banking System" envisages a *Zakāt* Fund and a "local and public Islamic Fund", besides organising the normal banking functions on the basis of *muḍārabah*. While the essential core of the model remains the same as stated above, the proposed scheme has a number of distinguishing features.

Depositors in the current accounts are offered, besides being free from service charges, "a part of the profits due to the bank as its contribution" (390: 20). They are given priority in banking services such as "accepting bills of exchange" without interest. Depositors in "savings accounts" are offered overdraft facility, without interest, as well as other services such as letters of credit and acceptance of their bills of exchange, besides their due share in profits on the basis of *muḍārabah* (390: 21).

As regards interest-free loans to the public, they may be given out of *Zakāt* funds. Regarding bills of exchange two ways are suggested. The bank may give cash to the creditor and become a sharer in the profits of the buyer, on the basis of *muḍārabah*. Alternatively, it may cash the bill (which amounts to an interest-free loan to the buyer) provided the parties concerned have a current account with the banks with an average annual balance amounting to a certain percentage of the value of the bill (390: 25). The second method is recommended only in case the first is not feasible. It might be noted that Mawdūdī (521) and Siddiqi (419) had suggested the same.

Ali Abdur Rasul allows discount on bills of trade.[51] The legal principle involved in "leaving a part of a loan to (be appropriated by) the one who gets that loan repaid (by the borrower) as a reward of this service of securing the repayment".[52] It follows that if a loan is not actually repaid no reward can be paid.[53] This view does not find support in the literature for the obvious reason that it amounts to charging interest on the advance made against a bill of exchange. While Ali Abdur Rasul's reference to Maliki jurists deserves consideration by experts on Islamic law, a look at the economic implications of his suggestions is more appropriate for us in this study. It would not be objectionable if a reasonable service charge was allowed to the bank which makes an interest-free loan against a bill of exchange, subject to the condition that the borrower will repay the loan if the bill is not honoured by the drawee on maturity. The intent and impact of a discount is different, being similar to interest on the sum lent, irrespective of profit or loss in the business which is financed. Ali Abdur Rasul says nothing as to the rate of this discount, maybe its determination is left to the market, as is the rate of interest. Some writers have rightly pointed out that a profit arrangement should be possible in case of most of the bills of exchange.

Uzair thinks the annual rate of return in an enterprise can be applied for calculating the returns on advances made for a period of one to three months.[54] Alternatively we can try to determine the specific rate of return on the funds advanced. But it may not be possible to do so in many cases. For short-term loans for less than a month, Uzair suggests "service charges" on a per transaction basis.[55] The bank would not get any reward for lending as service charges will have to correspond to the actual costs of servicing these loans. Uzair has rejected the idea of arranging the supply of short-term credit as a free service on the ground that "the solution for a business problem has to be found on business lines rather than as a goodwill gesture".[56] One wonders how lending could be a business proposition once interest is abolished. Defining business as an activity directed at profits, a "business loan" is a contradiction in terms as a "loan" cannot carry a profit under Islamic law. The need to "modify the conceptual framework of economics to suit the requirements of Islamic economics"[57] is not confined to the concept of capital alone. The concept of "loan" also qualifies for this purpose.[58]

The problem of bad debts is solved by means of "Co-operative Insurance" to which "borrowers contribute a certain sum of money to cover the possible risk" (390: 43). *Zakāt* funds provide the other source out of which bad debts can be recovered.

Local banks may carry out direct investment besides advancing capital on the basis of *muḍārabah*.

The Egyptian study also spells out the salient features of central banking and international banking. The International bank would serve as a link between the national banking, commercial, developmental and *Zakāt*-based institutions in Muslim countries. It would finance commercial and developmental institutions in these countries. It would also organise commercial exchange between Muslim and non-Muslim countries, besides functioning as a clearing house for intra-Islamic transactions. The study also envisages the setting-up of an investment and development body of Islamic countries.

The "Kuwaiti Investment House" project which antedates the Egyptian study, and also the works of al-Araby and Siddiqi, was much limited in scope (405). It was to be a joint stock banking institution making diversified investments on the basis of *muḍārabah*. An outstanding feature of that project was its elaborate scheme of precautionary reserves and profit distribution designed to protect the interests of the depositors and shareholders. It envisaged collection and disbursement of *Zakāt* funds and the supply of interest-free loans on a limited scale. Recently a number of banks have been established which are committed to eschew interest and promote Islamic ideals, the foremost being the Islamic Development Bank at Jeddah.

B: The Islamic Development Bank

The purpose of the bank is "to foster economic development and social progress of member countries and Muslim Communities individually as well as jointly in accordance with the principles of the *Sharī'ah*" (389: Article 1). It will "participate in equity capital of productive projects and enterprises in member countries", "invest in economic and social infrastructure projects in member countries by way of participation or other financial arrangements", "make loans to the private and public sectors for the financing of productive projects, enterprises and programmes" and "establish and operate special funds for specific purposes including a Fund for assistance to Muslim communities in non-member countries" (Article 2, i–vii). It will also operate Trust Funds, accept deposits and raise funds in any other manner. It will provide technical assistance to member countries and assist in promotion of foreign trade, especially in capital goods, among member countries (Article 2: vii, ix). It intends "to co-operate . . . with all bodies, institutions and organisations having similar purposes, in pursuance of international economic co-operation" (Article 2, xii). An important function of the bank shall be "to undertake research for enabling the economic, financial and banking activities in Muslim countries to conform to *Sharī'ah*" (Article 2: xi).

"The authorised capital stock of the Bank will be two thousand million (2,000,000,000) Islamic Dinars . . ." (Article 4, 6), one Islamic Dinar having the value of one special Drawing Right of the IMF (Article 4a).

As to financing "the Bank shall seek to maintain a suitable ratio between equity investment made in, and loans granted to, member countries" (Article 16, 4). "The Bank shall retain the option to sell its equity participation" (Article 17, 4). Normally it will not provide loans to an enterprise in whose equity it has participated (Article 17, 6). It shall "seek to maintain reasonable diversification in its equity investment" (Article 17, 8).

"The bank shall levy a service fee to cover its administrative expenses" (Article 20, 3).

Regarding the distribution of profits it has been provided that "no part of the net income or surplus of the Bank shall be distributed to members by way of profit until the General Reserve of the Bank shall have attained the level of twenty-five per cent of the subscribed capital" (Article 42, 1). This distribution "shall be made in proportion to the number of shares held by each member" (389: Article 42, 4).

Discussing the distinctive features of the Islamic Development Bank in the light of its Articles of Association and the highlights of the Islamic economic and banking systems, Shawi[59] points out that the crucial decision not to operate on the basis of interest has led the IDB to devise unique methods not traditionally adopted by development banks, such as participation in development projects at all levels – supply of capital, management and sharing of profits and losses.

The decision to attract deposits from the public (e.g. through issue of investment certificates) is another unconventional step the IDB has taken in view of the fact that it cannot go to the money market to obtain funds.

Shawi also points out the important place given to social progress side by side with economic development. This again is unique as conventional banks are financial institutions interested in profits or in the case of development banks, in "economic" development. The IDB is an expression of the solidarity of the Islamic peoples. The concept of the Islamic Dinar is a pointer towards a currency union of the Islamic countries.[60] Its adoption as the unit of account will protect the bank from the consequences of price fluctuations in the countries with which it is dealing. The provision that the value of the Islamic Dinar equals the value of one SDR is transitional. It suits the member countries under the present circumstances, but they can specify its value otherwise if and when they find it advisable to do so.

The evil consequences of interest have been well known to the economists as well as the laymen, but they had no alternative before them in banking and finance. Attempts at escaping from these evils through co-operative institutions of various types had failed because they catered only to the interests of particular groups of people and had to work as a part of the all-pervading interest-based system. The significance of the Islamic Development Bank lies in being the heralder of a viable and just alternative.

With the huge amount of investible funds available out of the oil revenues of some of the members of the Islamic Development Bank, and the vast opportunities of development waiting for investment in Asia and Africa, the stated objectives of the Bank charge it with great responsibilities and justifiably raise many expectations. Only the future can reveal how far these potentialities could be actualised. It seems however advisable to work for a network of similar institutions throughout the individual countries and communities involved in the process. Many writers mentioned above advocate this step. It is hoped that the subject will increasingly attract expert attention, now that an impetus has been provided by the establishment of the IDB.

The IDB has already gone into operation and a report on the first year of its working is available.[61] Large unused resources are understandably causing a problem as Islamic avenues for the profitable utilisation are not immediately available. Yet the Bank has successfully participated in a few projects in Algeria and elsewhere.

The establishment of the IDB has been followed by a few more Islamic Banks at Dubai (386), Cairo and Khartoum. The Dubai Islamic Bank established in 1975 has successfully completed the first year of its operation. It has mostly gone into real estate business and construction projects. No reports are available on the one established at Cairo in 1976 and its counterpart at Khartoum. The Philippines Amanah Bank has also been working without interest as a subsidiary of the Central Bank of the Philippines which, as the custodian of its reserves, earmarks the interest due for a special fund for Muslim welfare.

Industrial Relations, Labour and Population Policy

Those who have paid special attention to labour and industrial relations emphasise dignity of labour in Islam, the religious significance of good, honest work, and the labour's right to a decent wage commensurate with the average standards of living in the society. There is great emphasis on co-operation between labour and enterprise and on mutual consultation as a mode of decision making. Hameedullah (433), Yusufuddin (165: 365–388), Gamaluddin (425; 426), Chapra (115), Ṭaḥāwī (77), Ali Abdur Rasul,[62] Abdul Hadi[63] and Assal[64] are some of the writers sharing this emphasis. Abdul Majeed Qureshi, the *Jamā'at-i-Islāmī* labour expert in Pakistan, makes a strong plea for just wages for the labour and that the privileged position of capital be taken away from it and be restored back to labour. " 'Depreciation' of labour must be paid for: just as the expenses for maintenance, repair and reconditioning of buildings and machinery are accounted for in the expenditure of the business, similarly maintenance of health and medical aid should be fully accounted for in regular expenditure" (341: 27). Qureshi reserves half of the total profits of a concern for labour and would also like to see labour own 60 per cent shares in the concern at which they are working (441: 26–28). His notion of just wages are, however, regarded as undefinable by Faridi (431: 64) who thinks

Qureshi had adopted the Marxian approach. Shafi Malik too regards Qureshi to be vague and confused (435: 90). But the *Jamā'at-i-Islāmī* Pakistan Economic Committee report (126) echoes some of Qureshi's ideas. The just wages are defined by the report as a need-based minimum plus a differential according to nature of work, technical competence, course of work, productivity and profitability of the industry. These wages must be supplemented by a number of other facilities: residential, medical, educational, recreational, etc. Labour is also entitled to a bonus or profits and to the produce of the industry at commercial rates, if not free. He should be given financial aid or interest-free loans (repayable subject to capacity to pay) in case of emergency. The idea of making labourers shareholders in the concerns in which they are working also finds strong support in the report (126: 28–32). Mawdūdī has also endorsed this view "so that they (labourers) become interested in the growth of the industry in which they are employed" (51: 405). The suggestion finds a place in the *Jamā'at-i-Islāmī* Pakistan Manifesto for the 1970 elections (125: 29).

Examining the notion of "just wages" as elaborated in the above-mentioned report, Muhammad Akram finds its economic rationale dubious and suggests another model in which the wage rate is linked with the profits of the firm (613: 43–44). Distinguishing between need-based minimum wages and ideal wages which would "bridge the gulf between the living conditions of the employers and the employees" Chapra leaves the actual wages to be determined between these two limits "by the interaction of supply and demand, the extent of economic growth, the level of moral consciousness in the Muslim society and the extent to which the state plays its legitimate role" (115: 12–13).

Population Policy

Population control through family planning has been one of the most controversial subjects in the literature. The permission or otherwise of birth control by individuals in certain circumstances, in the light of the Qur'ān and the *Sunnah*, though relevant for this controversy, is not the matter that concerns us here. From the viewpoint of Islamic Economics we are interested mainly in two points. Does there exist an economic base for population control? And if it does, is family planning permitted by Islam, as a means to this end? It is only on these points that we will record the various opinions below.

Writing in the late thirties Mawlana Mawdūdī strongly opposed family planning. There is no economic case for population control. The argument based on scarcity of resources is dismissed as unrealistic and amounting to a loss of faith in God (458: 104–130). Population control has no place in Islamic culture (458: 67–80). God is the real planner of the human population (458: 150–153). Birth control leads to many physiological, moral and social ills (458: 81–98). Economically too, it is harmful. It will decrease aggregate demand, reduce employment and cause depression (458: 99–100). As to the argument that family planning enables better nourishment and education of children, Mawdūdī refers to the beneficial effects of adversity and wants on human character (458: 132).

According to him the only solution Islam presents for the problem of increasing world population is "augmentation and full utilisation of the resources of His bounty that God has created and a perpetual effort at discovering hidden resources" (457).

Endorsing Mawdūdī's views, Khurshid Ahmad (454), notes that the Malthusian prognosis on population growth has been belied by history (454: 168–172). There was never an economic case for birth control. This movement is a tool of Western imperialism to check the population of poor nations from rising and posing a threat to Western domination (454: 176–180). "Increase in population is generally beneficial economically" (454: 189). He has little faith in population projections. "If the organisational structure of the economy is developed in accordance with population there is no question of the population problem arising economically". . . . There is abundance of natural resources . . . if only the whole of the world was treated as one unit. "The real cause of economic decadence in the world is the selfishness of the Western man" (454: 191). "The real solution lies in improving economic and cultural resources and increasing production" (454: 201).

Similar views have been expressed by Sheikh Abu Zuhra who opposed population control through family planning on religious grounds (448; 449). He, along with Sheikh Khidr Husain, and most of those participating in a symposium held at Cairo in the early fifties (459) took this stand while allowing birth control for individuals in certain circumstances. The same is true of the deliberations at the international Islamic Congress at Cairo in 1965 (211). This is also the dominant view in India and Pakistan.

The International Planned Parenthood Federation organised a conference on this issue in December 1971 at Rabāṭ, of which the complete proceedings are now available in two volumes covering 1000 pages (452). Most of the participants considered population control through family planning as lawful in Islam and many regarded it as having become a necessity under the present circumstances. These scholars have discussed in detail the relevant issues of jurisprudence and the points of law involved. An appendix quotes a number of *fatwā* by eminent authorities on Islamic law such as Sheikh Abdul Majeed Saleem (which, however, touches only the individual aspect of the matter), Sheikh Mahmud Shaltūt (which goes only a little further), Sheikh Hasan Mamoon (which permits family planning but warns against coercion) and Sheikh Abdullah al Qalqīlī (which allows population control through family planning) (452: 541–566). Those who participated in the conference and supported family planning and population control include Ahmad al-Sharbasi (468) and Salam Madkoor (456). Another eminent scholar supporting population control through family planning is al Bahi al Khauli who declares that it is open to the rulers to appeal to the community to adopt this method, and to provide facilities for the same, when they find the social, economic, political and external circumstances of the community calling for such a policy (455: 192).

From among Islamic Economists who have discussed this issue, A. Mannan (132: 117–126, 138–147) admits that the issue is controversial, but he recommends population control through family planning, under the present circumstances and advances social, physiological and eugenic reasons in support.

Growth and Development

That one of the main objectives of modern Islamic states will be to achieve rapid economic development (221, II: 123–141) is a point stressed by all recent writings on the subject. Economic backwardness of the present-day Muslim countries and communities is seen as a hindrance to the fulfilment of their Islamic role in the world and a blot on their Islamic identity. What, then, is the strategy of economic development in the Economic system of Islam?

Some writers, including Akram (483) and Fanjari (477; 478) lay the main emphasis on the transformation of man, and the ethos of an Islamic society.

Abāẓa (473) like Fanjari (477) sees a great role for Islam in economic development as it regards developmental efforts to be *jihād*. Once that idea catches on we can expect big results. Ṭaḥāwī also thinks that invoking the Islamic injunctions in the context of developmental efforts will prove to be the most effective way of generating a powerful movement for economic development among the Muslim masses (77, II: 32).

According to Abāẓa (473: 1127) the *Sharī'ah* calls for interaction and co-ordination between production and distribution in the framework of comprehensive economic planning, but conditions prevailing in the Muslim countries at present necessitate that priority be given to directing maximum efforts towards increasing production. Distribution can take priority when the fruits of these efforts are available. It is not the distribution of a static quantity but that of a dynamic and growing one that is visualised by Islam.

Malik ben Nabi (484: 51) questions the thesis that the key to economic dynamism is capital investment. The source of dynamism lies in man and in the collective will of the society. Islamic strategy for economic development should not blindly accept the supremacy of capital lest it is frustrated because of capital shortage in Muslim countries. It should rely on awakening the man in the land of Islam and should generate a will for the performance of the Islamic mission for which economic development has become a necessary prerequisite. "The crucial issue in the world of Islam is not that of availability of capital, but that of harnessing the social forces: man, land and time, in a project propelled by a cultural will undeterred by any difficulties" (484: 84).

Malik ben Nabi regrets to note that countries in the Third World focus their attention on capital in planning for economic development. As they do not have enough capital they must borrow from others and depend on foreign expertise which has no intimate knowledge of the local situation. This strategy has failed to deliver the goods. He cites the experience of point Four programme to prove his point (484: 89–90).

As a recent example of economic regeneration based on the cultural will of the people and a strategy tailored for the local conditions Malik ben Nabi refers to China (484: 85, 90).

Malik ben Nabi is highly appreciated by Austervy who has some important points to make in an essay devoted to Islam and Economic Development (475). He finds the Islamic temperament uncongenial for the dynamic entrepreneurial role of Schumpeter's egotistic and highly individualistic innovators. The unsatiable urge for profits, the propensity to take risk and the will to dominate which lay at the root of the economic revolution in the West are conspicuous by their absence from the Islamic personality (475: 38–43). The motive force for economic development must, therefore, emerge from religion itself. Nourished by a desire to recapture the past glory of Islam, its mode has to be collective rather than individualistic, in consonance with the nature of the desire and the temperament of the Muslim *Ummah*. Economic development in an Islamic society has to be a co-operative affair (475: 96–113). He envisages a significant role for planning in economic development in Islam.

Faridi refutes the view that Islamic values are inimical to economic progress and points out that "the present acquiescence in established institutions and practices has been borne of internal political organisations, colonialism and other vested interests. Islam has little to do with it" (479: 53).

Kalim Siddiqi's Islamic development plan regards the "socialisation of surplus value" as the crucial issue and declāres that "only Islam can motivate voluntary sacrifice of it by the peasant and labourer" (494: 26–27). It is for the Islamic State to ensure correct motivation. He concludes on the need for a new Islamic model of industrialisation, finding the contemporary approach inept and unproductive.

While the afore-mentioned writers envisage a process of economic development that will be distinctively Islamic in view of the incentives, the collective mode and the way distributive justice is inalienably associated with the process of growth, there are others who regard development dependent on certain economic processes, of savings, investment and technological advancement and proceed to declare that all these shall find sufficient encouragement in the Islamic society to ensure growth. Listing the principal causes of growth as the effort to economise, knowledge of production and increasing amount of resources per head, Marghoob Qureshi cites the Qur'ān and the *Sunnah* to emphasise that Islam ensures all of them (492).

Zubair[65] finds Islam conducive to all the essential prerequisites of growth: it encourages accumulation of capital as well as human capital formation which leads to expansion in productive capacity. The resulting rise in income leads to increase in consumption as well as investment as Islam discourages idle cash balances.

Economic development in an Islamic framework has recently attracted several writers including Namiq[66], Khurshid[67] and Siddiqi.[68] Khurshid Ahmad notes the "crisis and revaluation" through which Development Economics is presently passing. Admitting the importance of technological relationship in any plan for development he stresses the point that technological decisions are made in the context of value relations. Man is the active agent of change, and change in the hearts of men is no less important than change in the environment.

He includes development of human personality as well as continuous sustained increase in national product with the correct product mix in goals of development policy in Islam. In this context he emphasises production of necessaries, defence goods and capital goods. Improvement in the quality of life involving distributive justice and employment come next. Balanced development, evolution of indigenous technology and "re-education of national dependency on the outside world and greater integration within the Muslim world" are the other goals listed.[69] Siddiqi regards increase in production, distributive justice, environmental balance and improvement in the quality of life in the cultural sense as the four necessary dimensions of development in an Islamic framework. Discussing the process of development in some detail and focussing on Africa and South and South East Asia, he concludes by enumerating the "main steps required for initiating and accelerating all-sided development" as under:

(1) Transforming the individual through a massive educational drive, aiming at 100 per cent literacy, commitment to social goals and inculcation of Islamic values.
(2) Strengthening the Muslim states through a powerful Islamic movement resulting in popular democratic Islamic regimes committed to the Islamic mission.
(3) Creating a popular will to develop, under the leadership of the state supported by the socially-oriented entrepreneurs, involving the

masses in productive work and fuller utilisation of natural and human resources.

(4) Curbing conspicuous consumption, both private and public, and guaranteeing a minimum level of consumption to all, accompanied by fiscal discipline ensuring the channelisation of the additional incomes generated to capital formation.

(5) Regional planning to ensure economic co-ordination of the countries in North Africa and South and South East Asia to effect a balanced development of the entire region making it self sufficient in food and agricultural products and most of the manufactured goods.

(6) Decreasing the dependence of the region on the developed countries by providing aid to the oil-poor countries out of the surpluses of the oil-rich countries and promoting trade between the countries of the region.

(7) Reorganising the financial institutions to free them from instruments of exploitation and the means through which the few centres of high finance exercise control on the economics and societies of the poor countries.

(8) National planning within the framework of the regional plan to ensure growth with justice, environmental balance and improvement of the cultural life.

(9) Increasing co-operation with all the developing countries of the world through trade, aid and other suitable means with a view to decreasing inequalities between nations.

(10) Vigorous participation in the efforts to secure a new world order ensuring peace, progress and social justice.

IV

ISLAMIC CRITIQUE OF CONTEMPORARY ECONOMIC THEORIES AND SYSTEMS

Criticism of Capitalism and Communism dates back quite early in the literature on Islamic Economics. It started during the twenties and the thirties and it was largely the challenge of these alien economic philosophies which provided the impetus for the first works on the subject that appeared during the fourth decade of this century.

Both *laissez faire* capitalism and Marxian socialism have been subjected to severe criticism. This criticism is generally based on the end products of these systems, in terms of injustice, human suffering and loss of individual freedom. But the philosophical and theoretical bases of the two systems have also been examined and refuted. The philosophy of Natural Law,

Individualism, Utilitarianism and the view that pursuit of self-interest by individuals results in ensuring the social good, have all been rejected as baseless. Similarly the Labour Theory of Value, the view that forces of production determine relations of production which determine "the superstructure of values" and the Marxian Theory of state have also been criticised and rejected. The two systems have been characterised as two extreme and unbalanced approaches to solving man's economic problems and Islam has been projected as the Middle Way assimilating the good points in both the systems and free from the imbalances from which they suffer. The great poet of Islam Muhammad Iqbal[70] (d. 1938) had already popularised this approach long before scholars and journalists took up the subject.

Capitalism

Mawdūdī (607: 26–51) mentions private property, freedom of enterprise, profit motive as the sole incentive, competition, discrimination between the rights of the employees and those of the employer, reliance on natural forces for growth and the principle of non-intervention by the state as the basic tenets of modern capitalism. He recognises an element of truth in these principles but finds them carried to extreme by capitalism. Undue emphasis on rights of individual ownership and freedom of enterprise played havoc during the industrial revolution causing widespread suffering and privation. The legalisation of usury added to the anti-social character of capitalistic enterprise leading to concentration of wealth and pauperisation of the masses. Undue emphasis on self-interest and the profit motive produced a society devoid of humane character, brotherhood, sympathy and co-operation. He reviews the reforms introduced in capitalistic countries allowing an active role for the state and a better deal for labour. Despite these changes, large-scale unemployment and the existence of unsatisfied needs when production resources lie unutilised, the occurrence of trade cycles and the domination of society by usurious financiers continue today (607: 100–106).

Mahmud Ahmad rejects capitalism's claim of being a self-adjusting process leading to maximum satisfaction of human wants, by pointing out the chaos it has led to. Economic crises are sufficient to refute such a claim (168: 4–17). Quoting Halm, A. Mannan (132: 37–38) criticises capitalism due to its failure in maintaining full employment and ensuring free competition.

The main weakness of capitalism according to Bāqir is its failure on the distribution front. Its emphasis on more and more production is misplaced as more production does not ensure greater welfare (171: 240–241). Mabid Mahmud (624) and Chawdhri (620) make the additional point that it is through equitable distribution of the social product that welfare and satisfaction can be ensured and the size of the cake is not always relevant in this context. Every increase in the size of the cake in the capitalist system decreases human welfare and satisfaction as it increases the gap between the rich and the poor.

A strong condemnation of capitalism comes from Syed Qutb (500) who finds it to be thoroughly inhuman and un-Islamic.

Modern Theories of Interest

While the main targets of attack have been the absolute conception of individual ownership rights and the unrestrained nature of freedom of enterprise in capitalism and the cut-throat competition, the inevitable rise of monopoly capitalism, exploitation of labour and emergence of imperialism, the most criticised institution is interest which is regarded as the source of many evils in the system. While we summarise the Islamic economists' views on the institution as such in the next chapter, here we note their criticism and rejection of the various theories which seek to explain and justify interest.

Mawdūdī (521) and Anwar Iqbal Qureshi (526) are the earliest contributors in this field in which Mahmud Ahmad (168), Issa Abdouh (504; 505), Mahmud Abu Saud[71] and Nasser A. Sheikh (154: 71–75) have also contributed.

Abstinence and waiting cannot entitle the capitalist to a reward unless it is proved that the use of borrowed capital necessarily results in profits. In the same manner merely taking a risk does not ensure augmentation of the capital risked. Productivity theory is without any proof as value-productivity of capital is subject to the uncertain conditions of demand and supply. Mawdūdī finds Time Preference and Liquidity theories as partly valid in so far as an *explanation* of interest in the modern economy is concerned. But an explanation does not amount to a *justification*. An institution can be justified only with reference to its role in society and its usefulness for mankind. Mawdūdī examines this role and finds interest to be the cause of many ills in society; economic and political as well as moral and spiritual.

Qureshi (526: 10–43) notes that there is no agreed theory of interest – a point emphasised by several writers on the subject. He criticises the classical theory of interest along familiar lines. Rejecting the Productivity Theory as circular in its reasoning and the Time Preference Theory as based on false psychological assumptions he finds the Monetary Theories of Interest in their neo-classical and Keynesian versions as less concerned with causes of existence of interest than with how its rate is determined. He quotes Keynes to establish the possibility and desirability of a zero rate of interest. Mahmud Ahmad (168) and Farid (514) cite Harrod to establish the same point. Siddiqi (158: 113–114) quotes Shackle to belittle the role of interest and underline its "paradoxical nature".

In his brilliant essay on "Semantics of the Theory of Interest" Mahmud

Ahmad (628)[72] notes the confusion that is found in economic literature between the terms profit and interest. He gives numerous excerpts from Smith, Ricardo, Say, Malthus, Sismondi, Marshall, Fisher and even Bhom Bawerk in this context. He distinguishes between the entirely different economic roles played by loan capital and risk capital. Defining capital as "that part of wealth which is used to create further wealth" he notes that "risk capital is that variety of capital which agrees to relate its reward for its service of participation in the productive process to the measure of value that its participation creates" (628: 179) but "loan capital dictates its price of participation in the shape of a fixed rate of interest. Its charge i.e. interest, is the first charge to be met out of the value of our product . . ." (628: 176). "Loan capital for this reason imparts a peculiar rigidity to the entire range of economic consideration, risk capital, on the other hand, projects a peculiar flexibility to the enterprises concerned. Loan capital by virtue of its interest, sets a limit to the marginal efficiency of productive effort, risk capital imposes no such limit and leaves it free to exploit all natural resources and employ all available manpower" (628: 176). He regards interest to be the "primary cause, with certain secondary causes which are themselves, reflex projections of this primary cause, which virtually perpetuates underemployment equilibrium". Interest raises prices, profits and rents (628: 182–187). Mahmud Ahmad examines the arguments in justification of interest by analogy with rent and hire and finds them faulty. As to rent he notes that land is essentially productive whereas money capital is not: "Money without labour will not produce anything at all. . . . Land even without labour will produce something, it may be only grass to graze cattle on or bushes to provide fuel" (628: 185).

In case of hire: "When there is loss by mischance or miscalculation, in the case of a hired item, it is the *lender* who suffers the loss; whereas in the case of money loan, every loss, whether by mischance, miscalculation or any other reason has to be borne by the *borrower*". He castigates Marshall for having invoked this false analogy between hire price and interest.

He concludes that interest is neither of the nature of profit nor of the nature of rent and hire. Mahmud Ahmad discusses the nature and purpose of savings and finds the claim that advancing savings as loan is equivalent to foregoing a need or that it involves a sacrifice, to be a false claim with no basis in reality (628: 191–192).

Uzair also notes that the origin of capital and the accompanying justification of its remuneration are derived from the concept of physical capital – capital goods – accumulated in the primitive society. When the same justification for reward is applied to money capital it creates confusion.[73] As stressed by several writers the uncertain world in which production takes place does not guarantee a positive value-productivity even to physical capital.[74]

A searching criticism of some recent attempts to justify interest has been made by Mahmud Abu Saud[75] who also warns "against the tendency of treating money capital as if it were capital goods or real assets, a tendency that has become quite frequent in modern literature".[76] He examines the views of Samuelson, Patinkin, Joe S. Bain besides those of Schumpeter and Keynes. Samuelson equates the price with the rental of use of money, giving the impression that to use the service of money is exactly as to use the service of a doctor. The obvious objections to treating interest as rent are that money as a medium of exchange is not supposed to depreciate and that you do not rent something that perishes or disappears once you use it.

Patinkin considers interest as one of the forms of income from property. The argument is fallacious as interest is paid not only before the realisation of income but also irrespective of such a realisation. Moreover, Patinkin's justification fails to cover the interest paid on consumption loans. Joe S. Bain equates the loanable funds with capital goods. Abu Saud points out that the owner of money capital is *not* the investor.

Of the two definitions of interest given by Keynes, the money rate and the commodity rate, the former is paramount to his time preference maxim as he considers that interest is the difference between the price of money today and its price at a future date. But what is that price? asks Abu Saud. "The only way to find the price of money is to define its purchasing power . . . this can be done for the present, but how can we find this price of money in the future?"[77]

Keynes implicitly mentioned another definition of interest, a definition more indicative about its *raison d'etre*. In the course of analysing the reasons that make money rates of interest more acceptable than commodity-rates, he mentioned that " . . . the power of disposal over an asset over a period may offer a potential *convenience* of *security*, which is not equal for assets of different kinds, though the assets themselves are of equal value. There is, so to speak, nothing *to show for this at the end of the period in the shape of output*, yet, it is something for which *people are ready to pay something*" (General Theory, p. 225). Is it a fact nowadays that we have more security in future payments in money than in any other asset? Or is it the contrary? It is of course more convenient to be paid in currency, but it is not safer at all, so much so that it would have been more true to say that the interest at present is a premium – not of security, but – of insecurity inherent in future money. Keynes went on describing his liquidity preference, ending by approving a "depreciating or stamped-money". If this is the case, then the whole concept of positive interest becomes void and the liquidity preference attribute would no longer be valid as a justification for interest.[78]

Turning to time preference Abu Saud notes that "the conception of future demand or the preference of present goods over future ones, seems to me more of an arbitrary postulate than a real fact".[79] With reference to Bhoem Bawerk's first two grounds of time preference he asks how come the lender charges a majoration because the *borrower* prefers present to the future? And what is the countervalue of the agio, or what right has the money lender acquired to entitle him to this extra amount?[80] As to the third ground, technical superiority of present over future goods, a reference is made to its refutation by Keynes. Further "it is extremely important to notice that neither Bhoem Bawerk nor Irving Fisher distinguished between *liquid* or *money* capital and *capital goods*,"[81] and in fact Fisher is telling us why there is interest by assuming the existence of interest, as the word "capitalized values" inevitably implies interest.[82] Thus the confusion between money capital and capital goods is the bane of all modern theories of interest.

To emphasise again the importance of discriminating between the two terms, one would simply consider the case of an investor who is in need of tangible assets (capital goods) and who goes into the market for buying them. The "price" is then negotiated on the basis of the conditions prevailing strictly in this specific market of capital goods. In course of settling the price of the purchased goods, the buyer takes into consideration the three Fisherian elements: time preferences, capital productivity and approximations or enterprise risks. On the sellers side there would be the cost of production, the profit, the risk (here represents the price of replacement plus the carrying cost plus obsolescence).

If the buyer has got the money in cash, the deal would be smoothly concluded. If he has no liquid means of exchange he will have to go to a money holder who would charge a price for the money needed. This new deal is completely different and independent from the first. To start with, there are no real goods involved, and if we apply the term "medium of exchange of a good for another" adopted by the neo-Keynesians, and taking for granted that money in this second transaction would be rendering a service to the investor by facilitating his deal, we are now talking of a different transaction of a different nature. Here we have the capital market where savings are mainly decided by incomes and where the final price – if it is a price at all – will be decided on elements other than the simple demand of investors.[83]

For Schumpeter the socially significant kind of interest is the payment made by the entrepreneurs to the capitalist for the use of purchasing power which enables him to earn profit. What if the entrepreneur fails to earn profit? asks Abu Saud. The argument is hardly convincing in periods of depression and cases of loss and failure. As to Schumpeter's argument that "the demand for productive loan funds with interest at zero would always be greater than supply which is always limited", Abu Saud regards it to be the old classical theory, linking saving and investment via interest, which has been refuted by Keynes.

Schumpeter implied that there would be no positive rate of interest unless there is either innovation or some positive demand for capital goods with marked time preference. Abu Saud regards it to be a description of the actual practice rather than a valid explanation or justification of interest. Would there be no innovation at zero rate of interest? he asks. In conclusion he notes that Schumpeter was convinced that interest is a tax on profits and suggests that "its elimination would be an extra stimulation to more developments as long as funds are available".[84]

Speculation and Forward Transactions

Another institution of capitalist economy severely criticised by Islamic economists is speculation. Many writers have briefly referred to this institution and have noted that Islam does not permit it.

Maulana Muhammad Taqī Amīnī, in a detailed juridical discussion on speculation and stock exchange transactions, declared purchase and sale on the stock exchange to be illegal (556: 118–155). Qureshi had also characterised speculation to be unlawful in Islam. He considers trade cycles to be the result of brisk activity of foreign transactions (526: 101–102). Naseer A. Sheikh (154: 128–135) regards speculation to be anti-social. He examines the arguments given in defence of forward trading and finds them to be unconvincing. A great harm done by speculation is that "money that ought to have been invested in industry and commerce finds its way into the speculative market where it is feeding disguised and parasitical workers like brokers and shrewd operators" (154: 132). A. Mannan (132: 195–197) thinks that "in so far as speculation renders social service by helping production and controlling sudden fluctuation of prices it is in conformity with the spirit of Islam". But speculators being interested in private gains create artificial scarcities which result in inflationary pressure on the economy". Such speculative practices, as well as forward transactions, were condemned by Islam.

Kahf notes (612: 75–76) that Islamic economists' disapproval of speculation is based on two reasons. Firstly, it is considered as a kind of gambling, and secondly, it involves a sale of what one does not own. Discussing speculation in the context of international monetary crises Akram notes that it is not generally acknowledged "that until speculation is retired, stability for the world economy would remain an illusion" (558: 15). Efficient arbiterage through time is, however, as much a social need as is the one through space, and the Islamic economists' discussion on speculation has yet to come to grips with this issue.

Lottery

Another modern institution attacked by our scholars is the system of lotteries. While the *ulema* giving their opinion on the subject have unanimously declared it to be unlawful on account of gambling, and have indicated the economic and social evils consequent upon the adoption of this method (560; 561; 562), a thorough analysis by some economist is still awaited.

Socialism and Communism

Islamic criticism finds Socialism in conflict with the basic requirements of the moral and spiritual growth of human personality, chief among them being freedom of choice and action. Private property and freedom of enterprise, within certain limits and subject to public good, are regarded essential for such freedom. Total nationalisation of means of production is considered to be incongruous with democracy which is an essential feature of the political structure of Islam. The methodology of change adopted by communism is bound to lead to a coercive regime. Materialism, class conflict and moral relativism, essential tenets of communism, are inimical to the Islamic way of life. As an economic system socialism is found to be wanting in many respects as it fails to answer important questions relating to organisation of society and strategy of economic development.

Exploitation of man by man cannot be eliminated by changing the hands that control the means of exploitation. The only way to achieve this end is a moral reorientation of the individuals which makes them servants of society and workers for the social good. This is what Islam does by relating man to God and making him live in accordance with His will so that he treats property as a trust and exercises his freedom with restraint. As a trustee of God he looks upon the welfare of fellow human beings as his own responsibility for which he will be accountable to Allah on the Day of Judgment. The extent of this accountability is directly related to the wealth and power possessed by one.

Mawdūdī, examining the various schools of socialism, finds that evolutionary socialism failed to make any headway and it was Communism that actually took roots. It succeeded in appropriating the Social Surplus for the state which could now use it for furthering the social good. Centralised planning succeeded in removing unemployment and decreasing waste. But this was achieved at a great cost in terms of human lives. Communism deprived people of their liberty and denied moral values. Corruption became rife and a totalitarian regime took recourse to more and more repressive measures. A sizeable portion of the social surplus had to be spent on internal security and defence (607: 52–83).

Bāqir regards the Marxian approach to be no less individualistic than that of capitalism, as it appeals to the self-interest of the have-nots to seize power and wealth from the capitalists. Real socialism required a change of attitude and not merely a change of the hands that wield power and wealth (171: 218).

Masud Alam Nadvi (589) regards the undue emphasis on distribution and the move to abolish private property to be mere reactions to the evils of capitalism. Man does not have to opt for such an extreme solution as the

Middle Path shown by Islam is sufficient to ensure the elimination of these evils and secure the legitimate ends of socialism.

Siddiqi examines and rejects the arguments in favour of socialisation of all means of production (221; I: 93–118) and concludes that individual ownership is a necessary condition for democracy and spiritual and moral growth (221, I: 119–124). A balanced approach would accommodate individual ownership under social supervision as well as socialisation whenever necessary.

Mirza Muhammad Husain condemns socialistic doctrines as they ferment class war (580). Dawālībi also finds instigation of the have-nots against the haves and a belief in the inevitability of class war to be the distinguishing features of Revolutionary Socialism (575). Abdul Hameed Siddiqi (181) refutes the Marxian theories and finds that Communism has created more problems than it has solved. Husain Khan (584: 198–284) seeks to establish, on the basis of the historical experience of Socialism, that it is a hindrance in economic development. Mahmud Ahmad (168: 77–78) regards the problem of efficiency as the greatest one faced by Communism which completely disregarded incentives and rewards. A. Mannan (132: 48–52) accuses Communism of having grossly over-emphasised the problem it sought to solve, with the result that the solutions are highly unrealistic and unworkable.

In his comprehensive study, Khurshid Ahmad accepts economic planning as a useful contribution of Socialism which should be assimilated by contemporary Islam without recourse to totalitarianism (584: 138). The bold and forward looking exposition of Islam's Economic System by Mustafa Sibai finds Islam to be far superior as a system ensuring social justice while upholding human dignity and liberty. Yet Muslims can benefit from the Communist experiment, as an economic system seeking to bring about social justice which was denied to mankind by Feudalism and Capitalism (70: 237–238).

Dialectical Materialism, Labour Theory of Value and Surplus Value

Time and space do not permit us to summarise Islamic criticism of the various Marxian theories. They have been examined in detail, among other writers, by Mazheruddin Siddiqi (595), Bāqir (171: 17–212), Taḥāwi (77: II: 111–196), Khurshid Ahmad (584: 15–160), Siddiqi (221, I: 96–112), Mirza Muhammad Husain (580: 18–20), Dawālībi (595) and Abāẓa (598).

Other Systems

Besides Capitalism, Socialism and Communism, Islamic writers have also criticised State Socialism, Fascism and Nazism (607: 84–95; 168: 136–168; 132: 53–60). These systems were reactions to the other systems, and they achieved very little, at great cost to humanity (for sake of brevity we do not go into details).

V

DEVELOPMENT OF ECONOMIC ANALYSIS IN THE ISLAMIC FRAMEWORK

As the number of trained economists taking up our subject increases analytical approach to the issues under discussion gains in strength. The generation represented by Dr. Anwar Iqbal Qureshi and Sheikh Mahmud Ahmad is followed by a number of younger economists like Khurshid Ahmad, Monzer Kahf, Abu Sulaiman, Muhammad Sakr, Anas Zarqā, Faridi, Chapra, Abdul Mannan, Masudul Alam Chawdhri, Uzair, Mohammad Akram and Siddiqi, who go further and deeper into the analysis of abolition of interest, *Zakāt* and *muḍārabah* and analyse the behaviour of economic units under the influence of Islamic teachings. Though most of these attempts are still rudimentary, they indicate uncharted explorations which might lead to new insights and better policy prescriptions. It is the promise and not the performance that persuades us to pay closer attention to the contributions relevant for this section. This we do under the following heads:

(i) Consumption
(ii) Production
(iii) Factors of Production
(iv) Exchange and Determination of Prices and Profits
(v) Profit Sharing (*Muḍārabah* or *Qirāḍ*)
(vi) The Role of *Zakāt*
(vii) Interest and its Abolition
(viii) Nature of Islamic Economics

(i) Consumption

Both Siddiqi (619: 88–90) and Kahf (612: 7–13) discuss economic rationality assumed by modern economics and indicate the various ways in which this concept must be modified and made broader before it is applied to the behaviour of the consumer in an Islamic society. Kahf notes that "the time horizon of an Islamic individual is extended to include the hereafter" which implies that he "should not limit his behaviour to doing things which he can collect the benefits resulting from them in this life, he is so oriented that he will do what is good or useful for its sake" (612: 10). According to Siddiqi the consumer "must, first of all, be satisfied that he is living up to the Islamic standards. To get this satisfaction he can forgo any satisfaction in the economic or utilitarian sense of the term" (619: 89). Despite this modification which introduces non-temporal, non-individualistic elements in the objectives of the consumer, these writers still find the principle of rationality applicable. As Siddiqi puts it Islamic rationality implies "orientation of action towards maximal conformity with the Islamic norms" (619: 90). Kahf proceeds to affirm, on the basis of this point, the validity of the maximisation proposition in the context of consumer behaviour in Islam (612: 13).

Siddiqi's attempt to trace the impact of "Islamic rationality" on the pattern of demand throws up some interesting points. Obviously, prohibited articles of consumption will go out of demand, but that is followed by the observation that "the extent of complementarity" amongst these goods (along with items of luxury whose demand he expects to decrease, relatively speaking) is greater than "in the group that constitutes the necessaries of life". "The abandonment of 'wine, women and gambling' as a way of life, is therefore sure to tell upon a host of other goods and still more upon services attached to this way of life" (619: 93). He also makes a point made earlier by Hameedullah in a different context (433: 229), that "leisure" may be in greater demand in an Islamic society (456: 95). Social wants are also visualised as gaining ascendancy on the ladder of priorities (619: 97–98).

While the above-mentioned points relating to the pattern of demand have several precedents in the literature, Kahf has sought to present a model of household decision assuming an Islamic system with *Zakāt*, replacement of interest by profit sharing (*Qirāḍ*) and of competition by co-operation, where economic units maximise utility of profit (615). He describes the behaviour of the consumer as maximisation of utility subject to two constraints, the size of income and a desire to maintain wealth. Abolition of interest encourages current consumption at the expense of deferred consumption but *Zakāt* urges a higher savings ratio.[85] It also raises the aggregate consumption by redistributing wealth in favour of classes having a higher propensity to consume. The combined effect of *Zakāt* and non-interest is called the "Consumption effect" (615: 22). A resolution of these conflicting "effects" takes place by the direct linkage between savings and earnings (profits) through investment on the basis of *Qirāḍ* (profit sharing) that the abolition of interest ensures in the system. This leads Kahf to the most important conclusion of his brilliant paper: "saving is positively related to investment opportunities and expectations. This relationship implies that at times of declining investment expectations saving will decline and consumption will rise, this in turn increases aggregate demand and raises business expectation" (615: 26). The question arises, however, what might happen to the level of income if the volume of investment decreases "at times of declining investment expectations", and if a fall in the level of income may not *decrease* aggregate demand despite a rise in the *propensity* to consume? Kahf has neither raised this question nor answered it.

Najjar (58: 280–286) questions the validity of the proposition that savings are a function of income. With reference to poor developing countries, availability of suitable channels of investment play a significant role in mobilising voluntary savings, as experienced by Najjar while conducting the experiments of interest-free banks in Egypt in the early sixties. Failure to note this possibility has led to a policy of forced savings and deficit financing with disastrous consequences.

Recently Anas Zarqa had a closer look at the utility function of a Muslim community which "has a new variable in it, namely, the reward of penalty in the hereafter".[86] Using a diagram to explain interaction between consumption and reward, he concludes that "rational Islamic behaviour should lead the individual to settle somewhere between the sufficiency threshold and the prodigality frontier".[87]

(ii) Production

Siddiqi summarises the main aspects of business motivation in Islam as under (619: 103):

(1) "Full compliance with the Islamic idea of justice.
(2) An urge to serve the society which makes the entrepreneur take the welfare of others into consideration, while he makes his entrepreneurial decisions.
(3) Profit maximisation within the limits set by the operation of the above principles."

The last point is seen to imply that:

(1) Producers would not be maximising their profits if, and when, they feel that by lowering their profit margins they can further the good of the society by satisfying unsatisfied needs.
(2) No producer, in any circumstances, shall increase his profits at the cost of explicit injury to the consumers or to his competitors. . . .
(3) Producers will generally be content with satisfactory profits. . . . (619: 136).

He tries to define "satisfactory profits" with reference to an upper limit permitted by the circumstances (without violating the legally-binding part of the Islamic code of conduct) and a lower limit affording the entrepreneur a decent living and a surplus to average out the losses. "Satisfactory profit . . . is any profit, in between the two limits defined above, which satisfies the entrepreneur's sense of goodness as well as his urge to earn money, maintain and develop his enterprise, and keep it in the good books of the customers, the government, and the people in general" (619: 107). This notion of satisfactory profits has, however, been criticised as subjective and vague (616).

Reviewing the subject, Kahf rejects "profit maximisation because it does not fit the Islamic rationale as far as the time horizon and the connotation of 'success' are concerned". He thinks, however, "that profit maximisation can be used as fair approximation if we look at it as constrained not only by cost but also by a minimum level of goodness guaranteed by both ethical values and legislation" (612: 20). The notion of constrained profit maximisation is also upheld by Chapra (115: 20–21) and Taḥāwi (77, I: 227–230).

Whether we regard it as multiplicity of goals (including non-economic goals) or interpret it as constrained profit maximisation, entrepreneurial behaviour ceases to be predictable and uniform once the simple maximisation hypothesis is abandoned. Tracing the unpredictable and potentially varied behaviour of the Islamic entrepreneur is therefore a hazardous task few have attempted. Siddiqi's rudimentary analysis indicates a weakening of the competitive process and its inevitable transformation into a "co-operative" one (619: 137–141).

(iii) Factors of Production

It is interesting to note that Islamic economists have given different answers to the question: what are the factors of production? Mawdūdī endorses the traditional list: land, labour, capital and organisation and finds its justification in the Islamic law relating to profit sharing (*muḍārabah*) (51: 159). It also fits in with his views on the legitimacy of share-cropping (*muḍārabah*).

Abu Saud reduces the list to three: elements of nature, good work and capital (5: 54–55), subsuming labour and organisation under one category. He views capital as resulting from the operation of human labour on elements of nature. Baqīr notes these three factors as they are so characterised by Political Economy but remarks that labour (including organisation) is not material wealth subject to ownership but the human element in production. Capital results from the operations of this factor. Hence nature is the chief source of production (171: 396–397). A. Mannan also proceeds on the basis of this tripartite categorisation of the factors of production, considering capital "not as a fundamental factor of production but as an embodiment of past land and labour" (132: 126).

Taḥāwī (77, I: 277) includes land and capital in "wealth" so that there remain only two factors of production "wealth" and labour, which includes enterprise. As all wealth belongs to God, He is the real owner of the return to this factor, i.e. of the return to land (rent) and capital (interest). He notes, however, that rent is sometimes allowed to be appropriated by the "owner" of land in view of man's needs. The return to labour belongs to the labourer. Najjar would also confine the list to labour and capital, including land in capital and entrepreneurship in labour (58: 106).

Abdul Ḥamīd Abu Sulaiman rejects the idea of characterising "labour" as a factor of production, regarding it as a result of the capitalistic philosophy which views production as an end in itself. He would characterise only land and capital as factors of production, labour – or more exactly man – being the entity for whose benefit these factors are created (7: 16–17). As a corollary to this distinction between capital and land on the one hand and labour or man on the other hand he lays down the rule that the entire produce of land and capital must be distributed among those who work on them. To regard labour itself as a "factor" of production might pave the way for their subjugation by others.

Of special interest is Malik ben Nabi's concept of Capital as stored by surplus labour (484: 81). As a result of the process of accumulation capital became a "prison house" for labour, denying to labour every right except that of serving its (capital's) interest. Our thinking on economic development is also clouded by the newly assumed importance of capital as we tend to forget its real nature and the fundamental importance of labour and enterprise. This, he regards to be a curse for the Third World. Man, land and time, are the only factors crucial for the destiny of the backward nations, a fact recently demonstrated by China. These factors guided by a "cultural will" and not capital is the condition for economic development of the under-developed countries. For him the prime value rests in Man (484: 79–94).

It is clear from this brief resume that the divergent approaches to the apparently innocuous issue of what are the factors of production are not without a deeper significance. They have important bearings on the authors' views on distribution and growth. Further development of thought in this area might produce some thesis of greater significance.

An important point has been made by some writers relating to the definition of capital. Wealth granted as loan or borrowed does not become capital, says Alavi (10: 30–31) and Mahmud Ahmad clarifies that it is only risk capital that actually participates in production and can be characterised as productive. "Loan capital" does not do so (628).

Stressing the "need to modify the conceptual framework of economics to suit the requirements of Islamic economics" Uzair[88] says that "a beginning will have to be made by redefining the factors of production. . . . Capital as a separate factor of production does not exist but it is a part of another factor of production, namely enterprise".[89] In his opinion "the separation of enterprise and capital has created not only conceptual problems but has also caused practical problems in the operation of the economy".[90]

(iv) Exchange and Determination of Prices and Profits

While the analysis of the functioning of a "co-operative" market guided by Islamic norms has yet to yield any formal results, attempts have been made to analyse exchange and discover the root cause of the malaise in the free economy. Bāqir's analysis (171: 326–328) lays the blame on the use of money as a store of value which makes exchange a means to the accumulation of wealth. This distorts the equilibrium between supply and demand. The Islamic remedy lies in *Zakāt* and the abolition of interest which will confine money to its basic role of mediating between production and consumption.

Freed of monopoly, hoarding, speculation and other un-Islamic practices the free working of the competitive forces is expected to result in prices which may be regarded as normal. This seems to be the assumption underlying the following definition of just profits given by Khurshid Ahmad and Naiem Siddiqi (126: 33).

> "That which is determined in average and normal conditions according to the law of demand and supply in a free market – provided that the laws of the state, its plans and policies, or any other controls are not interfering with the system of sales and purchase, production and supply of commodities and with free competition. Monopoly should not be allowed to influence the market and there should be no emergencies and accidents affecting the market."

In the same vein Kahf declares, after defining the framework within which the market would function in an Islamic society, that:

> "All prices, whether of the factors of production or of products, stem out of this mechanism, these prices are looked at as just or fair prices in this respect" (612: 44).

In the context of "just price" Kahf disagrees with Siddiqi's reference to cost of production (612: 88) and refers to Ibn Taimīya's "price of the equivalent". This concept originated in juridical literature to serve as a guide to the judges in the courtroom. According to Kahf, Ibn Taimīya's norm was a price determined in a market free of imperfections (663: 23).

In view of what has been noted above about the role of government in the market, it can be safely concluded that Islamic analysts are not quite sure if the working of the market will ever result in prices, rates of profit and wages that satisfy the Islamic norms. The concept of just or fair prices and profits oscillates between what the modern economists regard as "normal" and what the Islamic economists will find satisfying to their norms. Najjar (58: 123–124) has some new points to add in this connection.

There is some disagreement among our economists regarding the nature of profit. According to Bāqir, Islam does not consider "risk" to be a factor of production (171: 558) and profit is not the reward of risk bearing. It devolves on present work or past labour congealed in the form of property. He disagrees with the view that the share of the supplier of capital in *muḍārabah* contract can be regarded as a reward of uncertainty bearing (171: 559). This is in sharp contrast to Siddiqi's point of view (221, I: 157–171). Bāqir explains rents also with reference to labour that originally resulted in ownership of property.

(v) Profit Sharing (*Muḍārabah*) or *Qirāḍ*

Profit-share, defined as the percentage share of the supplier of capital in the profits of the entrepreneur, or the working partner, in the *muḍārabah* contract is compared and contrasted with the rate of interest in its function and role in the economy. The rate of profit-sharing is also being explored as a tool of analysis and a possible instrument of fiscal policy.

Kahf defines *Qirāḍ* (*muḍārabah*) as "the act of transforming money assets into factors of production as a result of a joint action between the two parties". Two crucial differences between profit-share and interest are stated. Firstly, "the profit-sharer has direct interest and real concern in the activity of the firm"; second, "profit-share is a long run phenomenon in which the preference for liquid assets is almost neglected, whereas interest is a dual phenomenon, short and long run, for which the economic thought could not provide any serious theory to provide the term structure. . . . In profit-share the short run changes do not interfere in the finance of investment unless through their effect on the rate of return expectations only, so that one source of long run fluctuations is eliminated, namely variation in short run interest rate" (612: 62–63).

He proceeds to discuss the equilibrium rate of profit-share which should be equal to the return on partnership, i.e. on share capital in joint stock companies (612: 85–86).

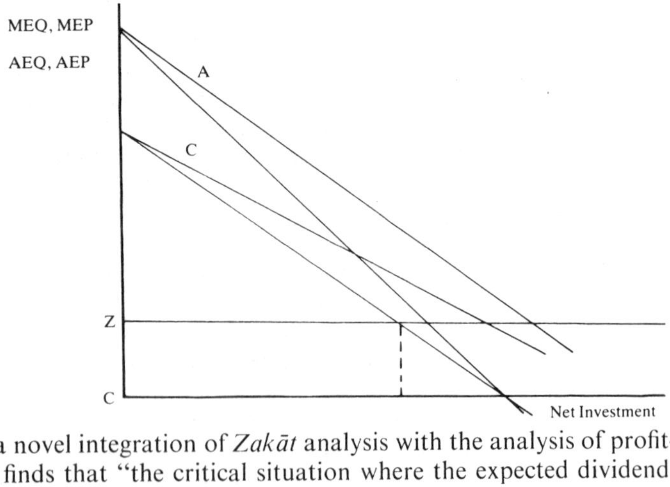

In a novel integration of *Zakāt* analysis with the analysis of profit-share Kahf finds that "the critical situation where the expected dividend (considered in percentage terms) . . . is below az-*Zakāt* line can be distinguished from the situation where the expected dividend is at or above az-*Zakāt* line" (drawn at a height of 2.5 per cent above X axis in the diagram reproduced above), "the difference between M and O is the remuneration of the entrepreneur" which he calls profit (612: 91–82). Then he proceeds to analyse the behaviour of investment, depending on the elasticity of Q curve and the determination of profit. Traditional economic theory fails to determine profits (612: 82, fn. 84) whereas his own theory is able to do so. Turning then to the capital market he notes that "in the traditional theory this market determines the rate of interest but not the entrepreneurial profit, whereas by having prices to be sought in percentage terms both profit-share and profit are determined simultaneously" (612: 85–86). "It is noted that the demand and supply functions in this (capital) market are really more likely to offer curves known in international trade theory than ordinary demand and supply curves. The other difference lies in the slope of the demand for finance which is positive in this market; this, in fact, reflects that, as the ratio of capital/entrepreneur rises, the profit-share offered by entrepreneur increases in order to attract more capital" (612: 86).

Kahf's analysis goes further than the earlier attempts by Muhammad Akram and Siddiqi. Akram's attempt is vitiated by his misconception about liability to losses in the *muḍārabah* contract and some of his assumptions relating to supply of savings in an Islamic society (404). Siddiqi pointed out the elasticity of the savings curve in relation to profit-share (417: 24).

A recent contribution to the subject is a paper by Chowdhury (620) in which he shows that the only value which comes nearer to a suitable capitalisation rate or acts as a reasonable substitute for the interest rate, is the rate of profit actually realised by the firm or the economy or the individual at any time during the period and process of capital formation.

(vi) The Role of *Zakāt*

Zakāt one of the main pillars of Islam's economic system, has attracted the attention of almost every writer on the subject, who emphasise its redistributive function, besides emphasising its educative role in giving the individual the right approach towards society and its needs. Since it is difficult to record these contributions with names we confine ourselves to a statement of the points made, mentioning only some recent contributors distinguished by their analytical insight.

1. *Zakāt* transfers part of the wealth of the haves to the have-nots, lessening the inequality in the distribution of income and wealth, and counteracting any tendency towards concentration of wealth.

In a recent contribution (624) Mabid Mahmud correlates the distribution of political power and the distribution of wealth. He finds that:

(1) "The degree of association between the distribution of wealth and that of power increases with the size of the political unit measured in terms of the number of voters.

(2) That degree of association increases with the degree of monopoly in information media" (624: 41–42).

He concludes that "the association between the distribution of wealth and that of political power can be broken by a redistributive scheme. This scheme must operate on wealth, not income. . . . It should be designed to check accumulation on an asset by asset basis, taxing more remunerative assets more heavily, for they provide a greater prospect for power accumulation . . . the conditions of such a redistributive scheme are all fulfilled in az-*Zakāt*" (624: 43).

2. As a result of this transfer there is an upward shift in the aggregate demand function because the marginal propensity to consume of those who receive the transfer payments is comparatively higher.

As noted above, Kahf finds the "consumption effect" of *Zakāt* re-enforced by abolition of interest (615: 22).

3. *Zakāt*'s distributive role involves an allocative role, too, as the *Zakāt* funds are mostly used on essential goods and services. Factors of production are thus diverted to the production of necessaries from that of luxuries on which the taxed persons might have spent these amounts. Hasanuzzaman argues that *Zakāt* will also lead to "a fall in the rich man's demand for imported luxury items"[91] thus resulting in foreign exchange savings.

4. *Zakāt* discourages hoarding and accumulation of idle wealth. It tries to put the waiting resources back into economic activity as increased capacity, through the investment of such wealth, or as increased demand for consumption. "It helps in pushing every bit of wealth into productive activity by increasing the cost of waiting" (612: 51). This point has been made by several writers including Mahmud Ahmad (168: 124), Nasir A. Sheikh (154: 90) and Hasanuzzaman.[92]

Afazuddin (621: 9) points out that "the incidence of *Zakāt* falls on liquidity preference and negates its influence on the rate of interest". The latter part of this statement means that *Zakāt* would encourage the cash holder to employ it in a profitable manner so that *Zakāt* is paid out of the profits and no depletion is caused in the assets. This would cause an addition to the supply of cash while liquidity preference works the other way round. But Afazuddin has apparently ignored the fact that cash is very often held in expectation of better investment prospects in the future and in that situation *Zakāt* would fail to negate "liquidity preference".

5. Kahf ascribes a "savings effect" to *Zakāt* assuming a desire on the part of the household to maintain its level of wealth intact and a similar urge on the part of the firm to maintain non-decreasing capital (615: 21; 612: 51). . . . If the rate of return on wealth is 10 per cent, one needs to save 27.5 per cent of one's income in order to keep one's wealth constant.[93] What is significant is that "it makes every individual merge . . . the decision of income allocation with that of savings utilisation". Obviously, Kahf's "savings effect" assumes a positive return to its utilisation through investment.

Qarḍāwī's comprehensive work on *Zakāt* compares it with modern taxation and explains the virtues of *Zakāt* as a tax on capital (313, II: 1027–30). *Zakāt* on agricultural produce, mineral wealth and salaries and rents can, however, be treated as a tax on income (313, II: 1033–1034). After making a comparative study of *Zakāt* and other taxes in the light of universally acclaimed principles of taxation (313, II: 1038–1052) he proceeds to explain why there is no progression in the rate of *Zakāt*, and dispels the misconception about there being a negative progression in the rates of *Zakāt* on livestock (313, II: 1054).

Mawdūdī has pointed out that the burden of *Zakāt* on merchandise cannot be shifted to the consumers (51: 362–363), but the reasoning is weak and unconvincing.

(vii) Interest and its Abolition

Islamic economists have analysed the role of interest in the economy and have traced the consequences of its abolition. They also compare interest and "profit-share" as means of mobilising savings and channelising them into the productive process. A discussion of these points necessitates a restatement of the causes why Islam has abolished interest.

A: Rationale of Prohibition

The main reason why Islam abolishes interest is that it is oppression (*Zulm*) involving exploitation. In the case of consumption loans it violates the basic function for which God has created wealth, which envisages that the needy be supported by those who have surplus wealth. In the case of productive loans, guaranteed return to capital is unjust in view of the uncertainty surrounding entrepreneurial profits.

The second reason why interest has been abolished is that it transfers wealth from the poor to the rich, increasing the inequality in the distribution of wealth. This is against social interest and contrary to the will (*marḍī*) of God, Who would like an equitable distribution of income and wealth. Islam stands for co-operation and brotherhood. Interest negates this attitude and symbolises an entirely different way of life.

A third reason why interest is abolished is that it creates an idle class of people who receive their income from accumulated wealth. The society is deprived of the labour and enterprise of these people. Such a way of life is also harmful for their personalities.

Mawdūdī has pointed out that a basic imbalance is caused between production and consumption by the phenomenon of interest. This happens in two ways. Firstly, interest on consumption loans transfers part of the purchasing power from a group of people with high propensity to consume to a group with low propensity to consume. This latter group mostly reinvests its income from interest which means that the decrease in consumption demand is accompanied by an increase in production.

Secondly, interest on productive loans raises the cost of production, hence the prices of consumption goods. Once again the amount taxed away from the people, in the form of higher prices falls in the hands of a class with a lower than average propensity to consume.

This imbalance is seen as the source of many evils such as stagnation and depression, monopoly and ultimately imperialism (521: 85–87).

Supply of interest-free loans to needy consumers and denial of a guaranteed return to capital removed this basic imbalance. The incomes generated by the process of production in the form of wages profits and profit-share are more equitably distributed. *Zakāt*-based transfer of wealth from the rich (profit earners) to the poor (wage earners) removed the remaining imbalance.

Hameedullah (433) pointed out that the institution of interest introduces an essential duality of interest between the capitalist and the entrepreneurs, which is a source of fluctuation in the system. By abolishing interest and bringing the capitalists and the entrepreneurs together on the basis of profit-sharing, Islam ends this duality and harmonises the interests of the two classes.

The above point is made by almost every writer on the subject. Mawdūdī points out that this removes the premium set on capital and shifts the emphasis on to the entrepreneur whose activity becomes the only source of income besides labour. The hold of the "rentier class" on society is destroyed and dynamic entrepreneurs are given the upper hand (521).

Elaborating on the first reason for the abolition of interest stated above, Hameedullah notes that the principle of unilateral risk involved in the institution of interest is the basis of its prohibition in Islam (119: paragraph 372). Ganameh (392: 86) also regards it to be the chief economic reason for Islam's prohibition of interest along with two other reasons: that it violates justice and is contrary to the Islamic dictum: no reward without effort.

Siddiqi argues (221, I: 173-75) that the borrowed capital whose repayment to the lender is guaranteed takes no part in the enterprise in which it is invested and is, therefore, not entitled to any returns even when the enterprise does make a profit. This capital does not expose itself to the risks and uncertainties of the enterprise.

These are borne by the collateral pledged by the borrower as security, and by the alternative source of finance to which the borrower must turn for repaying the loan, in case there are losses in the enterprise. He cites the famous tradition from the Prophet (al Khirāj bi'l dimān) "income devolves on liability" in this context.

B: Interest, Savings and Investment

This brings us to the impact of the abolition of interest on savings and investment and on the level of economic activity and allocation of resources in the economy.

Many writers have dispelled the doubt that abolition of interest will decrease the propensity to save. Quoting Keynes they argue that savings are a function of income and earning interest is only a minor motive of savings. In the absence of interest the possibility of earning profits on common stock or through *muḍārabah* contract will serve the same purpose. Moreover, the bulk of the savings in a developed economy arise from institutional sources. Siddiqi gives an analytical exposition of the subject (417: 180–190) which has been discussed earlier.

As regards investment, it is argued that "interest holds back investment in production" (A. Mannan[94] (132: 169). Mawdūdī (521 : 110; 51 : 270) and Dr. Qureshi (526: 218) point out that interest prevents the flow of capital towards projects with a low yield even though they are socially most useful. It is argued that in the absence of interest the margin of investment could be extended till the rate of return approaches zero. As regards the supply of savings making such an extension of investment possible, it is pointed out that investment creates its own savings by increasing incomes – a view which is hardly tenable unless qualified carefully.

Mahmud Ahmad points out (168: 36–37) that "the institution of interest provides banks with unproductive channels to employ their capital". This causes scarcity of capital available for productive enterprise which raises the rate of interest. In the absence of interest people's money will either be spent on consumption causing demand to rise or be invested in productive enterprise. Both ways there will be greater production and larger employment. Obviously the argument presumes taxation of hoarded money.

Mawdūdī has argued that the institution of interest discourages long-term investment, as the capitalist has a strong desire for liquidity. This is detrimental to the real interests of society (521 : 105–106). Furthermore, long-term loans based on a fixed rate of interest introduce an element of rigidity in costs which investment on the basis of profit-sharing would not.

The discouragements to long-term investment are not, however, confined to the interest cost. The real discouragement comes from the fact that uncertainties surrounding the returns to investment increase with the length of the time period involved. It is reasonable to assume that capitalists or banks advancing long-term capital on the basis of profit-sharing will do so only when the expected rate of return on long-term investment is higher than that expected on short-term investment by a margin that compensates for the greater uncertainties involved. It is also doubtful if the "real" interests of the society always favour longer-term investment. The above argument, therefore, remains inconclusive.

Chawdhri (620) has tried to demonstrate how ensuring a zero rate of interest which is a condition for Golden age equilibrium (in which capital labour and output are all growing at a constant relative rate) guarantees the best solution of resource allocation. He analyses the role of actually realised rate of profit in this context. Siddiqi also argues that "it is not the rate of interest but the priorities of a modern state and the rates of profit in various sectors of the economy that are decisive so far as allocation of investible funds is concerned" (158: 112).

Tracing the consequences of interest in a recent paper, Siddiqi[95] notes that fixed interest charges curtail the freedom of the entrepreneur who wishes to go by social priorities. The society is therefore obliged to admit low yield high priority undertakings into the public sector.

C: Abolition of Interest and Demand for Consumption Loans

Hasanuzzaman (629: 147–164) examines the argument that abolition of interest will increase the demand for consumption loans, accelerating inflation and, in under-developed countries, worsening the balance of payments. He finds little functional relationship between demand for consumer credit and the rate of interest. It is "increase in income and not the rate of interest that governs the demand for loans" (629: 160). Hence "abolition of interest even in the developed countries would not cause any substantial change in the existing set up" (629: 160). As regards the under-developed countries, he concludes that "when the supply of consumer loans and of goods is limited, the increase in demand, if at all, will be ineffective and will not materially disturb the economy and finance of the country" (629: 162).

D: Interest on Internal and External Debt

The "tyranny of interest" reaches its peak in relation to the public debt whose servicing has become a great headache for the modern state. Mawdūdī (521), Qureshi (526: 189–201) and A. Mannan (132) decry interest on this basis. Abolition of interest and replacement of interest-bearing public debt by interest-free debt and funds obtained for the public sector projects on the basis of profit-sharing (Siddiqi: 417: 185–170) will relieve the state of this crippling burden.

Foreign debts based on interest have done irreparable harm to the poor nations of the world. Issa Abdouh (505) focuses attention on this role of interest and Mawdūdī (521: 113–114) describes interest as the greatest instrument of exploitation at the international level.

E. Interest and Trade Cycles

Interest is seen as the root cause of the instability characterising the modern economic system. Interest creates "liquidity preference" for speculative purposes and results in keeping a large part of the money supply in hoards waiting for the rate of interest to rise. It encourages speculation which is the cause of instability in the system (Mawdūdī, 521: 194, Mahmud Ahmad, 168: 13–14).

Several writers including Hameedullah (433), Mahmud Ahmad (168: 13–14, 45–50), Mawdūdī (521: 104), Muhammad Uzair (422) and A.

Mannan (132: 170) have emphasised a causal link between the institution of interest and the occurrence of crises in the economic system, postulating that abolition of interest will contribute decisively towards elimination of trade cycles. Hameedullah regards the institutions of interest as the villain of the piece'; "just when the vital interests of the entrepreneur demand that they should have financial resources to cope with the situation, the interest of the lending class demands a payment of the loans and are against their renewal. . . . The institution of lending on interest causes the whole trouble. It makes the lowering of prices so harmful and withholding of supplies impossible" (433: 221). Analysing in detail the role of interest in the various phases of the trade cycle, Mahmud Ahmad concludes that "the abolition of interest can abolish the crises" (168: 49). Abdul Hameed Siddiqi (631) disagrees with this view. A change of the entire system, involving a change in the basic attitude of economic agents, specially in the "acquisitive mentality" is a pre-condition to the solution of this problem.

Siddiqi,[96] however, envisages a reduction in the volume of credit instruments and public debt, consequent upon the abolition of interest, will have important implications for business cycles. Moreover, investment based on production possibilities directly assessed by businessmen and bankers, in a profit-sharing banking system, are not likely to overstep themselves to an extent that makes a crash in share prices inevitable at a later stage.

F: Prohibition of *Ribā Al-Faḍl*

The prohibition of *ribā al faḍl* (interest involved in barter) has been looked upon as a discouragement of barter and a step directed at monetisation of the economy (519: 9; 403). The primary aim of this injunction is, however, to eliminate the possibilities of exploitation and injustice similar to that which is the target or prohibition of interest on money loans. There is some controversy regarding the coverage of this prohibition, which is a juridical issue not concerning us in this paper.

G: Accounting Concept of Interest

Waqar Husaini (121: 191) pleads for using an accounting concept of interest in economic planning and for project evaluation. Awsaf Ali (114: 199, 264) also thinks that in an Islamic economy the accounting rate of interest must of necessity be used and it is only in the sense of abolishing interest as a source of private income that the Islamic economy can function as an interestless economy. It is not entirely clear, however, why an estimated average rate of profit should not be sufficient for this purpose.

Abdul Bāqi[97] also suggests that the Islamic Bank should fix an accounting rate of interest to serve as a guide in allocation of investible resources, especially as a criterion for giving priority to one project over others. But the underlying assumption that the use of such a rate is inevitable has not been fully justified by him nor the possible alternatives examined in detail. Why are the social priorities and the expected rates of profit not sufficient guides to allocation of resources and selection of projects? If the idea is that the Central Bank keep a certain rate of profit in view and reject such projects as fail to promise a return commensurate with that rate, why insist on calling it an accounting rate of interest?

Sabri F. Ulgener notes that interest serves as "the most dependable factor in evaluating and comparing different investments" (632: 11). Without raising or answering the point why the current "rate of profit-share" paid by *muḍārabah*-based interest-free banks should not form the basis of such an evaluation, supplemented by other estimates based on realised profits, he proceeds to declare that there is no escape from modern bank interest. Hence "the crux of the problem for under-developed countries is to differentiate between interest as a surplus and interest as a factor in computing the overall efficiency of their economies" (632: 14). He does not refer to the various techniques of "computing the overall efficiency" developed in the socialist countries, nor does he clarify how interest as a surplus can be denied to the capitalists while using interest as a factor in computation.

(viii) Nature of Islamic Economics

An important theoretical issue discussed by Islamic economists is the nature, scope and methodology of Islamic economics. They have tried to distinguish Islamic economics from economics as such and state its *raison d'etre*.

Bāqir al Sadr distinguishes between the science of economics which deals with production and the laws that govern it, and the art of economic policy which is concerned with distribution and social justice. The function of an economic system is to solve the economic problems in the context of the ideal state of justice (171: 343–347). Capitalism and Marxism are "schools of economics" advocating different economic systems. Islamic economics is akin to political economy, its function being "the discovery of laws and analysis of real life in the context of an Islamic society in which the Islamic way of life is fully established" (171: 291). Such a science can appear only after the real Islamic society has come to exist – a condition yet to be fulfilled. It is, however, possible "to start investigation on certain given assumptions and derive the economic tendencies and course of events from them" (171: 226–227).

Bāqir considers modern economics to be relevant for modern capitalist societies and not for all societies all the time. Examining its laws, he finds that the only ones having universal validity are the laws of returns (in the theory of production), based as they are on nature rather than on man. All "laws" relating to man are relative as human behaviour depends on human volition which is shaped by beliefs and ethical ends. The celebrated law of demand and supply is no exception (171: 226–227).

Siddiqi also thinks that "Islam's science of economics or the economic analysis relevant to an Islamic society . . . will come into being when we have a people whose behaviour is Islamic, an economy which is truly Islamic" (73: 32). But he proceeds to define Islamic economics "in the context of the endeavour of the present-day Islamic peoples to live according to Islamic injunctions and ideals. It requires a study of the contemporary economic behaviour and socio-economic institutions, comparing and contrasting them with what could be their Islamic alternatives, with a view to defining the changes required to effect a transition to modes of behaviour and institutional arrangements conforming to the Islamic norms" (73: 22). Accordingly, "the task of Islamic economics lies in building bridges between the is and the ought" (73: 33). Both Kahf (611) and Khurshid Ahmad (47) seem to have this role of Islamic economics in mind when they outline the task of Islamic economists today. Kahf wants Islamic economists "to visualise" an economic theory based on "free co-operation rather than on free competition" and to "reformulate" consumer's utility theory "in a way which makes it to cover morals and the consent of Allah". His Islamic economics will be a behavioural science which takes as given the framework provided by "all the religious, moral, social, political and legal rules which constitute the surroundings of the behaviour of any member in the Islamic society" (611: 5–6). For Khurshid Ahmad, "Islamic economics is borne of the challenge thrown to a Muslim economist by the incongruities, paradoxes and complex problems" he observes in the contemporary Muslim world. This calls for "a critical reappraisal of the contemporary economic situation of the Muslim world", "A study of economic teachings of Islam", "an appraisal of the different variants of modern economic theory and policy", and, finally, for a "reconstruction and reformulation of the theory and policy of Islamic economics so as to identify the objectives and the modes of operation of economic activity in an Islamic or Islamising society" (644: 1–3).

This stress on contemporaneity is quite recent in origin, the earlier emphasis being on model building. Shabbir Khan wanted us "to prepare a simple model based on certain simplified assumptions and then introduce the Islamic code of economic life into that model" (643), a suggestion appreciated by Faridi (637). Medhat Hassanain also emphasised the need for building the Islamic economic model (641). A similar view has been expressed by Fanjari (636) and Fareed Naggar.[98]

A. Mannan is closer to Bāqir when he defines Islamic economics as "a social science which studies the economic problems of a people imbued with the values of Islam" (132: 3). Of special interest is Professor Farooqi's stress on the need for "meta-economics" which could judge human processes according to moral norms – "the divine pattern relevant to man's economic life" (638). The idea has been further explicated in a later note (639).

In one of the earliest contributions to this discussion Abdul Hameed Siddiqi (71) finds that economics ignored free will and focused its attention on "the animal aspects" of human behaviour, seeking to discover "laws" which had the finality of the physical laws of nature, thus severing all relations between the principles of economics and morality. Economics of Islam rectifies this error. Taking human volition into account it seeks to guide man in the light of the Islamic injunctions and to orient man's economic attitudes towards the Islamic ends and ideals.

Bāqir's discussion of the process through which the economic philosophy and economic policies of Islam can be "discovered" is detailed and illuminating (171: 341–390). Siddiqi (647), A. M. Manzar (645), Fanjari (636), Khurshid Ahmad (644: 34) and Kahf (611) have indicated some of the areas for research in Islamic economics and the methods which should be adopted.

The methodology of Islamic Economics necessitates a fresh look at the role of values in economics. Sakr (646) finds recent thinking gravitating towards the view that all economic thinking is value loaded and it would be better for an economist to be aware of his value premises and state them clearly. Islam's contribution in this regard lies in providing a set of values which is, because of its divine origin, universal, permanent and immune from tampering by man. The subject has been taken up at a philosophical level by Faruqi.[99]

VI

ECONOMIC THOUGHT IN ISLAM

The advent of Islamic Economics directed the attention of scholars towards the economic thinking of the Muslim thinkers in the past, of which the works on history of economic thought had taken no notice at all, with the sole exception of a casual mention of Ibn Khaldun in Schumpeter's compendium.[100]

Besides the economic thinking of the early jurists and the great philosophers in the later Abbasid period, attention has been paid to such writers as Abū Yūsuf, Abū 'Ubaid, Yahyā Ibn Ādam, Qudāma bin Ja'far, Ibn al-Muqaffa', al-Jāḥiẓ, al-Māwardī, Ibn Ḥazm, Ibn Taimīyah, Ibn Qayyim, Shātibī, Dimashqī, Ibn Khaldūn, Ṭūsī, Ghazālī, al-Ḥarīrī, Aḥmad 'Alī al-Dalajī and Shāh Walīallāh al-Dehlavi.

A: Ibn Khaldūn (1332–1406)

Ibn Khaldūn has rightly been hailed as the greatest economist of Islam. Besides Ezzat's doctoral thesis (655) and Nasha't's work (659) we have contributions by Rosenthal (661), Spengler (664), Boulakia,[101] Ahmad Ali

(656), Ibn al Sabil (192), Abdul Qadir (651; 652), Rifa't (660), Somogyi (650), Ṭaḥāwī (77), T. B. Irving (657) and Abdu Saṭṭar (654).

Ibn Khaldūn has a wide range of discussions on economics including the subjects of value, division of labour, the price system, the law of supply and demand, consumption and production, money, capital formation, population growth, public finance, trade cycles, etc. He discusses the various stages through which societies pass in economic progress. We also get the basic idea embodied in the backward-sloping supply curve of labour (664: 303). Spengler (664: 293) compares and contrasts his cycle theory of civilisation with Hicks' theory of trade cycles and Abdus Saṭṭar ascribes to him the theory that economic development passes through stages (654). We get the macro-economic view that "income and expenditure balance each other in every city . . . and if both income and expenditure are large . . . the city grows". He also noticed, in the Keynesian sense, the importance of the demand side, particularly government expenditure, in avoiding business slumps and maintaining economic development (654: 161). T. B. Irving also notes that according to Ibn Khaldūn "taxes have a point of diminishing returns and pump priming is important to keep the business running smoothly" (657: 32).

Abdul Qadir (651: 438) notes that labour has the central place in Ibn Khaldūn's theory of value, and Abdus Saṭṭar ascribes a labour theory of value to him (654: 164). Somogyi (650) rightly points out that Ibn Khaldūn anticipated Adam Smith on several points, and Abdul Qadir regards him as a precursor of the mercantilists, because of his views on the importance of Gold and Silver (651: 439). He highlights Ibn Khaldūn's emphasis on economic factors in the interpretation of history and his effort to relate economic progress with political stability (651: 434, 441). Ibn al-Sabil regards Ibn Khaldūn a precursor of Proudhon, Marx and Engels on the basis of his views on poverty and its causes (192: 154).

Rifa't refers to Ibn Khaldūn's discussion on utility which anticipates later analysis (660: 26). To money, he ascribed the two roles of standard of exchange and store of value (654: 165).

Rifa't compares his theory of population with that of Malthus and finds a number of common points, though Ibn Khaldūn did not mention preventive checks (660: 26).

In his exhaustive discussion on Ibn Khaldūn, Ṭaḥāwī (77, I: 473–603) explains how population and economic progress are related to one another in his model. Ibn Khaldūn also warned against state intervention in the economy and thought that a free market ensured proper distribution (77, I: 633). Ṭaḥāwī summarises Ibn Khaldūn's views on determination of prices by the forces of supply and demand, money, its values and its functions and the principles of taxation and government expenditure.

Boulakia notes Ibn Khaldūn's emphasis on the importance of social organisation of production whose main factor is human labour. Then comes the role of international division of labour which is based more on the skill of the inhabitants of various regions than their natural resources.[102] "His theory constitutes the embryo of an international trade theory, with the analysis of terms of exchange between rich and poor countries, of the propensity to import and export, of the influence of economic structures on development and of the importance of intellectual capital in the process of growth".[103] After surveying the wide-ranging contributions of Ibn Khaldūn on money, prices, distribution, public finance, trade cycles and population, Boulakia concludes that "Ibn Khaldūn discovered a great number of fundamental economic notions a few centuries before their official birth. He discovered the virtue and the necessity of a division of labour before Smith and the principle of labour value before Ricardo. He elaborated a theory of population before Malthus and insisted on the role of the state in the economy before Keynes. But much more than that, Ibn Khaldūn used these concepts to build a coherent dynamic system in which the economic mechanism inexorably led economic activity to long-term fluctuations. . . . ."[104] Boulakia can, therefore, feel more than justified in affirming that "His name should figure among the fathers of economic science".[105]

B: Ibn Taimīya (1262–1328)

Ibn Taimīya's economic views have been discussed by Muhammad al-Mubārak (134), Sherwani (667), Ilyas Ahmad (665), Kahf (666) and Siddiqi (221, II: 189–203).

Kahf discusses his notion of "price of the equivalent" and the complementary concept of "fair profit". Ibn Taimīya wanted to investigate what the price would be if there were no imperfections in the market. He held that the price of labour was determined in the same way as the other prices (666). Siddiqi has discussed Ibn Taimīya's view on price control at some length (221, II: 189–203).

He justified state intervention in the market on account of monopoly, monopsony, hoarding and speculation. Mubārak (134) discusses his work on *Hisbah*. Maintenance of fair competition and honest dealings were to be ensured through enforcement of the Islamic code of conduct on producers, traders and the middle men. Mubārak has also highlighted Ibn Taimīya's views on other responsibilities of the state, including that of ensuring fulfilment of the basic needs of the people by organising production and distribution (134: 106–127).

Sherwani (667) focuses his attention of Ibn Taimīya's views on the concept of ownership in Islam, emphasising the right of the state to abridge or abrogate this right in certain circumstances.

Ṭahāwī (77, I: 455) regards Ibn Taimīya's emphasis on the state's responsibility to ensure the fulfilment of the basic needs of the people as his unique contribution.

C: Abū Yūsuf (731–798)

Abū Yūsuf's main subject was taxation and the economic responsibilities of the state. His contribution lies in demonstrating the superiority of proportional taxation over the system of fixed levy on land, both from the viewpoint of revenue and equity. In his discussion he also refers to the other canons of taxation: capacity to pay, a consideration for the convenience of assessees in fixing the time of collection and its mode, and centralisation of decision making in tax administration. Siddiqi (671: 83–84) discusses these points along with Abū Yūsuf's emphasis on public works especially irrigation facilities and highways. He also urges upon the ruler to take other measures to ensure the development of agriculture (671: 89).

Siddiqi notes that Abū Yūsuf's brief comments on the relation between the supply of goods and their prices do not go deep enough and his advice to the ruler against price control is not accompanied by a thorough discussion on the subject (671: 78–79).

D: Nasiruddīn Ṭūsī (1201–1274)

Ṭūsī's contribution has been discussed by Rifa't (679), A. Mannan (132: 8), Anzarul Haq (678) and Habibul Haq Nadwi (235). Ṭūsī discussed the revenue and expenditure of the household as well as those of the ruler. He emphasised saving and warned against extravagance and expenditure on unproductive assets such as jewellery and uncultivable land (679: 124). He accorded supreme importance to agriculture giving trade and other vocations a second place (235: 148). He also discussed exchange and division of labour. His brief work on Public Finance has been reviewed by Rifa't (679) wherein he disapproves of certain taxes which had no sanction in Islam.

Jalāl al Din al Dawwani (678) closely follows Ṭūsī in his discussion of the household and the public treasury.

E: Shāh Walīullāh (1702–1763)

A resume of Shāh Walīullāh's broad sweep on the subject has been given by Tufail Ahmad Qureshi.[106] He regarded economic well-being to be a prerequisite of a good life and proceeded to discuss needs, ownership, means of production, co-operation, distribution and consumption with remarkable insight. Discussing the evolution of society from the primitive stages to the affluent culture of his day he points out the decadence that sets in with the growth of conspicuous consumption. In his discussion on means of production he tends to place a number of natural resources in the public sector.[107] He condemned hoarding and profiteering on economic as well as social grounds.[108]

The economic philosophy of Shāh Walīullāh had been earlier interpreted by Ubaidullah Sindhi (688). Ibn al Sabil compares Walīullāh's analysis of the decline of the Mughal with Marx's critique of capitalism (192: 515). Walīullāh's *Ḥujjatullāh al Bālighah* offers a wealth of material on the subject that awaits the attention of economists.

F: Other Thinkers

Kifayatullah[109] has recently reported on a work by Imām Muḥammad Ibn Ḥasan al Shaibānī (750–804) entitled "The Earning", which discusses what is right and what is wrong in ways of earning and spending. He regarded agriculture as the noblest of all professions because it is the most useful for the entire society, a view which sharply distinguishes Imām Muḥammad from most of his contemporaries who preferred trade and commerce over agriculture.

Ṭaḥāwī (77, I: 151–154) takes some notice of those Islamic thinkers who paid special attention to eradication of poverty and to ensuring social justice. He mentions Abu Dharr Ghifārī (d. 654), Ibn Hazm (d. 1064) and Ahmad 'Alī al Dalajī (d. 1421). Ibrahim Labban (614) also discusses the views of Abu Dharr Ghifārī and Ibn Hazm.

It could not be possible for the present writer to consult the numerous works on Ghazālī, Fārābī, Ṭūsī, Ibn Qayyim, Shāh Walīullāh and others for brief references to their economic views. Nor could he do justice to the works on the few thinkers discussed in this section. Here is a field that awaits the attention of researchers in Islamic Economics. But the material listed in our own bibliography should be sufficient to refute the thesis recently propounded by Meyer (648) that the "Arabic, Turkish and Persian speaking East has experienced no continuity of economic ideas such as those which come from the Judeo-Christian West". The West experienced systematic economic thinking since the time of the Renaissance and Economics came into its own in the wake of the Industrial Revolution – a period of history in which the East was sliding down the scale of decadence. The ascendancy of the Islamic civilisation and its dominance of the world scene for a thousand years could not have been unaccompanied by economic ideas as such. From Abū Yūsuf in the second century to Ṭūsī and Walīullāh we get a continuity of serious discussion on taxation, Government expenditure, home economics, money and exchange, division of labour, monopoly, price control, etc. Unfortunately, no serious attention has been paid to this heritage by centres of academic research in Economics.

Epilogue

The variety of subjects discussed by Islamic economists and their distinctive approach to some of the economic problems is brought out in our survey of the literature presently available. The new approach has a clearly defined frame of reference and there are certain common premises shared by all writers on the subject. The issues raised and discussed by them are relevant to the human situation and have a direct bearing on contemporary life. These discussions have a special significance for the Muslim countries and communities, but their relevance for a comparative study of economic systems and philosophies is universal and general.

To the students of Islamic economics in particular and the Muslim students of economics in general the survey provides an opportunity of stock-taking and programming for further research. Both Islam and economics would be benefited if closer attention is paid to an approach that seeks to relink economics with moral values and to evolve a framework in which man's quest for justice achieves fulfilment while ensuring maximum efficiency and satisfying the will to economise.

Notes

1 Research Report 1: Contemporary Literature on Islamic Economics, 1978. 69p.

2 "Allah coineth a similitude: a township that dwelt secure and well content, its provisions coming to it in abundance . . . ." (XVI: 112.)
"So let them worship the Lord of this House, Who hath fed them against hunger; and hath made them safe from fear." (CVI: 3–4).

3 'Alī 'Abd al-Rasūl: "*Sulūk al Mustahlik wa'l munsh'ah fi'l 'itar al Islāmī*". Paper presented at the First International Conference on Islamic Economics, Makka, 1976. Mimeo 31p.

4 Morris Bernstein: *Comparative Economic Systems*, Richard & Irwin Inc. Homewood, Illinois, 1965, Preface.

5 Also his paper, "The Islamic Welfare State and its Role in the Economy", p. 17. Presented at the First International Conference on Islamic Economics, Makka, 1976. Mimeo 51p.

6 Manna' Qaṭṭān: *Mafhūm wa manhaj al-iqtiṣād al Islāmī*, pp. 1–5. Paper presented at the First International Conference on Islamic Economics, Makka, 1976. Mimeo 11p.

7 Ali Abd al Rasul: *Salūk al mustahlik wa'l munsha'ah fi'l 'itar al-Islāmī*. Paper presented at the First International Conference on Islamic Economics, Makka, 1976. Mimeo 31p.

8 Chapra, Muhammad Umar: "The Islamic Welfare State and its Role in the Economy", p. 17. Paper presented at the First International Conference on Islamic Economics, Makka, 1976. Mimeo 51p.

9 Op. cit. p. 18.

10 Shihab, Rafiullah, *Islāmī riyāsat kā māliyātī Nizām*, Islamabad: Islamic Research Institute, 1973, 157p.

11 Also the following papers presented at the First International Conference on Islamic Economics, Makka, 1976.
Hasanuzzaman, S. M.: "Zakāt and Fiscal Policy". Mimeo 52p.
al-Syed, 'Atif: "Fikrat al-'Adālah al ḍarībīyah fi'l Zakāt fī ṣadr al Islām." Mimeo 67p.
Salih Tug: "The Centralization of *Zakāh* and Individual Freedom". Mimeo 18p.
Faridi, F. R.: "*Zakāt* and Fiscal Policy". Mimeo 28p.
Qardāwī, Yusuf: "Athar al Zakāh fi 'ilāj al mūshkilāt al īqtisādīyah". Mimeo 44p.
Gorayah, Muhammad Yusuf: *Nizām-e-Zakāt aur jādid ma'āshī masā'īl*, Islamabad: Islamic Research Institute, 1972, p. 158.

12 Op. cit., pp. 12–13.

13 Al Fanjari, Muhammad Shauqi: "al Maḍhab al-iqtiṣādī fi'l Islām", p. 38. Paper

presented at the First International Conference on Islamic Economics, Makka, 1976. Mimeo 74p.

14 Hasanuzzaman, S. M.: "Zakāt and Fiscal Policy", pp. 27–28. Paper presented at the First International Conference on Islamic Economics, Makka, 1976. Mimeo

15 *ibid.* p. 205.

16 'Abd al-Salām, Muhammad Said: *Daur al fikr al mālī wa'l muhāsibī fī taṭbīq al-Zakāt*, p. 21. Paper presented at the First International Conference on Islamic Economics, Makka, 1976. Mimeo 30p.

17 al-Sayyīd, 'Ātif: *Fikr al-'Adālah al ḍarībīyah fi'l Zakāt fī ṣadr al-Islām*, pp. 5–17. Paper presented at the First International Conference on Islamic Economics, Makka, 1976. Mimeo 67p.

18 Kashif, Ahmad Sami Musa: Al Islām wa'l amn al-īqtiṣādī wa'l ījtimā'ī—ishārah khāṣṣah ilā al-ta' mīnāt al-ījtimā'īyah, pp. 12–22. Paper presented at the First International Conference on Islamic Economics, Makka, 1976. Mimeo 26p.

19 Zarqa, Mustafa Ahmad: "Niẓām al ta'min: mawqafahū fi'l maidān al-iqtiṣādī bi-wajhin 'ām wa-mawqif al Sharī'āh al Islāmīyah minhu". Makka, 1976. Mimeo 40p.

20 Shaheedi, Jafar: al-Ta'mīn: hukmuhū fi'l fiqh al Islāmī-wa-ārā' al-madhāhib al Islāmīyah fīh. Makka, 1976. Mimeo 14p.
Awad, Ali Jamaluddin: al-Ta'mīn fī 'itar al-Sharī'āh al Islāmīyah. Makka, 1976. Mimeo 39p.

21 Khan, Shaukat Ali: al-Ta'mīn wa badīluhū fī naẓar al-Islām. Makka, 1976. Mimeo 40p.

22 al Sayyad, Jalal Mustafa: al-Ta'mīn wa ba'ḍ al-shūbhāt, Makka, 1976. Mimeo 14p.

23 As in 21 above.

24 Abu Sunnah, Ahmad Fatimi: Al-Ta'mīn 'ind al-nawāzil wa'l ḥawa' ij. Makka, 1976. Mimeo 15p.

25 At Attār, 'Abd al Nasir Tawfīq: Hukm ash-Sharī'ah al Islāmīyah fi'l ta'min, Makka, 1976. Mimeo 42p.
All papers presented at the First International Conference on Islamic Economics, Makka, 1976.

26 Also Zarqā, Mustafa Ahmad, op. cit., p. 35.

27 First International Conference on Islamic Economics, Makka, 1976. General Recommendations, No. 6.

28 Khafif, Sheikh Ali: al-Ta'mīn wa hukmuhū 'alā hadī al-Sharī'ah wa Uṣūlihā al-'āmmah, pp. 19–20. Paper presented at the First International Conference on Islamic Economics, Makka, 1976. Mimeo 64p.
Attar, Abd al Nasir Tawfiq, op. cit., pp. 20–22.

29 Awad, Ali Jamaluddin, op. cit., pp. 15, 17–18, 20.
al Sayyad, Mustafa Jalal, op. cit., pp. 11–12.

30 Fanjari, Muhammad Shauqi: Al-Ta'āwun lā al-istighlāl asās 'aqd al-ta'mīn al-Islāmī. Paper presented to the Council of *ulema* in Saudi Arabia, Makka, May, 1976. Mimeo 56p.

31 Also his paper at the First International Conference on Islamic Economics, Makka, 1976. "Interest-Free Banking", Mimeo 164p.
Ahmad, Shaikh Mahmud: "Man and Money". Mimeo 380p. (Under print.)

32 It implies "creating artificial carrying costs for money through the device of requiring legal tender currency to be periodically stamped at a prescribed cost in order to retain its quality as money" (Keynes, J. M.: *General Theory*, London, 1957, p. 234). Though Keynes thought the proposal "deserves consideration" he pointed out the difficulties involved (pp. 357–358).

33 The same proposal had been made earlier by Arthur Birnie in his thought provoking pamphlet: *The History and Ethics of Interest* (William Hodge & Co., London, 1952, 40p.). Birnie, however, notes that the proposal "excites so much

misunderstanding and alarm". He, therefore, suggests "the issue of a currency of dated notes, which would be recalled at intervals and exchanged for a new dated currency" (p. 38).

34 al Jarhi, Mabid Ali Mohammad Mahmoud: *The Relative Efficiency of Interest-Free Monetary Economics: The Fiat Money Case*. Paper presented at the First International Conference on Islamic Economics, Makka, 1976. Mimeo 44p.

35 Al-Assāl, Ahmad Muhammad and Fathi Ahmad Abdul Karim: *al Niẓām al-iqtisādī fi'l Islām*, p. 21. Paper presented at the First International Conference on Islamic Economics, Makka, 1976. Mimeo 111p.

36 Muslehuddin, Muhammad: Interest-Free Banking and the Feasibility of Muḍārabah. Paper presented at the First International Conference on Islamic Economics, Makka, 1976. Mimeo 37p.

37 al Shawi, Muhammad Tawfiq: al Khaṣā'iṣ al-mumaiyyazah li'l bunk al-Islāmī li-tanmiyah min khilāl al-nuṣūṣ itti fāqīyah ta'sīsuhū wa malāmih al-niẓām al-maṣrafī wa'l iqtiṣād al-Islāmī. Mimeo 47p. Paper presented at the First International Conference on Islamic Economics, Makka, 1976.

38 Siddiqi, Muhammad Nejatullah: Banking in an Islamic Framework. Paper presented at the International Economic Conference: The Muslim World and the Future Economic Order, London, July, 1977. Mimeo 22p.

39 Op. cit. p. 10.

40 Siddiqi, Muhammad Nejatullah: "Interest-Free Banking—Problems and Prospects". Mimeo 15p. Paper presented at the University of Petroleum and Minerals, Dhahrān, 1976.

41 Op. cit. p. 34.

42 Abu Saud, Mahmud: "Interest-Free Banking". Mimeo 164p. Paper presented at the First International Conference on Islamic Economics, Makka, 1976.

43 *Ibid*, p. 114.

44 *Ibid*, p. 115.

45 *Ibid*, p. 116.

46 *Ibid*, p. 117.

47 *Ibid*, p. 153.

48 *Ibid*, p. 112.

49 Hamud, Sami Hasan Ahmad: Tatwīr al-a'māl al maṣrafiyah bi mā yattafiqu wa'l Shar'īyah al-Islāmīyah. Dār al-ittihād al-'Arab li'l tibā'ah, 1976. 552p.

50 Siddiqi, Muhammad Nejatullah: *Banking in an Islamic Framework*. Paper presented at the International Economic Conference: The Muslim World and the Future Economic Order, London, July, 1977. Mimeo 22p. See also his Dhahrān paper cited above.

51 Abdur Rasul, Ali: *Bunūk bilā fawāi'd*. Paper presented at the First International Conference on Islamic Economics, Makka, 1976. Mimeo 31p.

52 *Ibid*, p. 2.

53 *Ibid*, pp. 9–11.

54 Uzair, Muhammad: *Some Conceptional and Practical Aspects of Interest-Free Banking*. p. 26. Paper presented at the First International Conference on Islamic Economics, Makka, 1976. Mimeo 34p.

55 *Ibid*, pp. 26–27.

56 *Ibid*, p. 25.

57 *Ibid*, p. 2.

58 Siddiqi, Muhammad Nejatullah: *Teaching of Economics at the University Level in Muslim Countries—Challenge of Alien Concepts and Formulation of Islamic Concepts*. Paper presented at the First World Conference on Muslim Education, Makka, 1977. Mimeo 17p.

59 Shawi, Muhammad Tawfiq: al Khaṣā'is al mumaiyyazah li'l bunk al-Islāmī li'l tanmiyah min khilāl nuṣūṣ ittifāqīyah ta'sīsihī wa malāmih al-niẓām al-maṣrafī

wa'l iqtiṣād al-Islāmī. Paper presented at the First International Conference on Islamic Economics, Makka, 1976. Mimeo 47p.

60 *Ibid*, p. 31.

61 Islamic Development Bank: The First Annual Report 1395/96 H—1975/76 Jeddah, 36p.

62 Abdur Rasul, Ali: Sutūk al mustahlik wa'l munsha'āt fi'l 'iṭar al Islāmī. Paper presented at the First International Conference on Islamic Economics, Makka, 1976. Mimeo 31p.

63 Abdul Hadi, Hamdī Amīn: Muqawwinat idārah al-tanmiyah fi'l fikr al Islāmī. Paper presented at the First International Conference on Islamic Economics, Makka, 1976. Mimeo 27p.

64 al Assal, Ahmad Muhammad and Fathi Ahmad Abdul Karim: al-Niẓām al iqtiṣādī fi'l Islām. Paper presented at the First International Conference on Islamic Economics, Makka, 1976. Mimeo 111p.

65 Zubair, Muhammad Umar: "al iqtisād al Islāmī wa dauruh fi tanmiyat al mujtama," in *Nadwah al Shabāb al 'Ālamiyah li'l Da'wah al-Islāmīyah*, pp 192–201. Riyadh, 1972, 344p.

66 Namiq, Salāh al Dīn: *Limādhā lā yakūn lanā mafhūm Islāmī akhlāqī jadīd li tanmiyah al-iqtiṣādiyah*. Paper presented at the First International Conference on Islamic Economics, Makka, 1976. Mimeo 19p.

67 Khurshid Ahmad: *Economic Development in an Islamic Framework—Some Notes on the Outline of a Strategy*. Paper presented at the First International Conference on Islamic Economics, Makka, 1976. Mimeo 30p.

68 Siddiqi, Muhammad Nejatullah: *An Islamic Approach to Economic Development*, the Muslim Institute for Research and Planning, Slough, Berks, U.K. 1977, 8p.

69 Khurshid Ahmad, op. cit., pp. 23–26.

70 Shahin, Rahim Bakhsh: Iqbal kē ma-ashī nazariyāt. Lahore: All Pakistan Islamic Educational Congress. n.d. 118p.

71 Abu Saud, Mahmud: "Interest-Free Banking". Paper presented at the First International Conference on Islamic Economics, Makka, 1976. Mimeo 164p.

72 Also, Shaikh Mahmud Ahmad: "Social Justice in Islam", pp. 1–31. Lahore: Institute of Islamic Culture, 1975, 120p. and "Man and Money", Mimeo 380p (under print) by the same author.

73 Uzair, Muhammad: "Some Conceptual and Practical Aspects of Interest-Free Banking". Paper presented at the First International Conference on Islamic Economics, Makka, 1976. Mimeo 36p.

74 e.g. Siddiqi, Muhammad Nejatullah: "Teaching of Economics at the University Level in Muslim Countries: The Challenge of Alien Concepts and the Formulation of Islamic Concepts". Paper presented at the First World Conference on Muslim Education, Makka, 1977. Mimeo 17p.

75 Abu Saud, Mahmud, op. cit., pp. 34–70.

76 *Ibid*, p. 35.

77 *Ibid*, p. 39.

78 *Ibid*, p. 41.

79 *Ibid*, p. 46.

80 *Ibid*, p. 50.

81 *Ibid*, p. 52.

82 *Ibid*, p. 52.

83 *Ibid*, pp. 53–54.

84 *Ibid*, p. 62.

85 See under V.

86 Zarqa, Muhammad Anas: "Social Welfare Function and Consumer Behaviour: An Islamic Formulation of Selected Issues". p. 30. Paper presented at the First International Conference on Islamic Economics, Makka, 1976. Mimeo 65p.

87 *Ibid*, p. 42.
88 Uzair, Muhammad: "Some Conceptual and Practical Aspects of Interest-Free Banking", p. 12.
89 *Ibid.*
90 *Ibid.*
91 Hasanuzzaman, S. M.: "Zakāt and Fiscal Policy", p. 37. Paper presented at the First International Conference on Islamic Economics, Makka, 1976. Mimeo 52p.
92 *Ibid*, p. 35.
93 So that the saved part of income earns additional income equal to the *Zakāt* payable on wealth plus new income, as $\frac{10}{100} \times 27.5 = 2.75 = \frac{(100 + 10)\ 2.5}{100}$
94 He quotes Keynes: *General Theory*, p. 235. "It seems that the rate of interest on money plays a peculiar part in setting a limit to the level of employment, since it sets a standard to which marginal efficiency of a capital asset must attain if it is to be newly produced."
95 Siddiqi, Muhammad Nejatullah: "Banking in an Islamic Framework". Paper presented at the International Economic Conference: "The Muslim World and Future Economic Order", London, 1977. Mimeo 22p.
96 Siddiqi, Muhammad Nejatullah: "Banking in an Islamic Framework". Paper presented at the International Economic Conference: The Muslim World and the Future Economic Order, London, 1977. Mimeo 22p.
97 Abdul Bāqi, Mahmud Salāh: *al Iqtiṣād al Islāmī: farḍiyat al Zakāt wa ḥurmat al Ribā*. Paper presented at the First International Conference on Islamic Economics, Makka, 1976. Mimeo 10p.
98 el Naggar, Fareed: "The Methodology of Islamic Economics: A Systems Approach". Paper presented at the First International Conference on Islamic Economics, Makka, 1976. Mimeo 30p.
99 Faruqi, Ismail Ragi: "Islamicising the Social Sciences". Paper presented at the First World Conference on Muslim Education, Makka, 1977. Mimeo.
100 Schumpeter, J. A.: History of Economic Analysis, Oxford University Press, London, 1959, p. 136 and p. 788.
101 Boulakia, Jean David C.: "Ibn Khaldūn: A Fourteenth Century Economist"—Journal of Political Economy 79 (5) September–October 1971: 1105–1118.
102 Boulakia, Jean David C.: op. cit. pp. 1107–1108.
103 *Ibid*, p. 1109.
104 *Ibid*, p. 1117.
105 *Ibid*, p. 1118.
106 Qureshi, Tufail Ahmad: "Shāh Walīullāh kī naẓar men musalmānon kē ma'āshī masā'il kā ḥal", *Fikr-o-Nazar* (Islamabad) 7 (3) September 69: 218–226; 7 (4) October 69: 304–310.
107 *Ibid*, pp. 223–225.
108 *Ibid*, pp. 309–310.
109 Kifayātullah: "Economic Thought in the Eighth Century: The Muslim Contribution", *Voice of Islam* (Karachi), March, 1976, pp. 301–304.

Appendix to Chapter Ten

CLASSIFIED BIBLIOGRAPHY

Contents

1. ECONOMIC PHILOSOPHY OF ISLAM
[1–80]

1.	'Abd al-Mujeeb	"Ma'īshat-e-Islām: fikr-o-niẓām" (Islam's economy: philosophy and system), *Tarjumān al-Qur'ān* (Lahore) 74(2), 91–108; 74(3), 165–173. (U)
2.	'Abd al-Rasūl, 'Alī	*al-Mabādi'l-iqtiṣādīyah fi'l-Islām wa'l-binā' al-iqtiṣādī li'l-dawlat al-Islāmīyah* (Economic principles of Islam and the Economic structure of Islamic State). al-Qāhirah, Dār al-Fikr al-'Arabī, 1968. 294p. (A)
3.	Abū Aiman	"Ma'ālim al-Ṭarīq: al-nāḥīyah al-iqtiṣādīyah" (Guideposts of the road: The Economic aspect), *al-Muslimoon* (Dimashq), 3(5), July 55: 20–25. (A)
4.	Abu 'l-Makārim, Zaidān	*Binā al-iqtiṣād fi'l-Islām* (Structure of economy in Islam). al-Qāhirah, al-Dār al-'Arabīyah, 1951. 210p. (A)
5.	Abū Sa'ūd, Maḥmūd	"The Economic Order within the General Conception of the Islamic Way of Life", *Islamic Review* (London) 55(2), Feb. 67: 24–26; 55(3), Mar. 67: 11–14.
6.	,, ,, ,,	*Khuṭūṭ ra'īsīyah fi'l-iqtiṣād al-Islāmī* (Salient Features of Islamic Economy). Beirut, Maṭba'ah Ma'tūq Ikhwān, 1965. 96p. (A)
7.	Abū Sulaimān, 'Abdul Ḥamīd Aḥmad	*Naẓarīyat al-Islām al-iqtiṣādīyah: al-falsafah wa'l-wasā'il al-mu'āṣirah* (Economic Theory of Islam: The Philosophy and Contemporary Means). al-Qāhirah, Dār Miṣr li'l-Ṭibā'ah, 1960. 124p. (A)
8.	,, ,, ,,	"The Theory of the Economics of Islam: The Economics of Tawhīd and Brotherhood; Philosophy, Concept and Suggestions", in: *Contemporary Aspects of Economic and Social Thinking in Islam*. Gary, Indiana, M.S.A. of U.S. & Canada, 1973: 26–78.
9.	Afzal-Ur-Rehman	Economic Doctrines of Islam. Lahore, Islamic Publications, 1974. 3v. v.I, 224p.; v.II, 275p. v.III, 273p.
10.	Alavi, Q. Ahmadur Rahman	"An Introduction to the Economic Philosophy of Islam", *Islamic Literature* (Lahore) 2(4), Apr. 50: 25–34.
11.	'Alī, Ibrāhīm Fu'ād Aḥmad	"Naḥwa iqtiṣād Islāmī mutaḥarrir" (Towards a free Islamic Economy), *al-Wa'y al-Islāmī* (Kuwait) (109), Jan. 74: (114), June 74: 99–103. (A)
12.	Ali, Syed Ahmad	*Economic Foundations of Islam—a Social and Economic Study*. Calcutta, Orient Longmans, 1961. 203p.
13.	Amīnī, Muḥammad Taqī	*Tahdhīb kī jadīd tashkīl* (Reconstruction of Civilisation). Delhi, Nadwat al-Muṣannifīn, 1974. 339p. (U)

14.	al-'Araby, Muḥammad 'Abdullāh	"Economics in the Social Structure of Islam", *World Muslim League* (Singapore) 3(7), July–Aug. 66: 10–25.
15.	,, ,,	*al-Iqtiṣād al-Islāmī fī taṭbīqihi 'ala'l-mujtama' al-mu'āṣir* (Islamic Economics as applied to Contemporary Society). Kuwait, Maktabah al-Manār, n.d. (A)
16.	,, ,,	"Some Aspects of Islamic Economics", *Islamic Thought* (Aligarh) 6(2), Mar.–Apr. 57: 8–19.
17.	,, ,,	*Ta'ālīm al-Islām al-iqtiṣādīyah* (Economic Teachings of Islam). Kuwait, Maktabah al-Manār, n.d. (A)
18.	Ashraf, Muḥammad	"Ḥuḍūr Anwar Ṣallallāh 'alaihi wa ṣallam aur ma'āshī niẓām" (The Prophet of Allah, peace be upon him, and the Economic System), *Bayyināt* (Karachi) 16, (6), Aug. 70: 22–40. (U)
19.	Ashraf, Shaikh Muḥammad	"Islāmī ma'īshat" (Islamic Economy), *Salsabīl* (Karachi) 8, July 70: 19–23. 208p. (U)
20.	Bābullī, Maḥmūd Muḥammad	*Al-Iqtiṣād fī ḍau' al-sharī'at al-Islāmīyah* (Economics in the light of Islamic Law). Beirut, Dār al-Kitāb al-Lubnānī, 1975. (A)
21.	,, ,,	"Khaṣā'iṣ al-iqtiṣād al-Islāmī" (Characteristics of Islamic Economy), *Nadwat al-Muḥāḍarāt, Rābiṭat al-'Ālam al-Islāmī*, Makka, 1969: 79–102. (A)
22.	Dastgīr, Ghulām	*Islām kē ma'āshi taṣawwurāt* (Economic Concepts of Islam), Karachi, 'Abbāsī Kutub Khāna (U)
23.	al-Fanjarī, Muḥammad Shauqī	*al-Madkhal ila'l-iqtiṣād al-Islāmī* (Introduction to Islamic Economics). al-Qāhirah, Dār al-Nahḍat al-'Arabīyah, 1972. V.1 235p. (A)
24.	Farīdī, Fazlur Rahman	*Nature and Significance of Economic Activity in Islam*. Aligarh, Muslim University, Theological Society, n.d. 19p.
25.	al-Fāsī, 'Allāl	"Islām kā ma'āshī naẓarīyah" (Economic Theory of Islam), *Fikr-o-Naẓar* (Islamabad) 7(II), May 70: 814–30. (U)
26.	,, ,,	*al-Naqd al-Dhātī* (Self Criticism). Beirūt, Dār al-Kashshāf, 1966. 477p. (A)
27.	Fazlur Rahman	"Economic Principles of Islam", *Islamic Studies* (Islamabad), 8(1), Mar. 69: 1–8.
28.	Gīlānī, Sayyid Manāẓir Aḥsan	"Ahammīyat al-iqtiṣād fī ḍau' al-sunnah" (Importance of Economics in the light of Sunnah), *al-Ba'th al-Islāmī* (Lucknow) 10(4), Dec. 65: 55–61. (A)
29.	,, ,,	*Islāmī ma'āsniyāt* (Islamic Economics). Hyderabad, Idāra Ishā'at-e-Urdū, 1947. 453p. (U)
30.	Hameedullah, Muḥammad	"Review on J. Hans: *Homo Oeconomicus Islamicus* (Vienna, Austria, Joh, Sen. Klegnfurt, 1952, 144p.) with a map showing Foreign Investment in Muslim Petro Countries", *Islamic Quarterly* (London) 2(2), July 55: 142–146.
31.	Ḥamūda, 'Abd al-Wahhāb	"Siyāsat al-māl fi'l-Islām" (Financial Policy in Islam), *Liwā' al-Islām* 13(10), Dec. 59: 592–594. (A)
32.	Ḥasan, Ḥasan Ibrāhīm	*Islam: A Religious, Political, Social and Economic Study*. Beirut, Khayats, 1967.
33.	Ḥasan al-Bannā, Shaikh	*Mushkilātunā fī ḍau' al-niẓām al-Islāmī* (Our Pro-

		blems in the light of Islamic System). al-Qāhirah, Dār al-Kitāb al-'Arabī, 1952. 96p. (A)
34.	Huda, M. N.	"Islam and Economics", in: *Some Economic Aspects of Islam*, Karachi, Motamar Alam-e-Islami, 1965: 15–26.
35.	Ḥusainī, Aḥmad	*al-'Iml wa'l-māl fi'l-Islām* (Knowledge and Wealth in Islam). al-Qahirah, Dār al-Taḥrīr li'l-Tibā'ah wa'l-Nashr, 1971. 126p. (A)
36.	Ibrāhīm, 'Issa 'Abdou	"Ḥaula al-siyāsāt al-iqtiṣādīyah" (Regarding Economic Policies), *al-Muslimoon* (Dimashq), 3(1), Mar. 55: 52–55. (A)
37.	Idrīs, Gaafar	"Economics Sans Man Sans Purpose: review Article on J. K. Galbraith's *Economics and the Public Purpose*", *Impact* (London) 4(12), 28 June, 11 July 74: 8.
38.	Ja'farī, Ra'īs Aḥmad	*Islam aur 'adl-o-iḥsān* (Islam, Justice and Benevolence). Lahore, Idāra-e-Thaqāfat-e-Islāmiyah, 1960. 391p (U)
39.	Jāmi'ah Fu'ād al-Awwal, Kullīyat al-Tijārah, Jam'īyat al-Dirāsāt al-Islāmīyah	al-Iqtiṣād fī ḍau' al-Islām (Economics in the light of Islam) al-Qāhirah, Dār al-Kitāb al-'Arabī, 1951. 114p. (A)
40.	Kagaya, Kan	"Islam as a Modern Social Force", *Developing Economics*.
41.	Khān, Muḥammad 'Abdur Raḥmān	"Islāmī ma'āshiyāt" (Islamic Economics), *Burhān* (Delhi) 12(2), Feb. 44: 125–132. (U)
42.	Khān, Muḥammad Murtaḍā	"Islām kī ma'āshī aqdār" (Economic Values of Islam), *Sayyārah* (Lahore) 16(xvi), 27–31. (U)
43.	al-Khaṭīb, 'Abd al-Karīm	"Naḥwa iqtiṣād Islāmī mutaḥarrir" (Towards a Free Islamic Economy), *al-Wa'y al-Islāmī* (Kuwait) (113), May 74: 32–37. (A)
44.	al-Khaṭīb, Muḥibb al-Din	"Daulah ta'āwunīyah wa ummah muta'āwanah" (Cooperative State and a Cooperating People), *al-Azhar* (Cairo) 29(4), Oct. 57: 289–294. (A)
45.	,, ,, ,,	"al-Māl fī niẓām al-Islām" (Wealth in Islamic System) *al-Azhar* (Cairo) 26 (17, 18), May 55: 945-953. (A)
46.	al-Khaulī, Amīn	*Fī Amwālihim* (In their Wealth). Cairo. Dār al-Hana li'l Ṭibā'ah, 1963, 142p. (A)
47.	Khurshīd Ahmad	*Islam and the Contemporary Economic Challenges*. Xerox Unpublished, 1973.
48.	al-Labbān, Ibrāhīm	"Haqq al-fuqarā' fī Amwāl al-Aghniyā' " (Right of the Poor in the Wealth of the Rich). *Kitāb al-mu'tamar al-awwal li majma' al-buḥūth al-Islāmīyah*, Cairo, Mar. 64. (A) Eng. Tr. "The Right of the Poor to the Wealth of the Rich", *al-Azhar* (Cairo) Mar. 64: 167–187.
49.	Mawdūdī Sayyid Abul A'lā	"Economic and political teachings of the Quran" in Sharif, M. M. (ed.) *A History of Muslim Philosophy*, V. I. Wiesbaden, Otto Harrassowitz, 1963: 178–90.
50.	,, ,, ,, ,,	*The Economic Problem of Man and its Islamic Solution*. Lahore, Islamic Publications, 1975. 40p.
51.	,, ,, ,, ,,	"*Ma'āshiyāt-e-Islām* (Economics of Islam). Lahore, Islamic Publications, 1969. 436p. (U)

52. Mawdūdī Sayyid Abul A'lā — "Principles and Objectives of Islam's Economic System", *Criterion* (Karachi), 4(2), Mar.–Apr. 69: 44–58.

53. al-Miṣrī, 'Abd al-Samī' — *Naẓarīyat al-Islām al-iqtiṣādīyah* (Economic Theory of Islam). al-Qāhirah, Maktabah al-Anjalū al-Miṣrīyah, 1972. 246p. (A)

54. Moulavi, C. N. Ahmad — *Principles and Practice of Islamic Economy* tr. from Malyalam by K. Hasan. Calicut (Kerala, India) Ansari Press, 1964. 200p.

55. Muslehuddin, Muhammad — *Economics and Islam*. Lahore, Islamic Publications, 1974. 112p.

56. Muzaffar Hussain — *Motivation for Economic Achievement in Islam*. Lahore, All Pakistan Educational Congress, 1974. 50p.

57. Nadwī, 'Abd al-Bārī — *Tajdīd-e-ma'āshiyāt* (Reconstruction of Economics). Ṣidq-e-Jadīd Book Agency, 1955. 518p. (U)

58. al-Najjār, Aḥmad — *al-Madkhal ila'l-naẓarīyat al-iqtiṣādīyah fi'l-minhāj al-Islāmī*. (Introduction to Economic Theory in the Framework of Islamic Methodology). Beirut, Dār al-Fikr, 1973. 315p. (A)

59. ,, ,, — *al-Naẓarīyat al-iqtiṣādīyah fi'l-Islām* (Economic Theory of Islam). al-Qāhirah, Dār al-Ṭaḥrīr li'l-Ṭibā'ah wa 'l-Nashr, 1973. 85p (A)

60. Parwez, G. A. — *Quranic Economics*. Lahore, Quranic Research Centre, n.d. 24p.

61. Qādrī, Sayyid Aḥmad — "Islāmī ma'āṣhiyāt kē chand rahnumā uṣūl" (Some guiding principles of Islamic Economics), *Zindagī* (Rāmpur) 41(2), Aug. 68: 31–40. (U)

62. Quṭb, Sayyid — *al-'Adālat al-ijtimā'īyah fi'l-Islām* (Social Justice in Islam). 7th ed. 1967 294p. (A). (First published in 1948.) Urdu tr. by Siddiqi, Muhammad Nejatullāh: *Islam meṇ 'adl-e ijtimā'*. Lahore, Islamic Publications, 1969. 576p. English tr.: *Social Justice in Islam* by John D. Hardie, American Council of Learned Societies, New York, 1970, 298p.

63. Quṭb, Muḥammad — *Shubhāt ḥaul al-Islām* (Islam: the Misunderstood Religion). Beirut, Dār al-Shurūq, 1973. 242p. (A) (First published in 1953.) English tr.: Islam: the Misunderstood Religion, Islamic Publications, Lahore, 1972. 199p.

64. Rafī'uddīn — "'Usus al-iqtiṣād al-Islāmī' " (Fundamentals of Islamic Economics) *al-Ba'th al-Islāmī* (Lucknow) 8(1), Sept. 63: 32–40 (A)

65. Ra'ūf al-Ḥasan, Shaikh — "Islām kē iqtiṣādī nazarīyāt" (Economic theories of Islam) *al-Balāgh* (Karachi) 3(10), Jan. 70: 15–23 (U)

66. Riḍwī, Sayyid Zāhid Qaiṣar — "Islām meṇ daulat-o-iflās kā tawāzun" (Balancing between wealth and poverty in Islam), *Burhān* (Delhi) 12(2), Feb. 44: 133–150. (U)

67. Shalbī, Aḥmad — *al-Ḥayāt al-ijtimā'īyah fi'l-tafkīr al-Islāmī* (Social life in Islamic Thought). al-Qāhirah, Maktabah al-Nahḍat al-Miṣrīyah, 1968. 392p. (A)

68. ,, ,, — *al-Siyāsah wa'l-iqtiṣād fi'l-tafkīr al- al-Islāmī* (Politics and Economics in Islamic Thought).

		al-Qāhirah, Maktabah al-Nahḍat al-Miṣrīyah, 1964. (A)
69.	al-Sharbāsī, Aḥmad	*al-Dīn wa'l-mujtama'* (Religion and Society) al-Qāhirah, al-Maṭba't al-'Arabīyah, 1970. 255p. (A)
70.	al-Sibā'ī, Muṣṭafā	*Ishtirākīyat al-Islām* (Socialism of Islam) 2nd ed. Dimashq, Mu'assasa al-Maṭbu'āt al-'Arabīya, 1960. 423p. (A)
71.	Ṣiddīqī, 'Abdul Ḥamīd	"Islām kā falsafa-e-ma'āshiyāt" (Economic Philosophy of Islam), *Chirāgh-e-Rāh* (Karachi), Sept. 51 : 17–36. (U)
72.	Ṣiddīqī, Muḥammad Maẓharuddīn	*Islām kā ma'āshī naẓarīya* (Economic Theory of Īslam) 2nd ed. Lahore, Idāra-e-Thaqāfat-e-Islāmiyah, 1955. 92p. (U)
73.	Ṣiddīqī, Muḥammad Nejatullāh	"Economics of Islam", *Islamic Thought* (Aligarh) 14(3), 71 : 22–33.
74.	Ṣiddīqī, Na'īm	"Chand ma'āshiyātī ḥaqīqateṇ" (Some Economic Truths) *Tarjumān al-Qur'ān* (Lahore) 33(6), May 50: 340–360. (U)
75.	Ṣiddīqī, Ṣiddīq Jamāl	*Islām aur ma'īshat* (Islam and the Economy) Hyderabad (Dn), Nizam Silver Jubilee Press, nd. 64p. (U)
76.	Syed, J. W.	"Islam and Material Progress", *Islamic Literature* (Lahore) 6(7), July 54 : 15–9.
77.	al-Ṭaḥāwī, Ibrāhīm	*al-iqtiṣād al-Islāmī madhhaban wa niẓāman wa dirāsah muqāranah.* (Islamic Economics—a School of Thought and a System, a Comparative Study). al-Qāhirah, Majma' al-Buḥūth al-Islāmīyah, 1974. 2v. 616, 400p. (A)
78.	Ṭāsīn, Muḥammad	"Islām kē ma'āshī maqāṣid (Economic Objectives of Islam), *Fikr-o-Naẓar* (Karachi) May 65 : 668–677. (U)
79.	'Uthmān, Shaikh Muḥammad	"Qur'ān kā ma'āshī rujḥān" (Economic attitude of Islām) *Fikr-o-Naẓar* (Islamabad) 3(9–10) Mar.–Apr. 66 : 647–660. (U)
80.	'Uthmānī, Muḥammad Fahīm	"Islāmī ma'āshiyāt : tana'uum wa 'aish koshī" (Islamic Economics : Affluent and Luxurious Living). *al-Ḥaqq* (Karachi), 5, Aug. 70 : 39–48. (U)

2. ECONOMIC SYSTEM OF ISLAM [81–498]

i. Sources and Precedents: 81–102

81.	'Abd al-Bārī	" 'Ahd-e-Hishām kā ma'āshī jāi'zah" (Economic Survey of the reign of Hishām) *Ma'ārif* (Azamgarh) 110(4), Oct. 72 : 267–281. (U)
82.	al-Afghānī, Sa'īd	*Aswāq al-'Arab fi'l-jāhilīyah wa'l-Islām* (The Arab Markets during Jāhiliyyah and Islam). Dimashq, Dār al-Fikr, 1960. 528p. (A)
83.	Amīnī, Muḥammad Taqī	"Ḥaḍrat 'Umar kī ma'āshī iṣlāḥāt" (Economic Reforms of 'Umar) *al-Furqān* (Lucknow) 38 (9, 10) Dec. 70 : 15–26. (U)
84.	,, ,, ,,	"Khilāfat-e-Fārūqī meṇ arāḍi kī tanẓīm-o-tansīq" (Land Organisation during the Caliphate of

'Umar), *Ma'ārif* (Azamgarh), 91(6) June 63: 405–409. (U)

85. Ḍanāwī, Muḥammad 'Alī — *'Umar bin 'Abd al-'Azīz fi'l-ḥukm wa'l-iqtiṣād wa'l-qaḍā'* ('Umar bin 'Abd al-'Azīz: Governance, Economics and Justice) Beirut, al-Dār al-'Arabīyah, 1966. (A)

86. Fāriq, Khurshīd Aḥmad — " 'Ahd-e-Fārūqī kā iqtiṣādī jā'izah" (Economic Survey of the Era of 'Umar) *Burhān* (Delhi) 64(6), June 70: 81–98. (U)

87. ,, ,, ,, — " 'Ahd-e-Ṣiddīqī kā iqtiṣādī jā'izah" (Economic Survey of the Era of Abū Bakr), *Burhān* (Delhi) 64(3), Mar. 70: 167–180; 64(4), Apr. 70: 241–255; 64(5), May 70: 324–337. (U)

88. ,, ,, ,, — "Daur-e-Ḥaidarī kā iqtiṣādī jā'izah" (Economic Survey of the Era of 'Alī), *Burhān* (Delhi) 65(6), Dec. 70: 392–409. (U)

89. Fischel, W. — "The Bait Māl al-khāṣṣa: a contribution to the History of 'Abbasid Administration", 19th Cong. Int. degli. Or, 1935: 538–541.

90. Gibb, H. A. R. — "The Fiscal Rescript of 'Umar II", *Arabica* 2(1955), 1–16.

91. Goitein, S. D. — *A Mediterranean Society*, Vol. I *Economic Foundation—the Jewish Communities of the Arab World as portrayed in the documents of the Cairo Geniza.* Berkley, Calif., Univ. of Calfornia Press, 1967. 550p.

92. Ḥameedullah, Muḥammad — *Jāhilīyat-e-'Arab ke ma'āshī niẓām kā athar pehlī mamlakat-e-Islāmīya kē qiyām par* (Impact of the Economic System of Arab Jāhiliyah Period on the Establishment of the First Islamic State). Hyderabad (Dn.), Habib Co., 1362 A.H. 103p.(U)

93. Imamuddin, S. M. — "Bayt al-Māl and Banks in the Medieval Muslim World", *Islamic Culture*, 34(1), Jan. 60: 22–30.

94. Kister, M. J. — "The Market of the Prophet" *Journal of the Economic and Social History of the Orient* (Leiden) 8(3), Jan. 65: 272–276.

95. Ra'nā, 'Irfān Maḥmūd — *Economic System under Omar the Great.* Lahore, Muḥammad Ashraf, 1970. 152p.

96. al-Rīs, Muḥammad Ḍiyā' al-Dīn — *al-Kharāj wal'l-nuẓum al-mālīyah fi'l-Islām ḥattā muntaṣif al-Qarn al-thālith al-hijrī* (Kharāj and the Financial Systems in Islam till the Middle of the Third Century Hijra) Ph.D. Thesis, Kulliyat al-Ādāb, Jāmi'ah al-Qāhirah, 1959.(A)

97. Ṣāliḥ, Muḥammad Amīn — *al-Nuẓum al-iqtiṣādīyah fī Miṣr wa'l-Shām fī ṣadr al-Islām* (Economic Systems in Egypt and Syria in the beginning of the Islamic Era). al-Qāhirah, Maktabah Sa'id Rifa't, 1971. 228p. (A)

98. al-Shāfi'ī, Aḥmad — *al-Niẓām al-iqtiṣādī fī 'ahd 'Umar bin al-Khaṭṭāb* (Economic System in the Era of 'Umar bin Khaṭṭāb) Ph.D. Thesis, Cairo University. (A)

99. Shalbī, Maḥmūd — *Ishtirākīyatu Muḥammad* (Socialism of Muḥammad) Cairo, Maktabat al-Qāhirah al-Ḥadīthah, 1962. (A)

100. ,, ,, — *Ishtirākīyatu 'Umar* (Socialism of 'Umar). Cairo,

		Maktabat al-Qāhirah al-Ḥadīthah, 1965. (A)
101.	Shalbī, Maḥmūd	Ishtirākīyatu 'Uthmān (Socialism of 'Uthmān). Cairo, Maktabat al-Qāhirah al-Ḥadīthah, 416p. (A)
102.	Ṣiddīqī, Muḥammad Maẓharuddīn	"Haḍrat 'Umar kī Zar'ī iṣlāḥāt" (Agricultural Reforms of 'Umar) *Thaqāfat* (Lahore) 1(8), Aug. 55: 7–14. (U)

ii. General: 103–166

103.	Abāẓah, Ibrāhīm Dasūqī	*al-Iqtiṣād al-Islāmī: muqawwimātuhū wa minhājuhū* (Islamic Economics: its Elements and Methodology). Cairo, Dār al-Sha'b, 1974. (A)
104.	,, ,, ,,	"al-Islām wa'l-binā' al-iqtiṣādī" (Islam and the Economic Structure) *al-Taḍāmun* (al-Rabāṭ) 1(3), Feb. 74: 166–173. (A)
105.	Abū Sa'ūd, Maḥmūd	"Economic Policy in Islam", *Islamic Review* (London) 45(5), May 57: 7–15.
106.	Abū Zuhra, Muḥammad	*Tanẓim al-Islām li'l-mujtama'* (Islamic Organisation of Society). Cairo, Maktabah al-Anjalū al-Miṣrīyah. 208p. (A)
107.	al-'Ādil, Fu'ād	*al-'Adālat al-ijtimā'īyah* (Social Justice). Beirut, Dār al-Kitāb al-'Arabī, 1969. (A)
108.	Afghānī, Shams al-Ḥaqq	"Islām kā ma'āshī niẓām" (Economic System of Islam) *Fikr-o-Naẓar* (Islamabad) 2, 89–100; 3, 276–284. (U)
109.	Aḥmad, Manẓūr al-Raḥmān	"Takwīn jadīd li'l-iqtiṣād al-Islāmī (Reconstruction of Islamic Economy). *al-Ba'th al-Islāmī* (Lucknow) 13(10), July 69: 51–55; 14(1), Aug. 69: 58–64; 14(2), Sept. 69: 67–74. (A)
110.	Amīn al-Ḥaqq	"Ma'āshī buḥrān aur Islām (Economic Crisis and Islam) *al-Ḥaqq* (Pakistan) 5(10), July 70: 41–48. (U)
111.	,, ,,	"Maujūdah ma'āshī buḥrān aur Islām" (Contemporary Economic Crisis and Islam) *al-Ḥaqq* (Pakistan) 5, (9) June 70: 50–59. (U)
112.	al-'Araby, Muḥammad 'Abdullāh	"Ṭuruq istithmār al-amwāl wa mauqif al-Islām minhā" (Islamic Viewpoint Regarding the Ways of Productive Employment of Property) *al-Azhar* (Cairo) al-Mu'tamar al-thānī li majma' al-buḥūth al-Islāmīyah, May 65: 124–136. (A)
113.	al-'Ashmāwī, Yāqūt	*al-Khuṭūṭ al-Kubrā li'l-niẓām al-iqtiṣādī fi'l-Islām* (Prominent Features of Economic System in Islam) al-Qāhirah, al-Idārat al-'Āmmah li'l-Thaqāfat al-Islāmīyah bi'l-Jāmi' al-Azhar, 1959. 32p. (A)
114.	Ausaf Ali	*Political Economy of the Islamic State*. Ph.D. Thesis, University of Southern California, 1970. 280p.
115.	Chāprā, M. 'Umar	*The Economic System of Islam—a Discussion of its Goal and Nature*. London, Islamic Culture Centre, 1970. 54p.
116.	Faiḍullāh, Muḥammad Fawzī	"Minhāj al-Islām fi'l-takāful al-ijtimā'ī" (Islamic Method of Collective Responsibility) *al-Wa'y al-Islāmī* (Kuwait) 115, July 74: 52–61. (A)
117.	Ghaznavi, Syed Abu Bakr	*Circulation of Wealth in Islam*. Lahore, Islamic

Society, West Pakistan University of Engineering & Technology. n.d. 14p.

118. al-Ghazzālī, Muḥammad — *al-Islām wa'l-awḍā' al-iqtiṣādīyah* (Islam and the Economic Institutions). al-Qāhirah, Dār al-Kutub al-Ḥadīthah, 1961. (First published in 1947.) (A)

119. Hameedullah, Muhammad — "The Economic System of Islam" in: *Introduction to Islam*. I.I.F.S.O., 1970: 140–168.

120. Ḥifẓur Raḥmān, Muḥammad, Seohārwī — *Islām kā iqtiṣādī niẓām* (Economic System of Islam). 2nd ed. Delhi, Nadwat al-Muṣannifīn, 1942. 359p. (U)

121. Husaini, S. Waqar Ahmad — "Principles of Environmental Engineering Systems Planning in Islamic Culture, Law, Politics, Economics, Education, and Sociology of Science and Culture", *in* Programmes in Engineering, Economic Planning: Stanford University Report EEP–47, December 1971: 281p.

122. Ibn 'Āshūr, Muḥammad al-Ṭāhir — *Uṣūl al-niẓām al-ijtimā'ī fi'l-Islām* (Principles of Social System in Islam). Tunis, al-sharikat al-Qaumīyah li'l-Nashr, 1964. 236p. (A)

123. ,, ,, — "al-Iqtiṣād al-Islāmī" (Islamic Economics) *al- Fikr al-Islāmī* (Beirut) 1(8), June 70: 32–58. (A)

124. 'Izz al-Dīn, Mūsā — *al-Islām wa qaḍāyā al-Sā'ah* (Islam and the Issues of the Day). Beirut, Dār al-Undulus, 1966. (A)

125. Jamā'at-e-Islāmī Pakistan — *Manshūr barā'ē intikhābāt 1970* (Manifesto for 1970 Elections) Lahore, 20 December 1969, 40p. (U)

126. ,, ,, — *Maujūdah iqtiṣādī buḥrān aur Islāmī ḥikmat-e-ma'īshat* (Contemporary Economic Crisis and the Economic Policy of Islam). Comp. by Khurshīd Aḥmad and Na'īm Ṣiddīqī. Lahore, Shu'bah Nashr-o-Ishā'at, 1970. 271p. (U)

127. Kāndhlawī, Iḥtishām al-Ḥaqq — *Ādāb-e-ma'īshat* (Rules of Economic Life). Delhi, Kutub Khāna Anjuman Tarraqī-e-Urdū, 1954. (U)

128. al-Kattānī, Muḥammad al-Muntaṣir — *Mudhakkirāt fi'l-amwāl fi'l-Islām* (Discourses on Wealth in Islam). Dimashq, Kullīyat al-Sharī'ah bi-Jāmi'ah Dimashq. (A)

129. Khān, Ḥāmid 'Alī — *Kasb-e ma'āsh kā Islāmī naẓarīyah* (Islamic Theory of Earning). Delhi, Jamāl Press, 1968. 115p. (U)

130. al-Khaulī, al-Bahī — *al-Tharwah fī Ẓill al-Islām* (Wealth in Islam) al-Qāhirah, Maṭba'ah al-Istiqlāl al-Kubrā, 1971. 161–340p. (A)

131. Makhlūf, Ḥasnain — *Fatwā Shar'īyah fī Shu'ūn iqtiṣādīyah* (Religious Verdict on Economic Issues Relating to Islam). Cairo, Maṭba'ah Muṣṭafā al-Bābī al-Ḥalabī, 1948. 16p. (A)

132. Mannan, M. A. — *Islamic Economics—Theory and Practice*. Lahore, Muḥammad Ashraf, 1970. 386p.

133. Mawdūdī, Sayyid Abul A'lā — *Rasā'il wa masā'il* (Letters and Problems) Vol. I. Delhi, Markazī Maktabah Jamā'at-e-Islāmī Hind, 1960. 415p. (U)

134. al-Mubārak, Muḥammad — *Niẓām al-Islām-al-iqtiṣād, mabādī wa gawā'id 'āmma* (Islamic System: The Economy, Elements and General Principles) Beirut, Dār al-Fikr, 1972. 160p. (A)

135. Muḥammad Miyāṇ — *Daur-e ḥāḍir kē siyāsī aur iqtiṣādī masā'il aur*

		Islāmī ta'līmāt-o-ishārāt (Economic and Political Problems of the Present Age and the Teachings of Islam). Delhi, Kitābistān, 1970. (U)
136.	Mustafizul Hasan, Syed	"The Quranic Way Out of the Present Economic Tangle", *Islamic Thought* (Aligarh) 1(2), May–June 54: 17–19.
137.	Mu'tamar al-Buḥūth al-Islāmīyah al-Sābi' (al-Qāhirah, Sept. 1972)	*Buḥūth iqtiṣādīyah wa tashrī'īyah* (Economic and Legal Discourses) al-Qāhirah, Majma' al-Buḥūth al-Islāmīyah, 1973. 410p. (A)
138.	Nabhān, Muḥammad Fārūq	*al-Ittijāh al-jimā'ī fi'l-tashrī' al-iqtiṣādī al-Islāmī* (Social trend in the Economic Legislation of Islam) Beirut, Dār al-Fikr, 1970. 528p. (A)
139.	al-Nabhānī, Taqī al-Din	*al-Niẓām al-iqtiṣādī fi'l-Islām* (Economic System of Islam) 3rd ed. al-Quds, Ḥizb al-Taḥrīr, 1953. 266p. (A)
140.	Nadhīr Aḥmad	"Uṣūl-e-taqsīm-e-daulat aur Islām" (Principles of Distribution of Wealth in Islam) *Ma'ārif* (Azamgarh) 14(2) Aug. 24: 130–132. (U)
141.	Nadwī, Abu'l Ḥasan 'Alī	"Mu'āsāt ṭau'īyah au musāwāt jabrīyah" (Voluntary Mutual Assistance or Forced Equality) *al-Ba'th al-Islāmī* (Lucknow) 11(1), Sep. 66: 63–83. (A)
142.	al-Nowaihī, Muḥammad	"Fundamentals of Economic Justice in Islam" in: *Contemporary Aspects of Economic and Social Thinking in Islam*, Gary, Indiana, M.S.A. of U.S. & Canada, 1973: 100–124.
143.	Parwez, Ghulām Aḥmad	*Niẓām-e rubūbīyat* (System of Divine Sustenance). Karachi, Idāra-e Ṭulū'-e Islām. 1954. 296p. (U)
144.	Qureshī, 'Abdul Majīd	"*Ma'āshiyāt kā bunyādī muṭāli'ah*" (Basic Study of Economics) *Zindagī* (Rampur) 14(4, 5), July–Aug. 55: 81–87.(U)
145.	Rodinson, Maxime	*Islam and Capitalism*, tr. by Brian Pearce, Suffolk, Allen Lane, 1974. 308p. Arabic tr. Nuzbah al-Ḥakim: *al-Islām wa'l-ra'smālīyah*. Beirut, Dār al-Ṭalī'ah, 1968.
146.	Sālim, Aḥmad Mūsā	*al-Islām wa qaḍāyāna'l-mu'āṣirah* (Islam and our Contemporary Problems). al-Qāhirah, Dār al-Hanā li'l-Ṭibā'ah, 1970. 293p. (A)
147.	Shabāna, Zakī Maḥmūd	"Ma'ālim ra'īsīyah iqtiṣādīyah Islāmīyah li muwājaha al-mushkilāt al-iqtiṣādīyah al-ḥāḍirah" (Salient Economic Features of Islam for Meeting the Challenges of Present Economic Problems) *al-Muslimoon* (Dimashq) 3(2–6). (A)
148.	Shafī', Muftī Muḥammad	"Distribution of Wealth in Islam", *Muslim News International* (Karachi) 7(8), Feb. 69: 5–10; 7(9), Mar. 69: 3–8.
149.	,, ,, ,,	"Taqsīm-e daulat kā Islāmī niẓām" (Islamic System of Distribution of Wealth) *al-Furqān* (Lucknow) 35(12), Apr. 68: 25–37 (U) Arabic tr. "Mauqif al-Islām min tauzī' al daulah" in *al-Ba'th al Islāmī* (Lucknow) 13(1), Sep. 68: 57–65; 13(2), Oct. 68: 57–68.
150.	Shākir, 'Abdul Mun'im Aḥmad	*Individual and Social Responsibility in Islamic Thought*. Ph.D. Thesis, 1966, New York University.

151. Shaltūt, Maḥmūd — "Money and the Economic Independence in Islam", *al-Azhar* (Cairo) 33(3), Aug. 61 : 5–18. (A)

152. Shamsul Hoda, Mīr — "Islamic Economy", *Islamic Literature* (Lahore) 5(5), May 53 : 17–25.

153. al-Sharbāṣi, A. — *al-Islām wa'l-iqtiṣād* (Islam and the Economy). al-Qāhirah, Dār al-Qaumīyah li'l Ṭibā'ah wa'l-Nashr, 1965. 276p. (A)

154. Sheikh, Nasir Ahmad — *Some Aspects of the Constitution and the Economics of Islam*. Woking, England, The Woking Mission & Literary Trust, 1967. 246p. (First Published in 1957.)

155. Ṣiddīqī, Ḥaīdar Zamāṇ — *Islām kạ ma'āshiyātī niẓām* (Economic System of Islam). Karachi, Feroz Sons. (U)

156. Ṣiddīqī, Muḥammad Maẓharuddīn — "Islam and Economic Exploitation", *Islamic Literature* (Lahore) 14(6), June 68 : 25–40.

157. ,, ,, — "Islam kī ma'āshī Ta'līmāt aur hamāra Jadid Mu'-āsharah" (Economic Teaching of Islam and the Modern Society) *Fikr-o-Nazr* (Rawalpindi) 4(5), Nov. 66 : 285–97. (U)

158. Ṣiddīqī, Muḥammad Nejatūllah — *Some Aspects of the Islamic Economy*. Lahore, Islamic Publications, 1970; Delhi, Markazī Maktabah Islāmī, 1972. 137p.

159. Ṣiddīqī, Na'īm — *Ma'āshī nāhamwāriyoṇ kā Islāmī ḥal* (Islamic Solution of Economic Inequities). Karachi, Maktabah Chirāgh-e-Rāh, 1958. (U)

160. Wāfī, 'Alī 'Abd al-Wāḥid — *al-Musāwāt fi'l-Islām* (Equality in Islam). Cairo, Dār al-Ma'ārīf, 1962, 112p. (A)

161. Yamānī, Aḥmad Zakī — " 'Adālatuna'l-ijtimā'ī" (Our Social Justice) *al-Muslimoon* (Geneva) 9(9), July 65 : 12–24; 9(10), Nov. 65 : 55–62. (A)

162. ,, ,, ,, — "Social Justice in Islam", *World Muslim League* (Singapore) 3(4), Apr. 66 : 11–33.

163. Yunus, H. Kahruddīn — "Economic System of Islam", *Islamic Thought* (Aligarh) 10(3 & 4), Jan. 65 : 33–60.

164. Yusuf, S. M. — *Economic Justice in Islam*. Lahore, Muḥammad Ashraf, 1971. vii, 116p.

165. Yūsufuddīn, Muḥammad — *Islām kē ma'āshī naẓariyē* (Economic Theories of Islam) 2nd ed. Hyderabad, Maṭba' Ibrāhīmīyah, 1950. 2v. 756p. (U)

166. World Muslim Congress — *Some Economic Aspects of Islam*. Karachi, Umma Publishing House, n.d. 164p. Arabic tr. *Ba'ḍ al-nawāḥī al-iqtiṣādīyah fi'l-Islām*. Karachi, 1964.

iii. Comparative Studies: 167–181

167. Abdur Rauf, M. — "Islam and Contemporary Economic Systems" in: *Contemporary Aspects of Economic and Social Thinking in Islam*. Gary, Indiana, M.S.A. of U.S. & Canada, 1973 : 79–84.

168. Ahmad, Sheikh Mahmud — *Economics of Islam: A Comparative Study*. Lahore, Muhammad Ashraf, 1972. xv, 227p.

169. al-'Araby, Muḥammad 'Abdullāh — "al-Iqtiṣād al-Islāmī wa'l-iqtiṣād al-mu'āṣir" (Islamic Economics and Contemporary Economics) *al-Azhar, Majma' al-Buḥūth al-Islāmīyah, al-Mu'tamar al-thālith*, 1966 : 209–313. (A)

170.	al-ʻAwadī, Rifʻat	*al-Iqtiṣād al-Islāmī wa'l-fikr al-muʻāṣir: naẓarīyat al-tauzīʻ*. Risālat al-Mājistir, Jāmiʻat al-Qāhirah (Islamic Economics and Contemporary Thought: Theory of Distribution). Master's Thesis, Cairo University. (A)
171.	Bāqir al-Ṣadr, Muḥammad	*Iqtiṣādunā* (Our Economics). Beirut, Dār al-Fikr, 1968. 2 V. 694p. (A) (First published in 1961.)
172.	al-Būṭī, Muḥammad Saʻīd Ramaḍān	*al-Madhhab al-iqtiṣādī bain al-shuyūʻīyah wa'l-Islām* (Economic Ideology in Communism and Islam). Dimashq, al-Maktabat al-Umawīyah, 1959. (A)
173.	al-Ghazālī, Muḥammad	*al-Islām al-muftarā ʻalaihi bain al-shuyūʻīyīn wa'l-r'asmālīyīn* (Islam the Misinterpreted Religion Contrasted with Communism and Capitalism). al-Qāhirah, Maktabah Wahbah, 1960. (A) (First Published 1950).
174.	Ḥaqqī, Iḥsān	*al-Islām wa'l-Shuyūʻīyah* (Islam and Communism). Jeddah, al-Dār al-Saʻūdīyah, 1970. (A)
175.	Imran, Muhammad	"Islamic Social Justice: the Alternative to the Curse of Capitalism and Socialism", *Criterion* (Karachi) 5(1), Jan.–Feb. 70: 21–31.
176.	Khurshid Ahmad	"Limādhā Yufaḍḍal al-iqtiṣād al-Islāmī ʻalā ghairihā?" (Why Islamic Economic System is Regarded Superior to Other Systems?) *al-Baʻth al-Islāmī* (Lucknow) 14(10), June 70: 71–75. (A)
177.	Maudūdī, Sayyid Abul Aʻlā	*Usus al-iqtiṣād bain al-Islām wa'l-nuẓum al-muʻāṣirah wa Muʻḍalāt al-Iqtiṣād wa ḥalluhā fi'l-Islām* (Fundamentals of Economics in Islam and the Contemporary Systems and Economic Problems of Man and their Islamic Solutions). 2nd ed. Jeddah, Dār al-Saʻūdīyah li'l-Nashr, 1967. 189p. (A) tr. Muḥammad ʻĀṣim al-Ḥaddād.
178.	al-Nabhān, Muḥammad Fārūq	"Makānat al-iqtiṣād al-Islāmī bain al-nuẓum al-iqtiṣādīyah al-muʻāṣirah" (The Place of Islamic Economy in the Contemporary Economic Systems) *al-Nadwah* (Makka) 26 Feb. 1967. (A)
179.	al-Nimr, ʻAbd al-Munʻim	"al-Islām wa'l-madhāhib al-iqtiṣādiyah al-ḥadīthah" (Islam and Modern Systems of Economics) *al-Baʻth al-Islāmī* (Lucknow) 2(8), May 57: 9–14. (A)
180.	Qadri, Anwar Ahmad	"The Sharīʻa and Other Economic Systems", *Criterion* (Karachi) 4(5), Sept.–Oct. 59: 39–53.
181.	Ṣiddīqī, ʻAbdul Ḥamid	*Insāniyat kī taʻmīr-e-nau aur Islām* (Reconstruction of Humanity and Islam) Ichra, Lahore, Markazī Maktabah Jamāʻat-e-Islāmī (Pakistan), 1956. 304p. (U)

iv. Socialistic Trends: 182–208

182.	Abu 'l-ʻUyūn, Maḥmūd	"al-Ishtirākīyah fi'l-Islam" (Socialism in Islam) *al-Azhar* (Cairo) 23(2), Ṣafr 51: 89–95. (A)
183.	Cragg, K.	"The Intellectual Impact of Communism Upon Contemporary Islam", *Middle East Journal* 8(2), 54: 127–138.
184.	Farrāj, Aḥmad (ed.)	*al-Islām din al-Ishtirākīyah* (Islam—a Religion of

Socialism). al-Qāhirah, al-Dār al-Qaumīyah, 1961. (A)

185. Faudah, 'Abd al-Raḥim — "al-Mujtama' al-ishtirākī fī ẓill al-Islām" (Socialistic Society under Islam) *al-Azhar* (Cairo) 37(8) Feb. 68: 438–441; 37(9, 10), Mar.–Apr. 66: 525–528. (A)

186. Gardner, G. H. and Hanna, S. A. — "Islamic Socialism", *Muslim World* 56(2), Apr. 66: 71–86.

187. Ḥafīẓ, 'Abbās — *al-Shuyū'īyah fi'l-Islām* (Communism in Islam). 3rd ed. al-Qāhirah, Maktabat al-'Arab, 1955. (A)

188. Halpern, M. — "The Implications of Communism for Islam", *Muslim World* 43(1), Jan. 53: 28–41.

189. al-Ḥanbalī, Shākir — "al-Ishtirākīyat al-Islāmīyah" (Islamic Socialism) *al-Tamaddun al-Islāmī* (Dimashq) 13(4, 5), Rabī' II 1366 A. H. 55–57. (A)

190. Hanna, Sami A. — "al-Takāful al-ijtimā'ī and Islamic Socialism", *Muslim World* 59(3, 4), Jul.–Oct.; 69: 275–286.

191. Ḥijāzī, 'Abd al-Badī' — *al-Musāwāt wa'l-ishtirākīyah fi'l-Islam* (Equality and Socialism in Islam). (A)

192. Ibn al-Sabīl, Waiṭlīf Khālid — "Islāmī ishtirākīyat kē chand pahlū" (Some Aspects of Islamic Communism) *Fikr-o-Naẓar* (Karachi) 7(7), Jan. 70: 513–526. (U)

193. Inamul Haq — *Principles and Philosophy of Democratic Socialism in Islam*. Karachi, The Author, 1966.

194. al-Khaṭīb, Anwar — *al-Naz'at al-ishtirākīyah fi'l-Islām* (Socialist Trend in Islam), Beirut, Dār al-'Ilm li'l-Malāyīn. (A)

195. al-Khaulī, al-Bahī — *al-Ishtirākīyah fi'l-mujtama' al-Islāmī bain al-naẓarīyah wa'l-taṭbīq* (Socialism in Islamic Society: Theory and Application). al-Qāhirah, Maktabah Wahbah, 181p. (A)

196. Marek, J. — "Socialist Ideas in the Poetry of Muhammad Iqbāl", *Studies in Islam* (Delhi) 5(1–3), 68: 167–179.

197. al-Miḥṣār, Hāmid — *Li man al-māl? 'alā ḍau' Ṣariḥ al-Kitāb wa Ṣahīḥ al-Sunnah* (To Whom Belongs the Wealth? In the Light of Explicit Provisions of the Qur'ān and Authentic Sunnah), al-Fajālah, Maṭba'ah al-Ḥaḍārah al-'Arabīyah 1974. (A)

198. al-Munajjid, Ṣalāḥ al-Dīn — *Balshafat al-Islām* (Bolshevism of Islam). Beirut, Dār al-Kitāb al-Jadīd, 1966. 144p. (A)

199. Muslehuddin, Muhammad — "Islamī Socialism—What is Implies?" *Criterion* (Karachi) 7(9), Sep. 72: 34–39; 7(10), Oct. 72: 19–29.

200. Parwez, Ghulām Aḥmad — *Economics in the Social Structure of Islam*. Lahore, Quranic Research Centre, n.d. 12p.

201. ,, ,, ,, — "Rizq-e-Muḥammadī kī taqsīm" (Distribution of 'Muhammadī' Provisions) *Ṭulū'-e-Islām* (Karachi) 23, June 70: 18. (U)

202. Riḍwān, Aḥmad Muḥammad — *Ishtirākīyat al-Islām* (Socialism of Islam). al-Qāhirah, Dār al-Kitāb al-'Arabī, 1950. 136p. (A)

203. Sarkar, Abdul Bari — *The Concept of Islamic Socialism*, Dacca, The Author, 1964.

204. Sharbāṣī, Sa'īd al-Shirabīnī — *Mabādi'l-ishtirākīyah fi'l-Islām* (Socialist Elements in Islam). al-Qāhira Dār al-Qaumīyah, n.d. 86p. (A)

205. Sharqāwī, Maḥmūd — "Ṣūrah min ishtirākīyat al-Islām" (A form of

		Islam's Socialism) *al-Azhar* (Cairo) 37(4), Oct. 65: 236–239. (A)
206.	Ṣiddīqī, Muḥammad Maẓharuddin	"Socialistic Trends in Islam", *Islamic Literature* (Lahore) 4(10) Oct. 55: 5–18. (Also published in *Iqbal* (Lahore) 1(1), 52: 65–82).
207.	Wāfī, 'Alī 'Abdul Wāḥid	"Islamic Socialism: The Best Guard Against Communism", *al-Azhar* (Cairo) 31(2), Aug. 59: 58–64; 31(3), Sep. 59: 91–93.
208.	Yūsuf Ludhyānwī, Muḥammad	"Islāmī ishtirākīyat ba-silsila-e-Kitāb al-Amwāl" (Islamic Communism in connection with 'Kitāb al-Amwāl') *Bayyināt* (Karachi) 115, Jan. 70: 44–54; Feb. 70: 37–47. (U)

v. Ownership: 209–223

209.	Abū-Sunnah, Aḥmad Fahmī	"Taḥdīd al-milkīyah fi'l-Islām" (Ceiling on Property in Islam) *al-Azhar* (Cairo) 24(3), Nov. 52: 300–363. (A)
210.	'Abdullah Knoun	"Private Property and its Limits in Islam" *Al-Azhar Academy of Islamic Research, First Conference*, Mar. 64.
211.	al-'Araby, Muḥammad 'Abdullāh	"al-Milkīyat al-Khāṣṣah wa ḥudūduhā fi'l-Islām" (Private Property and its Limits in Islam) *Kitāb al-Mu'tamar al-Awwal li-majma' al-buḥūth al-Islāmīyah*, Cairo, 1964. (A)
212.	al-'Araby, Muḥammad 'Abdullāh	"Private Property and its Limits in Islam" *al-Azhar Academy of Islamic Research, First Conference*, Mar. 64.
213.	'Arafah, Muḥammad	"Taḥdīd al-milkīyah fi'l-Islām", *al-Azhar* (Cairo) 24(2) Oct. 52: 141–145. (A)
214.	'Audah, 'Abd al-Qādir	*al-Māl wa'l-ḥukm fi'l-Islām* (Property and Government in Islam), 4th ed. Beirut, Manshūrāt al- 'Aṣr al-Ḥadīth, 1971. 116p. (A)
215.	Ḥasan, 'Abd al-Ghaffār	"Infirādī milkīyat" (Individual Ownership) *Mīthāq* (Lahore) 17, May–June 70: 47–54. (U)
216.	al-Ḥusainī, al-Sayyid Abu'l-Naṣr Aḥmad	*al-Milkīyah fi'l-Islām* (Property in Islam). al-Qāhirah, Dār al-Kutub al-Ḥadīthah, 1952. (A)
217.	Ittiḥād Ṭullāb Handasat al-Qāhirah, al-Lajnat al-Thaqāfīyah, al-Jam'īyah al-Dīnīyah	*al-Māl wa'l-milkīyah fi'l-Islām* (Property and Ownership in Islam). al-Qāhirah, Maṭba'ah al-Jīlādī, 1972. (A)
218.	Jamāl al-Dīn, Aḥmad	*Naz' al-Milkīyah fī aḥkām al-sharī'ah wa nuṣūṣ al-qānūn* (Confiscation of Property According to the *Sharī'ah* and Positive Law). Ṣaidā', al-Maktabat al-Miṣrīyah, 1966. (A)
219.	al-Khafīf, Shaikh 'Alī	"al-Milkīyat al-fardīyah wa taḥdīduhā fi'l-Islām" (Individual Property and its Limits in Islam) *Mu'tamar 'Ulamā' al-Muslimīn al-Awwal, Kitāb al-Mu'tamar* (al-Qāhirah), Mar. 64: 128 ff (A) Eng. tr. "Individual Property and its Limits in Islam" *al-Azhar, Academy of Islamic Research, First Conference*, Mar. 64: 79–103.
220.	Ṣiddīqī, Muḥammad Maẓharuddin	"Islām aur ijtimā'ī milkīyat" (Islam and Collective Ownership) *Thaqāfat* (Lahore) 3(5) Nov. 56: 46–51. (U)

221. Ṣiddīqī, Muḥammad Nejatullāh — *Islām kā naẓarīya-e-milkīyat* (Islam's Theory of Property). Lahore, Islamic Publications, 1968. Vol. I 304. 299p. (U)

222. 'Uthmānī, Muḥammad Fahīm — "Infirādī milkīyat par Islām kī 'ā'id Karda ḥudūd wa quyūd" (Restrictions Placed by Islam on Individual Ownership) *al-Ḥaqq* 5 June 70: 23–33. (U)

223. 'Uthmānī, Muḥammad Muḥtaram Fahīm — "Islām Meṇ shakhṣī milkīyat "(Private Property in Islam), *al-Ḥaqq* 5, Apr. 70: 40–49. (U)

vi. Land: Ownership and Tenure: 224–242

224. Abd al-Kader, Ali — "Land Property and Land Tenure in Islam", *Islamic Quarterly* (London) 5(1, 2), Apr.–July 59: 4–11. (Also published in *Islamic Review* (London) 47(12), Dec. 59 (20–23)

225. Aḥmad, Shaikh Maḥmūd — *Mas'ala-e-Zamīn aur Islām* (The Problem of Land and Islam). Lahore, Institute of Islamic Culture, 1955. 234p. (U)

226. Amīnī, Muḥammad Taqī — *Islām kā zar'ī niẓām* (Agricultural System of Islam). Delhi, Nadwatul-Muṣannifīn, 1955. 303p. (U)

227. A'ẓamī, Nūr Muḥammad — "Ẓamīn aur us kē masā'il" (Land and its Problems) *al-Balāgh* (Karachi) 4(2–3): 46–53. (U)

228. Gabaliah, al-Syed — "The Significance of Some Aspects of Islamic Culture for Tenure Adjustment: a Comment", *Land Tenure*. Proceedings of the International Conference on Land Tenure and Related Problems in World Agriculture held at Madison, Wisconsin, 1956: 109–110.

229. Ḥāmid, Muḥammad — "Naẓarun fī istighlāl al-arḍ fi'l-Islām" (A Glance at Exploitation of Land in Islam) *al-Muslimoon* (Dimashq) 3(1), Mar. 55: 77–83; 3(2), Apr. 55: 54–59. (A)

230. al-Kattānī, Muḥammad Muntaṣir — "al-Arḍ: milkīyatuhā wa Kirā'uhā fi'l-Islām" (Land, its Ownership and Lease in Islam), *al-Muslimoon* (Dimashq) 6(1), Feb. 58: 33–41; 6(2), Mar. 58: 35–44; 6(3), May 58: 43–53; 6(4), Sep. 58: 24–30. (A)

231. al-Khaṭīb, Syed 'Abdul Ḥamīd — "Landed Property and Ownership of Land in Islam" in: *Some Economic Aspects of Islam*. Karachi, Motamar, al-Alam al-Islami, 1965: 109–119.

232. Mawdūdī, Sayyid Abul A'lā — *Mas'ala-e Milkīyat-e Zamīn* (The Problem of Land Ownership). Lahore, Maktabah Jamā'at-e Islāmī, 1950. 76p. (U) Arabic tr. *Mas'alat milkīyat al-arḍ fi'l-Islām*. Kuwait, Dār al-Qalam, 1969.

233. " " " — "Mauqif al-Ikhwān al-Muslimīn min taḥdīd al-milkīyah: ḥadīth ma' al-Murshid al-'Āmm" (Stand of al-Ikhwān al-Muslimūn on Ceiling on Property —Interview with Murshid al-'Āmm) *al-Akhbār* (Cairo) 2 Sept. 52: 6. (A)

234. Muḥammad Aḥmad — *Mas'ala-e-Zamīn* (The Problem of Land). Lahore, Idrāra-e Thaqāfat-e Islāmīyah. (U)

235. Nadwī, Syed Habeebul Haq — "al-Iqṭā': A Historical Survey of Land Tenure and Land Revenue Administration in some Muslim

Countries with Special Reference to Persia", *Contemporary Aspects of Economic and Social Thinking in Islam*. Gary, Indiana, M.S.A. of U.S. and Canada, 1973: 125–156.

236. Poliak, A. N. — "Classification of Land in Islamic Law and its Technical Terms", *American Journal of Semetic Languages and Literatures* 57: 50–62.

237. Qureshi, Ishtiāq Ḥussain — "Islām meṇ milkīyat-e-Zamīn kā mas'ala" (The Problem of Land Ownership in Islam) *Thaqāfat* (Lahore) 6(4), Apr. 58: 9–21. (U)

238. Rashad, Shah Muhammad — "Land Ownership and Tenure in Islam", *Islamic Thought* (Aligarh) 6(2), 59: 29–34.

239. Ṣakr, Manṣūr Muḥammad — "al-Islām wa Kirā' al-'ard". (Islam and the Rent of Land) *Liwā' al-Islām* (Cairo) 16(8), Aug. 62: 511–514. (A)

240. al-Sāyis, Shaikh Muḥammad Alī — "Milkīyat al-afrād li'l-arḍ wa manāfi'uhā fi'l-Islām" (Individual Ownership of Land and its Benefits in Islam) in: *al-Azhar, al-Mu'tamar al-awwal li-majma' al-buḥūth al-Islāmīyah*, Cairo. 1964. (A) Eng. tr. "Ownership of Land and its Benefits in Islam" *Al-Azhar Academy of Islamic Research*, First Conference, Mar. 64: 127–151.

241. Shafī', Muftī Muḥammad — *Islām kā niẓām-e arāḍī* (Land Tenure in Islam), Karachi, Idārah al-Ma'ārif, 1383 A.H. 288p. (U)

242. Yusuf, S. M. — "Land, Agriculture and Rent in Islam", *Islamic Culture*, 31(1), Jan. 57: 27–39.

vii. Share Cropping: 243–244

243. Ḥasan, 'Abd al-Ghaffār — "Muzāra'at par taḥqīqī naẓar" (A Critical Evaluation of Share Cropping), *Tarjumān al-Qur'ān* (Lahore) 33(1, 2, 3), Dec. 49–Jan. 50: 89–112. (U)

244. Ṣiddīqī, Ḥaidar Zamāṇ — "Muzāra'at par taḥqīqī naẓar" (A Critical Evaluation of Share Cropping), *Tarjumān al-Qur'ān* (Lahore) 34(2, 4, 5) July–Aug.–Sep. 50: 121–168. (U)

viii. Partnerships and Profit-Sharing: 245–250

245. Gaiani, A. — "The Juridical Nature of the Moslem Qirāḍ", *East & West* (Rome) (1953) 81–86.

246. al-Khafif, Shaikh 'Alī — *al-Sharikāt fi'l-figh al-Islāmī: buḥūth muqārinah* (Partnerships in Islamic Law: Comparative Studies). al-Qāhirah, al-Jāmi'ah al-'Arabīyah, 1962. (A)

247. Khan, Muḥammad Akram — "Types of Business Organisations in Islamic Economy", *Islamic Literature* (Lahore) 17(8), Aug. 71: 5–16.

248. al-Khayyāt, 'Abd al-'Aziz — *al-Sharikāt fi'l-sharī'at al-Islāmīyah wa'l-qānūn al-waḥ'ī* (Partnerships in Islamic Law and Positive Law). 'Ammān, Wizārat al-Auqāf, 1971. 2v. 378, 342p. (A)

249. Ṣiddīqī, Muḥammad Nejātullāh — *Shirkat aur muḍārabat kē Shar'ī uṣūl* (Islamic Legal Principles of Partnership and Profit Sharing). Lahore, Islamic Publications, 1969. 159p. (U)

250. Udovitch, Abraham L. — *Partnership and Profit in Medieval Islam*. Princeton, N.J. Princeton Univ. Press, 1970. 282p.

ix. Consumption: 251–252

251. 'Abbāsī, Muḍṭar — "Isrāf kā ma'āshī pahlū" (Economic Aspect of Extravagance), *al-Ḥaqq* (Pakistan) 5(1), Jan. 70: 41–50. (U)

252. Khurshīd Aḥmad — "Islam and Simple Living", *Criterion* (Karachi) 5(4) July–Aug. 70: 5–12.

x. Business and Trade: 253–260

253. 'Alī Naqī — *Tijārat aur Islām* (Trade and Islam). Lucknow, Imamia Mission, 1933. 73p. (U)

254. Hasanuzzaman, S. M. — *Trade in Islam: Principles and Practices*. Karachi, Motamar al-Alam-al-Islami, n.d. 64p.

255. Ibrāhīm, Muḥammad — "The Standard of Business Morality in Islam", *Islamic Literature* (Lahore) 23(5), May 71: 281–289.

256. Mūsā, Muḥammad Yūsuf — *Fiqh al-Kitāb wa'l-sunnah: al-buyū' wa'l-mu'āmalāt al-mu'āṣirah* (Jurisprudence of the Qur'ān and Sunnah: Contemporary Trade and Transactions). Miṣr, Dār al-Kitāb al-'Arabī, 1373/1954. (A)

257. Nadwī, 'Abd al-Qayyūm — *al-Tijārāt fi'l-Islām* (Trades in Islam). Lahore, Kutub Khana Punjab. 160p. (U)

258. De Somogyi, J. — "Trade in Classical Arabic Literature", *Muslim World* 55(2), Apr. 65: 131–134.

259. ,, ,, — "Trade in the Qur'ān and Ḥadīth", *Muslim World* 52(2), Apr. 62: 110–114.

260. Ṭihrānī — *al-Bai' min Sharā'i' al-Islām* (Trade in Islamic Law). Tehran, 1320/1902. (A)

xi. Hisbah: 261–273

261. 'Abd al-Wahhāb, Ḥasan Ḥasanī — "Aṣl al-Ḥisbah bi'l-Ifrīqiyā: taḥlīl Kītāb Aḥkām al-Sūq li Yaḥyā b. 'Umar." (Basis of *Ḥisbah* in Africa—an Analytical Study of Yaḥyā b. 'Umar's Book 'Rules of the Market'), *Hauliyāt al-Jāmi'ah, al-Jāmi'ah al-Tunīsīyah*, 4. 67: 5–21. (A)

262. Fahmī, 'Alī Ḥasan — "al-Ḥisbah fi'l-Islām Muqāranah ma' al-nuẓum al-mushābiha fi'l-tashrī' al waḍ'ī" (*Ḥisbah* in Islam: A Study in comparison with similar institutions in Positive Law) in: *Usbū' al-figh al-Islāmī*. Dimashq, 1961. (A)

263. Ḥusainī, Isḥāq Mūsā — "al-Ḥisbah fi'l-Islām" (*Ḥisbah* in Islam) *al-Muslimoon* (Geneva) 9(2), Sept. 64: 17–26; 9(4), Jan. 65: 37–44. (A)

264. ,, ,, ,, — "*Ḥisbah* in Islam" *al-Azhar, Academy of Islamic Research*, Cairo, First Conference. Mar. 64: 255–277.

265. al-Khafīf, Shaikh 'Alī — "al-Ḥisbah" (*Ḥisbah*) in *Usbū' al-fiqh al-Islāmī*, Dimashq, 1961.

266. Latham, J. D. — "Observations on the Text and Translation of Al-Jarsifi's Treatise on 'Ḥisba'," *Journal of Semetic Studies*, 5 (1960), 60: 124–143.

267. al-Sāmarrā'ī Ḥusām al-Dīn — *Nihāyat al-rutbah fī ṭalab al-ḥisbah li Ibn Bassām al-Muḥtasib* (Highest Standards in Organising

		Ḥisbah by Ibn Bassām al-Muḥtasib) 1968. (A)
268.	al-Shaḥāwī, Ibrāhim Dasūqī	*al-Ḥisbah fi'l-Islām* (*Ḥisbah* in Islam). al-Qāhirah Maktabah Dār al-'Urūbah, 1382–1962. (A)
269.	„ „	*al-Ḥisbah waẓīfah ijtimā'īyah* (*Ḥisbah* a Social Function). al-Qāhirah, Majma' al-Buḥūth al-Islāmīyah, 1973. 64p. (A)
270.	al-Shūrījī, al-Bushrā	*al-Tas'īr fi'l-Islam* (Price Control in Islam). Kuwait. 155p. (A)
271.	'Urnūs, Maḥmūd	"Sharī'at al-Ḥisbah fi'l-Islam" (The Law relating to *Ḥisbah* in Islam) *Liwā' al-Islām* (Cairo) 8(2), June 54: 99–103. (A)
272.	Wickers, G. M.	"Al-Jarsifī on the Hisba", *Islamic Quarterly* (London) 3(3), 1956–57: 176–187.
273.	Ziadeh, Nicola	*al-Ḥisbah and al-muḥtasib in Islam: Old Texts Collected and Edited with an Introduction*. Beirut, Catholic Press, 1962.

xii. Co-operation: 274–279

274.	Baryūn, Nūrī 'Abdussalām	*Mafhūm al-arbāḥ fi'l-iqtiṣād al-ta'āwunī ma' al-ishārah ila'l-fikr al-iqtiṣādī al-kilāsīkī* (Meaning of Profits in a Cooperative Economy with a Note on Islamic Economic Thought and the Classical Economic Thought). Tripoli, Libya, Dār al-Fikr, 1969. (A)
275.	Fahīm, Muḥammad	*Ṣuwar al-ta'āwun fi'l-Islām* (Forms of Cooperation in Islam) al-Qāhirah, Dār al-Kitāb al-'Arabī, 1968. 81p. (A)
276.	Ḥimādah, 'Abd al-Mun'im	*al-Islām wa'l-ta'āwun* (Islam and Cooperation). al-Qāhirah, al-Majlis al-A'lā li-Shu'ūn al-Islāmīyah, 1968. 186p. (A)
277.	„ „ „	"al-Sharikāt al-ta'āwunīyah" (Cooperative Partnerships) *Liwā' al-Islām* 19(11), 25 Oct. (A)
278.	Ṣiddīqī, Na'īm	"Islāmī niẓām meṇ imdād-e bāhamī kē idārāt" (Cooperative Institutions in Islamic System) *Chirāgh-e Rāh* (Karachi) Jan. 51: 33–43. (U)
279.	„ „	"al-Ta'āwun fi'l-Islām" (Cooperation in Islam) *Liwā' al-Islām* 14(8), 22 Sep. 60: 507–516. (A)

xiii. Hoarding: 280–282

280.	Abdul Majid	"Islam, Christianity and Monopoly", *Islamic Review* (London) Aug. 40: 287–290.
281.	„ „	"al-Iḥtikār wa'l-ribḥ al-fāḥish ḥarām ka'l-ribā" (Hoarding and Exhorbitant Profits are Prohibited like *Ribā*), *al-Azhar* (Cairo) 24(3), Nov. 52: 350–351 (A)
282.	Madkūr, Muḥammad Salām	"al-Iḥtikār wa tas'īr al-sila' wa ḥukmuhā fi'l-fiqh al-Islāmī (Hoarding and Price Control and their Position in Islamic Law) *al-Wa'y al-Islāmī* (Kuwait) (116), Aug. 74: 33–39. (A)

xiv. Public Finance: General: 283–299

283.	Abāẓah, Ibrāhīm Dasūqī	"al-Siyāsat al-mālīyah fī iqtiṣād al-Islāmī" (Financial Policy in Islamic Economy) *al-Manhal* (Jeddah) 34(10), Nov. 73: 712–717. (A)

284. Ahsan, M. Manāzir — "Baytul māl and its Role in the Islamic Economy", *Criterion* (Karachi) 10(9), Sept. 75: 14–27.

285. Aghnides, Nicholas P. — *Mohammaden Theories of Finance*. Lahore, Premier, 1961. iv, 532p.

286. Bravmann, Meir M. — "The Surplus of Property—an early Arab Social Concept", *Der Islam* (Berlin) 38(62): 28–50.

287. Hameedullah, Muhammad — "Budgeting and Taxation in the time of Holy Prophet", *Journal of the Pakistan Historical Society* 8(pt. I), Jan. 55.

288. Ḥasan, 'Abd al Raḥmān — "al-Mawārid al-'āmma fi'l-Islām" (Public Revenue in Islam) *Kitāb al-Mu'tamar al-Awwal li Majma' al-Buḥūth al-Islāmīyah*, Cairo, Mar. 64. Eng. tr. "Financial Resources in Islam" *al-Azhar, Academy of Islamic Research*, First Conference March 1964.

289. Hasanuzzaman, S. M. — *Economic Functions of the Islamic State* (up to the end of the Umayyad period) Ph.D. Thesis, 1973. Edinburgh University. (Unpublished) mimeo, 462p.

290. 'Iwaḍ, Badawī 'Abd al-Laṭīf — *al-Mizānīyah al-ūlā fi'l-Islām* (The First Budget in Islam). Beirut, Jām'iah Beirūt al-'Arabīyah, 1973. 39p. (A)

291. ,, ,, ,, ,, — *al-Niẓām al-mālī al-Islāmī al-muqārin* (A Comparative Study of the Islamic Financial System). al-Qāhirah, al-Majlis al-A'lā li'l-shu'ūn al-Islāmīyah, 1972. 124p. (A)

292. al-Jamāl, Muḥammad 'Abd al-Mun'im — *Dirāsāt ḍarībīyah Islāmīyah mu'āṣirah* (Studies in Contemporary Islamic Taxation). al-Qāhirah, Ma'had al-Dirāsāt al-Islāmīyah. (A)

293. al-Jaraf, Muḥammad Kamāl — *al-Niẓām al-mālī al-Islāmī* (Islamic Financial System). al-Qāhirah, Maktabat al-Nahḍat al-Jadīdah, 1970. (A)

294. Khaṭīb, 'Abd al-Karīm — *al-Siyāsat al-mālīyah fi'l-Islām* (Financial Policy in Islam). al-Qāhirah, Dār al-Fikr al-'Arabī, 1961. (A)

295. Lokkegaard, Frede — *Islamic Taxation in the Classical Period with Special Reference to Circumstances in Iraq*. Copenhagen, Branner & Korch, 1950. 286p.

296. Marsī, Muḥammad Kāmil — *al-Amwāl* (Wealth). 2nd ed. al-Qāhirah, Maṭba'ah Fatḥ Allāh Ilyās, 1937. (A)

297. Nadwī, Muḥammad Isḥāq — "Mālīyat al-daulah fi'l-Islām" (State Finance in Islam), *al-Ba'th al-Islāmī* (Lucknow) 8(3), Nov. 63: 64–69. (A)

298. Ṣiddīqī, S. A. — *Public Finance in Islam*. Lahore, Sheikh Mohammad Ashraf, 1975, 252p. first published in 1948.

299. 'Uwaiḍah, Aḥmad Thābit — *al-Islām waḍa'a al-usus al-ḥadīthah li'l-ḍarībah* (Islam Formulated the Modern Canons of Taxation). al-Jāmi' al-Azhar, 1959. 10p. (A)

xv. Public Finance: Zakāt: 300–321

300. Abū Zuhra, Shaikh Muḥammad — "al-Zakat" (*Zakāt*) *al-Azhar, al-Mu'tamar al-Thānī li-Majma' al-Buḥūth al-Islāmīyah*. Cairo, May 65: 137–201. (A)

301.	Ahmad, Shaykh (ed.)	*Some Socio-Economic Aspects of Zakāt*. Karachi, Pakistan Institute of Arts and Design. n.d.
302.	'Allām, Mahdī	"al-Ṣadaqah fi'l-Islām" (*Sadaqah*) in Islam *al-Azhar* (Cairo) 37(1), May 65: 90–100. (A)
303.	Ataullah, Sheikh	*Revival of Zakāt*. Lahore, Rippon Printing Press, 1949. 110p.
304.	al-Bassām, 'Abdullāh bin 'Abd al-Raḥmān	"al-Zakāt fi'l-Islām (*Zakāt* in Islam) Nadwah *Muḥāḍarāṭ, Rābiṭat al-'Ālam al-Islāmī* (Makka) 67: 198–212. (A)
305.	Faruki, Kamal A.	"Islam and Social Justice", *Criterion* (Karachi) 7(7), July–Aug. 72: 34–45.
306.	Ghulām, 'Alī, Malik	"Zakāt wa Ṣadaqāt kā niẓām" (The System of *Zakāt* and *Ṣadaqāt*) *Tarjumān al-Qur'ān* (Lahore) 60(2), May 63: 114–117. (U)
307.	Hussain, Mirza Moḥammad	"Zakāt—A Scheme of Social Insurance" in: *Islam and Socialism*. Lahore, 1947: 119–177.
308.	Ibrāhīm, Muḥammad Ismā'īl	*al-Zakāt* (*Zakāt*). al-Qāhirah, Dār al-Fikr al-'Arabī, 1959, 166p. (A)
309.	Iṣlāḥi, Amin Aḥsan	"Mas'ala-e-tamlīk aur Zakāt kē muta'alliq ba'ḍ dūsrē masā'il" (Transfer of Ownership and Some Other Problems Related to *Zakāt*) *Tarjumān al-Qur'ān* (Lahore) 44(6), Aug. 55: 395–410; 45(1), Sep. 55: 33–65. (U)
310.	Mawdūdī, Sayyid Abul A'lā	"Zakāt aur mas'ala-e tamlīk (*Zakāt* and Transfer of Ownership) *Tarjumān al-Qur'ān* (Lahore) 43(3), Nov. 54: 198–204. (U)
311.	,, ,, ,, ,,	"Naẓarāt fi'l-Zakāt min khilāl al-iṭār al-'āmm il'l-sharī'ah" (Observations on *Zakāt* in the Context of the General Framework of Islamic Law) *al-Fikr al-Islāmī* (Beirut) 1(3), Jan. 72: 84–88. (A)
312.	Niẓāmī, Khwāja Ḥasan	*Khudā'i income tax: aḥkām, masā'il aur maṣārif-e zakāt kā bayān*" (Divine Income Tax: A Statement of the Rules and Regulations relating to *Zakāt* and Heads of its Expenditure). Delhi, Dilli Printing Works, 1925. 80p. (U)
313.	al-Qarḍāwī, Yūsuf	*Fiqh al-Zakāt: dirāsah muqāranah li-aḥkāmihā wa falsafatihā fī ḍau' al-Qur'ān wa'l-sunnah* (Principles of *Zakāt*: A Comparative Study of its Philosophy and Laws in the Light of the Qur'ān and the *Sunnah*). Beirut, Dār al-Irshād, 1949. 2v. 1227p. (A)
314.	Rafiullah	"Niṣāb-e Zakāt par ēk taḥqīqī naẓar" (A Study of Exemption Limit in Relation to *Zakāt*) *Fikr-o-Naẓar* (Karachi) 3(5), Nov. 65: 349–362. (U)
315.	al-Sabsabī, 'Abd al-Qādir	"Ḥaula sharī'at al-*Ẓakāt*" (on Laws of *Zakāt*) *al-Muslimoon* (Dimashq) 6(8), June–July 59: 51–57; 6(9) Aug.–Oct. 59: 63–69. (A)
316.	Sakr, Muhammad Ahmad	*al-Zakāt wa muqāranatuhā bi'l-ḍarā'ib al-mu'āṣirah* (*Zakāt* and its Comparison with Contemporary Taxes). *Mimeo*, Baiḍā', Libya, 1972. 8p. (A)
317.	Shafī', Muftī Muḥammad	*Qur'ān meṇ niẓām-e Zakāt* (System of *Zakāt* in the Qur'ān). Karachi, Dār al-Ishā'at, 1963. 118p. (U)
318.	Shāh, Syed Ya'qūb	"Zakāt kē maṣārif" (Heads of *Zakāt* Expenditure) *Fikr-o-Naẓar* (Islamabad) 5(12), June 68: 917–927; 6(1), July 68: 46–55. (U)

319. Ṭasīn, Muḥammad — "*Ṣan'atī Sarmā'ē aur 'imārāt par Zakāt*" (*Zakāt* on Industrial Capital and Buildings) *Fikr-o-Naẓar* (Islamabad) 4(7): 435–448. (U)

320. Yūsuf, Mirzā Muḥammad — "Mas'ala-e tamlīk fi'l-Zakāt" (Transfer of Ownership and Giving Into Possession Regarding *Zakāt*) *Burhān* (Delhi) 37(9) Sept. 56: 150–161; 37(10) Oct. 56: 213–225; 37(11) Nov. 56: 273–291; 37(12) Dec. 56: 337–352; 38(1), Jan. 57: 24–38. (U)

321. de Zayas, Farishta G. — *The Law and Philosophy of Zakāt*. Damascus, al-Jadīdah Press, 1960. xxix, 420p.

xvi. Public Finance: 'Ushr, Kharāj, etc.: 322–329

322. Dennett, Danial C.Jr. — *Conversion and the Poll Tax in early Islam*. Cambridge, 1950. 13p. Urdu tr.: Mihr, Ghulām Rasūl, *Jizyah aur Islām*. Lahore, Ghulām Alī, 1962. 207p.

323. Khan, M. A. — "Jizyah and Kharaj (A Classification of the Meaning of the Terms as they were used in the 1st Century H.)" *Journal of Pakistan Historical Society* 4(76) (1956): 27–35.

324. Qādrī, Sayyid Aḥmad — " 'Ushr kē ēk Juz'iyē kī tauḍīḥ" (Classification of a Rule Relating to '*Ushr*). *Zindagī* (Rampur) 26(3), Mar. 66: 53–55. (U)

325. Qureshi, Aijaz Hasan — "A Critical Study of Wellhausen's Theory of Land and Poll Tax under Muslims" *Islamic Literature* (Lahore) 11(1, 2) Jan.–Feb. 59: 45–56.

326. ,, ,, ,, — "Assessment and Collection of Kharaj (Land Tax) under 'Umar I, the Second Caliph in Islam", *Journal of Punjab University Historical Society* 13(61): 83–92; *Voice of Islam* (Karachi) 10(11) Nov. 62: 531–541.

327. ,, ,, ,, — "The Terms *Kharāj* and *Jizya* and their implications", *Journal of Punjab Historical Society* 12 (June 1961): 27–38.

328. Tritton, A. S. — "Notes on the Muslim System of Pensions", *Bulletin of the School of Oriental and African Studies* 16(1), 54: 170–172.

329. De Zayas, Farishta G. — "Tithe Lands, Kharāj Lands, and the Law of *Zakāt*", *Islamic Literature* (Lahore) 13(5), May 67: 5–9.

xvii. Inheritance: 330–333

330. 'Abd al-Razzāq, Muḥammad — "Islāmī qānūn-e Wirāthat kī Khuṣūṣīyāt" (Characteristics of Islamic Law of Inheritance), *Ma'ārif* (Azamgarh) 34(1), July 34: 30–36. (U)

331. Abū Zuhra, Muḥammad — *Aḥkām al-tarikāt wa'l-mawārīth* (Laws of Inheritance and Legacies). Cairo. Dār al-Fikr al-'Arabī, n.d. 344p. (A)

332. Mūsā, Muḥammad Yūsuf — *al-Tarikah wa'l-mirāth fi'l-Islām, ma' madkhal fi'l-mirāth 'inda'l-'Arab wa'l-Rūmān, baḥth muqārin* (Inheritance and Legacy in Islam, with an Introduction to Inheritance amongst Arabs and the Romans—A Comparative Study). al-Qāhirah, Ma'had al-Dirāsāt al-'Arabīyah al-'Āliah, 1960. 396. (A)

333. al-Ṣa'īdī, 'Abd al-Muta'āl — *al-Mīrāth fi'l-sharī'at al-Islāmīyah wa'l-sharāi' al-Samāwīyah wa'l-waḍ'īyah* (Inheritance in Islamic Law, Other Divine Laws and the Positive Laws). al-Qāhirah, Maktabat al-Ādāb. 183p. (A)

xviii. Social Security: 334–344

334. Abū Zuhra, Muḥammad — *al-Takāful al-ijtimā'ī fi'l-Qur'ān* (Collective Responsibility in the Qur'ān). al-Dār al-Qaumīyah li'l-ṭibā'ah wa 'l-Nashr.

335. al-Fanjarī, Muḥammad Shauqī — "al-Islām wa mushkilat al-faqr" (Islam and the Problem of Poverty) *al-'Arabī* (Kuwait) (169), Dec. 72: 34–41. (A)

336. Ibrāhīm, Aḥmad Ibrāhīm — *Niẓām al-nafaqāt fi'l-sharī'ah al-Islāmīyah* (Rules Relating to Maintenance in Islamic Law). al-Qāhirah, Maṭba'ah Salafīyah, 1349 A.H. (A)

337. al-Labban, Ibrahim — "Islam and the Problem of Poverty", *Islamic Review* (London) 55(8), Aug. 67: 14–19.

338. al-Qarḍāwī, Yūsuf — *Mushkilat al-faqr wa kaifa 'ālajaha'l-Islām* (Problem of Poverty and how Islam has dealt with it). 'Ammān, Jordan, Maktabat al-aqṣā; Beirut, al-Dār al-'Arabīyah 1966. 168p. (A)

339. al-Ramadi, Gamal eldin — "Social Security in Islam", *al-Azhar* (Cairo) 36(10, Mar. 65: 9–12.

340. Rizq, 'Alī Shiḥateh — *Maṣra' al-faqr fi'l-Islām.* (Eradiction of Poverty in Islam), al-Qāhirah, Dār al-Ta'līf, 1951. 223p. (A)

341. al-Ṭanṭāwī, 'Alī — *Muḥāḍarah: Nafaqāt al-aqārib ka maṣdar li tamwīl mashrū'āt al-takāful al-ijtimā'ī. Ḥalqat al-dirāsat al-ijtimā'īyah li'l duwal al-'arabiyah, al-mun'aqad fī Dimashq* āmm 1953. (Discourse: Maintenance of Near Relatives as a Source of Financing Schemes for Social Security.
Series of Social Studies of Arab Countries, conducted in Damascus in 1953. (A)

342. 'Ulwān, 'Abdullāh — *al-Takāful 'al-ijtimā'ī fi'l-Islām* (Collective Responsibility in Islam). Jeddah, al-Dār al Sa'ūdīyah. (A)

343. 'Uthmān, Muḥammad Fatḥī — *al-Islām Yuḥārib al-faqr* (Islam at War with Poverty). (A)

344. al-Zayyāt, A. Ḥasan — "How Islam Tackles Poverty", *Azhar* (Cairo) 31(7), Jan. 60: 153–157. (A)

xix. Endowments: 345–348

345. Cattan, H. — "The Law of Waqfs" in: *Law in The Middle East*, V.I. 1955: 203–222.

346. Schacht, J. — "Early Doctrines on Waqfs", *Mél Köprülü* 1953: 443–452.

347. Shaṭā, Muḥammad — "al-Waqf Wasīlah li-taḥqīq al-'adālah al-ijtimā'īyah fi'l-tashrī' al-Islāmī" (*Waqf* a Means of Ensuring Social Justice in Islamic Law) *Nadwat al-Muḥāḍarāt. Rābiṭāt al-'Ālam al-Islāmī*, Makka 1959: 29–37. (A)

348. Suhrawardi, A. al-Mamoon — "The *Wakf* of Moveables", *Journal Proceedings of the Asiatic Society of Bengal N.S.*, 7(1911): 323–340.

xx. Insurance: 349–380

349. ʻAbdou, Muḥammad ʻIssa — "al-Ta'mīn" (Insurance), *al-Balāgh* (Kuwait) 9 July 69:20; 20 Aug. 69. (A)

350. „ „ „ — *al-Ta'mīn: al-aṣīl wa'l-badīl* (Insurance: Real and Substitute). Beirut, Dār al-Buḥūth al-Islāmīyah, 1972. 48p. (A)

351. al-Bahī, Muḥammad — *Niẓām al-Ta'mīn fī hadyi aḥkām al-Islām wa ḍarūrāt al-mujtamaʻ* (Insurance according to Islamic Laws and the Needs of Society) 1965. (A)

352. Dānish, Aḥmad — *Muḥāḍarah fi'l-ta'mīn* (A Lecture on Insurance). (A)

353. „ „ — "al-Ta'mīn wa hal huwa ḥill fī jamīʻ ṣuwarih?" (Insurance: Are All of its Forms Legal?). *al-Azhar* (Cairo) 26(5, 6), Nov. 54: 273–274. (A)

354. al-Dasūqī, Muḥammad — "al-Ta'min bain al-naẓarīyah wa'l-taṭbīq" (Insurance in Theory and Practice) al-Wa'y al-Islāmī (Kuwait) (60), Feb. 70: 12–19. (A)

355. al-Dasūqī, Muḥammad al-Syed — *al-Ta'min wa mauqif al-sharīʻat al-Islāmīyah minhu* (Insurance and the Standpoint of Islamic Law) al-Qāhirah, al-Majlis al-Aʻlā li'l-Shu'ūn al-Islāmīyah, 1967. 198p. (A)

356. al-Hindī, Abū Salmān — *Bīma-e-Zindagī Islāmī nuqṭa-e naẓar sē* (Life Insurance from Islamic Viewpoint). Karachi, Maktabah Saʻdīyah, n.d. (U)

357. Ibrāhīm, Aḥmad Muḥammad — " ʻAudah ilā'l-ta'mīn fi'l-sharīʻah wa'l-qānūn" (Insurance in Islamic Law and Secular Law) *al-Fikr al-Islāmī* (Beirut) 2(3), Mar. 71: 77–83; June 71: 67–71. (A)

358. „ „ — "al-Ta'mīn fi'l-sharīʻah wa'l-qānūn" (Insurance in Islamic Law and Secular Law), *al-Fikr al-Islāmī* (Beirut) 2(2), Feb. 70: 75–83. (A)

359. ʻĪsā, ʻAbd al-Raḥmān — *al-Muʻāmalāt al-ḥadīth wa aḥkāmuhā* (New Transactions and their Legal Position). 84p. (A)

360. Jārullāh, Mūsā — "Islām aur bīma" (Islam and Insurance) *al-Raḥīm* (Karachi) Mar. 67 (U)

361. al-Khafīf, Shaikh ʻAlī — "al-Ta'min" (Insurance), *al-Azhar* (Cairo) 37(1), May 65: 79–89; 37(2, 3), Sep. 65: 156–160; 37(4), Oct. 65: 268–274; 37(5, 6), Nov. Dec. 65: 353–357; 37(7), Jan. 66: 416–420; 37(8), Feb. 66: 478–485; 37(9, 10) Mar. 66: 534–546; 38(1), Apr. 66: 110–115. (A)

362. al-Khaṭīb, Muḥibb al-Dīn — "al-Ta'mīn" (Insurance), *al-Azhar* (Cairo) 26(3), Sep. 54: 130–133. (A)

363. al-Khizām, Anṭoun Ḥabīb — *al-Ta'mīn* (Insurance), al-Qāhirah, 1950. 350p. (A)

364. Kilingmulier, E. — "The Concept and Development of Insurance in Islamic Countries", *Islamic Culture* 43(1), Jan. 69: 27–37.

365. al-Majlis al-Aʻlā li-Riʻāyat al-funūn wa'l-Ādāb wa'l-ʻulūm al-ijtimāʻīyah — *Usbūʻ al-fiqh al-Islāmī wa Mahrajān Ibn Taimīyah.* (Islamic Jurisprudence Week and Ibn Taimīyah Celebrations). Cairo, 1963. 925p. (A)
Contributions:
al-Zarqā', Muṣṭafā Aḥmad:

'Aqd al-ta'mīn wa mauqif al-sharī'at al-Islāmīyah minhu (Insurance Contract and the Stand Point of Islamic Law).
al-Qalqīlī, Muḥammad:
'Aqd al-ta'mīn (Insurance Contract).
al-Amīn, Muḥammad:
Ḥukm 'aqd al-ta'mīn fi'l-sharī'at al-Islāmīyah (Position of Insurance Contract in Islamic Law).
'Īsā, 'Abd al-Raḥmān:
'Aqd al-ta'mīn (Insurance Contract);
Ḥilmī, Bahjat Aḥmad: *Mazāyā niẓām al-ta'mīn* (Distinguishing Features of Insurance).
'Umaruddīn, Muḥammad:
'Aqd al-ta'mīn (Insurance Contract).

366. Majlis Taḥqīqàt-e Shar'īyah, Lucknow — *Sawālnāma muta'alliqah insurance ma' jawābāt* (Questionnaire Relating to Insurance with Replies) n.d. (U)

367. Malik, Muḥammad Rāmīz — "Ra'yun ākhar fi'l-ta'min" (Another Opinion on Insurance) *al-Fikr al-Islāmī* (Beirut) 2(10), Oct. 71: 25–37. (A)

368. Muḥammad, Sa'd Ṣādiq — "al-Ta'mīn fi'l-sharī'ah wa'l-qānūn" (Insurance in Islamic Law and Positive Law) *al-Wa'y al-Islāmī* (Kuwait) (61), Mar. 70: 51–59. (A)

369. Muṣleḥuddīn, Muḥammad — *Insurance and Islamic Law*. Lahore, Islamic Publications, 1969. 202p.

370. Nadwī, Muḥammad Isḥāq — "Mas'alat al-ta'min kamā yarahā Majlis al-Dirāsāt al-shar'īyah" (The issue of Insurance as Viewed by *Majlis Dirāsāt Sharī'yah, al-Ba'th al-Islāmī* (Lucknow) 10(7), Apr. 66: 61–65. (A)

371. al-Qarḍāwī, Yūsuf — "Naẓarat al-sharī'ah ila'l-ta'āwun wa'l-ta'mīn" (Cooperation and Insurance as Viewed by *Sharī'ah*) *al-Ba'th al-Islāmī* (Lucknow) 12(6), Mar. 68: 44–52. (A)

372. al-Rūḥanī, al-Sayyid Muḥammad Ṣādiq — *al-Masā'il al-mustaḥdatha* (The New Issues). Qum, 1384 A.H. (A)

373. al-Sanūsī, Aḥmad Ṭāhā — "'Aqd al-tam'īn fi'l-tashrī' al-Islāmī" (Insurance Contract in Islamic Legislation) *al-Azhar* (Cairo) 25(2), 232–236; 25(3), 303–307. (A)

374. Ṣiddīqī, Muḥammad Nejatullāh — *Insurance Islāmī ma'īshat meṇ* (Insurance in Islamic Economy). Delhi, Islam and the Modern Age Society, 1975. 95p. (U)

375. Ṣiddīqī, Na'īm — *Bīma-e Zindagī Islāmī nuqta-e nigāh sē* (Life Insurance from Islamic Viewpoint). Lahore, Islamic Publications, 1960; Dehli, Markazī Maktabah Islāmī, 1974. 31p. (U)

376. ,, ,, — "al-Ṭa'mīn 'alā'l-Ḥayāt" (Life Insurance) Nadwah *Liwā' al-Islām* (Cairo) 8(11), 708–714. (A)

377. Tonkī, Muftī Walī Ḥasan — "Islām aur bīma" (Islam and Insurance) *Bayyināt* (Karachi) 5(5), Mar. 65: 18–40; 6(1), Apr. 65: 17–33. (U)

378. 'Uthmān, Muḥammad Fatḥī — *al-Fikr al-Islāmī wa'l-taṭawwur* (Islamic Thought, and Change) 2nd ed. Kuwait, al-Dār al-Kuwaitīyah, 1969. 559p. (A)

379. Wahbah, Taufiq 'Alī — "al-Ta'mīn fi'l-sharī'ah wa'l-qānūn" (Insurance in

Islamic Law and Positive Law), *al-Wa'y al-Islāmī* (Kuwait) (53), July 69: 16–21. (A)

380. al-Zarqā', Muṣṭafā Aḥmad — *'Aqd al-ta'mīn (al-saukarah) wa mauqif al-sharī'at al-Islāmīyah minhu* (Insurance Contract and the Standpoint of Islamic Law). Dimashq, Maṭba'ah Jāmi'ah Dimashq, 1962. 112p. (A)

xxi. Banking without Interest: 381–422

381. Abāẓah, Ibrāhīm Dasūqī — "Ḥaula msharū' al-bunūk al-Islāmīyah" (On the Project of Islamic Banks) *al-Manhal* (Jeddah) 33(7), Aug.–Sept. 72: 730–737. (A)

382. 'Abdou, Muḥammad 'Issa — *Bunūk bilā fawā'id* (Banks Without Interest). al-Qāhirah, Dār al-Fikr, 1970. (A)

383. Ahmad, Sheikh Mahmud — "Banking in Islam", *Muslim News International* 8(1), June 69: 5–11.

384. al-'Araby, Muḥammad 'Abdullāh — "Contemporary Bank Transactions and Islam's Views Thereon" *Islamic Thought* (Aligarh) 11(3, 4), July 67: 10–43.

385. ,, ,, — "al-Mu'āmalāt al-Maṣrifīyah al-mu'āṣirah wa ra'y al-Islām fīh" (Contemporary Bank Transactions and Islam's Views Thereon), *al-Azhar. al-Mu'tamar al-thānī li-Majma' al-Buḥūth al-Islāmīyah.* May. 65: 79–122. (A)

386. ,, ,, — *Bank Dubai al-Islāmī* (Dubai Islamic Bank). Dubai, Matba'ah Dubai, 1975. 40p. (A)

387. Bāqir al-Ṣadr — *al-Bank al-lā rabawī fi'l-Islām* (Interest Free Bank in Islam). Kuwait, Jāmi' al-Naqī. (A)
(Urdu tr. 'Ali Jawādī, *Islamic Bank*. Bombay, Jamali Publications, 1974. 208p.

388. Baryūn, Nūrī 'Abdussalām — *Kaifa Yakūn al-niẓām al-Maṣrifī fi'l-iqtiṣād al-Islāmī* (The Shape of the Banking System in Islamic Economy). Tripoli, Libya, Dār Maktabat al-Fikr, 1972. (A)

389. Conference of Islamic Finance Ministers, Jeddah, Aug. 1974. — *Islamic Development Bank. Articles Establishing the IDB.*

390. — *The Egyptian Study on the Establishment of the Islamic Banking System* (Economics and Islamic Doctrine), Cairo, 1972.

391. al-Gammāl, Gharīb — *al-Maṣārif wa'l-a'māl al-maṣrifīyah fi'l-sharī'at al-Islāmīyah wa'l-qānūn* (Banks and Banking Transactions in Islamic Law and Positive Law). al-Qāhirah, Dār al-Ittiḥād al-'Arabī li'l-Ṭibā'ah, 1972. 477p. (A)

392. Ghanameh, Abdul Hadi — "The Interestless Economy" in: *Contemporary Aspects of Economic and Social Thinking in Islam.* Gary, Indiana, M.S.A. of U.S. and Canada, 1973: 85–99.

393. Hammeedullah, Muḥammad — "Anjumanhā-e qarḍa-e bē sūd" (Interest Free Loan Societies), *Ma'ārif* (Azamgarh) 53(3) Mar. 44: 211–216. (U)

394. ,, ,, — "Bunūk al qarḍ bidūn rībā" (Interest Free Lending Banks) *al-Muslimoon* (Dimashq) 8(3), Dec. 62: 16–21. (A)

395. Hammeedullah, Muḥammad — "A Suggestion for an Interest Free Islamic Monetary Fund", *Islamic Review* (London) 43(6), June 55: 11–12.

396. al-Hamsharī, Muṣṭafā 'Abdullāh — *al-A'māl al-maṣrifīyah wa'l-Islām* (Banking Operations and Islam).

397. Huda, M. N. — "Economics Accepting Islam", *World Muslim League* (Singapore) 1(3), Jan. 64: 10–17.

398. „ „ — "Hal Yumkin 'an ta'mala al-bunūk bighair fā'idah" (Is it possible for Banks to function without Interest?) *al-Muslimoon* (Dimashq) 3(4), June 55: 36–40. (A)

399. Irshad, Shaikh Ahmad — *Interest Free Banking*. Karachi, Orient Press of Pakistan, n.d. 100p.

400. „ „ „ — *Bilā sūd bank kārī* (Banking Without Interest). Karachi, Maktabah Tahrīk Musāwāt, n.d. 152p. (U)

401. al-'Itr, Nūr al-Dīn — al-Mu'āmalāt al-maṣrifīyah wa ḥukmuhā fi'l-Islām (Banking Transactions and their Legal Position in Islam). (A)

402. Jamjūm, Aḥmad Ṣalāḥ — *al-Bank al-Islāmī* (Islamic Bank). Jeddah, Maṭābi' Dār al-Iṣfahānī wa Shurakā'hū. 33p. (A)

403. Khan, Muhammad Akram — "Interest Free Banking: Some Further Questions", *Islamic Education* (Lahore) 5(2), Mar.–June 72: 29–47.

404. „ „ „ — "Islāmī ma'īshat meṇ bank aur bachateṇ" (Banks and Savings in Islamic Economy), *Chirāgh-e-Rāh* (Karachi) May–June 65: 68–83. (U)

405. al-Lajnah al-Tahḍīrīah li Mashrū' Bait al-Tamwīl al-Kuwaitī — *Mashrū' al-niẓām al-asāsī li-bait al-tamwīl al-Kuwaitī*. Kuwait, n.d. 21p. (A)

406. Mannan, M. A. — "Consumption Loan in Islam", *Islamic Review* (London) 58(3), Mar. 70: 19–22.

407. „ „ — "Islam and Trends in Modern Banking—Theory and Practice of Interest Free Banking", *Islamic Review* (London) 56(11, 12) Nov.–Dec. 68: 5–10; 57(1), Jan. 69: 28–33.

408. „ „ — "A Muslim World Bank; Urgent Need", *Criterion* (Karachi) 6(1) Jan.–Feb. 71: 15–20.

409. Muslehuddin, Muhammad — *Banking and Islamic Law*. Karachi, Islamic Research Academy, 1974. 153p.

410. „ „ — *Commonwealth of Muslim Countries and the Muslim World Bank*.

411. al-Najjār, Aḥmad Muḥammad 'Abd al-'Azīz — Bunūk bilā fawā'id ka-istirātijīyah li'l-tanmīyah al-iqtiṣādīyah wa'l-ijtimā'īyah fi'l-duwal al-Islāmīyah. (Banks Without Interest as a Strategy for Economic and Social Development of Muslim Countries) Jeddah, Jāmi'at al-Malik 'Abd al-'Azīz, 1972. 104p. (A)

412. Ready, R. K. — "The Egyptian Municipal Savings Bank Project", *International Development Review* 9, June 67: 2–5.

413. Sakr, Muhammad Ahmad — *Tanẓīm al-maṣārif fī ḍau' al-Islām* (Organisation of Banks in the Light of Islam. Baiḍā', Libya, 1972. 20p. mimeo. (A)

414. Sattar, S. A. — "Interest Free Banking", *Criterion* (Karachi) 9(6), June 74: 15–26.

415. Shalbī, Aḥmad — "al-Bank al-Islāmī" (Islamic Bank) *al-Wa'y al-Islāmī* (Kuwait) 5(56) Oct. 69: 19–25. (A)

416. Siddīqī, Muhammad Nejatullah — "A Model of Interest Free Banking", *Criterion* (Karachi) 6(4), July–Aug. 61: 19–33; *Journal of Islamic Studies* (Cairo) 2(3), Oct. 69: 1–22.

417. „ „ — *Ghair sūdī bank kārī* (Banking Without Interest). Lahore, Islamic Publications, 1969. 224p.; Delhi, Markazī Maktabah Jamā'at-e-Islāmī Hind, 1969. 235p. (U) English tr. *Banking Without Interest*. Lahore Islamic Publications, 1973. 207p.

418. „ „ — "Islāmī ma'ishat kē ba'ḍ pahlū" (Some Aspects of Islamic Economy), *Chirāgh-e-Rāh* (Karachi) Oct. 65: 19–28. (U)

419. Ṣiddīqī, Na'īm — "Islamī uṣūl par banking" (Banking according to Islamic principles), *Chirāgh-e-Rāh* (Karachi) 1(11), Nov. 48: 60–64; 1(12), Dec. 48: 24–28. (U)

420. 'Uzair, Muḥammad — " 'Awāmil al-najāḥ fi'l-maṣārif al-lārabawīyah" (Factors Contributing to the Success of Interest Free Banks) *al-Muslimoon* (Dimashq) 6(1), Feb. 58: 81–85; 6(4), Sep. 58: 84–88; 6(5), Oct. 58: 70–77. (A)

421. „ „ — "Interestless Banking: Will it be a Success?", *Voice of Islam* (Karachi): 853–859.

422. „ „ — *An Outline of Interestless Banking*. Karachi; Dacca, Raihan Publications, 1955. 21p.

xxii. Foreign Trade: 423

423. 'Uzair, Muḥammad — "Foreign Trade in an Interestless Economy", *Voice of Islam* (Karachi) 7(2–3), Nov.–Dec. 58: 90–104.

xxiii. Labour and Industrial Relations: 424–445

424. Abū Zuhra, Muḥammad — "al Waẓīfah wa'l-muwaẓẓif fi'l-Islām" (Service and the (Public) Servant in Islam), *Liwā'al-Islām* (Cairo) 16(4), 5 May 62: 225–231; 16(5), June 62: 290–295. (A)

425. 'Ayyad, M. Gamāluddīn — *al-'Amal wa'l-'ummāl* (Labour and the Labourers). al-Qāhirah, sharikat al-Ittiḥād wa'l-Ṭibā'ah, 1967. 136p. (A)

426. „ „ — "Ḥuqūq al-'ummāl fi'l-Islām" (Rights of the Labourers in Islam), *al-Azhar* 37(4), Oct. 65: 247–250; 37(5, 6) Nov.–Dec. 65: 312–328. (A)

427. „ „ — "al-Islām wa'l-'alāqāt al-insānīyah fī majāl al-'amal" (Islam and Human Relations in the Field of Labour), *al-Azhar* 37(7), Jan. 66: 410–412. (A)

428. „ „ — "The Merits of Labour in Islam", *al-Azhar* 38(1), Apr. 66: 7–10.

429. „ „ — "Wājibāt al-'ummāl fi'l-Islām (Duties of the Labourers in Islam), *al-Azhar* 37(8), Feb. 66: 469–471. (A)

430. al-Bakr, 'Abd al-Raḥmān — 'Alāqāt al-'amal fi'l-Islam (Labour Relations in Islam). al-Qāhirah, al-Mu'assasah al-Thaqāfīyah al-'Ummālīyah 1970. 151p. (A)

431. Faridi, Fazlur Rahman — "On Wages in an Islamic Economy", *Islamic*

Thought (Aligarh) 7(1), Apr.–June 60: 61–66.

432. Faridi, Fazlur Rahman — "The Problem of Industrial Peace", *Islamic Research Circle Bulletin* (Rampur) 5(1), Oct. 53: 5–18.

433. Hameedullah, M. — "Islam's Solution to the Basic Economic Problems—the Position of Labour", *Islamic Culture (Hyderabad)* 10(2), Apr. 36: 213–233.

434. Khan, Muhammad Akram — "The Theory of Employment in Islam", *Islamic Literature* (Lahore) 14(4), Apr. 68: 5–16.

435. Malik, Muhammad Shafi — "Wages in an Islamic Economy", *Islamic Thought* (Aligarh) 7(2), July–Sep. 60: 62–67.

436. Mawdūdī, Sayyid Abul A'lā — "Bērozgārī kā mas'alah ḥal karnē kē liyē sarmāya-dārī socialism aur Islām kā ṭarīq-e-kār" (The Methods of Capitalism, Socialism and Islam in Solving the Problem of Unemployment), *Zindagī* (Rampur), 41(2), Aug. 68: 41–42. (U)

437. ,, ,, — "Taqrīr—Labour Convention (Speech in Labour Convention) 12 May 1957", *Chirāgh-e-Rāh* (Karachi) Oct. 57: 44–48. (U)

438. Nadwī, Mujībullāh — "Islāmī qānūn-e ujrat kā ēk bāb" (A Chapter of the Islamic Law of Wages), *Ma'ārif* (Azamgarh) 77(6), June 56: 405–421. (U)

439. Qureshī, 'Abdul Majīd — *Miḥnat kē masā'il aur unkē ḥal* (Labour Problems and their Solutions). Ichra, Lahore, al-Ḥabīb Publications, n.d. 60p. (U)

440. ,, ,, ,, — "On 'Wages' in an Islamic Economy", *Islamic Thought* (Aligarh) 7(3), Oct.–Dec. 60: 40–45.

441. ,, ,, ,, — "Wages in an Islamic Economy", *Islamic Thought* (Aligarh) 6(2), Oct.–Dec. 59: 24–28.

442. Siddīqī, Muhammad Nejatullah — "Industrial Peace", *Islamic Thought* (Aligarh) 1(1) Mar.–Apr. 54: 17–18.

443. Udovitch, A. L. — "Labour Partnership in Early Islamic Law", *Journal of the Economic and Social History of the Orient* 10(1), 67: 64–80.

444. 'Uthmānī, Muḥammad Muḥtaram Fahīm — "Mazdūr Islāmī mu'āshrē meṇ" (The Labourer in Islamic Society), *al-Balāgh* (Karachi) 4(4) July 70: 51–59. (U)

445. Zain al-'Ābidīn, Wajīh — "al-Islām wa'l-'ummāl" (Islam and the Labourers) *al-Ba'th al-Islāmī* (Lucknow) 11(5), Feb. 67: 53–59. (A)

xxiv. Family Planning: 446–472

446. 'Abd al-'Azīz Bin Bāz — "Ḥaula taḥdīd al-nasl" (On Population Control) *Majallat al-Ḥajj* (Makka) 19(2) Dec. 64: 75. (A)

447. 'Abdullāh Knoun — "Qarār al-Rābiṭah bi-sha'n al-nasl" (Resolution of the *Rabitāh* on Population Control), *Akhbār al-'Ālam al-Islāmī* (Makka) (438), 28 July, 75: 7. (A)

448. Abū Zuhra, Muḥammad — "Tanẓīm al-nasl" (Population Planning) *Liwā' al-Islām* (Cairo) 16(11), Nov. 62: 676–680. (A)

449. ,, ,, ,, — "Tanẓīm al-usrah wa tanẓīm al-nasl" (Family Planning and Population Planning) *al-Azhar. al-Mu'tamar al-thānī li-Majma' al-Buḥūth al-Islāmīyah* (Cairo), May 65: 247–303. (A)

450. ‘Īsā, ‘Abd al-‘Azīz Muḥammad
al-Islām wa tanẓīm al-usrah (Islam and Family Planning), al-Qāhirah, Jihāz Tanẓīm al-Usrah, 1973. 23p. (A)

451. „ „
al-Islam wa tanẓīm al-usrah (Islam and Family Planning) al-Qāhirah, Maṭba‘ah al-Abrām al-Tijārīyah, 1973. (A)

452. al-Ittiḥād al-‘Ālamī li-Tanẓīm al-Wālidīyah (International Planned Parenthood Federation).
al-Islām wa tanẓīm al-usrah (Islam and Family Planning). Beirut, 1973. 2v. 414, 596p. (A)

453. Khan, M. E.
"Is Islam against Family Planning?", *Islam and the Modern Age* (New Delhi) 6(2), May 75: 61–72.

454. Khurshīd Ahmad
"Taḥrik-e ḍabṭ-e Wilādat kā ‘Ilmī jā’izah" (Scientific Review of Birth Control Movement) in: Mawdūdī, Sayyid Abul A‘lā: *Islām aur ḍabṭ-e Wilādat*. Lahore, Islamic Publications, 1962: 163–204. (U)

455. al-Khaulī, al-Bahl
al-Islām wa’l-mar’at al-mu‘āṣirah (Islam and the Contemporary Woman). 3rd. ed. Kuwait, Dār al-Qalam. (A)

456. Madkūr, Muḥammad Salām
Naẓarat al-Islām ilā tanẓīm al-nasl (Islamic view point on family planning). al-Qāhirah, Dār al-Nahḍat al-‘Arabīyah, 1969. 98p. (A)

457. Mawdūdī, Sayyid Abul A‘lā
"Ḍabṭ-e Wilādat aur Waṣīyat al-‘ainain kē shar‘ī ḥaithīyat." (Position of Birth Control and Donation of Eyes in Islamic Law), *Tarjumān al-Qur’ān* (Lahore) 57(4), Jan. 62: 251–252. (U)

458. „ „ „
Islām aur ḍabṭ-e Wilādat (Islam and Birth Control), Lahore, Islamic Publications, 1962. 204p. (U)
First published in 1943.
English tr. *Birth Control, Its Social, Political, Economic, Moral and Religious Aspects* by Khurshid Ahmad and M. I. Faruqi. Lahore, 1968. 182p.

459. „ „ „
"Nadwat Liwā’ al-Islām: baḥth taḥdīd al-nasl", (Liwā’ al-Islām Conference: Discussion on Population Control), *Liwā’ al-Islām* (Cairo) 7(2), June 53: 117. (A)

460. al-Nadwī, Khaṭīb Aḥmad
"Taḥdīd al-nasl fī ḍau’ al-Kitāb wa'l-sunnah" (Population Control in the Light of the Qur’ān and the Sunnah), *al-Ba‘th al-Islāmī* (Lucknow) 14(1), Aug. 69: 64–69. (A).

461. Population Council. New York
Muslim Attitudes Towards Family Planning, New York, The Council, Aug. 1967.

462. al-Qūbanī, Muḥammad ‘Abd al-Salām
"Taḥdīd al-nasl" (Population Control) *al-Azhar* 29(6) Dec. 57: 550–552. (A)

463. Rābiṭat al-‘Ālam al-Islāmī. al-Majlis al-Ta’sīsī.
Taḥdīd al-nasl ibādah li'l-‘ālam al-Islāmī" (Population Control is Destruction of the Muslim World), *al-Mujtama‘* (Kuwait) (247) 29 Apr. 75: 31. (A)

464. Rafiullah
"Birth Control in the Light of Islamic Jurisprudence", *World Muslim League* (Singapore) 3(7), July–Aug. 66: 26–31.

465. „
"Ḍabṭ-e Wilādat kī fiqhī ḥaithīyat (Status of Birth

Control in Fiqh) *Fikr-o-Naẓar* (Karachi). Nov.–Dec. 64: 332–334. (U)

466. Sambhalī, 'Atīqur Raḥmān — "Nas bandī barā'ē Khāndānī manṣūba bandī" (Sterilization as means of Family Planning), *al-Furqān* (Lucknow) 35(10, 11, 12), Jan., Feb., Mar, 68: 73–88; 36(1), Apr. 68: 39–54. (U)

467. ,, ,, ,, — "Taḥdīd al-nasl min wijhat naẓar al-Islām" (Population Control from Islamic View Point), *al-Ba'th al-Islāmī* (Lucknow) 12(8), May 68: 58–66; 12(9), June 68: 66–72. (A)

468. al-Sharbāsī, al-Shaikh Aḥmad — *al-Dīn wa ṭanẓīm al-Usrah* (Religion and Family Planning). al-Qāhirah, Matābi' al-Sha'b, 1384/1968. (A)

469. al-Shūrī, Ibrāhīm — "al-Nasl bain al-taḥdīd wa'l-tanẓīm" (Population, its Control and Planning) *Akhbār al-'Ālam al-Islāmī* (Makka) (435) 7 July 75: 11. (A)

470. Siddīque, Kaukab — "Population Explosion and Mankind's Future: a Scientific Reply" *Criterion* (Karachi) 3(2), Mar.–Apr. 68: 55–64. (Review of 'Nigel Colder: *The Environment Game*', London, Secker & Warburg, 1957. 240p.).

471. Zerruq, A. R. M. — "Islam and Family Planning", *Islamic Literature* (Lahore) 10(8–9), Aug.–Sep. 58: 71–74.

472. Zohurul Hoque — "Religion of Islam and Family Planning", *Islamic Review* (London) 58(1), Jan. 70: 6–11.

xxv. Economic Development 473–494

473. Abaẓah, Ibrahīm Dasūqī — "al-Islām wa'l-tanmīyat al-iqtiṣādīyah" (Islam and Economic Development) *al-Manhal* (Jeddah) 33(11), Dec. 72–Jan. 73: 1123–1132. (A)

474. Alexander, A. P. — "Industrial Entrepreneurship in Turkey, its origin and Growth", *Economic Development and Cultural Change* 8, 1960: 349–365.

475. Austruy, Jaques — *al-Islām wa'l-tanmīyat al-iqtiṣādīyah* (Islam and Economic Development) tr. from French by Nabīl Ṣubḥī al-Ṭawīl. Dimashq, Dār al-Fikr, 1960. 118p. (A)

476. Berger, Morroe — *The Arab World Today*. London, Weidenfeld & Nicholson, 1962. 480p.

477. al-Fanjarī, Muḥammad Shauqī — "al-Iqtiṣād al-Islāmī wa'l-daur alladhī yumkin 'an yal'abah" (Islamic Economics and the Role it can Play) *al-Wa'y al-Islāmī* (Kuwait) (112), Apr. 74: 35–42. (A)

478. ,, ,, — "al-Islām wa'l-mushkilat al-iqtiṣādīyah (Islam and the Economic Problem) *al-Wa'y al-Islāmī* (Kuwait) (95), Dec. 72: 23–33. (A)

479. Faridi, Fazlur Rahman — "Economic Development and Islamic Values", *Islamic Thought* (Aligarh) 10(1, 2) Apr. 64: 9–53.

480. Haffar, Ahmed R. — "Economic Development in Western Scholarship", *Islam and the Modern Age* (New Delhi) 6(2), May 75: 5–22; 6(3), Aug. 75: 5–29.

481. Issawi, Charles — *Egypt at Mid-century; An Economic Survey*. London, O.U.P., 1954. xiv, 289p.

482. ,, ,, — "The Entrepreneur Class" in Fisher, S. N. (ed.):

Social Forces in the Middle East, Ithaca, N.Y., Cornell U.P., 1955: 116–136.

483. Khan, Muhammad Akram — "Concept of Development in Islam", *Criterion* (Karachi) 4(4), July–Aug. 69: 7–16.

484. Mālik ben Nabī — *al-Muslim fī 'ālam al-iqtiṣād* (The Muslim in the Economic World). Beirut, Dār al-shurūq, 1972. 132p. (A)

485. „ „ „ — *Shurūṭ al-nahḍah* (Conditions of Progress) tr. from French by 'Abd al-Ṣabūr Shāhīn wa 'Umar Kāmil Masqāwī, 1960. (A)

486. Manzar, Abdul Moiz — "On Economic Development and Islamic Values", *Islamic Thought* (Aligarh) 10(3, 4), Jan. 65: 66–70.

487. al-Mashriqī, Muḥammad Muḥyuddīn — "Ẓāhirat al-takhalluf al-iqtiṣādī fi'l-duwal al-Islāmīyah al-nāmīyah" (The Phenomenon of Economic Backwardness in the Developing Islamic Countries), *al-Baḥth al-'Ilmī* (Rabāt) 3(17), Jan.–May 71: 44–133. (A)

488. Meyer, A. J. — "Entrepreneurship and Economic Development in the Middle East", *Public Opinion Quarterly*, 22 (1958): 391–396.

489. „ „ — "Entrepreneurship, the Missing Link in the Arab States", *Middle East Economic Papers* (Beirut) 54: 121–132.

490. „ „ — *Middle Eastern Capitalism*. Cambridge, Mass., Harvard U.P. 1959. 161p.

491. al-Najjār, Aḥmad Muḥammad 'Abd al-'Azīz — "al-Tarbīyat al-Islāmīyah wa mushkilātūna'l-iqtiṣādīyah" (Islamic Education and our Economic Problems), *al-Wa'y al-Islāmī* (Kuwait) (50) 18 Apr. 69: 41–46. (A)

492. Quraishi, Marghoob A. — "Investment and Economic Development in Muslim Countries", *Association of Muslim Social Scientists, Proceedings, Third Seminar*, Gary, Indiana, U.S.A. May 74: 1–8.

493. Sayigh, Y. A. — *Entrepreneurs of Lebanon: the Role of the Business Leader in a Developing Economy*. Cambridge, Mass., Harvard U.P., 1962. 181p.

494. Siddīqī, Kalim — "Islamic Development Plan", *al-Islam* (Singapore) 5(1), Jan.–Mar. 74: 24–30. (Also printed separately: Karachi, Umma Publishing House, 1970).

xxvi. Audit and Accounts: 495–498

495. Quraishi, Marghoob Ahmad — *Annual Zakāt Payment Form*. Palo Alto, California. Al Manar Press, 1970. 19p.

496. Shiḥātah, Shauqī Ismā'īl — *al-Mabādi'l-Islāmīyah fī naẓarīyāt al-ṭaqwīm fi'l-muḥāsabah* (Islamic principles in the theory of value Assessment in Accounting), Ph.D. Thesis, Kullīyat-al-Tijārah, Jāmi'at al-Qāhirah, 1960. (A)

497. „ „ „ — *Muḥāsabah Zakāt al-māl 'ilman wa 'amalan*. (A Scientific and Practical Accounting of *Zakāt* on Property). Cairo, Maktabah al-Anjalū al-Miṣrīyah, 1970. (A)

498. „ „ „ — *Niẓām al-muḥāsabah li-ḍarībat al-Zakāt wa'l-dafātir al-musta'malah fī bait al-māl* (System of Accounting for *Zakāt* tax and the Registers used in *bait-al*

māl). M.A. Dissertation. Kullīyat al-Tijārah Jāmi'at al-Fu'ād al-Awwal. 1951. (A)

3. ISLAMIC CRITIQUE OF CONTEMPORARY ECONOMIC THEORIES AND SYSTEMS [499–609]

i. Capitalism: 499–500

499. Parwez, Ghulām Aḥmad — *Khudā aur sarmāyadār* (God and the Capitalist). Lahore, Idāra-e-Ṭulū'-e Islām, 1967. (U)
500. Quṭb, Sayyid — *Ma'rikat al-Islām wa'l-ra's mālīyah* (Confrontation of Islam and Capitalism). 3rd ed. al-Qāhirah, 1966. 122p. (A)

ii. Interest: 501–533

501. Abbasi, Masud Ahmad — "Interest—An Economic Study on the Three Economic Systems", *Islamic Review* (London) 57(3–4), Mar.–Apr. 69: 28–32.
502. 'Abd al-Bāsiṭ, Badr al-Mutawallī — "al-Ribā dā' al-bashariyah al-Wabīl" (*Ribā*, the Disastrous affliction of Mankind) *al-Azhar* 22(9), Ramaḍān 1370: 797–800. (A)
503. 'Abdou, Muḥammad 'Īssa — *al-Fā'idah 'alā ra's al-māl ṣūrah min ṣuwar al-ribā* (Interest on Capital is a Form of *Ribā*). Beirut, Dār al-Fatḥ, 1970. (A)
504. ,, ,, ,, — *Limādhā ḥarrama Allāh al-ribā* (Why Allah has Prohibited *Ribā*?). Kuwait, Maktabah al-Manār, n.d. 33p. (A)
505. ,, ,, ,, — *al-Ribā wa dauruhū fī istighlāl mawārid al-shu'ūb* (*Ribā* and its Role in the Exploitation of the Incomes of Nations). Kuwait, Dār al-Buḥūth al-'Ilmīyah, 1969. 86p. (A)
506. ,, ,, ,, — *Waḍ' al-ribā fī binā' al-iqtiṣādī* (Position of *Ribā* in the Economic Structure), Kuwait, Dār al Buḥūth al-'Ilmīyah, 1973. 190p. (A)
507. Abū Sa'ūd, Muḥammad — "Islamic View of *Ribā*", *Islamic Review* (London) 45(2), Feb. 57: 9–16.
508. Abū Shaḥbah, Muḥammad — *Naẓarat al-Islām ilā'l-ribā* (Islam's Viewpoint of *Ribā*). al-Qāhirah, Majma' al-Buḥūth al-Islāmīyah, 1971. (A)
509. Abū Zuhra, Muḥammad — *Buḥūth fi'l-ribā* (Discourses on *Ribā*). Kuwait, Dār al-Buḥūth al-'Ilmīyah, 1970. 94p. (A)
510. ,, ,, ,, — "al-Ribā (tafsīr al-Qur'ān)" (*Ribā*, exegesis of the Qur'ān), *Liwā al-Islām* (Cairo) 8(3), July 54: 137–145. (A)
511. Ahmad, Sheikh Mahmud — "Interest and Unemployment" *Islamic Studies* (Islamabad) 8(1), Mar. 69: 9–46.
512. ,, ,, ,, — "Sūd kā mas'alah" (The Problem of Interest) *Thaqāfat* (Lahore) 2(2), Feb. 56: 33–43. (U)
513. Darāz, Muḥammad 'Abdullāh — *al-Ribā fī naẓar al-qānūn al-Islāmī* (*Ribā* according to Islamic Law) Kuwait, Maktabat al-Manār. n.d. (A) Also in *al-Azhar* 23(1), 51: 11–17; 23(2), Ṣafar 1371: 105–112; 23(3) Rabī' I, 1371: 193–195. (A)
514. Farid, Q. M. — "Is Interest Obsolete?", *Voice of Islam* (Karachi) 8(10), Jul. 64: 495–502.

515.	al-Ghawālī, Ḥāmid	"al-Ribā bain al-ṭibb wa'l-Islām" (*Ribā* according to the Science of Medicine and Islam), *Liwā' al-Islām* (Cairo) 13(4), June 59: 246–248. (A)
516.	Ghulām, 'Alī, Malik	"Jawāz-e sūd kē ḥaq meṇ ēk riwāyat sē ghalāṭ istidalāl." (Wrong Argument in Favour of Permissibility of interest derived from a tradition), *Tarjumān al-Qur'ān* (Lahore) 60(5), Aug. 63: 306–309. (U)
517.	Ḥāmid, Muḥammad	"Ḥaula mushkilat al-ribā" (On the Problem of Interest) *al-Muslimoon* (Dimashq) 6(4) Sep. 58: 75–81. (A)
518.	Hussain, S. Mushtaq	"Interest on Money and Islam—A Suggested Analysis", Report of *First Regional Conference of the M.S.A. of U.S. & Canada*. Stanford University, California, June 10–12, 1966: 9–14.
519.	Irshad, Sheikh Ahmad	"Islamic Economy and the Elimination of Interest", *Voice of Islam* (Karachi) 12(2), Nov. 63: 78–85.
520.	Kharūfah, 'Alā al-Dīn	"al-Ribā wa'l fā'idah" (*Ribā* and Interest), *Majma' al-'Ilmī al-Irāqī* 10(1), 63: 353–354. (A)
521.	Mawdūdī, Sayyid Abul A'lā	*Sūd* (Interest). Lahore, Islamic Publications, 1961, 410p. (U) Arabic tr. *al-Ribā*, Dimashq, Dār al-Fikr.
522.	Muslim, A. G.	"The Early Development of the Islamic Concept of *Ribā*", *Current British Research in Middle Eastern and Islamic Studies*, University of Durham, Centre for Middle Eastern and Islamic Studies, 1971.
523.	Nadwī, 'Abd al-Salām	"Taḥrīm-ē sūd" (Prohibition of Interest) *Ma'ārif* (Azamgarh) 14(1), July 24: 9–31; 14(2) Aug. 24: 93–128; 14(3), Sep. 24: 170–184. (U)
524.	Nadwī, Muḥammad Na'īm	"Tāḥrīm-e- sūd 'ilm wa 'aql kī raushnī meṇ", (Prohibition of Interest in the Light of Science and Reason). *Zindagī* (Rampur) 38(1, 2) Jan. Feb. 67: 25–35. (U)
525.	Qādrī Sayyid Mu'īnuddīn	"Sarmāyakārī kī ma'āshī ḥaqīqat aur Islāmī nuqṭaenaẓar sē us kē mu'āwaḍē kī wajh-e jawāz" (The Economic Nature of Investment and the Basis of Permission of its Reward from Islamic Viewpoint), *Burhān* (Delhi) 55(3), Sep. 65: 159–176; 55(4), Oct. 65: 221–229. (U)
526.	Qureshi, Anwar Iqbal	*Islam and the Theory of Interest* with an Introduction by Syed Sulaiman Nadvi. Lahore, Muhammad Ashraf, xxiv, 223p. Arabic tr. *al-Islām wa'l ribā* by Fārūq Ḥilmī. al-Qāhirah, Maktabah, Miṣr, 158p.
527.	Quṭb, Sayyid	*Tafsīr āyāt al-ribā* (Exegesis of the Verses (of the Qur'ān) related to *Ribā*). Kuwait, Dār al-Buḥūth al-'Ilmīyah, n.d. 66p. (A)
528.		"*al-Ribā*" (Interest), *Liwā' al-Islām* (Cairo) 8(10), Feb. 55: 648–657. (A)
529.		*al-Ribā fi'l-Islām wa fi'l-naẓarīyāt al-iqtiṣādīyah al-ḥadīthah* (*Ribā* in Islam and in recent Economic Theories). Kuwait, al-Dār al-Kuwaitīyah li'l-ṭibā'ah wa'l-Nashr, n.d. 72p. (A)

530.	Riḍā, Muḥammad Rashīd	*al-Ribā wa 'l-mu'āmalāt fil-Islām* (*Ribā* and Transactions in Islam). al-Qāhirah, Maktabat al-Qāhirah, 1960. (A)
531.	Shafī', Muftī Muḥammad	*Mas'ala-e-sūd* (The Problem of Interest). Karachi, Idārat al-Ma'ārif, 3rd edition, 1390 A.H., 148p. (U)
532.	Ṣiddīqī, Muḥammad Maẓharuddīn	"Sūd kā mas'alah" (The Problem of Interest), *Thaqāfat* (Lahore) 4(5), May 57: 54–62. (U)
533.	Zakī al-Dīn, Ibrāhīm	*Naẓarīyat al-ribā al-muḥarram* (The Theory of the Prohibited interest).

iii. Commercial Interest: 534–553

534.	'Abbāsī, Manẓūr Aḥsan	"Qurūḍ wa ribā" (Loans and Interest), *Thaqāfat* (Lahore) 8(8), Aug. 60: 43–62. (U)
535.	Anwārullāh, Muḥammad	*Mas'alat al-Ribā* (The Problem of Interest). Hyderabad (Dn.), Majlis Ishā'at al-'Ulūm, n.d. 27p. (U)
536.	Ḍanāwī, Muḥammad 'Alī	"Hal bai' al-taqsīṭ Jā'iz?" (Is Instalment Purchase Legal?), *al-Ba'th al-Islāmī* (Lucknow) 11(5), Feb. 67: 60–65. (A)
537.	Fazlur Rahman	"Riba and Interest", *Islamic Studies* (Karachi) 3(1), Mar. 64: 1–43.
538.	Fazlur Rahman (Gunnauri)	"Mabḥath taḥlīlī ḥaula al-ribā al-tijārī" (An Analytical Study of Commercial Interest), *al-Ba'th al-Islāmī* (Lucknow) 12(7), Apr. 68: 48–57; 12(8), May 68: 67–71. (A)
539.	,, ,, ,,	"A Study of Commercial Interest in Islam", *Islamic Thought* (Aligarh) 5(4 & 5) July–Oct. 58: 24–46.
540.	,, ,, ,,	*Tijāratī sūd tārīkhī aur fiqhī nuqṭa-e naẓar sē* (Commercial Interest from the Stand Point of History and Islamic Law). Aligarh Muslim University, 1967. xv, 176p. (U)
541.	Ḥasan, Abū 'Usāmah	"Faẓlur Raḥmānī taḥqīq-e ribā kī ḥaqīqat" (An Evaluation of Fazlur Rahman's Study on *Ribā*), *Bayyināt* (Karachi) 3(2) Jan. 64: 105–123; 3(3) Feb. 64: 177–189; 3(4) March 64: 231–251; 3(5) April 54: 311–317. (U)
542.	'Imādī, Tamannā	"Ribā aur bai'" (*Ribā* and Trade), *Fikr-o Naẓar* (Karachi) 2(7), Jan 65: 429–434. (U)
543.	Ismā'īl, Ch. Muḥammad	"Mas'ala-e sūd (The Problem of Interest), Thaqāfat (Lahore) 9(1, 4, 6): 37–47, 35–50, 53–61, 40–50. (U)
544.	Ja'far Shāh, Muḥammad, Phulwārwī	*Commercial Interest kī fiqhī ḥaythīyat* (Commercial Interest in Islamic Law). Lahore, Idāra-e Thaqāfat-e Islāmiyah, 1959. 234p. (U)
545.	Khan, Mir Sa'ādat Ali	"The Mohammadan Laws Against Usury and how they are Evaded", *Comparative Legislation* 11 (1920): 233–244.
546.	al-Nabhān, Muḥammad Fārūq	*al-Qurūḍ al-intājīyah wa mauqif al-Islām minhā* (Islam's Stand on Production Loans), M.A. Dissertation. Unpublished. Cairo University.
547.	Nadwī, Muḥammad Na'īm	"Bank kā sūd" (Bank Interest), *Zindagī* (Rampur) 40(3), Mar. 68: 22–37. (U)

548. Nadwī, Muḥammad Na'īm — "Mahājanī aur tijāratī sūd" (Money Lenders Interest and Commercial Interest), *Zindagī* (Rampur) 40(2–3). (U)

549. Nāṣif, Hafnī Beck — "Bank aur sūd" (Banks and Interest), *Thaqāfat* (Lahore) 9(2), Mar. 61 : 57–64. (U)

550. Shāh, Syed Ya'qūb — *Chand ma'āshī masā'il aur Islām* (Some Economic Problems and Islam). Lahore, Idāra-e Thaqāfat-e Islāmīyah, 1967. 259p. (U)

551. „ „ „ — "Islam and Productive Credit", *Islamic Review* (London) 47(3) Mar. 59 : 34–37.

552. Shāmī, Amīr Ḥamza — "Commercial Interest aur Islām" (Commercial Interest and Islam) *Tarjumān al-Qur'ān* (Lahore), 57(1), Oct. 61 : 32–46. (U)

553. Suhail, Iqbāl Aḥmad — *Haqīqat al-ribā* (Nature of *Ribā*), Badāyūn, Niẓāmī Press, 1936, 14, 178p. (U)

iv. Ribā'l-Faḍl: 554–555

554. al-'Itr, Nur al-Dīn — " 'Illat ribā'l-faḍl" (Legal Basis of (Prohibiting) *Ribā'l-faḍl*) *al-Wa'y al-Islāmī* (Kuwait) (116), Aug. 74 : 51–53. (A)

555. 'Iwaḍ, Aḥmad Ṣafī al-Dīn — "Taṣawwur jadīd li ribā'l-faḍl" (A New Conception of *ribā'l-faḍl*), *al-Wa'y al-Islāmī* (Kuwait) (111), Mar. 74 : 57–69. (A)

v. Speculation and Stock Exchange: 556–559

556. Amīnī, Muḥammad Taqī — *Maqālāt-e-Amīnī* (Essays of Amini), Aligarh Muslim University Press, 1970. 268p. (U)

557. Hārūn, Abdussalām Muḥammad — *al-Maisir wa'l-azlām* (Games of Chance and Raffles), al-Qāhirah, Dār al-Fikr al-'Arabī, 1953. 106p. (A)

558. Khan, Muḥammad Akram — "International Monetary Crisis: Causes and Cure", *Criterion* (Karachi) 62(2), Mar. Apr. 71 : 5–19.

559. „ „ „ — "Stock Exchanges: Function and Need to Reform", *Criterion* (Karachi) 7(1), Jan. 72 : 28–38.

vi. Lottery: 560–562

560. Pīrzāda, Shams — *Lottery*. Delhi, Markazī Maktabah Jamā'at-e-Islāmī Hind 1971, 23p. (U)

561. Syed 'Alī — "Lottery" *Zindagī* (Rampur) 44(4), Apr. 70 : 47–50. (U)

562. Ṣiddīqī, Na'īm — "Qur'ah aur lottery" (*Qur'ah* and lottery), *Tarjumān al-Qur'an* (Lahore) 41(3), Dec. 53 : 205–206. (U)

vii. Socialism and Communism: 563–597

563. 'Abd al-Bārī, Muḥammad — "Islam and Socialism", *Islamic Literature* (Lahore) 3(8), Aug. 51 : 21–27.

564. Abdul Hakim, Khalifa — *Islam and Communism*. Lahore, Institute of Islamic Culture, 1953. 262p.

565. Abū Zuhra, Muḥammad — "al-Shuyū'īyah wa'l-Islām" (Communism and Islam), *Liwā' al-Islām* (Cairo) 13(9), 2 Nov. 59 : 535–538; 13(10), Dec. 59 : 599–604; 13(11), Jan. 60 : 663–668; 13(12), Feb. 60 : 727–733. (A)

566.	Akbar Murādpūrī, Muḥammad	*Conflict between Socialism and Islam*, Lahore, Muhammad Ashraf, 1970. 125p.
567.	al-'Aqqād, 'Abbās Maḥmūd	"A Doctrine in Bankruptcy (Communist Materialism Incapable of Survival)", *al-Azhar* 31(1), June 59: 26–30.
568.	al-'Aqqād, 'Abbās Maḥmūd	*al-Shuyū'īyah wa'l-insānīyah* (Communism and Humanity). Cairo, 1956, 335p. (A)
569.	al-'Aqqād, 'Abbās Maḥmūd; 'Aṭṭār, Aḥmad 'Abd al-Ghafūr	*al-Shuyū'īyah wa'l-Islām* (Communism and Islam). 2nd ed. Beirut, 1072. 213p. (A)
570.	al-Badrī, 'Abd al-'Azīz	*Ḥukm al-Islām fi'l-Ishtirākīyah* (Islam's Verdict on Socialism). al-Madīnat al-Munawwarah, al-Maktabat al-'Ilmīyah, 1969. 172p. (A)
571.	al-Bahī, Muḥammad	"Communism and Religion", *al-Azhar* 31(3), Sep. 59: 76–90.
572.	al-Bannā, Muḥammad Kāmil	"al-Shuyū'īyah (Communism), *Liwā' al-Islām* (Cairo) 13(10), Dec. 59: 605–608. (A)
573.	al-Bārūdī, 'Alī	*Durūs fi'l-ishtirākīyat al-'Arabīyah* (Discourses on Arab Socialism). Alexandria, Maktabat al-Ma'ārif, 1967. 262p. (A)
574.	Bashīr al-'Auf	*Ishtirākīyatuhum wa Islāmunā* (Their Socialism and Our Islam). Beirut, Mu'assasat al-Intāj al-Ṭibā'ī, 1966. 158p. (A)
575.	Dawālībī, Ma'rūf	*Naẓaratun Islāmiyah fi'l-Ishtirākiyat al-thauriyah* (An Islamic Review of Revolutionary Socialism). Beirut, Dār al-Kitāb al-Jadīd, 1965. 144p. (A)
576.	Enayat, Hamid	"Islam and Socialism in Egypt", *Middle Eastern Studies* 4(2), Jan. 68: 141–172.
577.	al-Ghazālī, Muḥammad	*al-Islām wa'l manāhij al ishtirākīyah* (Islam and the Socialistic Methods). Cairo, 1951. 120p. (A)
578.	Ghulām Rasūl, Sayyid	"Islām aur socialism kā bunyādi farq" (Basic Difference between Islam and Socialism), *Fārān* (Karachi) 22(1), Apr. 70: 11–12. (U)
579.	Ḥussain, Mirzā Muḥammad	*Islam and Socialism: A Critical Study of Capitalism, Socialism, Fascism and Nazism as contrasted with the Quranic Concept of a New World Order*. Lahore, Muhammad Ashraf, 1947. xii, 446p.
580.	„ „	*Islam versus Socialism*. Lahore, Muhammad Ashraf, 1970. 170p. (First Published in 1947.)
581.		"al-Ishtirākīyah" (Socialism), *Liwā' al-Islām* (Cairo) 14(7), 23 Aug. 60: 443–453. (A)
582.	Kerr, M. H.	"Islam and Arab Socialism", *Muslim World* 56(4) Oct. 66: 276–281.
583.	Khan, Muḥammad Ihsanullah	"Communism and Islam Contrasted", *Islamic Literature* (Lahore) 3(4), Apr. 51: 11–21.
584.	Khurshīd Aḥmad (ed.)	"*Chirāgh-e Rāh*". Socialism Number (Karachi) Dec. 1967. 525p. (U)
585.	„ „	*Socialism Yā Islām* (Socialism or Islam). Karachi, Maktabah Chirāgh-e-Rāh, 1969, 320p. (U)
586.	Lewis, Bernard	"Communism and Islam", *International Affairs* (London) 30(1), 54: 1–12.
587.	Mubārak, Muḥammad	"Ishtirakīyāt aur Islām" (Communism and Islam), *Bayyināt* (Karachi), 15(1) Jan. 70: 24–33. (U)
588.	al-Munajjid, Ṣalāḥ al-Dīn	*al-Taḍlīl al-ishtirākī* (The Socialist Misguidance).

Beirut, Dār al-Kitāb al-Jadīd, 1966. 144p. (A)

589. Nadwī, Mas'ūd 'Ālam — *Ishtirākīyat aur Islām* (Communism and Islam) Karachi, Maktabah Chirāgh-e-Rāh, 1949. 80p. (U)

590. al-Nawawī, Maḥmūd; Khafājī, 'Abd al-Mun'im — *Bain al-shuyū'īyah wa'l-Islām* (Between Communism and Islam). al-Qāhirah, Dār al-'Ahd al-Jadīd, 1959. 102p. (A)

591. Sa'īd, 'Abd al-Mughnī — *al-Islām wa'l-uṣūl al-fikrīyah li'l-ishtirākīyat al-'Arabīyah* (Islam and the Intellectual Bases of Arab Socialism). al-Qāhirah, Maktabat al-Anjalū Miṣrīyah, n.d. 109p. (A)

592. Shaltūt, Maḥmūd — "Socialism and Islam" in Karpat, Kemal H. (ed) *Political and Social Thought in the Contemporary Middle East*. New York, Praeger, 1970: 126–132.

593. Shamsī, Syed Mughni al-Dīn — "Taḥrīk-e-socialism par ēk tanqīdī naẓar" (A Critical Study of the Socialist Movement), *Burhān* (Delhi) 3(2), Aug. 39; 3(5), Nov. 39: 119–134. (U)

594. Ṣiddīqī, 'Abd al-Ḥamīd — "Ishtirākīyat aur 'amal-e taṭhir" (Purges in Communism), *Zindagī* (Rampur) 45(6), Dec. 70: 15–24. (U)

595. Ṣiddīqī, Muḥammad Maẓharuddīn — *Ishtirākīyat aur niẓām-e Islām* (Communism and the Islamic System). Lahore, Markazi Maktabah Jamā'at-e-Islāmī, 1949. (U) (Earlier Published under the Title: *Hegal, Marx aur niẓām-e-Islām* (Hegal, Marx and the Islamic System). Pathankot, Daftar Risālah Tarjumān al-Qur'ān, 1943. 240p.

596. " " — *Marxism or Islam*, Lahore, Orientalia, 1952. 168p.

597. Zayīd, Sa'īd — "al-Islām wa'l-ishtirākīyah" (Islam and Socialism), *al-Azhar* 22(7), Rajab 1370: 665–669; Ram. 1370: 826–828; 22(10) Shaw. 1370: 921–923; Muhar. 1371: 61–63. (A)

viii. Marxian Theories: 598–599

598. Abāẓah, Ibrāhīm Dasūqī — "Naqd al-naẓarīyat al-mārxīyah" (Critique of Marxian Theory), *al-Baḥth al-'Ilmi* (Rabāṭ) 8(17), Jan.–May 71: 97–131. (A)

599. 'Abdullāh, Syed — "Karl Marx kē naẓarīyāt maghribī naqqādoṇ kī naẓar meṇ." (Western Critics on the Theories of Karl Marx), *Tarjumān al-Ḥadīth*, Jan. 70: 37–42. (U)

ix. Socialism and Capitalism, etc.: 600–610

600. 'Abdullāh, Amin 'Afīfī — "Islām aur daur-e jadīd kē iqtiṣādī madhāhib" (Islam and the Economic Ideologies of Modern Age), tr. by Ḍiyā' al-Dīn Iṣlāhī, *Ma'ārif* (Azamgarh) 88(3), Nov. 61: 391–396. (U)

601. Darwish, Muṣṭafā — *al-Islām fī muwājahat al-ra'smālīyah wa'l ishtirākīyah* (Confrontation of Islam with Capitalism and Socialism). al-Qāhirah, al-Jāmi' al-Azhar, 1959. 20p. (A)

602. Dawālībī, Ma'rūf — *al-Islām amām al-ra'smālīyah wa'l-Marksīyah* (Islam versus Capitalism and Marxism). Beirut, Dār al-Kitāb al-Jadīd. n.d. 22p. (A)

603. Dawalībī, Ma'rūf — "Islam versus Capitalism and Marxism", *World Muslim League* (Singapore) 3(5), May 66: 14–24.

604. Ismā'īl, Ibrāhīm Muḥammad — *Islam and Contemporary Economic Theories*, tr. from Arabic by Ismā'īl Kashmīrī. Cairo, Supreme Council for Islamic Affairs. n.d. 100p.

605. al-Khaulī, al-Bahī — *al-Islām-lā shuyū'īyah wa lā ra'smālīyah* (Islam—neither Communism nor Socialism). (A)

606. Mahmud Javed — "Capitalism and Socialism", *Criterion* (Karachi) 8(9), Sep. 73: 25–35; 9(4), Apr. 74: 14–31.

607. Mawdūdī, Sayyid Abul A'lā — *Islam aur jadīd m'āshī naẓarīyāt* (Islam and Modern Economic Theories). Delhi, Markazi Maktabah Jamā'at-e-Islāmī (Hind) 1969. 136p. (U)

608. ,, ,, ,, ,, — "Mauqif al-Islām min al-shuyū'īyah wa'l-ra'smālīyah" (Islamic Stand *vis à vis* Capitalism and Communism), *al-Azhar* 24(4), Dec. 52: 458–460. (A)

609. Shafī', Muftī Muḥammad — "Ishtirākīyat, qaumīyat aur sarmāyadārī" (Communism, Nationalism and Capitalism), *Zindagī* (Rampur) 44, May 70: 29–39. (U) (Also Published in *al-Balāgh* (Karachi) 3, Mar. 70: 15–22.

610. Ṭamān, 'Alī Fahmī — *al-Fikrat al-Islāmīyah bain al-shuyū'īyah wa'l isti'mār* (Islamic Thought versus Communism and Imperialism). al-Qāhirah, al-Mu'allif, 1948. (A)

4. ECONOMIC ANALYSIS IN AN ISLAMIC FRAMEWORK [611–648]

i. General: 611–614

611. Kahf, Monzer — *Challenges Confronting Islamic Economist*. Utah, U.S.A., Univ. of Utah, S.L.C., July 1972. 8p. mimeo.

612. ,, ,, — *A Contribution to the Study of the Economics of Islam*. Utah, U.S.A., Univ. of Utah, S.L.C., July 1973. 110p. mimeo.

613. Khan, Muhammad Akram — *A Survey of Contemporary Economic Thought in Islam*, mimeo.

614. Ṣiddīqī, Muhammad Nejatullah — *A Survey of Contemporary Literature on Islamic Economics*. Jeddah, First International Conference on Islamic Economics. 1975. 174p. mimeo.

ii. Consumption: 615

615. Kahf, Monzer — "A Model of the Household Decisions in Islamic Economy" in: *Association of Muslim Social Scientists, Proceedings, Third National Seminar*. Gary, Indiana, May 1974: 19–28.

iii. Production and Enterprise: 616–619

616. Hamid, Habeeb — "On Economic Enterprise in Islam", *Islamic Thought* (Aligarh) 5(3), May–June 55: 17–18.

617. Mohiuddin, Ghulam — "On Market Mechanism under the Influence of Islamic Spirit", *Islamic Thought* (Aligarh) 5(1), Jan.–Feb. 58: 32.

618. Ṣiddīqī, 'Abdul Hamid — "Economic Enterprise in Islam", *Islamic Thought* (Aligarh) 6(2) Mar.–Apr. 57: 27.

619. Ṣiddīqī, Muhammad Nejatullah — *Economic Enterprise in Islam*. Lahore, Islamic Publications, 1972. 179p.; Delhi, Markazī Maktabah-Islāmī, 1972. 179p.

iv. Profit-Sharing: 620

620. Chawdhari, A. B. M. Masudul Alam — "A Mathematical Formulation of 'Muḍārabah' the Profit Sharing in Islam", in: *Association of Muslim Social Scientists, Proceedings, Third National Seminar*. Gary, Indiana, May 1974: 19–28.

v. Zakat: 621–627

621. Ahmad, Afazuddin — "Economic Significance of *Zakāt*", *Islamic Literature* (Lahore), 4(8), Aug. 52: 5–11.

622. Hasanuzzaman, S. M. — "*Zakāt*, Taxes and Estate Duty", *Islamic Literature* (Lahore) 17(7), July 71: 407–411.

623. Izadi, Ali, M. — "The Role of az-Zakat (An Institutionalised Charity) in the Islamic System of Economics in Curing the Poverty Dilemma" in: *Association of Muslim Social Scientists, Proceedings, Third National Seminar*. Gary, Indiana, May 1974: 9–18.

624. Mahmoud, Mabid — "Frictions, Power Rationing and *al-Zakāt*" in: *Association of Muslim Social Scientists, Proceedings, Third National Seminar*. Gary, Indiana, May 1974: 29–43.

625. Mohammad bin Jamāl — "*Zakāt*—A Socio Economic Power for the Development and Progress of the Muslim Community', *World Muslim League* (Singapore) 1(6), May 64: 47–52.

626. — "Waẓīfat al-Zakāt fi'l-mujtama' (Function of *Zakāt* in Society), *Liwā' al-Islām* (Cairo) 15(8), Sep. 61: 463–469. (A)

627. De-Zayas, Farishta G. — "The functional role of *Zakāt* in the Islamic Social Economy", *Islamic Literature* (Lahore) 15(3), Mar. 69: 5–10.

vi. Abolition of Interest: 628–632

628. Ahmad, Mahmud — "Semantics of Theory of Interest", *Islamic Studies* (Rawalpindi) 6(2), June 67: 171–196.

629. Hasanuzzaman, S. M. — "Islām aur sharḥ-e sūd" (Islam and the Rate of Interest), *Burhān* (Delhi) 53(6), Dec. 64: 325–341. (U)

630. ,, ,, — "Islam *vis-à-vis* Interest Rate", *Islamic Culture* 40(1) Jan. 66: 1–12. Arabic tr. "Mauqif al-Islām min si'r al-fā'idah", *al-Muslimoon* (Dimashq) 9(6), Apr. 65: 36–53.

631. Siddiqi, Abdul Hamid — "Islāmī niẓām aur tijāratī chakkar" (Islamic System and Trade Cycles), *Tarjumān al-Qur'ān* (Lahore) 42(1). Apr. 54: 64–66 (U)

632. Ulgener, Sabri F. — "Monetary Conditions of Economic Growth and the Islamic Concept of Interest", *Islamic Review* (London) 55(2), Feb. 67: 11–14.

vii. Nature of Islamic Economics: 633–647

633. Alan, Hashmat — *Distribution Theory under Islamic Law*. Ph.D. Thesis, 1953, George Town University. 174p.
634. Chawdhri, A. B. M. Masudul Alam — "Foundations of Islamic Economics, Pt. I: General Methodology of Islamic Economics", *Criterion* (Karachi), 9(1) Jan. 74: 17–25.
635. Durrānī, Muḥammad Murtaḍa Aḥmad Kḥān — *Ma'āshīyāt (Islāmī nuqṭa-e naẓar sē)*. Lahore, 1952. (U)
636. al-Fanjarī, Muḥammad Shauqī — "al-Iqtiṣād al-Islāmī—kaifa aghfal'l-Muslimūn tadrīsahū wa taṭbiqahū" (Islamic Economics: How Muslims have Neglected its Study and Application), *al-'Arabī* (Kuwait) (164), July 72: 64–67. (A)
637. Faridi, Fazlur Rahman — "Need for a Scientific Study of Islamic Economy", *Islamic Thought* (Aligarh) 2(5), Sep.–Oct. 55: 34–35.
638. al-Faruqi, Isma'il R. A. — "Foreword" in: *Contemporary Aspects of Economic and Social Thinking in Islam*. Gary, Indiana, M.S.A. of U.S. & Canada, 1973: 1–8.
639. ,, ,, ,, — "Introduction" in: *Association of Muslim Social Scientists, Proceedings, Third National Seminar*, Gary, Indiana, May 1974: V–IX.
640. Hamid, Habeeb — "On 'Problems of Islamic Research in Economics'," *Islamic Thought* 5(2) Mar.–April 58: 31–32; 5(3), May–June 58: 19–20.
641. Hassanein, Medhat — "Towards a Model of the Economy of Islam" in: *Contemporary Aspects of Economic and Social Thinking in Islam*. Gary, Indiana, M.S.A. of U.S. & Canada, 1973: 17–25.
642. Khan, Muhammad Akram — "Islamic Economics: An Outline Plan for Research" *Criterion* (Karachi) 10(4), Apr. 75: 27–35.
643. Khan, Muhammad Shabbir — "A Suggestion to the Students of Economics" *Islamic Thought* (Aligarh) 2(4), July–Aug. 55: 27.
644. Khurshid Ahmad — "Method of Approach to Economics", *Islamic Thought* (Aligarh) 2(2), Mar.–Apr. 55: 37.
645. Manzar, Abdul Moiz — "Economics Needs a Reconstruction", *Islamic Thought* (Aligarh) 2(2), Mar.–Apr. 55: 7–21.
646. Sakr, Muhammad Ahmad — al-Iqtiṣād al-Islāmī: mafāhim wa murtakazāt (Islamic Economics: Its Foundations and Concept). Paper Presented at the First International Conference on Islamic Economics held at Makka on Feb. 21–26, 1976. *Mimeo*. 51p.
647. Siddiqi, Muhammad Nejatullah — "Problems of Islamic Research in Economics", *Islamic Thought* (Aligarh) 6(4, 5), Oct. Dec.– 57: 1–8.

5. HISTORY OF ECONOMIC THOUGHT IN ISLAM [648–691]

i. General: 648–649

648. Meyer, A. J. — "Economic Thought and its Application and Methodology in the Middle East", *Middle East Economic Papers* (Beirut) 56: 66–74.

649. Ṣāliḥ, Muḥammad Zakī — "al-Fikr al-iqtiṣādī al-'Arabī fi'l-qarn al-khāmis 'asharah" (Arab Economic Thought in the Fifteenth Century, *al-Qānūn wa'l-Iqtiṣād* (Cairo), Mar., Oct. 33.

650. De Somogyi, Joseph — "Economic Theory in the Classical Arabic Literature", *Studies in Islam* (Delhi) 2(1), Jan. 65: 1–6.

ii. Ibn Khaldūn: 651–664

651. 'Abd al-Qādir, Muḥammad — "Ibn Khaldūn kē ma'āshī khayālāt" (Economic Views of Ibn Khaldūn), *Ma'ārif* (Azamgarh) 50(6), Dec. 42: 433–441. (U)

652. „ „ „ — *Ibn Khaldūn kē ma'āshiratī, siyāsī, ma'āshī khayālāt* (Social, Political and Economic Ideas of Ibn Khaldūn) Hyderabad (Dn.), A'zam Steam Press, 1943. (U)

653. „ „ „ — "The Social and Political Ideas of Ibn Khaldun", *Indian Journal of Political Science* (Delhi), 3(2), Jul.–Sept. 41.

654. Abdus Sattar, M. — "Ibn Khaldun's Contribution to Economic Thought" in: *Contemporary Aspects of Economic and Social Thinking in Islam.* Gary, Indiana, M.S.A. of U.S. & Canada, 1973: 157–168.

655. el-Alfi, Ezzat S. — *Production, Distribution and Exchange in Khaldun's Writings.* Ph.D. Thesis, Univ. of Minnesota, 1968.

656. Ali, Syed Ahmad — "Economics of Ibn Khaldūn—A selection", *Africa Quarterly* (New Delhi) 10(3) Oct.–Dec. 70: 251–259.

657. Irving, T. B. — "Ibn Khaldūn on Agriculture", *Islamic Literature* (Lahore) 7(8), Aug. 55: 31–32.

658. Maharjān Ibn Khaldūn — "*A'māl Maharjān Ibn Khaldūn al-mun'aqid fi'l-Qāhirah min 2 ilā 6 yanāyir 1962.* (Proceedings of Ibn Khaldūn Celebrations held at Cairo from 2 to 6 January 1962). al-Qāhirah, al-Markaz al-Qaumī li'l-Buḥūth al-ijtimā'īyah wa'l-Jinā'īyah, 1962. (A)

659. Nash'at, Muḥammad 'Alī — *al-Fikr al-iqtiṣādī fī muqaddimat Ibn Khaldūn* (Economic Thought in the Prolegomena of Ibn Khaldūn). Ph.D. Thesis, Cairo University, Maṭba' Dār al-Kutub al-Miṣrīya, 1944. (A)

660. Rif'at, Sayyid Mubāriz al-Dīn — "Ma'āshīyāt par Ibn Khaldūn kē Khayālāt" (Ibn Khaldūn's Views on Economics), *Ma'ārif* (Azamgarh) 40(1) July 37: 16–28; 40(2), Aug. 37: 85–95. (U)

661. Rozenthal, Franz — *Ibn Khaldūn: The Muqaddimah, An Introduction to History*, V.I. London, Routledge & Kegan Paul, 1958. 481p. (Complete History is 3 Volumes.)

662. Sharif, M. Raihan — "Ibn Khaldūn, The Pioneer Economist", *Islamic Literature* (Lahore) 6(5), May 55: 33–40.

663. Sherwani, H. K. — "Ibn-e-Khaldūn and His Politico-Economic Thought" *Islamic Culture* 44(2), Apr. 70: 71–80.

664. Spengler, J. J. — "Economic Thought of Islam: Ibn Khaldūn", *Comparative Studies in Society and History* (The Hague), VI, 64: 268–306.

iii. Ibn Taimīyah: 665–667

665. Ahmad, Ilyas — "Ibn Taimiyah on Islamic Economics", *Voice of Islam* (Karachi) 9(11), Aug. 61: 557–569.

666. Kahf, Monzer — *The Economic Views of Taqiuddin Taimeyah* (1263–1328): *The Great Radical Reformist of the Islamic Middle Ages*. 1973. 29p. *mimeo.*

667. Sherwani, H. K. — "Ibn-e-Taimiyah's Economic Thought", *Islamic Literature* (Lahore) 8(1), Jan. 56: 9–23.

iv. Abū Yūsuf: 668–672

668. Abū Yūsuf — *Kitāb al-Kharāj: Taxation in Islam*, tr. by Ben Shemesh. Leiden, Brill; London, Luzac, 1969, vii, 155p.

669. Ben Shemesh, A. — *Taxation in Islam* V.2: Qudāma B. Ja'far's Kitāb al-Kharāj, Part Seven, and Excerpts from Abū Yūsuf's Kitāb al-Kharāj. Leiden, Brill; London, Luzac, 1965. 146p.

670. Iṣlāḥī, Ḍiyā al-Dīn — "AbūYūsuf aur unkē fiqhī wa qānūnī Kārnāmē" (Abū Yūsuf and his Juridical and Legal Works), *Ma'ārif* (Azamgarh) 95(5), May 65: 361–384. (U)

671. Siddiqi, Muhammad Nejatullah — "Abū Yūsuf kā ma'āshī fikr" (Economic Thought of Abū Yūsuf), *Fikr-o-Naẓar* (Aligarh) 5(1), Jan. 64: 66–95. (U)

672. Siddiqi, Muhammad Nejatullah — *Islām kā niẓāme maḥāṣil, tarjuma kitāb al-Kharāj: Qāḍī Abū Yūsuf* (Islam's Tax System, translation of Qāḍī Abū Yūsuf's Kitāb al-Kharāj). Lahore, Islamic Publications, 1966. 635p. (U)

v. Yahyā Ibn Ādam: 673–675

673. Ben Shemesh, A. — *Taxation in Islam*, V.I: *Yaḥyā Ben Ādam's Kitāb al-Kharāj*. Leiden, Brill, 1958. 172p.

674. Kister, M. J. — "The Social and Political Implications of Three Traditions in the *Kitāb al-Kharāj* of Yahya b. Adam", *Journal of Economic and Social History of the Orient* (Leiden) 3(3), Oct. 60: 326–334.

675. Nadwī, Mujībullāh — "Yaḥyā ibn Ādam aur unkī *kitāb al-Kharāj*" (Yaḥyā ibn Ādam and his *Kitāb al-Kharāj*), *Ma'ārif* (Azamgarh) 64(4), Oct. 49: 293–300; 64(5), Nov. 49: 367–375. (U)

vi. Abū Ja'far Dimashqī: 676–677

676. 'Āshūr, al-Sayyid Muḥammad — *Dirāsah fi'l-fikr al-iqtiṣādī al-'Arabī: Abu'l-Faḍl Ja'far bin 'Alī al-Dimashqī (Abu'l-iqtiṣād)* (A Study of Arab Economic Thought: Abū'l Faḍl Ja'far bin 'Alī al-Dimashqī—Father of Economics). al-Qāhirah, Dār al-Ittiḥād al-'Arabī li'l Ṭibā'ah, 1973. 69, 191p. (A)

677. al-Dimashqī, Abul Fadl Ja'far bin 'Alī — *Kitāb al-ishārah ilā maḥāsin al-tijārah wa ma'rifat jaiyid al-a'rāḍ wa radīyihā wa ghushūsh al-mudallisīn fīhā* (A Guide Book on Virtues of Trade, and Distinction between Good and Bad Commodities and the Frauds Played by Adultrators). Cairo, Maṭba'at al-Mu'ayid, 1318 A.H. 76p. (A)

vii. Naṣīr al-Dīn Ṭūsī: 678–679

678. Anzarul Haque, Muhammad — *A Critical Study of Jalāl al-Dīn al-Dawwānī's Contribution to Social Philosophy*. Aligarh Muslim University, Ph.D. Thesis (Unpublished) 443p.

679. Rif'at, Sayyid Mubāriz al-Dīn — "Naṣīr al-Dīn Ṭūsī kā risāla-e māliyāt" (Treatise on Economics by Naṣīr al-Dīn Ṭūsī), *Majallah 'Uthmānīyah* (Hyderabad) 7(2, 3): 1–14. (U)

viii. Others: 680–691

680. Abū 'Ubaid, al-Qāsim bin Sallām — *Kitāb al-amwāl* (Treatise on Wealth), Urdu tr. by A. R. Surti. Islamabad, Islamic Research Institute, 1968. 2v. (A), 543p, 408p.

681. Amedroz, H. F. — "The Ḥisba Jurisdiction in the Aḥkām Sultaniyyah of Mawardi", *Journal of the Royal Asiatic Society of Great Britain & Ireland* (London) 1916: 77–101; 287–314.

682. Ehrenkreutz, A. S. — "al-Būzanjānī (A.D. 939–997) *The Ma'āṣir*", *Journal of Economic and Social History of the Orient* (Leiden) 8(1), Aug. 65: 90–92.

683. Hanna, S. A. — "al-Afghānī; A Pioneer of Islamic Socialism", *Muslim World* 57(1), Jan. 67: 24–32.

684. al-Labbān, Ibrāhīm — *Ḥaqq al-fuqarā' fī amwāl al-Aaghniyā' 'ind Ibn Ḥazm*. (Right of the Poor to the Wealth of the Rich according to Ibn Hazm). (A)

685. Muḥsinī, Shams al-Raḥmān — *Shāh Walīullāh kē 'Umrānī naẓarīyē* (Sociological Theories of Shāh Walīullāh). Lahore, Sind Sagar Academy, 1946. 142p. (U)

686. Sharafuddīn, Abu 'l-Muḥsin Muḥammad — "Abū Ja'far al-Dāwūdī's Kitāb al-Amwāl" *Islamic Studies* (Rawalpindī) 4(4), Dec. 65: 441–448.

687. 'Ubaidullāh Sindhī — *Imām Walīullāh Dehlavī aur unkā falsafa-e-'Umrāniyāt wa ma'āshiyāt*. (Imām Walīullah of Delhi and His Sociological and Economic Philosophy), Tr. by Bashīr Aḥmad. Lahore, Kitab Manzil, 1953. (U)

688. ,, ,, — *Shāh Walīullāh aur unkā falsafah ya'nī Imām Walīullāh kī ḥikmat kā ijmālī ta'āruf* (Shāh Walīullāh and his Philosophy, i.e., A Brief Introduction to the Wisdom of Imām Walīullāh). Lahore, Sind Sagar Academy, 1944. 240p. (U)

689. Yādullāhī, Shihābuddīn — *Abū Dharr Ghifārī kā madhhab* (Viewpoint of Abū Dharr). Shahdadpur (Sind), Bazm-e-Adab, 1374/1954. (U)

690. al-Yāfī, 'Abd al-Karīm — "al-Nasl wa qaḍīyah taḥdīd 'ind al-Ghazālī, *Mahrajān al-Ghazzalī, Dimashq*, Mar. 61. (Population and its Control according to al-Ghazzālī—al-Ghazzālī Celebrations, Damascus, Mar. 61). al-Qāhirah (al-Majlis al-A'lā li-Ri'āyat Funūn wa'l-Ādāb wa'l-'Ulūm al-Ijtimā'īyah: 415–429. (A)

691. De Zayas, Farishta G. — "Considerations on al-Ghazzālī's Pragmatical and Mystical Approach to Zakāt" *Mahrajān al-Ghazzālī*, Dimashq—Mar. 61. al-Qāhriah, al-Majlis al-A'lā li-Ri'āyat al-Funūn wa'l-Ādāb wa'l-'Ulūm al-Ijtimā'īyah: 271–275.

6. MISCELLANEOUS [692–698]

692. Akbarābādī, Sa'īd Aḥmad — *Islām meṇ Ghulāmī kī ḥaqīqat* (*al-Riqq fi'l-Islām*), (Nature of Slavery in Islam). Delhi, Nadwatul Muṣannifin, 1357 A.H. 272p. (U)

693. Ghoraba, Hammoudah — "Islam and Slavery". *Islamic Quarterly* (London) 2(3) Oct. 55: 153–159.

694. a-Hadāwī, Muṣṭafā — *al-Riqq fi'l-ta'rikh wa fi'l-Islām* (Slavery in History and in Islam). al-Qāhirah, al-Sharikat al-'Arabīyah al-Sa'ūdīyah al-Muttaḥidah, 1963. (A)

695. Hasan, Riaz — "The Nature of Islamic Urbanization—A Historical Perspective", *Islamic Culture* (Hydrabad) 43(3), July 69: 233–237.

696. Iṣlāḥī, 'Abdul 'Aẓīm — "Qurbānī ma'āshi nuqṭa-e naẓar sē" (Immolation from Economic Viewpoint), Ta'mīr-e Ḥayāt (Lucknow) 12(4), 25 Dec. 74: 6, 13. (U)

697. Nadwī, Sayyid Sulaimān — "Qurbānī kā iqtiṣādī pahlū" (Economic Aspects of Immolation), *Ma'ārif* (Azamgarh) 39(2), Mar. 37: 170–176. (U)

698. al-Najjār, Aḥmad 'Abd al-'Azīz — *al-Mujtama' al-'Arabī fī marhalat al- taghyīr* (The Arab Society in Transition Phase). Beirut, Dār al-Fikr, 1970. (A)

7. BIBLIOGRAPHIES [699–700]

699. 'Aṭiyyah, Jamāl al-Dīn — "Dalīl al-bāḥith fi'l-iqtiṣād al-Islāmī" (A Guide to Researcher in Islamic Economics) *al-Muslim al-Mu'āṣir* (Beirut) Nov. 74: 142–151.

700. Khan, Muḥammad Akram — *Annotated Bibliography of Contemporary Economic Thought in Islam and Glossary of Economic Terms in Islam. Islamic Education* (Lahore). All Pakistan Education Congress, July–Aug., 1973.

CHAPTER ELEVEN

Contemporary Turkish Literature on Islamic Economics

*Professor Dr. Sabahuddin Zaim**

Introduction

We are in this research report concerned with the mass of material on Islamic Economics, written in Turkish language during the last fifty years of Republican Period. Therefore the very rich materials, written during the Ottoman Period, are not covered.

More than four thousand books are published, during the last fifty years, related to the topics of Islam. Out of them, about seven per cent are related to the specific subject of Islamic Economics, which are composed or translated by Turkish authors. The articles published in periodicals are excluded in these figures. Actually they are incomplete. Because, systematic classification of articles in National Library started only after 1950.

Totally, four per cent of publications related to Islamic Economics were printed before 1950, 22 per cent were published during the period of 1950 to 1960, and 74 per cent, that is, three-quarters are outcome of the last period of after 1960.

In the original text, these publications were classified according to the periods, topics, writer, publisher, etc., and the contents of the composed books summarized and *annotated*. In other words, this research report was originally arranged as an Annotated Bibliography, and on a subject-classification system slightly different from the one developed by Dr. Siddiqi in the Research Report No. 1 on the Contemporary Literature on Islamic Economics.

Later on, it was rearranged on the basis of the last mentioned system so

---

* Professor Dr. Sabahuddin Zaim is Professor of Economics and the head of the Institute of Social Development and Research of Faculty of Economics, University of Istanbul, Turkey.

as to create uniformity as well as to reap the benefits of a prearranged classification—without annotation.

Therefore I would like to express my gratitude to Mr. Azmatullah Khan of the Islamic Foundation who has rearranged the material and edited it for publication.*

---

* There is nothing new to be pointed out in this note. Thus, (i) inverted commas are used to differentiate an article from a book (for which no commas are used); (ii) the English translation of a work is given in parenthesis; (iii) the name of the journal is also made distinct from the name of the publisher, etc.; (iv) in the case of a book (T) indicates that the work is a translation and an asterisk (*) denotes that there is an introductory note about the relevant work in the appendix at the end of this bibliography. *Editor*.

The Structure of the Publication on Islamic Economics in Turkey by percentage (%)

Subject	Composed books	Transl. books	Composed articles	Transl. articles	Total
1 ECONOMIC PHILOSOPHY OF ISLAM	39	52	9	–	100
2 ECONOMIC SYSTEM OF ISLAM					
i Sources and Precedents ...	29	18	46	7	100
ii General	43	14	43	–	100
iii Comparative Studies	46	31	23	–	100
iv Socialistic Trends	70	30	—	–	100
v Ownership	—	100	—	–	100
vi Land: Ownership and Tenure	—	—	100	–	100
vii Sharecropping	—	—	—	–	100
viii Partnership and Profit Sharing	50	50	—	–	100
ix Consumption	—	50	50	–	100
x Business and Trade	75	—	25	–	100
xi *Hisbah*	—	—	—	–	—
xii Co-operation	100	—	—	–	100
xiii Hoarding	—	—	—	–	—
xiv Public Finance: General ...	37	63	—	–	100
xv Public Finance: *Zakāt* ...	72	—	28	–	100
xvi Public Finance: *'Ushr*, *Kharāj*, etc.	50	50	—	–	100
xvii Inheritance	—	—	—	–	—
xviii Social Security	37	63	—	–	100
xix Endowments	—	—	—	–	—
xx Insurance	—	—	—	–	—
xxi Banking without Interest ...	—	20	80	–	100
xxii Foreign Trade	—	—	—	–	—
xxiii Labour and Industrial Relations	50	29	21	–	100
xxiv Family Planning	67	—	33	–	100
xxv Economic Development ...	—	33	67	–	100
xxvi Audit and Accounts	—	—	—	–	—
3 ISLAMIC CRITIQUE OF CONTEMPORARY ECONOMICS: THEORIES AND SYSTEMS					
i Capitalism	—	67	33	–	100
ii Interest	—	12	88	–	100
iii Commercial Interest	—	—	—	–	—
iv *Ribā'l Faḍl*	—	—	100	–	100
v Speculation, Stock Exchange	—	—	—	–	—
vi Lottery	—	—	—	–	—
vii Socialism and Communism ...	43	36	21	–	100
viii Marxian Theories	—	—	—	–	—
ix Socialism and Capitalism, etc.	—	—	100	–	100

Subject	Composed books	Transl. books	Composed articles	Transl. articles	Total
4 ECONOMIC ANALYSIS IN AN ISLAMIC FRAMEWORK					
i General	14	43	43	–	100
ii Consumption	—	—	—	–	—
iii Production and Enterprise ...	—	—	—	–	—
iv Profit Sharing	—	—	—	–	—
v *Zakāt*	67	—	33	–	100
vi Abolition of Interest	34	33	33	–	100
vii Nature of Islamic Economics	40	40	20	–	100
5 HISTORY OF ECONOMIC THOUGHT IN ISLAM					
i General	50	50	—	–	100
ii Ibn Khaldun	—	100	—	–	100
iii Ibn Taymiah	—	—	—	–	—
iv Abu Yusuf	—	100	—	–	100
v Yahya Ibn Adam	—	—	—	–	—
vi Abu Ja'far Dimashqi	—	—	—	–	—
vii Nasir al-Din Tusi	—	—	—	–	—
viii Others	—	100	—	–	100
6 MISCELLANEOUS	53	40	7	–	100
7 BIBLIOGRAPHIES...	100	—	—	–	100
TOTAL PUBLICATIONS OF ISLAMIC ECONOMICS	37	34	28	1	100

1. ECONOMIC PHILOSOPHY OF ISLAM [1–23]

1. Akseki, A. Hamdi — *Islām Dini, Itikạd, Ibadet ve Ahlāk* (Islam, Faith, Practice and Ethics). Ankara: Kanaat Basimevi, 1950. 442p.
2. Albayrak, Sadīk — *Sōmūrūye Karşi Islām* (Islām vs. Exploitation). Ankara: Akçağ Kitabevi, 1971. 197p.
3. Arslan, Ali (T) — *Islāmi Hareketin Ahlāki Temelleri* (Ethical Basis of Islamic Movement). Istanbul: Tūrkiye Basimevi, 1967. 73p.
4. Atay, Hūseyin (T) — *Islām Hukuku Felsefesi* (The Philosophy of Islamic Law). Ankara: Ankara University Basimevi, 1973. 391p.
5. Babanzade, Ahmet Naim — *Islām Ahlākinin Esaslari* (Ethical Principles of Islam). Istanbul: Yūcel Yayinlari, 1963. 88p.
6. Basrici, Bekir and Topuz, Mustafa (T) — *Islamda Hayat Nizami* (Islamic Way of Life). Istanbul: Hilāl Yayinlari, 1965.
7. Belli, Abdul Mecid — *Adalet Mūlkūn Temelidir* (Justice is the Basis of the Social Order). Istanbul: Ahmet Sait Matbaasi, 1964. 216p.
8. Davudoğlu, A. (T) — *Būlugul Meram Selāmet Yōllari* (The Way of Peace). Istanbul: Nurettin Yuycan Matbaasi, 1968. 4 vols.
9. Demircan, Ali Riza — *Islām Nizami, Suleymaniye Minberinden* (The Islamic Order from the Pulpit of the Sulemaniye Mosque). Istanbul: Fatih Matbaasi, 1974. 375p.
10. Demirer, Tūzūn (T) — *Islāmda Iktisat Nizami* (Iktisadi Meseleleri ve Islāmda Cōzūm Tarzi) (The Economic Problem of Man and its Solution in Islam). Istanbul: Turkiye Basimevi, 1966. 46p.
11. Eker, Hamid (T) — *Islām ve Modern Ilim* (Islam and the Modern Sciences). Istanbul: Dizerkonca Matbaasi, 1970. 224p.
12. En Nebhani, Tekiyuddin (T) — *Islām Nizami* (The Islamic Social Order).
13. Hallaf, Abdulvehhab — *Islām Hukuk Felsefesi* (Islamic Legal Philosophy). Ankara: University Basimevi, 1973. 391p.
14. Ilhami, Agar (T) — *Islām Inkilābi* (Islamic Revolution). Ankara: Sinan Matbaasi, 1959.
15. Karakoc, Sezai — "Insanliğin Dirilişi, Bunalimin Kaynaği." (Revival of Humanity—The Main Source of Trouble.) *Diriliş Aylik Dergi* No. 3, November, 1974, pp. 3–6.
16. Mansur, Adnan M. (T) — *Islāmda Sosyal Adalet* (Social Justice in Islam). Istanbul: Cağaloğhlu Yayinevi, 1962. 2 vols.

17. Özkan, Kāzim

Allahin Kanunlari, Islāmiyette Sasyal Adalat (Divine Laws and Social Justice in Islam). Istanbul: Burhaneddin Erenler Matbaasi, 1965. 64p.

18. Riza, M. Rashid

Kur'ani Kerim Göre Servet Haklari ve Iktisadi Islahat (Accumulation of wealth from the Quranic point of view).

19. Şener, Abdul Kadir (T)

Islāmda Ahlāk Nizami (Ethical Viewpoint of Islam). Istanbul: Turkiye Basimevi, 1966. 50p.

20. Tabbara, Afif Abdulfettah (T)

Islāmian Ruhu (The Spirit of Islam). Istanbul: Turkiye Basimevi, 1965. 159p.

21. Topçu, Nurettin

Ahlāk Nizami (The Ethical Order). Istanbul: Çeltūt Matbaasi, 1961. 109p.

22. Topuz, Mustafa and Basrici, Bekir (T)

Islāmda Yayat Nizami (The Islamic Way of Life). Istanbul: Hilal Yayinlari, 1965. 151p.

23. Ülkümen, Lūtfi

Muztarib Dūnya ve Kurtuluş Yolu (The Troubled World and its Salvation). Erzurum: Atatūrk Üniversitesi Basimevi, 1971. 47p.

2. ECONOMIC SYSTEM OF ISLAM [24–142]

i. Sources and Precedents: 24–51

24. Akif, Mehmet (T)

Hazreti Ali nin Bir Devlet Adamina Emirnamesi (Hazrat 'Ali's Instructions to an Administrator). Istanbul: Nur'u-osmaniye Matbaasi, 1963, 32p.

25. Ansay, Sabri Şakir

Hukuk Tarihinde Islām Hukuku (Islamic Law in Legal History). Ankara: Ajanstūrk Matbaasi, 1958. 323p.

26. Aydin, Mehmet (T)

Islām Medeniyeti Esas ve Menşei (Sources of Islamic Civilization). Istanbul: Turkiye Basimevi, 1968. 232p.

27. Ayiter, Ferit

"Eski Türk Hususi Hukuna Ait Bazī Notlar; Einige Bemerkungen Uber Das Alt Turkishe Privatrecht" (Some Notes on the Old Turkish Personal Law). *Iktisat Fakūltesi Mecmuasi*. Vol. 11, No. 1–4; 1949–50; pp. 417–436.

28. Berki, Ali Himmet

Hukuk Tarihinden Islām Hukuku (Islamic Law in Legal History). Ankara: Örnek Matbaasi, 1955. 163p.

29. Bilmen, Omer Nasuhi

Hukuki Islamiyye ve Istilahat-i Fikhiyye Kamusu (Islamic Law and Dictionary of Legal (Fiqhi) Terms). Istanbul: Istanbul University Yayinlari, 1970.

30. Dūzdag, Ertugrul M. — *Seyhulislam Ebusuud Efendi Fetvalari Işiğinda 16 Asir Turk Hayati* (Life in the 16th Century Turkey in the light of Ebusuud Efendi's Fetwas). Istanbul: Hikmet Gazetecilik Ltd., Şti., 1972. 245p.

31. Ed Dūrī, Abdulaziz — "Hicri Dōrdūncū Asirda Irak Iktisat Tarihi" (Economic History of Iraq in the 4th Century Hijri) *Iktisat Fakūltesi Mecmuasi*. Vol. 15, No. 1–4, 1953–54; pp. 344–351.

32. El Ali, Salih Ahmet — "Hicri I. Yūzyilda Basrada Sosyal ve Ekonomik Dūzen". (Social and Economic Structure of Basra Society in First Century Hijri). *Iktisat Fakūltesi Mecmuasi*, Vol. 15, No. 1–4, 1953–54; pp. 352–360.

33. Erim, Turgut — "Roma, Bizans ve Kilise Bankaciliği" (Banking in Rome during the Byzantium Period and the part Played by the Church). *Akbank Būlteni*, Vol. 10, No. 7, 1966, pp. 12–15.

34. Eyice, Semavi — "Ilk Osmanli Devrinin Dini—Içtimai Bir Mūessesesi Zaviyeler ve Zaviyeli Camiler (Zawia and the Mosque with the Zawia—A Religious Institution of the First Ottoman Era). *Iktisat Fakūltesi Mecmuasi*, Vol. 23, No. 1–2; 1962–63, pp. 3–80.

35. Filipovic, Nedim — "Bosna Hersekte Timar Sisteminin Inkişafinda Bazi Hususiyetler" (Some Characteristic Features of the Development of Timar System In Bosnia—Herzgovina). *Iktisat Fakūltesi Mecmuasi*, Vol. 15, No. 1–4, 1953–54; pp. 154–188.

36. Harufe, Alaeddin — "Yahudi, Hristiyan ve Islām Şeriatinda Riba" (The Institution of Interest in Jewish, Christian and Islamic Jurisprudence). *Gurbet Mecmuasi*, Vol. VII, 1965.

37. Inalcik, Halil — "XV. Asir Turkiye Iktisadi ve Içtimai Tarihi Kaynaklari". (Sources of Economic and Social History of 15th Century Turkey.) *Ankara University Ilahiyat Fakūltesi. Islām Ilmleri Enstitūtūsū Dergisi*. Vol. 15/16, No. 1–4, 1953–54, pp. 51–57.

38. „ „ — "Islām Arazi ve Vergi Sisteminin Teşekkūlū ve Osmanli Devrindeki Şekillerle Mukayesesi." (Operation of the Land Tax System and its Comparison with Prevalent Systems in the Ottoman Empire.) Ankara University. *Ilahiyat Fakūltesi Islam Ilimleri Enstitusi Sergisi*, Vol. 1, No. 1, 1959, pp. 29–46.

39. Karcioğlu, Nuri Akif (T) — *Islām Şeriati*. (Islamic Law.) Ankara: Baylan Basin ve Ciltevi, 1969, 95p.

40. Kreseviakovic, Hamdiya — "Eski Sarayevoda Esnaf ve Sanatlar." (Arts and Artisans in the Old Saray-Bosina.) *Iktisat Fakūltesi Mecmuasi*, Vol. 17, No. 1–4, 1955–56, pp. 359–379.

41.	Meylani, Ahmed (T)	*Fikh'i Islām Tarihi*. (History of Islamic Law.) Istanbul: Ōzdemir Basimevi, 1973. 496p.
42.	Ozek, Ali	"Hazreti Omerin Idaresi." (Administration of Hazrat Omer.) *Buyuk Tūrkiye Mecmuasi*, Vol. 1. No. 7–8, 1970.
43.	,, ,,	"Islām Iktisadina Dair Hadisler." (Hadith About Economic Activity.) *Buyuk Tūrkiye Mecmuasi*, Vol. 1, No. 7–8, Oct./Nov. 1971.
44.	Ōzturk, Osman	*Osmanli Hukuk Tarihinde Mecelle*. (Codification of Islamic Law in the Ottoman Period.) Istanbul: Irfan Matbaasi, 1973, 431p.
45.	Sahillioğlu, Halil	"Bir Multezimin Zimem Defterine Gōre XV. Yūzyil Sonunda Osmanli Darphane Mukataalari." (Minting of Coins During the Ottoman Period.) *Iktisat Fakūltesi Mecmuasi*, Vol. 23, No. 1–2, 1962–63, pp. 145–218.
46.	Togan, Zeki Velidi	"Reşideddin'in Mekutuplarinda Anadolunun Iktisadi ve Medeni Hayatina Ait Kayitlar." (Notes on Economic and Civic Life of Anatolia as Depicted in the Letters of Reşideddin.) *Iktisat Fakūltesi Mecmuasi*, Vol. 15, No. 1–4, 1953–54, pp. 33–50.
47.	Tuğ, Salih (T)	*Islāmin Hukuk Ilmine Yardimlari*. Makaleler Kūlliyati. (A Guide to Islamic Law.) Istanbul: Milliyetçiler Derneği Neşriyati, 1962, 146p.
48.	Turan, Osman	"Selçuklularda Faizle para Ikrazi Mūnasebetiyle Zoraki Tenkid." (A Critical Study of the Credit System During the Selzuk Period.) *Ilahiyat Fakūltesi Dergisi*, Vol. 1, 1955, pp. 23–30.
49.	Varli, Mustafa (T)	*Islāmda Helal ve Haram*. (The Halal and Haram in Islam.) Ankara: Ōzdemir Basimevi, 1970. 387p.
50.	Yavuz, Fikri	*Islām Fikhi ve Hukuku*. (Islamic Law and Fiqh.) Istanbul: Ahmed Sait Matbaasi, 1970. 349p.
51.	Zapsu, Ahdurrahim	Helal ve Haram. (Legitimate and Illegitimate.) Istanbul: Burhaneddin Matbaasi, 1947. 32p.

ii. General: 52–58

52.	Binatli, Yusuf Ziya	"Islam Dininin Ekonomik Alana Etkisi." (The Influence of Islam on Economic Activity.) *Ekischir Iktisadi ve Ticari Ilimler Akademisi Dergisi*, Vol. 1, 1965, pp. 193–199.
53.	En Nabhani, Tekiyuddin (T)	*Islam Nizami* (The Islamic Order.)

54. Karakoç, M. Sezai — *Islām Toplumunun Ekonomik Strūktūrū* (Economic Structure of an Islamic Society). Istanbul: Turkiye Basimevi, 1967. 62p.

55. Karagūlle, Suleyman — "Islāmiyette Iktisadi Deveran" (Circular Flow of Wealth in Islam). *Gurbet Mecmuasi*, Vol. 1, No. 7, 1965, p. 7.

56. Kozdal, Ismail — *Islām Būyūklerine Gōre Içtimai Yapi* (Social Structure of Islam) Ozdemir Basimevi, 1969. 183p.

57. Ozek, Ali — "Iktisadi Gerçekler" (Economic Realities). *Būyūk Tūrkiye Mecmuasi*, Vol. 1, No. 11–12, Feb., 1971,

58. Pişkin, Mehmet — *Islāmda Sosyal Dūzen* (The Islamic Social Order). Ankara: Ulusoğlu Matbaasi, 1960. 64p.

iii. Comparative Studies: 59–71

59. Akin, Ismail Hakki — *Islām Şahsiyetçiliği* (Individualism and Islam). Istanbul: Ahmet Said Matbaasi, 1972. 144p.

60. Aral, Namik Zeki — "Islām ve Iktisadi Liberalizm" (Islam and Economic Liberalism) *Tūrkiye Iktisat Gazetesi*, Vol. 15, No. 727, 1967, pp. 1–7.

61. Atilhan, Cevat Rifat — *Tarih Boyunca Islām Hukimiyeti ve Uğradiği Suikastlar* (Superiority of Islam and the Forces Sabotaging Islam). Istanbul: Çelikcilt Matbaasi, 1968. 222p.

62. Kuşçu, Kemal (T) — *Garb Materyalizmi Karşisinda Islām* (Islam vs. Western Materialism). Istanbul: Sōnmez Neşriyat ve Matbaacilik, 1967. 230p.

63. Kutbi, Muhammad Hasan — *Islām Her Zaman ve Her Yerde en Uygūn Kanundur* (Islam is the Best System for all Times and for all Places). Ankara: Şark Matbaasi, 1966. 18p.

64. Moldibi, Adnan — "Modern Iktisat ve Islām" (Modern Economy and Islam). *Hilāl Mecmuasi*, Vol. 5, No. 49, Feli, 1965, pp. 18–21.

65. Ozek, Sadik (T) — *Marksizm ve Kapitalizm Karşisinda Islām* (Islam vs. Marxism and Capitalism). Istanbul: Eskin Matbaasi, 1970.

66. Temel, Ali — *Islām Iktisadinin Ūstūnlūğū* (Superiority of Islamic Economics System). Istanbul: Fatih Matbaasi, 1971. 70p.

67. Tuğ, Salih (T) — *Modern Iktisad ve Islām* (Modern Economy and Islam). Istanbul: Yağmur Yayinlari, 1963. 47p.

68. Ūçişiklar, Hasan K. *Tūrkiyede Gizli Devletler: Islām Duşmanlari Kommunizm, Siyonizm, Masonluk Histiyanlik; Kurtuluş çareleri, Zaferler, Mūjdeler* (Secret Forces Against Islam in Turkey: Communism, Zionism, Freemasonry, Christianity, Solutions, Victories, Good News), Istanbul: Sinan Matbaasi, 1965, 32p.

69. Varli, Mustafa *Yagāne Dunya Nizami* (Islam The Only World Order). Ankara: Nur Yayinlari, 1966. 56p.

70. Zaim, Sabahuddin *Modern Iktisat ve Islām* (Modern Economy and Islam). Istanbul: Fatih Matbaasi, 1969, 31p.

71. ,, ,, "Modern Iktisat ve Islam" (Islam and the Modern Economy). *Islām Dusuncesi Mecmuasi*, Vol. 2, No. 5, 1968, pp. 317–328.

iv. Socialistic Trends: 72–81

72. Bercavi, Faik (T) *Islāmda Sosyalizm* (Socialism of Islam). Istanbul: Işik Basimevi. 1964. 54p.

73. Beder, Hakki *Islāmda Sol ve Hayat* (Life and Meaning of Left in Islam). Ankara: Bilgi Yayinevi, 1970, 108p.

74. Berkes, Niyazi *Arap Dūnyasinda Islāmiyet, Milliyetçilik ve Sosyalizm* (Islam, Nationalism and Socialism in the Arab World). Istanbul: Fono Matbaasi, 1969. 246p.

75. Cemal, M. *Islām Iktisadiyat ve Ictimayati Sosyalizm ile Kapitalizmi Telif Edebilir* (Sociology and Economics of Islam can be Reconciled with Socialism and Capitalism). Istanbul: Vakit Matbaasi, 1924. 15p.

76. Cerrahoğlu, A. *Islāmiyet ve Osmanli Sosyalistleri, Islāmiyet ve Yōncū Sosyalistler* (Islam and Ottoman Socialists, Islam and Socialists of Yon Group). Istanbul: Ersa Matbaacilik Kol, Sti. 1964. 34p.

77. ,, ,, *Islāmiyet ve Sosyalism Bagdaşabilir mi? Isa Sosyalist Midir? Yeni Asrin Dini* (Can Islam and Socialism be Reconciled? Was Eesa (peace be upon him) Socialist?—A Look at the Religion of the 20th Century). Istanbul: B. Kervan Matbaasi, 1962. 32p.

78. Doğanpala, Salih *Sağ Sol Meselesi, Islāmin Hūkmū* (The Problem of Right and Left in Islam). Bursa. Bursa Yayinevi, 1966. 77p.

79. Kayalar, Cevdet (T) *Islāmi Sosyalizm* (Islamic Socialism). Istanbul: Hūsnūtabiat Matbaasi, 1967. 61p.

80. Kayalar, Cevdet (T) — *Islāmi Sosyalizmin Ozeti Islāmin Degişmez Prensipleri Hakkinda Tartisma* (Summary of Discussions On Islamic Socialism and Unchallengeable Principles of Islam). Istanbul: Hūsnūtabiat Matbaasi, 1976. 61p.

81. Niyazoğlu, Y. A. (T) — *Islām Sosyalizmi* (Islamic Socialism). Hareket Yayinlari.

v. Ownership 82–84

82. Menna, El-Kettan (T) — "Islāmda Mūlkiyet" (Property Rights in Islam). *Hilal.* Vol. 5, No. 54, July, 1966, pp. 12–14.

83. Tarhan, Sami (T) — "Kur'ani Kerime Gōre Servet Haklari ve Iktisadi Islahat" (Rights of Possession of Wealth and Economic Reforms in Accordance with the Quran). *Islām*, Vol. 4, No. 8, May, 1961, pp. 233–235.

84. Varli, Mustafa (T) — *Islāmda Mulkiyet Nizami* (Property Rights in Islam). Istanbul: Turkiye Basimevi, 1967, 69p.

vi. Land: Ownership and Tenure: 85

85. Ōzek, Ali — "Islāmin Tarim Hakkindaki Gōrūsūa" (Islamic View About Agriculture). *Būyūk Tūrkiye Mecmuasi*, Vol. 1, No. 21, Nov. 1972.

vii. Sharecropping

viii. Partnership and Profit Sharing: 86–87

86. Dūlger, Bahadir (T) — *Kaynaklara Dōnūş* (Return on The Use of Resources). Izmir: Endūstri Basim ve Yayinevi, 1969. 33p.

87. Riza, M. Rashid — *Kurani Kerime Gōre Servet Haklari ve Iktisadi Islahat* (Accumulation of wealth from the Quranic viewpoint).

ix. Consumption: 88–89

88. Çiftçi, Ebusseyt (T) — *Islāmda Israf ve Lūks* (Islamic View About Luxury and Waste). Ankara: Elif Matbaacilik, 1972. 123p.

89. Karagūlle, Sūleyman — "Islāmda Fiyat Tahdidi Meselesi" (The Problem of Ceiling on Prices in Islam). *Islām Medeniyeti Mecmuasi*, Vol. 2, No. 8, 1969, pp. 22–24.

x. Business and Trade: 90–93

90. Inan, Yusuf Ziya — *Islāmda Ticari Ahlāk* (Business Ethics of Islam). Istanbul: Sinan Matbaasi, 1964. 240p.

91. Karaçōğūr, Osman — *Islāmda Ticaret Hukuku* (Islamic Commercial Law). Konya: Yeni Kitap Basimevi, 1966. 48p.

92. ,, ,, — *Islāmda Ticari Ahlāk ve Rizik Meselesi* (Business Ethics of Islam and the Problem of Providence). Istanbul: Fazilet Kitabevi, 1974. 80p.

93. Karagūlle, Sūleyman — "Islāmda Fiyat Tahdidi" (Ceiling Prices in Islam). *Gurbet Mecmuasi*, Vol. 1, No. 13, 1965.

xi. Hisbah

xii. Co-operation: 94

94. Bora, Cemal — *Toplum Kalkinmasinda Din Gorevlilerinin Ōdevi, Birlik Beraberlik ve Kooperatifiçilik* (The Co-operative Movement, Brotherhood and the Functions of Religion in Social Development). Ankara: Divan Matbaasi, 1970. 47p.

xiii. Hoarding

xiv. Public Finance: General: 95–102

95. Genceli, Ali (T) — *Islāmda Hūkūmet* (The Islamic Government). Istanbul: Ozdemir Matbaasi, 1971. 902p.

96. Hatemi, Hūseyin — *Islām Hukukunda Devlet Yapisi* (Organisation of State in Islam). Istanbul: Ahmet Sait Matbaasi, 1970. 120p.

97. Kuşçu, Kemal (T) — *Islāmda Siyasi Dūşūnce ve Idare Ūzerinde Araştirmalar* (Islamic Political Thought and Administration). Istanbul: Ahmed Sait Matbaasi, 1963. 181p.

98. ,, ,, — *Islāmda Devlet Idaresi* (The Islamic Conduct of State). Istanbul: Ahmed Sait Matbaasi, 1963. 302p.

99. Ōzdenōren, Rasim (T) — *Islām Devletinde Mali Yapi* (Public Finance in Islam). Istanbul: Fatih Matbaasi, 1972. 272p.

100. Tuğ, Salih — "Islām vergi Hukukunun Ortaya Çikişi" (The Development of Tax System in Islam). *Maliye Enstitūsū Konferanslari*, No. 7. Istanbul: University of Istanbul, 1973.

101. Zeydan, Abdulkerim (T) — *Islām Hukukunda Fert ve Devlet* (Islam Anaysa Hukuku) (State and the Individual in Islamic Law). Gary (Indiana), USA., IIFSO, 1970. 94p.

102. Zengin, Ali (T) — *Islāmda Siyaset Nizami* (Political Theory of Islam). Istanbul. Turkiye Basimevi, 1972. 56p.

xv. Public Finance: Zakāt: 103–109

103. Iz, Mahir — "Zekāt" (Zakāt). *Islām Düşüncesi Mecmuasi*. Vol. 2, No. 7, May, 1969, pp. 419–424.

104. Ozerdim, Yakup — *Islām Dininde Zekāt* (Zakāt in the Religion of Islam). Bursa. Emektar Matbaasi, 1962. 25p.

105. Salih, M. Erzurumlu Yeşiloğlu — *Islām Dini Celilinde Zekāt* (Zakāt in Islam). Istanbul: Burhaneddin Erenler Matbaasi, 1949. 16p.

106. Tanribuyruğu, H. H. Salih — *Zekāt, Sadaka-i Fitr ve Bayram Risalesi* (Zakāt, Sadaqat and Charity). Izmir: Izmir Basimevi, 1963. 24p.

107. Tuğ, Salih — "Zekātin Yeniden Merkezilestiril Mesi" (Collection of Zakāt). *Islām Medeniyeti*, Vol. 3, No. 28, Feb. 1973, pp. 30–33.

108. ,, ,, — *Islām Vergi Hukukunun Ortaya Çikişi* (The Development of Islamic Tax System). Ankara: Ankara University Basimevi, 1963. 112p.

109. Yavuz, Yunus Vehbi* — *Islāmda Zekāt Muessesesi* (The Institution of Zakāt). Istanbul: Ahmet Sait Matbaasi, 1972. 390p.

xvi. Public Finance: 'Ushr, Kharāj, etc.: 110–111

110. Dinyith, Daniel (T) — *Islām ve Cizye* (Islam and the Cizye Tribute).

111. Tuğ, Salih* — Islam Vergi Hukukunem Ortaya Çikişi (The Development of Islamic Tax System). Istanbul: Sermet Matbaasi, 1963, 17p.

xvii. Inheritance

xviii. Social Security: 112–115

112. Eskicioğlu, O. and Fiğlali, E. R. (T) — *Islāmda Sosyal Dayanişma* (Social Solidarity in Islam). Istanbul: Ahmed Sait, 1969. 199p.

113. Fiğlali, E. R. and Eskicioğlu, O. (T) — *Islāmda Sosyal Dayanişma* (Social Solidarity in Islam). Istanbul: Ahmet Sait Matbaasi, 1969. 199p.

114. Ōzakyol, Sami — *Cemiyetin Refahi* (Social Welfare). Islamda Ticaret, Zirat, ve Sanat Trade, Agriculture and Industry In Islam). Izmir: Bizim Yol Matbaasi, 1965. 229p.

115. Turgut, Ahmet Hamdi — *Islāmda Sosyal Hizmet Mūessesesi* (The Institution of Social Security in Islam). Ankara: Bayur Matbaacilik Ṣti, 1961. 11p.

xix. Endowments

xx. Insurance

xxi. Banking without Interest: 116–120

116. Aral, Namik Zeki — *Islām Bankasi* (Islamic Bank). *Tūrkiye Iktisat Gazetesi*, Vol. 2, No. 6–7.

117. Coṣkun, Mustafa — "Faiz, Banka ve Islām" (Interest, Banking and Islam). *Islām Medeniyeti Mecmuasi*, Vol. 3, No. 25, 29 and 30. Nov. 1972, pp. 38–41. March, 1973, pp. 36–40. April, 1973, pp. 27–32.

118. Cem, Ibnuttayyar — "Faizsiz Banka (Interest Free Bank). *Hilāl Dergisi*. Vol. 1, No. 48, 1964.

119. Gūran, M. T. (T) — *Faizsiz Banka—Islām ve Modern Bankacilikta Eḡilimler* (Interest Free Banking, Islam and the Trends in Modern Banking). Ankara: Ayyildiz Matbaasi, 1969. 79p.

120. Inalcik, Halil — "Islām ve Modern Bankacilik" (Islam and Modern Banking). Hilāl Mecmuasi, Vol. 9, No. 98, Dec. 1969, pp. 18–26.

xxii. Foreign Trade

xxiii. Labour and Industrial Relations: 121–134

121. Algūl, H. and Ṣekerci, O. (T) — *Islāmda Beṣeri Mūnasebetler* (Human Relations in Islam). Istanbul: Ṣamil Yayinevi, 1971. 204p.

122. Armaḡan, Nihat (T) — *Islāmda Ṣura* (The Counsel in Islam). Istanbul: Fatih Matbaasi, 1973. 124p.

123. Aslangūl, Halil — *Islāmda Çaliṣmanin Onemi* (The Importance of Work in Islam). Ankara: Kardeṣ Matbaasi, 1962. 18p.

124. Çakir, Musa — *Çaliṣmak Ibadettir. Islāmda Iṣçi ve Iṣverenin Hakki* (To Work is to Worship. Rights of Employees and Employers in Islam). Istanbul: Fatih Matbaasi, 1967. 50p.

125. Eygi, Mehmet — *Şevket Muslümanlar Nasil Çalişmali* (How a Muslim Worker Should Work). Istanbul: Bedir Yayinevi, 1970. 32p.

126. Inan, Yusu Ziya — *Islām Toplumunda Işçi ve Tacirin Sosyal Borcu* (Functions of Labour and Businessmen in an Islamic Society). Istanbul: Sinan Matbaasi, 1967. 211p.

127. Kaplan, Cemeleddin, Mūfti of Adana — *Islāmda Işçi Işveren Mūnaşebetleri* (Employee and Employer Relationship in Islam). Ankara: Elif Matbaacilik. 1971. 103p.

128. Okur, Rana — *Tūrk Islām Medeniyetinde iş Ahlaki* (Ethics of Labour in an Islamic Society). Ankara: Ayyildiz Matbaasi, 1969. 70p.

129. Şekerci, O. and Algūl, O. (T) — *Islāmda Beşeri Mūnasebetler* (Human Relations in Islam). Istanbul: Şamil Yayinevi, 1971. 204p.

130. Şevket, Eşrefefendizade — *Islāmda Emek sermaye* (*Saive Sermaye Mucadelatinin Dinen Sureti Halli*) Anglican Kilisesine Cevap (Labour and Capital in Islam for the Struggle between Labour and Capital—An Answer to the Anglican Church). Ankara: Kardes Matbaasi, 1964. 57p.

131. Toksari, Ihsan (T) — *Islāmda iş Ahkāmi ve Isci Haklai* (Labour Laws in Islam). Istanbul: Fatih Matbaasi, 1968. 109p.

132. Ūlgener, Sabri, F. — "XIV Asidanberi Esnaf Ahlaki ve Sikayeti Mucip Halleri (Artisan Character and the Problem of their Grievances since the 14th Century). *Iktisat Fakūltesi Mecmuasi*, Vol. 11, No. 1–4, 1949–50, pp. 388–396.

133. Zaim, Sabahuddin — "Işçi Meselesi Demokrasi ve Islam" (Labour Problems, Democracy and Islam). *Milli Isik Mecmuasi*, Vol. 7, No. 24, 1969, pp. 29–32.

134. „ „ — "Milli Mefkūremiz ve Sendikacilik" (National and Islamic Objectives of Trade Unionism). *Būyūk Tūrkiye Mecmuasi*, Vol. 1, No. 11–12, Feb./Mar., 1971, pp. 23–29.

xxiv. Family Planning: 135–137

135. Galip, Mūbarek — *Arzda Nufus-i Islām. Vesaike Mūstenit Istatistikler* (Muslim Population of the World—Some Authentic Statistical Information), 1923.

136. Nazmi, Ahmet — *Islāmda Tese'ul Yoktur* (Beggary in Islam). Istanbul: Ahmedi Matbaasi, 1929. 59p.

137. Zaim, Sabahuddin — "Nūfus Meselesi" (The Population Problem). Milli Işik Mecmuasi, Vol. 1, No. 25, May, 1969. pp. 27–28.

xxv. Economic Development: 138–142

138. Austrin, Jac — *Islām ve Iktisadi Gelişme* (Islam and Economic Development).

139. Barkan, O. Lūtfi and Ūlgener, Sabri — "Iktisadi Inhitat Tarihimizin Ahlāk ve Zihniyet Meseleleri" (Moral and Psychological Causes of Economic Deterioration). *Iktisat Fakūltesi Mecmuasi*, Vol. 11, No. 1–4, 1949–50, pp. 189–195. Vol. 12, No. 1–4, 1951, pp. 162–173.

140. Konur, Sabri (T) — "Ekonomik Gelişmenin Bazī Şartlari ve Islamin Faiz Telakkisi" (Economic Development and the Prohibition of Interest). *Kalkinan Dunya*, Vol. 23, No. 42–44, 1967.

141. Ūlgener, Sabri and Barkan, O. Lūtfi — "Iktisadi Inhitat Taihimizin Ahlāk ve Zihniyet Meseleleri" (Moral and Psychological Causes of Economic Deterioration). *Iktisat Fakūltesi Mecmuasi*. Vol. 11, No. 1–4, 1949–50, pp. 189–195; Vol. 12, No. 1–4, 1951, pp. 162–173.

142. Zaim, Sabahuddin — "Islami Ahlākin Iktisadi Gelismeye Tesiri" (The Influence of Islamic Character on Economic Development). *Milliyetci Tūrkiyeye Doğru*. Istanbul: Garanti Matbaasi, 1969, pp. 198–208.

xxvi. Audits and Accounts

3. ISLAMIC CRITIQUE OF CONTEMPORARY ECONOMICS [143–179]

i. Capitalism: 143–145

143. Ismail, Hakki (T) — *Islām Şahsiyetciliği* (Individualism and Islam). Istanbul: Ahmet Sait Matbaasi, 1972. 144p.

144. Aral, Namik Zeki — "Islām ve Iktisadi Liberalizm" (Islam and Economic Liberalism). *Tūrkiye Iktisat Gazetesi*, Vol. 15, No. 727, 1967, pp. 1–7.

145. (X) (T) — *Islām ve Kapitalizm* (Islam and Capitalism). Istanbul: Ūlke Matbaasi. 1969. 320p.

ii. Interest: 146–153

146. Aral, Namik Zeki — "Islam ve Faiz" (Islam and the Institution of Interest) *Tūrkiye Iktisat Gazetesi*, Vol. 8, No. 75.

147. Cenan, Mihriddin — "Bankalar ve Ikramiyeler" (Banking and Bonuses). *Islām Dergisi*, Vol. 8, No. 75.

148. Evrin, Sadettin — "Iktisat ve Faiz, Asrin Dini Muslumanlik" (Economics and Interest—Islam as a Religion of the Current Century). *Iktisadi Yūrūyūş*. No. 6.

149. Harufe, Alaeddin — "Yahudi, Hristiyan ve Islām Şeriatinda Riba" (The Institution of Interest in the Jewish, Christian and Islamic Jurisprudence). *Gurbet Mecmuasi*, Vol. 1, No. 4, 1965, pp. 4–6.

150. Imece, Basi — "Bankacilik Nezaman Başladī Ilk Bankalar ve Tekamul Safhalari" (When did the First Banking Start?). *Karinca Dergisi*, Vol. 32, No. 349, Jan. 1966, pp. 36–37.

151. Īşiksal, Cavide — "Kalkinmamizi Engelleyen Yūksek Faiz" (High Interest Rates Retard Economic Development). *Tūrkiye Iktisat Postasi*, Vol. 2, No. 25/26, 1968, pp. 23–28.

152. Kuşdemiroğlu, A. E. — "Sanayileşmiş Ūlkelerde Faiz Hadleri" (Interest Rates in the Industrialised Countries). *Istanbul Ticaret*, Vol. 12, No. 573, 1969, pp. 4–7.

153. Şekerci, Osman (T) — *Faiz Tarihi ve Islām* (History of the Institution of Interest and Islam). Istanbul. Toker Matbaasi, 1968. 45p.

iii. Commercial Interest

iv. Ribā'l Faḍl: 154–158

154. Aral, Namik Zeki — "Tefecilik ve Siyaset" (Usury and Politics). *Tūrkiye Iktisat Gazetesi*, Vol. 16, No. 768, 1968. pp. 1–7.

155 ,, ,, ,, — "Memlekette Tefecilik" (Usury and the Nation). *Tūrkiye Iktisat Gazetesi*, Vol. 16, No. 807, 1968.

156. ,, ,, ,, — "Tefecilik Hakkinda Meclis Araştirmasi" (Enquiries About the Institution of Usury—Report of the Parliamentary Sub-Committee). *Tūrkiye Iktisat Gazetesi*, Vol. 17, No. 829, 1969. pp. 1–8.

157. Ete, Muhlis — "Tefecilik" (Usury). *Iktisadi Yūrūyūş*, Vol. 28, No. 476, Dec. 1967. pp. 3–13.

158. Sevgen, Necibe — "Nasil Sōmūrūldūk Sarraflar" (How we are Exploited by the Saraffs). *Belgelerle Turk Taihi Dergisi*, Vol. 1, No. 13/15, Oct. 1968.

v. Speculation and Stock Exchange

vi. Lottery

vii. Socialism and Communism: 159–172

159. Aral, Namik Zeki — "Arap Sosyalizmi ve Islam Dini" (Arab Socialism and the Religion of Islam). *Türkiye Iktisat Gazetesi*, Vol. 15, No. 723, 1967, pp. 1–7.

160. Başaran, Cemali — *Islāmiyet ve Komunizm* (Islam and Communism). Balikesi. Alpkanlar Matbaasi, 1955. 41p.

161. Bercavi, Faik — *Islāmda Sosyalizm* (Socialism in Islam). Istanbul. Bozkurt Matbaasi, 1964. 56p.

162. Beylem, Erdinç — "Islamiyet ve Sosyalizm" (Islam and Socialism). *Hilāl Mecmuasi*. Vol. 5, No. 50, March, 1965, pp. 26–28.

163. Cerrahoğlu, A. — *Islāmiyet ve Osmanli Sosyalistleri; Islāmiyet ve Yōncū Sosyalistler* (Islam and the Ottoman Socialists; Islam and the Socialists of Yon Group). Istanbul: Ersa Matbaacilik Kollektif Sti, 1964. 34p.

164. Cumalioğlu, Fehmi — *Komunizm ve Islām* (Communism and Islam). Istanbul: Sōnmez Matbaacilik A.S., 1963. 129p.

165. Eygi, Mehmet Şevket — *Islāmiyet ve Sosyalizm* (Islam and Socialism). Istanbul: Ahmet Sait, 1969. 16p.

166. Hatiboğlu, Ahmed Hamdi (T) — *Islāmiyet ve Komunizm* Birbirine Zittīr (Islam vs. Communism). Istanbul: Sōnmez Matbaacilik, 1962, 38p.

167. Hatemi, Hūseyin Perviz — "Sosyalizm ve Islāmiyet Tartişmalari (Discussions on Islam and Socialism). *Fikir ve Sanatte Hareket*, Vol. 8, No. 5–9, 1966, p. 7.

168. ,, ,, ,, — *Islām Açisindan Sosyalizm* (Socialism from Islamic Point of View). Istanbul: Halk Matbaasi, 1967. 240p.

169. Kuşçu, Kemal (T) — *Komunizme Karşi Islām* (Islam vs. Communism). Istanbul: Sōnmez Neşriyat ve Matbaacilik A.Ş., 1961. 8p.

170. Kutlu Mustafa (T) — *Islām Gōzūyle Ihtilālci Sosyalizm* (Revolutionary Socialism from Islamic Point of View). Istanbul: Ozdemic Yayinlari, 1968. 103p.

171. Saran, A. K. (T) — *Sosyalizm ve Insan* (Socialism and Man). Istanbul: Şamil Yayinevi, 1970. 112p.

172. Tufekci, E. Avcioğlu (T) — *Sosyalizm ve Islāmiyet* (Socialism and Islam). Istanbul: Gūn Matbaasi, 1965. 88p.

viii. Marxian Theories

ix. Socialism and Capitalism: 173–174

173. Aral, Namik Zeki — "Çarpişan Iki Nizam" (The Two Conflicting Systems). *Türkiye Iktisat Gazetesi*, Vol. 15, No. 754, 1967, pp. 1–7.

174. Karagülle, Süleyman — "Marksizm ve Kapitalizm" (Marxism and Capitalism). *Gurbet Mecmuasi*, Vol. 1, No. 6, 1965, p. 7.

4. ECONOMIC ANALYSIS IN AN ISLAMIC FRAMEWORK [175–192]

i. General: 175–181

175. Karağaçli, Cemal (T) — *Islâm ve Çağdaş Ekonomik Doktrinler* (Islam and the Contemporary Economic Doctrines). Istanbul: Fatih Yayinevi. 144p.

176. Karagülle, Süleyman — *Islâmiyet ve Ekonomik Doktrinler* (Islam and the Economic Doctrines). Istanbul: Fatih Matbaasi, 1969. 94p.

177. ,, ,, — "Islâmda Iktisat Nizami" (Economic Doctrines of Islam). Gurbet Mecmuasi. Vol. 1, No. 8, 1965, p. 7.

178. Mert, Hamdi — "Islamin Iktisadi Esaslari" (Economic Principles of Islam). *Islâm Medeniyeti*, Vol. 1, No. 6, Jan, 1968, pp. 35–38.

179. Tabakoğlu, Ahmet — "Islam Iktisadina Giriş: Insan ve Madde" (Introduction to Economics of Islam, Materialism and Mankind). *Fikir ve Sanatte Hereket*, Vol. 7, No. 80, Aug., 1972, pp. 9–13.

180. Toksari, I. (T) — *Iktisat Prensipleri, Islâm ve Muasir Nizamlara Göre* (Economic Principles of Islam and Contemporary Doctrines). Istanbul: Fatih Matbaasi, 1968. 127p.

181. Zengin, Bahri (T) — *Islâm Ekonomisi, Teorik ve Pratik* (Economics of Islam in Theory and Practice). Istanbul: Özdemir Basimevi, 1973. 536p.

ii. Consumption

iii. Production and Enterprise

iv. Profit Sharing

v. Zakāt: 182–184

182. Carullah, Musa — *Zekāt* (Zakāt). Petrograd: Muhammed Alim Maksudef Matbaasi, 1916. 96p.

183. Dinçer, Nahit — *Zekāt* (Zakāt). Ankara: Guven Basimevi, 1954. 15p.

184. (X) — "Zekāt" (Zakāt). *Muslumanin Sesi*. Izmir, Vol. 4, No. 62, 1952, pp. 6–7.

vi. Abolition of Interest: 185–187

185. Aral, Namik Zeki — "Diyanet Işleri ve Faiz Meselesi" (The Problem of Interest). *Diyonet Isleri Baskanligi Dergisi*, Vol. 8, No. 90/91, 1969, pp. 362–365.

186. Beşer, Mehmet Hasan (T) — *Faiz* (Interest). Ankara: Tūrkiye Basimevi, 1966. 151p.

187. Tuğ, Salih — *Faiz Nazariyesi ve Islam* (Islam and the Theory of Interest). Istanbul: Ahmet Sait Matbaasi, 1966. 230p.

vii. Nature of Islamic Economics: 188–192

188. Çekmegil, Said M. — *Islāmda Iktisat Anlayisimiz* (Islāmda Iktisad) (An Understanding of Islam). Istanbul: Fakulteler Matbaasi, 1966. 113p.

189. Debbaoğlu, Ahmet — "Islām Iktisadina Giris: Fert, Cemiyet, Devlet" (Introduction to Economics of Islam: Individual, Society and the State). Fikir ve Sanatte Hereket Mecmuasi. Vol. 8, No. 85/86, 1973, pp. 13–18.

190. Ōzek, Ali (T) — *Islāmi Iktisadīn Esaslarī* (Principles of Islamic Economics). Istanbul: Fatih Matbaasi, 1969. 128p.

191. Ōzdenōren, Rasim (T) — "Islām Ekonomisi" (Islamic Economics). *Dirilis*. Vol. 1, Oct. 1969, pp. 30–36.

192. Papatya, Nail — *Islāmda Iktisat* (Economics of Islam). *Izmir Hoşgōnūl*, Matbaasi, 1967. 13p.

5 HISTORY OF ECONOMIC THOUGHT [193–204]

i. General: 193–194

193. Arslan, Ali — *Ihya'ul Ulumuddin* (Reconstruction of Islamic Knowledge). Yaylacik Matbaasi. 8 vols, 1973.

194. Fiğlali, E. R. and Eskicioğlu, O. (T) — *Islāmda Siyasi ve Iktisadi Mezhepler Tarihi* (History of Political and Economic Doctrines of Islam). Istanbul: Yağmur Yayinevi, 1970. 301p.

ii. Ibn Khaldun: 195

195. Kadiri, Zakir (T) — *Tercemei Mukaddeme-i Ibn'i Khalduns* (Translation of Ibn Khaldun's Muqqadima). Istanbul: Maarif Basimevi, 1957. 3 vols.

iii. Ibn Taymiah

iv. Abu Yusuf: 196–198

196. Erdoğan, Naim (T) — *Imami Azamdan Cevaplar* (Answers to Important Fiqha questions by Imam-e Azam). Istanbul: Yaylacik Matbaasi, 1969. 79p.

197. Ōzek, Ali (T) — *Kitabul Haraç* (Kitabul Kharaj). Istanbul: Fakulteler Matbaasi, 1970. 343p.

198. Uysal, Mustafa (T) — *Imami Azamin Būtūn Muslumanlara son Vasiyeti* (Imam Azam's Advice to Muslims). Konya: Kanaat Matbaasi, 1966. 31p.

v. Yahya Ibn Adam

vi. Abu Ja'far Dimashqi

vii. Nasir-al-din Tusi

viii. Others: 199–204

199. Fahri, S. (T) — *Abu el Hasan el Kudduri*. Istanbul: Ahmet Sait, 1967.

200. Kuşçu, Kemal (T) — *Imam-i Azam ve Eseri* (Imam-e Azam and his Works). Istanbul: Cağaloglu Yayinevi, 1963. 56p.

201. Ibn I Rusht (T) — *Bidayatul Muctehid.*

202. Miras, Kamil and Ahmed, Naim — *Tecrid'i Sarih Tecumesi* (A Translation of Tecrid-i-Sarih). Istanbul: Turk Tarih Kurumu Matbaasi, 1957.

203. Uysal, Mustafa (T) — Translation of *Multeka*. Konya: Ahmet Sait Matbaasi, 1973.

204. Yeniçeri, Cemil (T) — Translation of El Ihtiar, 5 vols.

6. MISCELLANEOUS [205–219]

205. Akseki, A. Hamdi — *Islām*. Istanbul: Evkaf Matbaasi, 1966. 413p.

206. Baltacioğlu, Ismail — *Din ve Hayat* (Religion and Life). Istanbul: Kader Matbaasi, 1939. 50p.

207. Başgil, Ali Fuat — *Din ve Laik lik* (Legal and Social Studies, Religion and Secularism). Istanbul: Sōnmez Nesriyat ve Matbaacilik, 1962. 319p.

208. Bekir, Sadiq (T) — *Cihan Sulhu ve Islām* (World Peace and Islam). Istanbul: Fatih Matbaasi. 191p.

209. Bennabi, Malik (T) — *Cezayirde Islāmin Yeniden Doğuşu* (Rebirth of Islam). Istanbul: Çeltūt Matbaasi, 1973.

210. Bilmen, Ōmer Nasuhi — *O. N. Bilmen Tafsiri* (Explanation of the Qur'ān). Istanbul: Basim ofset. 1966, 8 vols.

211. Gōze, Ergun (T) — *Islam Davasi*. Istanbul: Ahmet Sait Matbaasi, 1970. 167p.

212. ,, ,, ,, — *Islām ve Demokrasi* (Islam and Democracy). Istanbul: Ōtūken Yayinevi. 64p.

213. Karagūlle, Suleyman* — *Islāmi Gōrūş Açisindan Ekonomi ve Doktrinler*.

214. Milli Egitim Bakanliği — *Islām Ansiklopedisi* (Encylopaedia of Islam). Istanbul: University of Istanbul, 1950.

215. Nuri, Akif — *Işlam Dusuncesi* (Islamic Thought). Istanbul: Ōzdemir Basimevi, 1973. 342p.

216. Şekerci, Osman (T) — *Devlet Başkanlarina* (To the Statesman). Istanbul: Sinan Yayinevi, 1969. 175p.

217. Seri Mehmet Paşa — *Devlet Adamlarina Ōğūtler* (Some suggestions to a Statesman). Ankara: Turk Tarih Kurumu Basimevi, 1969. 133p.

218. Taeschner, Franz (T) — "Islam Ortacaginda Futuwa; Die Futuwa Bunde in Islamischen Mittelalten; Iktisat Kefultesi Mecmuasi. Vol. 15, No. 1–4, 1953–54, pp. 3–32.

219. Varli, Mustafa (T) — *Islām ve medeniyetin ornekleri* (Islam and other Models of Civilization). Istanbul: Tūrkiye Basimevi, 1967. 213p.

7. BIBLIOGRAPHIES [220]

220. Ōztūrk, Osman and Topaloğlu, Bekir. *Cumuriyetin Ellinci Yilinda Islāmi Neşriyat Bibliyografyasī* (Bibliography of Islamic Publications on the occasion of 50th Anniversary of the Republic). Ankara: Nūve Matbaasi, 1975.

Appendix A: Turkey: A Chronology of Events in Modern History

1920: March 16:	The invading Christian armies abolish the last Ottoman Parliament in Istanbul. The centre of war of independence moves from Istanbul to Ankara.
April 23:	Turkey elects a new parliament on the basis of direct adult franchise.
September:	The new Parliament declares that it has assumed power provisionally in order to pave the way for the restoration of the Caliphate and the establishment of an independent Islamic State.
1921: November 17:	The last Ottoman caliph ordered to leave the country.
November 22:	The abolition of the Ottoman dynasty by the Turkish Parliament declared in the words: "The Caliphate belongs to the Ottoman Dynasty." It also declared: "The Caliph will be elected by the parliament from the most suitable members of that dynasty." It further declared that "The Turkish state is the protector of the Caliphate".[1] Thus the Act made a distinction between the Caliphate and the monarchy.
1923: July 24:	Laussane Treaty signed and endorsed by the Parliament on the 23rd August.
September:	Republican People's Party formed with Secularism as one of its objectives.[2] Since it was the ruling party all the elected members of the Turkish parliament became members of that party.
1923: October 13:	Ankara declared as the capital. Istanbul which had served as the centre of Islamic culture for the last so many centuries is abandoned.
October 23:	Turkey declared officially as a Republican State.
1924: March 3:	The passing of the following Acts by the Parliament: Act 429 – the abolition of the Ministry of Religious Affairs. Act 430 – Abolition of all traditional religious schools and nationalisation of all educational institutions.[3] Act 431 – Abolition of the Caliphate system. The last Caliph – Sultan Abdul Majid – and all the members of the Ottoman dynasty expelled from

1. *Macmua-i-Kavanin* C.I. Sh. 448.
2. Other objectives being Republicanism, Statism, Democracy, Nationalism and Revolution.
3. Later on, a new legislation allowed some 29 schools of Islamic Studies to continue under the direct supervision of the Ministry of Education. This number dwindled to 26, 20 and finally to only 2 in 1925, 1926 and 1927 respectively. In 1930, a complete closure of all such schools was announced.

	Turkey. They were deprived of Turkish citizenship and their properties confiscated by the State.[4] The Parliament approves new constitution which declares the end of the Empire, the monarchy, the dynasty and the Caliphate. It stated, however, that "the official religion of the Turkish state is Islam".
1925: February:	The parliament abolishes old Islamic Tax system known as tithes.
November 25:	By an Act (No. 671), the western type of hat was introduced as a part of the military uniform. The fez cap and other items of eastern dress prohibited.
November 30:	The tombs, convents of dervishes and Zawiyya (Sufi circle) closed and people prohibited from joining any Tariqa order.[5] The sheikh and the dervish disallowed to collect any tithe from the members of the public.
December 31:	The Turkish parliament passed the Act (No. 618) to enforce the Christian calendar in place of the old Hijra calendar. It also enforced the new working hours in place of the old which had a provision for the prayer times.
1926: February 17:	A new civil code adopted after the abolition of the old Islamic Law.[6]
1928: April 20:	Turkey declared "a secular state" by a constitutional amendment of the Articles 2, 16, 26 and 38 which pertained to the Islamic character of the State.
November 3:	Arabic script abolished and the use of Latin script implemented (Act 1353).
1929: September:	Teaching of Arabic and Persian languages stopped in the high schools.
1934: January 3:	Use of garments worn in religious circles banned outside religious centres.
1935: May 27:	Friday ceased to be the day of religious significance and Sunday declared as a closed holiday of the week.

4. Sicilli Kevanin, C.I. Sh. 448.
5. This was contrary to the clauses of the new constitution (Article 75). The lacuna was removed by a constitutional amendment in 1937.
6. The new code incorporated following pieces of legislation which were borrowed *in toto* from the legal system of the country names in the parenthesis:
   a. Civil code 1926 (Switzerland).
   b. Liabilities Act 1928 (Switzerland).
   c. Trade Law 1928 (Germany).
   d. Law of Punishment 1928 (Italy).

1941: June 2: An old decision of the Department of Islamic Affairs (March 6, 1933) banning the use of Arabic for the call to prayer from the Minaret implemented and the use of Turkish language enforced (Act No. 4055).

1949: Lectures about Islamic religion introduced in the primary schools. Later on, Islamic Studies was introduced at the University level and the first Faculty of Theology was opened at the University of Ankara.

1950: The Parliament amended an Act (No. 677) passed earlier and allowed the tombs of famous Turkish saints to be reopened – including the tomb of Ayub al-Ansari (a renowned companion of the Prophet Muhammad, peace be upon him). Joining of Tariqas (Sufi orders) was also permitted. This was conceded under the Treaty of Human Rights which Turkey signed on November 4, 1950.
The members of the Ottoman dynasty permitted to come back and settle down in Turkey.

June 16: The parliament recognised the return to the use of Arabic language for the call to prayer. In fact, the Act made it optional either to use Arabic or Turkish for this purpose.

1951: October 13: The Ministry of Education decided to reopen the schools of Islamic Studies. This was followed by a series of measures towards the introduction of Islamic Education at different levels.

1960: Act 7344, decided to open High Islamic academies.

1965: June 26: The whole clerical officials of Islamic Religion, paid and supported by the State, and introduced into the State-budget.

1967: July 13: Act 903 re-established the legal ways for new private Islamic foundations.

1970: Presidency of Islamic Affairs officially supported the organisation of Koranic courses all over country.

Appendix B: Works on Economic History of Turkey (1–39)

1. Akdağ, Mustafa — *Turkiyenin Iktisadi ve Ictimai Tarihi* (Economic and Social History of Turkey). Istanbul: Yalkin Matbaasi, 1974, 3 vols.

2. Altayli, Mūrşid — *Turk Milliyetçi Toplumcun Doktrininin Umumi Esaslarī* (General Principles of Nationalist and Socialist Doctrines of Turkey). Istanbul: Çoker Matbaasi, 1969. 367p.

3. Ayiter, Ferit — "Eski Tūrk Hususi Hukukuna Ait Bazi Notlar Einige Bemerkungen Uber Das Alt Turkishe Privatrecht" (Some Aspects of Turkish Personal Law). *Iktisat Fakūltesi Mecmuasi*, Vol. 11, No. 1–4, 1949–50, pp. 417–436.

4. Barkan, Ōmer Lūtfi — "Fatih Aomii ve Imareti Tesislerinin 1489–1490 Yillarina Ait Muhasebe Blançolari" (Accounting Balance Sheet of the Building and the Mosque of Fatihi in the year 1489–1490). *Iktisat Fakūltesi Mecmuasi*, Vol. 23, No. 1–2, 1962–63, pp. 297–341.

5. ,, ,, ,, — "Osmanli Imparatorluğunda Imaret Sitelerinin Kuruluş ve Işleyiş Tarzina Ait Araştirmalar" (An Investigation into the Foundation and Function of the Imrat System in Ottoman Empire). *Iktisat Fakūltesi Mecmuasi*. Vol. 23, No. 1–2, 1962–63, pp. 239–296.

6. ,, ,, ,, — "Ayasofya Camii ve Eyup Tūrbesinin 1489–1491 Yillarina Ait Muhasebe Blançolari" (Accounting Balance Sheet of Tomb of Ayul Ansari and Aha Sophia in 1489–1491). *Iktisat Fakūltesi Mecmuasi*. Vol. 23, No. 1–2, 1962–63, pp. 342–379.

7. Barkan, Ōmer Lutfi — "Saaray Mutfağinin 849–895 (1489–1490) Yilina Ait Muhasebe Blançosu" (Balance Sheet of Palace Kitchen in 1489–1490). *Iktisat Fakūltesi Mecmuasi*. Vol. 23, No. 1–2, 1962–63, pp. 380–398.

8. Barkan, Ōmer Lūtfi and Uzuncarşili, Ismail — "Osmanli Devlet Teskilat ina Methal" (Introduction to the Organisation of the Ottoman State). *Iktisat Fakūltesi Mecmuasi*. Vol. 3, No. 1–2, 1941–42, pp. 228–238.

9. Belli, Abdulmecid — *Adaletin Zaferi, Maras 2 Sulh ceza Makemesinin din hurriyati ve laiklike ilgili Tarihi bir Karari* (Court Judgement on Problems of Secularism in Turkey). Istanbul: Ahmet Sait Matbaasi, 1963. 48p.

10. Çermen, Osman Nuri — *Dinde Reform Modern Turkiye Icin* (Religious Reform in Modern Turkey). Istanbul: Dizgi, Reklam, Matbaa ve Nesriyatevi, 1956, 40p.

11. ,, ,, ,, — *Kemalizm Reformuna Gore Dinimizin 54 Farzi* (54 Obligations of our Religion as Against Kemalist Reform).

12. Daver, Būlent — *Tūrkiye cumhuriyetinde Layiklik* (Secularism in Turkish Republic). Ankara: Son Havadis Matbaasi, 1955. 260p.

13. Dinçer, Nchit — *1913 Ten bu Yana Imam Halip Okullari Meselesi* (The Problem of Islamic Studies since 1913). Istanbul: Otaz Matbaasi, 1974.

14. Demirer, Ercumend — *Din, Toplum ve Kemal Atatürk* (Religion, Society and Kemal Ataturk). Ankara: Kardeş Matbaasi, 1969. 192p.

15. Dūzdağ, Ertuğrul M. — *Şeyhulislām Ebussud Efendi Fetvalari Işiğinda 16 Asir Turk Hayati* (The Life in the 16th Century Turkey in the Light of the Fetwas of Ebussud Efendi). Istanbul: Hikmet Cazetecilik Ltd., Sti. 1972. 245p.

16. Gōlpinarli, Abdūlbaki — "Islām ve Turk Illerinde Fūtuvet Teşkilāti ve Kaynaklari; les organizations de la Fatauvet dans les paiza Musulmans et Turcs et ses origines" (Sources of Futuvet in Islamic Turkish Province). Vol. 11, No. 1–4, 1949–50, p. 7.

17. " " — "Futuvet Name i Sultani ve Futuvet Hakkinda Bazi Notlar (Some Notes About Futuvet of the Sultan). *Iktisat Fakūltesi Mecmuasi*. Vol. 17, No. 1–4, 1955–56, pp. 156–178.

18. " " — "Şeh, Seyyid Gaybioğlu Seyyid Huseyin in 'Futuvet Name' si (Futuvet Name i Seyh Seyyid Huseyin Ilmi Gaybi). *Iktisat Fakūltesi Mecmuasi*. Vol 17, No. 1–4, 1955–56, pp. 27–72.

19. " " — "Burgazi ve Futuvetnamesi" (Burgazi and his Futuvet). *Iktisat Fakūltesi Mecmuasi*, Vol. 15, No. 1–4, 1953–54, pp. 76–153.

20. Inalcik, Halil — "XV Asir Tūrkiye Iktisadi ve Ictimai Tarihi Kaynaklari" (Sources of Economic and Social History of 15th Century Turkey). Ankara: University Ilahyat Fakūltesi, Vol. 15/16, No. 1–4, 1953–54, pp. 51–57.

21. Işiksal, Cavide — "Turkiyede Ilk Bankacilik Hareketi ve Osmanli Bankasinin Kurulmasi" (First Banking Movement in Turkey and the Opening of Ottoman Bank). *Belgelerle Turk Tarihi Dergisi*, Vol. 8, No. 10, July, 1968, pp. 72–79.

22. Kereseviakovic, Hamdiya — "Erki Sarayevoda Esnaf ve Senatler" (Arts and Artisans in the Old Saray Bosnia). *Iktisat Fakūltesi Mecmuasi*, Vol. 17, No. 1–4, 1955–56, pp. 359–379.

23. Kuşdemiroglu, A. E. — "Memlektimizde Ōdunç Para Verme Işleri" (The Problem of Credit in our Country). *Istanbul Ticaret*, Vol. 13, No. 610, 1970, p. 7.

24. " " — "Mevzuatimizda Faiz Kavrami" (The Concept of Interest in our Country). *Istanbul Ticaret*, Vol. 13, No. 622, 1970, pp. 5–7.

25. Ōzturk, Osman — *Osmanli Hukuk Tarihinde Mecelle* (Codification of the Islamic Law in the Ottoman Empire). Istanbul: Irfan Matbaasi, 1973. 931p.

26.	Sahillioglu, Halil	"Bir Multezimin Defterine Göre XV Yüzyil Sonunda Osmanli Darphane Mukataalari" (Coin Minting During the Ottoman Empire). *Iktisat Fakültesi Mecmuasi*, Vol. 23, No. 1–2, 1962–63, pp. 145–218.
27.	Saygin, M. Celal	*Diyanet Cephesinden Atatürk Inkilāplari* (Ataturk Reforms from the Religious Point of View). Ankara: Türk Tarih Kurumu Basimevi, 1972, 40p.
28.	Sencer, Muzaffen	*Dinin Turk Toplumuna Etkileri* (Influence of Religion on Turkish Society). Istanbul: Osmanbey Matbaasi, 1971. 235p.
29.	Togan, Zekivelidi	"Resideddinin Mekluplarinda Anadolunun Iktisadi ve Medeni Hayatina Ait Kayitlar" (Notes on the Economic and Civic Life of Anatolia as Depicted in the Letters of Residdedin). *Iktisat Fakültesi Mecmuasi*, Vol. 15, No. 1–4, 1953–54, pp. 33–50.
30.	Turan, Osman	*Türkiyede Manevi Buhran, Din ve Laiklik* (Moral Crisis in Turkey, Religion and Secularism). Ankara: Şark Matbaasi, 1964. 296p.
31.	Uzançarşili, Ismail and Barkan, O. Lutfi	"Osmanli Devleti Teskilatina Methal" (Introduction to the Organisation of Ottoman State). *Iktisat Fakültesi Mecmuasi*, Vol. 3, No. 1–2, 1941–42, pp. 228–238.
32.	Zaim, Sabahuddin	*Türkiyede Mufus Meselesi, Siyasi, Iktisadi ve Sosyal Yonleriyle* (The Population Problem in Turkey with Its Political, Economic and Social Implications). Istanbul: Boğaziçi Yayinlari, 1973. 158p.

Appendix C: Introductory Notes on some important works

1. Akdağ, Mustafa — *Turkiyenin Iktsadi ve Ictimai Tarihi* (Economic and Social History of Turkey). Istanbul: Yelken Matbaasi, 1974, 3 vols.

This is a standard work on Turkey's economic history during the period 1243–1623.

Contents:

Vol. 1: Turkey – During the great chaos after the Seljukes; transformation of Turkey from the Seljukes to an Ottoman Empire; organisation of the state and general economic condition at the turn of the 10th century.

Vol. 2: Social and economic structure of the Ottoman Turkey during the 11th century; state treasury and the beginning of the period of deterioration.

Vol. 3: Turkey's emergence in the 16th century.

2. Cekmegil, Said M. — *Islamda Iktisat Anlayişimiz* (Our understanding of Islamic Economics). Istanbul: Fakulteler Matbaasi, 1966. 113p.

This book is a perfect example of how a common Turk reacted to the onslaught of Western ideologies on Turkey's Islamic past. There is a useful bibliography at the end of the book.

Contents:

Recent economic theories; the Islamic order; Social Insurance; Zakāt; Prohibition of Interest; Austerity and Injunction against the waste of resources; rights of ownership; problems of industrial unrest and its solution in Islam.

3. Karagūlle, Sūleyman — *Islāmi Gōrūş, Açisindan Ekonomi ve Doktrinler.*

An unpublished work so far. It is a scholar's answer to the conflict of Islam and Western ideologies, specially capitalism and socialism. The author has analysed the existing economic systems and compared them with the Islamic economic system.

Contents:

1. Some familiar economic concepts.
2. Time as an economic resource.
3. Money – its investment and circulation.
4. Economic transformation.
5. Class structure of a society.
6. Economic ideologies.

4. Tuğ, Salih — *Islām vergi Hukukunun Ortaya Çikişi* (The Development of Taxation System in Islam).

Contents:

1. Taxation system before Islam.
2. Introduction of the taxation system in Madina.
3. Taxes for Muslims.
4. Taxes for non-Muslims.
5. Bibliography.

5. Yavuz, Yunus Vehbi — *Islāmda Zekāt Muessesesi* (The Institution of *Zakāt*). Istanbul: Ahmet Sait Matbaasi, 1972. 390p.

It is a comprehensive scholarly work on the subject.

Contents:

1. Principles of *Zakāt*.
2. Expenditure of *Zakāt*.
3. Collection of *Zakāt*.
4. Application of *Zakāt* in the present age.

6. Zaim, Sabahuddin — *Modern Iktisat ve Islām* (Modern Economy and Islam). Istanbul: Fatih Matbaasi, 1969. 31p.

This is an analytical study of the existing economic systems and their comparison with the Islamic economic system.

Contents:

1. The present day world crisis.
2. Ideological division of the world.
3. Comparison of Islam with capitalism and socialism.
4. Further description of Islamic economic system.

Appendices

APPENDIX I

Conference Communiqué

Thanks to Allah Almighty, the First International Conference on Islamic Economics was held in Holy Makka, Safar 21–26, 1396H. (February 21–26, 1976) at the invitation of King Abdul Aziz University and under the auspices of the faculty of Economics and Business Administration.

The Conference discussed all the papers and studies submitted to it on the following issues:

(1) Concept and Methodology of Islamic Economics.
(2) Survey and Examination of Contemporary Literature on Islamic Economics.
(3) Theories of Production and Consumption in an Islamic Community.
(4) The Role of the State in an Islamic Economy.
(5) Insurance within the Framework of the Islamic *Sharī'ah*.
(6) Interest-Free Banks.
(7) *Zakāt* and Financial Policy.
(8) Economic Development within the Framework of Islam.
(9) Economic Co-operation among Muslim Countries.

The Conference expressed its satisfaction at the general standard of these papers and the positive and constructive tone of deliberations, which together contributed to a clarification of the issues and an enrichment of the science of Islamic Economics.

The participants stressed the need for continuing research on various aspects of Islamic Economics, to add to its depth and proper organisation, and to create planned co-operation among scholars from all corners of the world to achieve this objective.

Contemporary civilisation, whether Capitalist or Marxist, despite its material achievements, has led both individuals and societies into conflict, division, anxiety and loss of purpose. Technology has been given preference over man's peace, security and stability.

The Muslim nation has suffered from imperialism and backwardness for generations and its peoples have been forced into an attitude of subservience and imitation. But now this nation has clearly realised the need for originality in thought and practice of true Islam, to realise the reason for its existence, to release its energies and to motivate it for action. It has to concentrate all its positive and constructive efforts in clarifying its course of action and surmounting the attitude of subservience and imitation. This needs to be done if this nation is to save itself from backwardness and humility and to play a leading role in the guidance of humanity.

The participants agreed that the Islamic faith does not merely define the relation of man to Allah, but also provides the *Sharī'ah* that safeguards human interests, harmonises all aspects of life and pays as much attention to economic affairs as to all other aspects of human welfare.

They agreed that the norms and values of Islam constitute the foundation of the economic system of Islam.

The participants confirmed that this economic system would be ineffective if it is not accompanied by the practise of all aspects of the comprehensive Islamic system.

The participants stated their belief that the Islamic economic system is a unique system based on a well-defined economic philosophy. The basic principles of the system are founded on *tawḥīd* and are derived from the Qur'ān and *Sunnah*.

The participants confirmed that Muslims ought to be the first in adopting this system. They should do their utmost to expound it, rather than waste their energies in forcing it into the mould of alien systems that have led them to false and confused solutions.

Islam is the only means of saving humanity from its present spiritual and material crises and of replacing the civilisation of matter with a civilisation for man. It is the moral obligation of Muslims to convey the message of this civilisation to humanity.

> "Verily this is My Way, heading straight; follow it; follow not other paths. They will scatter you away from this (great) path" (6: 153).

To realise these objectives, the Conference approved the following recommendations:

(1) Universities should carefully attend to the teaching of Islamic Economics, supporting research in this area and providing basic facilities for this purpose, whether through specialised libraries, research units, full time research scholarships, publication of periodicals, exchange programmes and the establishment of scientific associations.

(2) It is the duty of all universities and educational institutions of the Muslim world to develop their economics curricula along Islamic lines. This will help create an Islamic outlook in the new generation and leadership and help bring about conformity between the faith and practice of the Muslims.

(3) The King Abdul Aziz University should, as part of its constructive efforts in the academic field for the service of Islam and the *Ummah*, establish an international centre for the study of Islamic economics.

This centre should operate under the guidance of a Supreme Council composed of Muslim scholars in *Sharī'ah* and Economics from various countries. This centre should endeavour also to co-ordinate and support international research at the highest level of scholarship. The centre should direct its efforts to:

(a) the establishment of a specialised library that would collect scholarly works in the field of Islamic Economics in various languages and issue catalogues to research scholars everywhere;
(b) conduct and support theoretical and applied research in various fields of Islamic Economics, publish textbooks in this field for the use of Muslim universities, and organise training courses for Muslim economic establishments;
(c) provide research facilities and scholarships for visiting Muslim scholars to undertake research in their fields of interest;
(d) promote co-operation in the field of Islamic economic research among various universities and institutions;
(e) publish research papers and periodicals in Islamic Economics;
(f) help establish chairs for the teaching of Islamic Economics, provide scholarships for research in this field, and promote lectures with conferences and regional symposia.

(4) The International Conference on Islamic Economics should be reconvened every two years, with specialised seminars being held more often.

It was recommended that the theme of the next Conference should be "Development in the Framework of Islamic Economics" and that the first seminar be convened within nine months to discuss the subject of "Monetary Policy and Institutions within an Islamic Framework".

(5) A permanent secretariat should be established for the Conference on Islamic Economics with headquarters at the King Abdul Aziz University under the direction of the Chairman of the Conference or his Deputy.

The Secretariat should immediately begin preparations for the following conferences and seminars, implementing the recommendations of the Conference, drafting a charter and rules and regulations for this conference and the Secretariat, which may be presented to the next Conference.

To replace commercial insurance, it was recommended that a specialised committee of Muslim "*Ulamā*" and Economists should work on developing a system of insurance which is free from *ribā* and speculation, which would promote co-operation in the Islamic spirit and would conform to the conditions of the *Sharī'ah*.

(6) It was recommended that all Muslim countries should make their laws as well as social and economic institutions conform to the principles of the *Sharī'ah*.

The Conference felt that Commercial Insurance as presently practised does not realise the *Sharī'ah* aims of co-operation and solidarity because it does not satisfy the Islamic conditions for it to become acceptable.

(7) The King Abdul Aziz and other Muslim universities should develop an interim one-year graduate course of study in Islamic *Sharī'ah* specially designed for social scientists to help them in reformulating social sciences including economics to conform with Islamic Laws.

(8) The Conference Secretariat should prepare and publish the reports and recommendations of various committees on the proceedings of this Conference.

(9) The Chairman of the Conference was requested to submit to His Majesty King Khalid Bin Abdul Aziz and His Royal Highness Crown Prince Fahd Bin Abdul Aziz the participants' sincere thanks for the support and encouragement as well as heart-felt appreciation for the sincere efforts and generous support to the Muslim *Ummah* and *Da'wah*.

The Conference expressed its sincere gratitude to H.R.H. Prince Fawwaz Bin Abdul Aziz the Governor of the Province of Makka.

The Conference expressed its deep gratitude to H.E. the Minister of Higher Education, and Head of the World Association of Muslim Youth, Shaikh Husain Bin Abdullah Al-Shaikh for his great help and hospitality.

The Conference expressed its heart-felt gratitude to the Muslim people of Saudi Arabia for their hospitality and warm reception.

The Conference greatly appreciated the very extensive efforts of King Abdul Aziz University and its Acting President, the Steering Committee, the Executive Committee, the various Committees in the Conference, the Faculty of Economics and Administration and the Faculty of *Sharī'ah* at King Abdul Aziz University, and their staff.

In the Name of Allah, The Most Gracious, the Most Merciful
First International Conference on Islamic Economics

Suggestions and Recommendations of the Committees

1. Committee on the Concept and Methodology of Islamic Economics:

   – Development of the Islamic Economic concept is based on the following:

   (i) The belief that the universe belongs to Allah and that all wealth belongs to Allah.
   (ii) That Man is a trustee of what he possesses of the bounties of God.
   (iii) That private ownership approved by Islam is within the framework of the proper means of earning and spending and satisfaction of the obligations on wealth.
   (iv) The economic system of Islam achieves social equilibrium and solidarity.

2. Committee on the Survey of Contemporary Literature on Islamic Economics:

   (i) Formation of a Committee to compile a dictionary of Islamic Economics terminology in different languages.
   (ii) Survey and development of references and *Ijtihād* throughout the history of the Muslim nation to promote Islamic Economics.

3. Committee on a Study of the Theories of Production and Consumption in the Islamic Community:

   – Making use of mathematical analyses in the study of Islamic Economics.

4. Committee on the Teaching of Islamic Economics:

   – The need for teaching Islamic jurisprudence pertaining to human relations in transactions and its principles in the Faculties of Commerce, Economics and Administration in the universities of Muslim countries.

5. Committee on Interest-Free Banks:

   (i) Calling on Muslim Governments to bolster the existing Islamic banks and propagate and extend the scope of interest-free banking.

(ii) Arranging for the training of personnel in Islamic banks so as to achieve higher standards and greater efficiency.

6. Committee on *Zakāt* and Fiscal Policy:

   – Stressing the obligation of *Zakāt* with a view to ensure social justice in Muslim countries.

7. Committee on Economic development in an Islamic Framework:

   – Conduct a Comprehensive Survey of experiences in the field of Islamic Economics and encourage participation in scientific research in Muslim countries.

Our final call is:

Praise be to Allah
The Cherisher and
Sustainer of the Worlds.

STEERING COMMITTEE OF THE CONFERENCE

1. Dr. Muhammad Omar Zubeir (Chairman)
   Acting President, King Abdul Aziz University, Jeddah.
2. Dr. Hasan Abou Roukba
   Dean, Faculty of Economics and Administration, King Abdul Aziz University, Jeddah.
3. Dr. Muhammad A. Sakr
   Professor of Economics, King Abdul Aziz University.
4. Professor Khurshid Ahmad
   Director General, The Islamic Foundation, U.K.
5. Dr. Muhammad Nejatullah Siddiqi
   Reader in Economics, Aligarh Muslim University, Aligarh – India.
6. Dr. Muhammad Umar Chapra
   Economic Adviser, Saudi Arabian Monetary Agency.
7. Dr. Abdul Hamid Abu-Sulaiman
   Riyadh University.

8. Dr. Ahmad Totonji
   Riyadh University.
9. Dr. Bakor O. Al-Amri
   Assistant Professor of Political Science, King Abdul Aziz University.
10. Dr. Muhiadin R. Tarabzune
    Assistant Professor of Accounting, King Abdul Aziz University.
11. Dr. Hasan Balkhi
    Assistant Professor of Economics, King Abdul Aziz University.

EXECUTIVE COMMITTEE OF THE CONFERENCE

1. Dr. Hasan Abou Roukba
   Dean, Faculty of Economics & Administration, King Abdul Aziz University, Jeddah.
2. Dr. Bakor O. Al-Amri
   Assistant Professor of Political Science, King Abdul Aziz University.
3. Dr. Ahmed El-Naggar
   Professor, Head of Islamic Economics Research Unit.
4. Dr. Muhammad A. Sakr
   Professor of Economics, King Adbul Aziz University.
5. Dr. Muhiadin R. Tarabzune
   Assistant Professor of Accounting, King Abdul Aziz University.
6. Dr. Hasan Balkhi
   Assistant Professor of Economics, King Abdul Aziz University.

OFFICERS OF THE CONFERENCE

1.	Dr. Muhammad Omar Zubeir	Chairman
2.	Dr. Hasan Abou Roukba	Vice Chairman
3.	Professor Khurshid Ahmad	Vice Chairman
4.	Professor Sabahuddin Zaim	Vice Chairman
5.	Dr. Monzer Kahf	Rapporteur

APPENDIX II

Conference Participants

(List of Participants to the Conference from outside Saudi Arabia)

Amman
Foad H. Basiso
Ministry of Oil
Agriculture and Fishery

Australia
Dr. Delian Neor
Professor of Political Sciences

Bangladesh
Dr. Mirza Nurul Huda
Member
The Council of Advisers to the President
Government of Republic of Bangladesh

Brunei
Dato Utama Haji Ismail Omar Abdul-Aziz

Canada
Dr. Jamal Badawi
Assistant Professor

Egypt
Dr. Abdel Aziz Hegazy
Professor

Dr. Abdel El-Meneim A. H. El-Banna
Deputy Governor of the Central Bank of Egypt

Dr. Abdel Kerim S. Barkat
Professor
Beruit University

Dr. Ahmed Abdel Salam Heba
Professor and Head of Plantation Department
Faculty of Agriculture
Tauta

Dr. Ahmed Abou Ismail
Minister of Treasury

Dr. Eisa Abdou
Professor of Islamic Economics

Dr. El-Bahy El-Kholy
Professor
Islamic Higher Studies
Al-Azhar University

Dr. Gamal El-Din Awad
Professor and Head of Law Department
Cairo University

Dr. Hassen Tawfik
Dean
Faculty of Commerce
Cairo University

Dr. Hussein Ibrahim El-Ghamry
General Director of Dar-El-Maarif

Ibrahim Mahmoud Loutfy
Head of the Board of Directors
Nasr Bank

Imam Abul Halim Mohammed
Sheikh
Al-Azhar

Dr. Ismail Mohammed Hashem
Dean
Zakazik Faculty of Commerce

Dr. M. Helmi Morad
Professor of Economics

Dr. Mahmoud Loutfy Abdel Hakim
Advisor

Dr. Mahmoud Mohamed Nor
Faculty of Commerce
Azhar University

Mobid Ali Al-Garhi
Lecturer
National Institute of Planning

Dr. Mohammed Al-Gazer
Dean
Faculty of Azhar Commerce

Mohamed Kamal Al-Garf
Lecturing Professor
Sharī'ah Faculty

Mohamed Mohamed Al-Samari
Member of the Board of Directors of Journalist Syndicate

Dr. Mohamed Shafik Balba
General Secretary
The Higher Council of Universities

Omar Mario
Advisor

Dr. Salah El-Din Namak
Dean
Faculty of Azhar Commerce

Sheikh M. Khater
Mufti of Arab Republic of Egypt

Zaidan Abou El-Makarim
Headmaster

India

Abdul Haseeb
Director, Research Department
Central Bank of India

Dr. A. M. Khusro
Vice-Chancellor
Aligarh Muslim University

Dr. F. R. Faridi
Reader
Department of Economics
Aligarh Muslim University

Dr. Mohammad Shabbir Khan
Professor of Economics
Aligarh Muslim University

Mohammed Shamim

Dr. M. Nejatullah Siddiqi
Professor of Economics
Aligarh Muslim University

Indonesia

Dr. Ahmed Mofleh Safuddin
Lecturer at Agricultural University

Bashir Hasan
Associated Dean
University of Indonesia

Dr. Ismail Suny
Director of Mohammediah University
Jakarta

Muhammad Arayad
Vice Director
Institute of Economics

Dr. Nur Sal
Assistant Director
Trade Corporation

Iran
Dr. Ali Mohammed Eghtedari
Vice-Dean, Faculty of Business and Administration
Tehran University

Dr. Jaffar Niski
National University of Iran
Faculty of Economics

Dr. Jaffar Shahidi
Professor, Faculty of Literature

Dr. Sohrab Behdad
Assistant Professor
Faculty of Economics

Iraq
Dr. Hashim Y. H. Al-Mallah
Dean of Faculty of Literature
Mosel University

Dr. Khidr Ghasim M.Al-Doury
Assistant Professor
Faculty of Literature
Mosel University

Dr. Mahmoud M. Al-Habib
Assistant Professor
Basrah University

Japan
Khalid Kiba
Management Expert

Jordan
Dr. Adel Al-Hiari
Professor
University of Jordan

Fadilat Sheikh Mostafa Al-Zarka
Sharī'ah Faculty University of Jordan

Dr. Ibrahim Zied Kilani
Sharī'ah Faculty University of Jordan

Dr. Jawad A-Enani
Director of Research Department
Central Bank of Jordan

Dr. Salehf Hasawna
Head of Economic and Statistics Department
Jordan University

Dr. Taysir Abdel-Ghabir
Economic Expert
The Economic Committee for East Asia
United Nations

Kuwait
Dr. Farid Al-Naggar
Professor
Faculty of Commerce
Kuwait University

Dr. Midhat Hasnain
Social and Economics Development Fund

Dr. Mohamed Faroq Al-Nabhan
Professor
Faculty of Economics and Sharī'ah
Yousif Al-Refaie

Libya
Dr. Abdel Hafiz-Ziliety
Professor
Faculty of Economics
Libyan University

Abdel Hafoz-Ziliety
Professor
Faculty of Economics
Libyan University

Malaysia
Dr. K. A. M. Arief
Deputy Dean
Faculty of Economics and
Administration

Morocco
Abdel Rehim Bin Salem
Director
Justice Court

Dr. Ibrahim Discuki Abaza
Professor
Faculty of Law
Rabat

Mahdi Bin Abbo Ud
Professor
Philosophy Department
Mohammed Fifth University

Pakistan
Dr. Abdul Hameed Qureshi
National College of Engineering
and Technology

Dr. Amjed Saeed
Professor
University of Punjab
Department of Business and
Administration

Dr. Anwar Iqbal Qureshi
Economic Expert
Hafizulla Khan Niazi
Mathematics Department
University of Islamabad

Hassan Mahmoud Jaffrey
Islamabad University

Dr. Masood Akram
Chairman
Department of Economics
University of Peshawar

Matin Ansari
Director
Institute of Industrial
Accountants

Mohammad Akram Khan
Auditor

Mohammed Baker Nakawy
Director
Pakistan Broadcasting Station

Dr. Mohammed Uzair
Member (Additional Secretary)
Monopoly Control Authority
Government of Pakistan

Dr. Rafiq Ahmed
Professor
Faculty of Arts
University of Punjab

Sheikh Mahmoud Ahmed
Educational Advisor
Government of Pakistan

Dr. S. M. Hasan-uz-Zaman
Assistant Director Research
State Department of Pakistan
Central Directorate

Dr. Ziauddin Ahmed
Economic Advisor
State Bank of Pakistan
Central Directorate

Philippines
Ebrahim A. Mamao
Banking

Mohammed Anwar Basheer
Director
Mindano Arabic Islamic Institute

Qatar
Dr. Yosuf Abdollah Al-Qar Dawy
Professor and Head of The Department of Islamic Studies

Singapore
Dr. Azahari Zahiri
Economic Advisor

Sudan
Dr. Ahmed Al-Haj Ali-Azrak
Lecturer
Om-Dorman University

Dr. Ahmed Hasan Al-Jak
Head of Department of Management
Khartoum University

Dr. Ahmed Osman Al-Haj
National Planning Authority

Dr. Ali Abdul Rasoul
Professor
Om-Dorman University

Soliman Babkir
Ministry of Foreign Affairs

Dr. Yousif Hamid Alem
Om-Dorman Islamic University
Khartoum

Syria
Dr. Rafik Al-Misry
Head of Lending Department
Industrial Bank

Turkey
Dr. Aydin Yalcin
Professor of Economics
Ankara University

Dr. Nevzazad Yalcintas
Professor
Istanbul University

Dr. Mustafa Bilge
Member
Islamic Studies Institute

Dr. Sabahuddin Zaim
Professor
Istanbul University

Salih Tug
Professor
Institute of Islamic Studies
Istanbul University

Dr. Yusuf Zia
Associate Professor
Faculty of Islamic Studies
University of Ataturk

U.K.
Afzal-Ur Rehman
Chairman
Muslim Educational Trust

Dr. Kalim Siddiqi
Director
The Muslim Institute for Research and Planning, Preparatory Committee

Khurshid Ahmad
Director
The Islamic Foundation

Mashuq Ally
Researcher
Islamic Foundation

Dr. M. M. Ahsan
Assistant Director
The Islamic Foundation

Jamil Sharif
Researcher

Mohammed Iqbal Azaria
Economic Researcher

Dr. Omar Nur Eldayem
Engineer

U.S.A.
Dr. Abdul Munim Shakir
Director and Professor
Muslim World Studies

Dr. Ahmed Abdul Majid
Anis Ahmed
Department of Philosophy and Religion
Applachain State University

Ijaz Shafi Gilani
Economic Researcher

Mahmoud Abou Saud
Financial Adviser

Dr. Mahmoud Wahba
Professor
City University of New York

Marghoub Ali Quraishi
Director
Associated Management Systems

Mehmoud Saleh Abdel-Baki
The National Institute
Management of Development
Cairo

Dr. Mohammed Ishaq Nadiri
Department of Economics, Graduate, School of Arts and Sciences, New York University

Dr. Mohammed Kadri M. El-Araby
Assistant Professor Institute of Technology, New York

Dr. Monzer Kahf
Economic Researcher

Dr. Sulayman S. Nyang
Acting Director
African Studies and Research Programme
Harvard University

William Assoey
Consultant

West Germany
Dr. Heider Dawar
Professor

JOURNALISTS

No.

Egypt

1 Ahmed Sadik Farrag
2 Mahmoud Fahmy Howidy
3 Mostafa Ahmed Ali
4 Salah Azzam
5 Shawky Al-Sayed
6 Tawfik Ismail Al-Sayed

No.

England

1 Ebrahim Ahmed Bawany
2 Muhammad H. Faruqi

Kuwait

1 Abel Al-Walaity
2 Badr Soliman Al-Kassar
3 Mashary M. Al-Baddeh
4 Mohamad K. Al-Tounsy

LIST OF PARTICIPANTS TO THE CONFERENCE FROM SAUDI ARABIA

Dr. Muhammad Omar Zubair
Dr. Abdullah Omar Nasif
Sheikh Amad Muhammad Jamal
Secretary General, Word Muslim League
H.E. Prince Muhammad Al-Faisal
Secretary General, Foreign Ministers Conference
Dr. Gharib El-Gamal
Sheikh Ahmad Salah Jamjoom
Sheikh Wuhaib Bin Zaqar
Sheikh Mohsin Al-Baroom
Dr. Muhammad Abdul Wahid Jamjoom
Dr. Ahmad Muhammad Ali
Mr. Muhammad Zaki Azam
Mr. Shamshad Ali Khan
Dr. Saeed Minai
Dr. Hasan Zaki Ahmad
Mr. M. Muslehuddin
Shiekh Saleh Al-Hasin
Dr. Mohsin Shoukh, Al-Fanjari
Mr. Muhammad Babuli
Dr. Hamdi Abdul Adi
Dr. Hasan Balkhi
Dr. Abdul Nasir Al-Attar
Dr. Atif As-Sayyid
Dr. Muhammad Ahmad Sakar

Islamic University

Sheikh Abdul Aziz Albahsi
Sheikh Muhammad Aman

University of Petroleum and Minerals

Mr. Ali Al-Yousuf

University of Riyadh

Dr. Rafiq Al-Kusm
Dr. Amin Shaltouni
Dr. Younus Al-Bitriq
Dr. Muhammad Musa Al-Kashif
Dr. Ahmad Al-Assal
Dr. Abdul Hamid Abu Sulaiman
Mr. Saeed Al-Arabi
Dr. Ahmad Totonji
Dr. Anas Al-Zarqa

King Faisal University

Abdullah Al-Bishr
Saad Balghonaim
Ahmad Almotairi

Imam Muhammad Bin Saud University
Sheikh Mannaa Qattan

Faculty of Dawah Makka Mukarrama
Mr. Muhammad Qutb
Sheikh Muhammad Al-Mubarak
Dr. Rashid Al-Rajeh
Dr. Muhammad Saeed Al-Rashid
Dr. Hasan Hamid Khan
Dr. Mahmoud Al-Aroosi
Dr. Muhammad Saeed Abdussalam
Dr. Jalal Alsayyad
Mr. Fouad Al-Khatib
Dr. Abdul Malik Al-Sayyed
Dr. Kamil Salamah Al-Daqs
Dr. Tawfiq Al-Shawi
Dr. Ahmad Al-Najjar
Dr. Bakar Al-Qamari
Dr. Mohyiddin Tarbazooni

APPENDIX III

Conference Programme

INAUGURAL SESSION

Saturday, 21st February, 1976.
Main Hall, Hotel Intercontinental, Holy Makka.

HOLY QUR'ĀN RECITATION

Inaugural Speeches:	Part I
	Minister of Higher Education, and President of the Supreme Council of Universities, H. E. Hasan Al al-Shaikh, representing His Majesty the King
	Dr. Mohammed Omar Zubeir Chairman Steering Committee of the Conference,
	Dr. Hasan Abou Roukba Chairman Executive Committee of the Conference.
	Delegates Representative
	Part II
Speech:	Dr. A. M. Khusro Vice Chancellor, Aligarh Muslim University
Speech:	Professor Muhammad Qutb King Abdul Aziz University.

Sunday, 22nd February, 1976
Ibn Rushd Hall

CONCEPT AND METHODOLOGY

Chairman:	Dr. Muhammed Finaish
Co-Chairman:	Dr. M. N. Huda
Rapporteur:	Dr. Jamal Badawi
First Session:	Dr. M. S. Fanjeri
	Discussion
	Dr. Ahmed al-Assal and Dr. Fathi Abdul Karim
	Discussion

Second Session:	Sheikh Manna al-Qattan
	Discussion
	Isa Abduh
	Discussion
Third Session:	Dr. Ismail R. al-Faruqi
	Discussion
	Dr. Fareed Najjar
	Discussion

Main Hall

A SURVEY OF CONTEMPORARY LITERATURE ON ISLAMIC ECONOMICS

Chairman:	Dr. Ahmed Ali
Co-Chairman:	Dr. Nevzad Yalcintas
Rapporteur:	Dr. Faiz al-Habib
First Session:	Dr. M. Nejatullah Siddiqi
	Discussion
Second Session:	Dr. Sabahuddin Zaim
	Discussion
	Dr. Mustafa Bilge
	Discussion

Monday, 23rd February, 1976

Ibn Rushd Hall

CONCEPT AND METHODOLOGY

Chairman:	Dr. Mohammed Finaish
Co-Chairman:	Dr. M. N. Huda
Rapporteur:	Dr. Jamal Badawi
First Session:	Dr. Mohammed A. Sakr
	Discussion
	Dr. Hashim Samarrai
	Discussion
Second Session:	Discussion and Recommendations

PRODUCTION AND CONSUMPTION

Chairman:	Dr. Ehsan R. Siddiqi
Co-Chairman	Dr. Ibrahim Ayagi
Rapporteur:	Dr. Ahmad Qatnani
Third Session:	Dr. Anas Zarqa
	Discussion

Main Hall

THE ROLE OF THE ISLAMIC STATE IN A MODERN ECONOMY

Chairman:	Dr. Mahdi ben Abboud
Co-Chairman:	Dr. Ismail Nawab
Rapporteur:	Dr. Azahar Zahiri
First Session:	Dr. M. Umar Chapra
	Discussion
	Sheikh Mohammed al-Mubarak
	Discussion
Second Session:	Dr. Sulayman Nyang
	Discussion
	Ijaz Shafi Gilani
	Discussion
Third Session:	Discussion and Recommendations

PLENARY SESSION:

TEACHING ISLAMIC ECONOMICS

Leader:	Dr. Abdul Hamid Abu Sulaiman
Rapporteur:	Dr. Anas Zarqa

Ibn Seena Hall

INSURANCE WITHIN THE FRAMEWORK OF ISLAMIC SHARĪ'AH (JURISPRUDENCE)

Chairman:	Dr. Rashid al-Rajih
Co-Chairman:	Dr. Ali M. Eghtedari
Rapporteur:	Dr. M. Farouq al-Nabhan
First Session:	Sheikh Mustafa Zarqa
	Dr. Husain Hamid
	Dr. A. F. Abu Sunnah
	Discussion
Second Session:	Sheikh Ali al-Khalif
	Dr. Jaffer Shaheedi
	Dr. Ali Jamal Awad
	Discussion
Third Session:	Dr. A. Nasir al-Attar
	Dr. Jalal al-Sayyad
	Dr. Gherib al-Jammal
	Discussion

Tuesday, 24th February, 1976.
Ibn Rushd Hall
PRODUCTION AND CONSUMPTION

Chairman:	Dr. Ehsan R. Siddiqi
Co-Chairman:	Dr. Ibrahim Ayagi
Rapporteur:	Dr. Ahmed Qatnani
First Session:	Dr. Hasan Balkhi
	Discussion
	Dr. Munzer Kahf
	Discussion
Second Session:	Dr. Ali Abdul Rasul
	Discussion
	Discussion and Recommendations

INTEREST-FREE BANKING

Chairman:	Sheikh Ahmed S. Jamjoum
Co-Chairman	Ibraheem Lutfi
Rapporteur:	Dr. Hasan Balkhi
Third Session:	Mahmud Abu Saud
	Discussion
	Dr. M. N. Huda
	Discussion

Main Hall

Chairman:	Dr. S. A. Minai
Co-Chairman:	Dr. Ahmed Ibrahim
Rapporteur:	Dr. Yunus al-Batriq
First Session:	Dr. Yusuf al-Qaradawi
	Discussion
	Dr. Arif al-Sayed
	Discussion
Second Session:	Dr. Hasanuzzaman
	Discussion
	Dr. Salih Tug
	Discussion
Third Session:	Dr. Mohammed Abdul Salam
	Discussion
	Mohammed Abdul Baqi
	Discussion

Main Hall	
Public Lecture:	Dr. Yusuf al-Qaradawi

Ibn Seena Hall

ECONOMIC DEVELOPMENT IN AN ISLAMIC FRAMEWORK

Chairman:	Dr. A. M. Khusro
Co-Chairman:	Dr. Dellar Noer
Rapporteur:	Dr. Ahmed S. Osman
First Session:	Khurshid Ahmad
	Discussion
	Dr. Bakor al-Amri
	Discussion
Second Session:	Dr. Hamadi A Abdul Hady
	Discussion
	Discussion and Recommendations

INSURANCE WITHIN THE FRAMEWORK OF ISLAMIC SHARĪ'AH (JURISPRUDENCE)

Chairman:	Dr. Rashid al-Rajih
Co-Chairman:	Dr. Ali M. Eghtedari
Rapporteur:	Dr. M. Farouqi al-Nabhan
Third Session:	Discussion and Recommendations

Wednesday, 25th February, 1976

Ibn Rushd Hall

INTEREST-FREE BANKING

Chairman:	Sheikh Ahmed S. Jamjoum
Co-Chairman:	Ibraheem Lutfi
Rapporteur:	Dr. Hasan Balkhi
First Session:	Dr. Mohammed Uzair
	Discussion
	Dr. Mobid A. al-Jarhi
	Discussion
Second Session:	Dr. Ahmed A. Najjar
	Discussion
	Dr. Taufiq al-Shawi
	Discussion
Third Session:	Dr. M. Muslehuddin
	Dr. Afzalur Rehman
	Discussion

Main Hall

ZAKĀT AND FISCAL POLICY

Chairman:	Dr. S. A. Minai
Co-Chairman:	Dr. Ahmed Ibrahim
Rapporteur:	Dr. Yunus al-Batriq
First Session:	Dr. F. R. Faridi
	Discussion
	Dr. A. M. al-Sayed
	Discussion
	Discussion and Recommendations

Main Hall

PLENARY SESSION — Reports from Conference Sessions

Ibn Seena Hall

ECONOMIC CO-OPERATION AMONG ISLAMIC STATES

Chairman:	Dr. Mohammed Natsir
Co-Chairman:	Dr. Umar Nuruddin
Rapporteur:	Dr. Z. I. Ansari
First Session:	Dr. Ziauddin Ahmed
	Discussion
	Hasan Abbas Zaki
	Discussion
Second Session:	Dr. Qadri al-Arabi
	Discussion
	Dr. Ahmed Abdul Majeed
	Discussion
Third Session:	Discussions and Recommendations

Thursday, 26th February, 1976

Main Hall

PLENARY SESSION:	Reports and Recommendations
	Business Session
	Concluding Session
	Achievements of the Conference
	President of the Conference

Indexes

A. GENERAL

B. SPECIAL INDEX TO CHAPTER TEN (pp. 271–315)*

* **Bold figures relate to books. Numbers refer to lists, not pages.**

C. SPECIAL INDEX TO CHAPTER ELEVEN (pp. 325–347)*

* **Bold figures relate to books. Numbers refer to lists, not pages.**